Leaving Babylon

An Essential Guide for Walking in the Light

Todd D. Bennett

Shema Yisrael Publications

Leaving Babylon – An Essential Guide for Walking in the Light

First printing 2023

ISBN-13: 978-0-9863032-5-8

Printed in the United States of America.

Please visit our website for other titles:
www.shemayisrael.net

For information write:
Shema Yisrael Publications
123 Court Street
Herkimer, New York 13350

For information regarding publicity for author interviews call:
(315) 866-6648

Leaving Babylon

An Essential Guide for Walking in the Light

"*[6] Flee from the midst of Babylon,
and every one save his life! Do not be cut off in her
iniquity, for this is the time of YHWH's vengeance;
He shall recompense her. [7] Babylon was a golden cup
in YHWH's hand, that made all the earth drunk.
The nations drank her wine;
therefore the nations are deranged.*"
Jeremiah 51:6-7

Table of Contents

Acknowledgments

I must first and foremost acknowledge my Creator, Redeemer and Savior who opened my eyes and showed me the Light. He never gave up on me even when, at times, it seemed that I gave up on Him. He is ever patient and truly awesome. His blessings, mercies and love endure forever and my gratitude and thanksgiving cannot be fully expressed in words.

Were it not for the patience, prayers, love and support of my beautiful wife Janet, and my extraordinary children Morgan and Shemuel, I would never have been able to accomplish this work.

They gave me the freedom to pursue the vision and dreams that my Heavenly Father placed within me, and for that I am so very grateful. I love them all more than they will ever know.

I also want to thank my Aunt Nora who planted the seeds of righteousness in my life when I was very young. She gave me my first Bible, as well as the book Pilgrim's Progress. It gave me an early understanding that we are all "pilgrims" on a journey that ultimately led me to this path that leads out of Babylon.

Introduction

This book is written for all of those who are searching for truth in a world filled with confusing and conflicting religious systems and denominations. Man-made religions have made it extremely difficult for people to walk in the light of truth. In fact, most are leading people down a wide path of destruction.

The Messiah made a very chilling statement: *"¹³ Enter by the narrow gate; for wide is the gate and broad is the way that leads to destruction, and there are many who go in by it. ¹⁴ Because narrow is the gate and difficult is the way which leads to life, and there are few who find it."* Matthew 7:13-14

So, the way to life is narrow, but I found myself in a religion and denomination that seemed to be very popular and not difficult at all. In fact, I was taught as a child that all I had to do was say a prayer and believe I Jesus and I would be saved through a doctrine know as eternal security. In other words, no matter how I lived my life I could not lose that salvation – once saved always saved.

Now this did not seem to agree with the clear words of the Messiah. In fact, having grown up in a major protestant denomination since I was a small child, I had been steeped in many doctrines and traditions that often seemed to contradict the very words contained within the Scriptures. This was something that I grappled with, but I was limited in resources and not able to figure out the source of the problem.

Regardless of these inconsistencies, I always considered myself to be a Christian, although I never took the time to research the origins of Christianity or to understand exactly what the term Christian meant. I simply grew up believing that Christianity was right and every other religion was wrong or deficient.

Now my beliefs were founded on more than simply blind faith. I had experienced a "living God," my life had been transformed by a loving Redeemer and I had been filled with a powerful Spirit. I knew that I was on the right track, regrettably I always felt something was lacking. I was certain that there was something more to this religion called Christianity; not in terms of a different God, but what composed this belief system that I subscribed to, and this label which I wore like a badge.

Throughout my Christian walk I experienced many highs and some lows, but along the way I never felt like I fully understood what my faith was all about. Sure, I knew that "Jesus died on the cross for my sins" and that I needed to believe in my heart and confess with my mouth in order to "be saved." I "asked Jesus into my heart" when I was a child and sincerely believed in what I had done, but something always felt like it was missing. As I grew older, I found myself progressing through different denominations, each time learning and growing, always adding some pieces to the puzzle, but never seeing the entire picture.

College ministry brought me into contact with the baptism of the Holy Spirit and more charismatic assemblies yet, while these people seemed to practice a more complete faith than those in my previous denominations, many of my original questions remained unanswered and even more questions arose. It seemed that at each new step in my faith I added a new adjective to the already ambiguous label "Christian". I went from being a mere Christian to a Full Gospel, New Testament, Charismatic, Spirit Filled, Born Again Christian; although I could never get away from the lingering uneasiness that something was still missing.

For instance, when I read Matthew 7:21-23 I always felt uncomfortable. In that Scripture most English Bibles indicate that Jesus says: "*Not everyone who says to Me, Lord, Lord, will enter the kingdom of heaven, but he who does the will of My Father Who is in heaven. Many will say to Me on that day, Lord, Lord, have we not prophesied in Your name and driven out demons in Your name and done many mighty works in Your name? And then I will say to them openly (publicly), I never knew you; depart from Me, you who act wickedly [disregarding My commands].*" The Amplified Bible.

This passage of Scripture always bothered me because it sounded an awful lot like the modern-day Christian Church, in particular, the charismatic churches which I had been attending where the gifts of the Spirit were operating. According to the Scripture passage it was not the people who **believed** in the spiritual manifestations that were being rejected, it was those who were *actually doing* them. I would think that this would give every Christian pause for concern.

First of all "in that day" there are *many* people who will be calling Him "Lord." They will also be performing incredible spiritual acts in His Name. Ultimately though, the Messiah will openly and publicly tell them to depart from Him. He will tell them that He never knew them and specifically He defines them by their actions, which is the reason for their rejection; they acted wickedly or lawlessly. In short, they disobeyed His commandments. Also, it seems very possible that while they thought they were doing these things in His Name, they were not, because they may have never known His Name. In essence, they did not know Him and He did not know them.

I think that many Christians are haunted by this Scripture because they do not understand who it applies to or what it means and if they were truly honest they must admit that there is no other group on the face of the planet that it can refer to except for the "Christian Church."

Ultimately, my search for answers brought me right back to the starting point of my faith. I was left with the question: "What is the origin and substance of this religion called Christianity?" I was forced to examine the very foundations of my faith and to examine many of the beliefs which I subscribed to and test them against the truth of the Scriptures.

What I found out was nothing short of earth

shattering. I experienced a "parapettio," which is a moment in Greek tragedies where the hero realizes that everything he knew was wrong. I discovered that many of the foundations of my faith were not rocks of truth, but rather the sands of lies, deception, corruption and paganism.

I saw the Scripture in Jeremiah come true right before my eyes. In many translations, this passage reads: *"O LORD, my strength and my fortress, My refuge in the day of affliction, The Gentiles shall come to You from the ends of the earth and say, "Surely our fathers have inherited lies, worthlessness and unprofitable things. Will a man make gods for himself, which are not gods?"* Jeremiah 16:19-20 NKJV

I discovered that I had inherited lies and false doctrines from the fathers of my faith. I discovered that the faith which I had been steeped in had made gods which were not gods and I saw very clearly how many could say "Lord, Lord" and not really know the Messiah. I discovered that these lies were not just minor discrepancies but critical errors which could possibly have the effect of keeping me out of the New Jerusalem if I continued to practice them. (Revelation 21:27; 22:15)

A good example is the next verse from the Prophet Jeremiah where most translations provide: *"Therefore behold, I will this once cause them to know, I will cause them to know My hand and My might; and they shall know that My Name is the LORD."* Jeremiah 16:21 NKJV.

Could our Heavenly Father really be telling

us that His Name is "The LORD"? This is a title, not a name and by the way, won't many people be crying out "Lord, Lord" and be told that He never knew them?

It is obvious that you should know someone's name in order to have a relationship with them. How could you possibly say that you know someone if you do not even know their name. So then we must ask: "What is the Name of our Heavenly Father?"

The answer to this seeming mystery lies just beneath the surface of the translated text. In fact, if most people took the time to read the translator's notes in the front of their "Bible" they would easily discover the problem.

You see the Name of our Creator is found in the Hebrew Scriptures almost 7,000 times. Long ago a false doctrine was perpetrated regarding speaking the Name. It was determined that the Name either could not, or should not, be pronounced and therefore it was replaced.

Thus, over the centuries the Name of the Creator which was given to us so that we could know Him and be, not only His children, but also His friends, was suppressed and altered. You will now find people using descriptions, titles and variations to replace the Name. Some examples are: God, Lord, Adonai, Jehovah and Ha Shem ("The Name"). These titles, particularly The LORD, are inserted in place of the actual Name that was given in the Hebrew text. What a tragedy and what a mistake!

One of the Ten Commandments, also known

as the Ten Words, specifically instructs us not to take the Name of the Creator "in vain" and "*He will not hold him guiltless who takes His Name in vain.*" (Exodus 20:7)

Most Christians have been taught that this simply warns of using the Name lightly or in the context of swearing or in some other disrespectful manner. This certainly is one aspect of the commandment, but if we look further into the Hebrew word for vain - שָׁוְא (pronounced shav) we find that it has a deeper meaning in the sense of "desolating, uselessness or naught."

Therefore, we have been warned not only to avoid using the Name lightly or disrespectfully, but also not to bring it to naught by carrying it.

Well this is exactly what has been done over the centuries. The Name of our Creator, which we have the privilege of calling on and praising, has been suppressed to the point where most people do not even know the Name, let alone use it. In fact, the trues depth of that Commandment extolls us to "carry" the Name.

It sounds like a conspiracy of cosmic proportions, and it is. Anyone who believes the Scriptures must understand that there is a battle between good and evil. There is an enemy, ha shatan (the adversary), who understands very well the battle that has been raging since the beginning. He will do anything to distract or destroy those searching for the truth, and he is very good at what he does.

In fact, this conflict originates in the Garden

as the serpent sought to defile mankind – the very image of the Creator. This struggle is between two Kingdoms – the Kingdom of Light and the Kingdom of Darkness.

The Kingdom of Darkness is often represented by Babylon – that ancient kingdom that originated with Nimrod, and sought to unify mankind in rebellion against their Creator. That conflict has continued through the ages. In fact, it was represented through an image revealed to the King of Neo-Babylon. That has spanned through the ages and the head of the image is Babylon.

The existence of this Babylonian system is hidden from most, and is described as a mystery. Most of us have been born and raised in the Mystery Babylon referred to in the Book of Revelation.

All of these revelations started me on a sort of archaeological dig into my religion to get to the source. This dig was sometimes literal as I travelled to the Land of Israel for two decades.

During that process I hit bedrock, and I found the treasure that I was looking for. That resulted in my writing the Walk in the Light series. Those books lay out the foundation of the belief system that I held to, but it was not properly represented by any mainstream religious system.

Once you understand that you have been misled and deceived by your culture and your religion, the question that many ask is: "What next?" That same book warns us to *"Come out of her, my people, lest you share in her sins, and lest you receive of her plagues."* Revelation 18:4

The message is clear. We need to get out of Babylon. This is actually not a new message. Thousands of years ago, a man named Abram found himself in a similar situation in ancient Babylon. He was immersed in a system that worshipped gods. He had a mainstream religion and everything seemed normal until he too had a parapettio.

He had an encounter with the Most High Elohim and he needed to separate from the land and the culture that he was born in. He had to leave his comfortable existence and venture into a land filled with giants.

As we examine the Scriptures we see patterns for this process as we journey out of the kingdom of darkness to the Kingdom of Light. This book is intended to help those who find themselves searching for those ancient paths. It is not the only way, since we all come from different backgrounds and circumstances, but it points the way and acts as a guidebook for all those . . . Leaving Babylon.

I

The Awakening

It's hard to remember exactly when it happened. That's because my awakening was a process. It began as a lingering question, and it ultimately morphed into a frequent nagging.

I found myself regularly questioning the methodology and teachings of the religious construct that I was raised within. Ultimately, I was confronted with an avalanche of information that literally rocked my entire worldview, and the understanding of my faith.

You see, I was raised in a mainline Christian denomination. I learned at a young age to regularly read my Bible, and pray every night. For some reason, I focused on the Psalms and the Proverbs. As a result, I prayed for wisdom, knowledge and understanding regularly over the course of almost thirty years.

When I left my small hometown and my church, in order to attend college, I had no real foundation to resist the worldly temptations that awaited me. Since my Christian training taught me that the Law was abolished, along with even some of the Ten Commandments,[1] I had very little guidance concerning how to live a righteous life.

While Christianity taught me that God loved me, and that Jesus died for my sins, it did not prepare me for how to

---

[1] There is a common misconception in Christianity regarding "the Law." Known as "Torah" in Hebrew, "the Law" is better defined as "the instructions in righteousness." The Torah consists of the Commandments that give us guidance in the realm of right and wrong, righteousness and wickedness, clean and unclean. The Torah actually defines sin, so without the Torah as the guide, many Christians are relegated to the realm of lawlessness, which leads to separate from the Messiah according to Matthew 7:21-23.

live in a pagan and lawless society that I refer to as Babylon.[2]

After spiritually floundering for a couple years, I found a college ministry where I was introduced to the "gifts of the Spirit." It was a very different religious environment than the one I was raised within.

It shared the same fundamental beliefs, but it was much more exciting. They sang modern songs with words projected on a screen. They used drums and guitars with amplifiers, and mixing boards. For special events, there might even be a light show!

Their worship was far different from the pipe organ, robed choir and traditional hymns sung from hymnals that I was accustomed to. This style of Christianity was very modern, and appealed to people raised in a western culture – a people used to being entertained. In fact, going to church was kind of like going to a concert. Of course, at the time it all seemed great to me.

As I progressed through college and graduate school, I traversed my way through various denominations and movements in Christianity. Along the way, I was met with many interesting questions, and apparent contradictions.

There was a time when it became popular to ask "What Would Jesus Do?" Of course, that's a great question that often brings into focus the conflict between ancient cultures and modern cultures. In fact, it was also a good question to ask when confronted with Christian traditions that directly contradicted the Scriptures.[3]

Through the years, I often read specific instructions in the Scriptures that I was not obeying. In fact, I was taught that I didn't have to obey them. Take for instance the dietary

---

[2] Babylon is a vast subject that will be discussed further in this book. For now, it simply refers to modern pagan society and culture that I grew up within that rejects the way of the Scriptures. In Daniel 2:31-35, a succession of world empires was represented by an image, whose head was Babylon. It continues to this day, and the use of that term will become evident as this discussion continues.

[3] Just what exactly are the Scriptures is discussed in detail in Chapter 14 of this book.

instructions detailed in the "Old Testament."[4] The Creator actually provided very specific instructions for a "holy"[5] people. Those instructions showed them how to live, including what they were to eat. He actually provided the definition for food.

My Christian training taught me that those Commandments given to the "holy" (Set Apart) Assembly of Yisrael[6] were not relevant to Christians.[7] I never understood why the Creator would tell a set apart people known as Yisrael how to eat yet, for some reason, that did not apply to Christians, who purported to be the Bride of Christ. The explanation that I was given was that the Yisraelites did not have refrigeration, so that is why some animals were prohibited.

Ok, so the Creator meticulously defined what could be eaten by His chosen people. He called those items "clean." He also defined items that could not be eaten. He classified them as unclean, and even abominable. And I was supposed to believe this was all about food spoilage, and a refrigeration issue? Somehow this seemed to involve much more than the temperature we store our food.

It simply did not make sense to me. Well, people would also point out that Jesus actually declared all foods clean, so now we could eat anything. They would rely upon an obscure

---

[4] I place the term Old Testament within quotation marks because we shall see that the term is really not a good descriptor of the texts contained therein. By calling them "old" it makes them appear to be outdated and irrelevant because they have been replaced by something newer. As we shall see in this book, that is not an accurate notion.

[5] The term "holy" is better described by the Hebrew word "qodesh" (קֹדֶשׁ) which literally means: "set apart". We will be discussing the notion of being set apart in Chapter 5.

[6] Yisrael is the proper transliteration of the Hebrew word יִשְׂרָאֵל, that is often spelled Israel. This can cause confusion with the modern State of Israel and the citizens of that country, which is very different from the Covenant Assembly described in the Scriptures.

[7] This is a critical issue that strikes to the heart of Christian doctrine and Christian identity. Due to various false doctrines such as Replacement Theology, the Christian Church has separated itself from the Covenant Assembly of Yisrael, described in the Scriptures. Christianity has relegated Yisrael to "the Jews," and Judaism. It promotes a belief that the Church is now "spiritual" Yisrael while the Jews are "physical" Yisrael. This is such a confused and distorted understanding that most Christians never get past the smokescreen and recognize that there is only one Covenant Assembly, and it does not belong to Judaism, but rather to those who follow Yahushua the Messiah.

passage in Mark 7 to support that claim. Here is a quote from the English Standard Version:

"*¹⁴ And He called the people to Him again and said to them, 'Hear me, all of you, and understand: ¹⁵ There is nothing outside a person that by going into him can defile him, but the things that come out of a person are what defile him.' ¹⁷ And when He had entered the house and left the people, His disciples asked Him about the parable. ¹⁸ And He said to them, 'Then are you also without understanding? Do you not see that whatever goes into a person from outside cannot defile him, ¹⁹ since it enters not his heart but his stomach, and is expelled?' (Thus, he declared all foods clean.)*" Mark 7:14-19

Note the words in the parenthesis – "Thus, he declared all foods clean." The reason those words are in parenthesis is because the one called Jesus did not say them. Those words in parenthesis were only an opinion – they were actually a translator's insertion. That is why they are in parenthesis.

Well, I never realized that. I thought the Bible was the "inerrant word of God." I had no idea that translators actually inserted their comments and opinions into certain manuscripts. If you read the introductory notes in Bibles, they might explain these things, but I don't think that most Christians reading the English text understand the distinction.

But wait a minute. Isn't the Bible actually the inerrant Word of God? I always thought my Bible was perfect - dropped straight from Heaven – in the King James English no less. How could someone just insert their opinion into the text of my Bible?

That led me on another journey involving the compilation, contents and translation of my Bible. I later discovered that the Mark 7 insertion was not the only problem with my English translation of Scriptures – originally written mostly in Hebrew.

I found this to be a big deal, because millions of Christians for centuries have been willing to toss out the dietary commandments due to six words inserted by a translator. What else was there to find?

It is critical to understand that translations from one language to another always involve human intervention, and some subjective opinions. This is especially true when converting an eastern language (ie. Hebrew) into a western language (ie. English). That is a subject all of its own.[8] For now, we will simply look further at the issue discussed in the text of Mark.

In order for something to qualify as food it had to be "clean" or "sanctified" by the Scriptures. So, the statement in Mark doesn't even make sense. In fact, the context of the passage has nothing to do with abrogating the dietary instructions, and everything to do with disregarding a tradition of men – the washing of hands.

Incredibly, most Christians currently believe that Jesus abolished the dietary instructions, because of a translator's insertion – one that doesn't even make sense.[9] What an eye opener!

This was just the beginning of my awakening. Once I recognized that "Jesus"[10] never told us we could eat anything we wanted, I started to put the WWJD test to everything that I considered normal in my Christian faith. It didn't take too long for my whole religious paradigm to get turned upside down.

I began to discover that Christianity does not promote, or follow, the teachings of the true Messiah. In fact, it really has a poor understanding of His purpose, teaching, and identity. Most Christians don't even use His correct Name – which is Yahushua.[11]

---

[8] The subject of translations and the Scriptures is discussed in detail in the Walk in the Light series book entitled *The Scriptures*.
[9] The subject of the dietary instructions is discussed in detail in the Walk in the Light series book entitled *Kosher*.
[10] I place the name Jesus in quotes because it is not an accurate depiction of the Name of the Messiah. We will discuss that issue shortly.
[11] It is well understood that the Name of the Messiah is the same name as the Patriarch named Joshua. There is no "J" in Hebrew and a proper transliteration of Joshua is Yahushua or Yahshua. The subject of the Names of the Father and the Son are discussed in detail in the Walk in the Light series book entitled *Names*.

They call the Father "the LORD," but He also has a Name provided in the Hebrew Scriptures as יהוה – in modern Hebrew script.

The Hebrew language consists of 22 characters, originally written as pictographs. Each pictograph has a meaning, and by combining them together they form words with meanings. The Name of the Creator is depicted in the Ancient Hebrew Script as ᴬᵞᴬᴢ. In the even more ancient Paleo-Hebrew Script, it might appear as ⵂⵏⵀ.

The Name is often pronounced as Yahweh and Yehovah, but it is probably better pronounced as Yahuwah.[12] Because of the differences in scripts and pronunciations, we will represent the Name through the English consonants of YHWH, which correlate with the Hebrew consonants.

Understanding and recognizing the Name of my Creator is fundamental to my faith and belief system. Amazingly, I had never been given any of this information through my years in the Christian religion. Instead, the Name had been replaced and hidden from me by my pastors, teachers and Bible translators.

Interestingly, most Bibles actually provide this information in the preliminary pages, but I never knew enough to look.

The problem is that most Christians end up following traditions that do not necessarily synchronize with the words and teachings of their Messiah as recorded in the Gospels. All one has to do is read what He said, and believe Him.

For instance, He specifically stated – I did not come to destroy the Law. But wait a minute. I was taught that when He died, the Law was "nailed to the cross" and done away with.

Again - not so! That is a tradition which directly

---

[12] Pronouncing the Name is an area of dispute and sometimes contention. We simply do not know for certain based upon changes that have occurred in the Hebrew language and due to the influence of Masoretic vowel pointing. The subject of pronouncing the Name is examined further in the Walk in the Light series book titled *Names*.

conflicts the specific words of Yahushua. In Matthew, Yahushua is recorded as saying: "*17 Do not think that I came to destroy the Law (Torah) or the Prophets. I did not come to destroy but to fulfill. 18 For assuredly, I say to you, till heaven and earth pass away, one jot or one tittle will by no means pass from the Law (Torah) till all is fulfilled.*" Matthew 5:17-18

Since heaven and earth have not passed away, according to Yahushua, not the slightest part of the Law (Torah)[13] has passed away. So why do Christians contradict the Messiah, and state that it was "nailed to the cross" and abolished? This understanding is primarily due to the mistranslation of a statement from one of Paul's epistles.[14]

Sadly, most of Christianity completely misses the purpose and context of the Messiah's ministry. He came to fulfill prophecy, and restore the divided Kingdom of Yisrael through a renewed Covenant. That is why He was referred to as the "Son of David," and the "King of the Jews."

He did not come to start a new religion. He had no intention of scrapping all of the past history with Yisrael, and starting out fresh with a new entity called "the Church."

Yisrael had broken the Covenant because of their disobedience. Yahushua came to provide the atonement needed so that the Lost Sheep of the House of Yisrael could be regathered and restored back into the Kingdom through a Covenant renewed by His blood. That is why He taught His

---

[13] The Hebrew word "Torah" (תורה) refers to the instructions in righteousness provided by YHWH. It is often translated into English as "Law," which often gives in a negative inference by those who advocate against "legalism." Laws of man can be unfair and oppressive. This is not the case with YHWH. The instructions contained in the Torah are intended to provide guidance for people who desire to be in Covenant with a "holy" Elohim. So to use the same generic word "law," can be misleading and inaccurate.

[14] The understanding is taken from the text of Colossians which states "*having wiped out the handwriting of requirements that was against us, which was contrary to us. And He has taken it out of the way, having nailed it to the cross.*" Colossians 2:14 The problem is that the text is not talking about the Torah. The "handwriting of requirements" that Paul was referring to is our sins. Whenever a person was crucified, their crime was posted on the cross so everyone knew why the person was being punished. In Colossians, Paul was referring to the fact that "our crimes" were affixed to His execution stake, and He bore the punishment for our sins. The subject of Paul and the impact of including his letters into the Bible is discussed in the book titled *The Christian Conundrum.*

disciples to pray "Your Kingdom come."[15]

The Kingdom of Yisrael represented the Kingdom of YHWH. Yisrael had broken the Covenant with YHWH. It was divided, and needed to be reunited and restored to YHWH, through a "renewed" covenant.

The renewed Covenant was all about the Torah, as described by Jeremiah.

> "[31] Behold, the days are coming, says YHWH, when I will make a renewed covenant with the House of Yisrael and with the House of Yahudah - [32] not according to the covenant that I made with their fathers in the day that I took them by the hand to lead them out of the land of Egypt, My covenant which they broke, though I was a husband to them, says YHWH. [33] But this is the covenant that I will make with the House of Yisrael after those days, says YHWH: **I will put My Torah in their minds, and write it on their hearts;** and I will be their Elohim, and they shall be My people." Jeremiah 31:31-33

If you read this passage in a popular English translation, there are many words that would be different from what you read above.

For instance, you would read "the LORD" in each instance where we have YHWH. You would also read the word "God" instead of the Hebrew word "Elohim."[16]

So, this text actually provides the Name of the Elohim

---

[15] See Matthew 6:10 and Luke 11:2

[16] The Hebrew word "Elohim" (אלהים) is not exclusive to the Creator of the Universe, commonly described as "God" or "G-D". The word in Hebrew simply means "powers" and can generically refer to any "powerful spiritual entity". That is why it is important to know the Name of the Creator as opposed to other "elohim" (gods) worshipped by the pagans. Most pagan cultures either intentional or inadvertently worship the fallen angels, referred to as elohim and gods. They are certainly powerful beings, but they were created by YHWH, thus they mat be classified as "elohim" and "gods", but they are below YHWH – the Most High Elohim.

Who made the original Covenant, and Who is promising to renew the Covenant. It is hard to enter into a Covenant relationship with someone when you do not even know their name. This exemplifies the need to know and use the Name of the Creator.

You might also find the word "new" instead of "renewed." The use of the word "new" gives the impression that it is a brand new covenant, but that is not consistent with the text. It will differ from the previous covenant, because of where the Torah is placed.

Instead of on tablets of stone, the Torah would be written in their minds, and on their hearts. Of course, most translations will use "Law" instead of "Torah."

The reason for the renewed Covenant is because we need His instructions in our minds and on our hearts. This is what Moses referred to as a circumcised heart,[17] and only the Spirit can accomplish this internal change. That is why Yahushua sent the Spirit to comfort and help those who follow Him. This is done so that we can truly follow Him, and walk out the Commandments as He lived and taught.

Incredibly, most Christians entirely miss the point that Yahushua was teaching people how to obey the Commandments, while pointing out the error of the traditions being promoted by the Sadducees and the Pharisees.

He specifically said "*If you love Me keep My Commandments.*" John 14:15 Since He stated that He and the Father are One[18], and since He specifically stated that He did not come to destroy the Torah, there can be no question that His Commandments are contained in the Torah.

The Torah constitutes His instructions, and the marriage contract for His Bride.[19] He wants us to follow His

---

[17] "*And YHWH your Elohim will circumcise your heart and the heart of your descendants, to love YHWH your Elohim with all your heart and with all your soul, that you may live.*" Deuteronomy 30:6

[18] "*I and My Father are one.*" John 10:30

[19] In ancient times a wedding was preceded by negotiations that led up to an agreement. The agreement, often called a "ketubah," was set forth in writing and constituted the terms of the

instructions, which provide the way of righteousness.[20] It is sin not to obey the Commandments, and sin is lawlessness.[21]

Did you catch that? If not, let me provide the Scripture that defines sin.

> *"Whoever commits sin also commits lawlessness,*
> *and sin is lawlessness."*
> 1 John 3:4

The term "lawlessness" is "anomia" (ἀνομία) in the Greek, and literally means "against the Torah" or "violates the Torah."

The Scriptural definition of sin is a violation of the Torah. So much for Jesus abolishing the Torah. He would have to abolish sin altogether. Of course, that is unthinkable.

There is sin, and there is righteousness. Yahushua died to forgive us from our sins, and lead us into the ways of righteousness. And again, the Commandments are righteousness. (Psalm 119:172)

Ultimately, I kept returning to one passage in the text of Matthew 7 that nagged at me my entire life. Yahushua was providing instructions, and just finished saying that we need to enter by the narrow gate that leads to life which is difficult and few will find it.[22] He then warned about false prophets, and the need to bear good fruit in our lives.[23]

After that He made the following powerful statement: *"[21] Not everyone who says to Me, 'Lord, Lord,' shall enter the kingdom of heaven, but he who does the will of My Father in heaven. [22] Many will say to Me in that day, 'Lord, Lord, have we not*

---

marriage covenant. This is the process that we see occurring at Sinai between YHWH, the Husband, and Yisrael, the Bride. The terms of the Covenant have not changed. The Covenant has simply been renewed and elevated through the Messiah.

[20] "My tongue shall speak of Your word, for all Your commandments are righteousness." Psalm 119:172
[21] "Whoever commits sin also commits lawlessness, and sin is lawlessness." 1 John 3:4
[22] "[13] Enter by the narrow gate; for wide is the gate and broad is the way that leads to destruction, and there are many who go in by it. [14] Because narrow is the gate and difficult is the way which leads to life, and there are few who find it." Matthew 7:13-14
[23] Matthew 7:15-20

prophesied in Your name, cast out demons in Your name, and done many wonders in Your name?' [23] *And then I will declare to them, 'I never knew you; depart from Me, you who practice lawlessness!'"*
Matthew 7:21-23

For much of my life I grappled with this passage, because I did not know what to make of it. To me, these people were bearing good fruits. They were prophesying, casting out demons and doing wonders.

These people were calling Jesus "Lord," and it sounded very much like the Pentecostal Movement – the ones who were supposed to be operating in the power of the Spirit. If these people were getting rejected by the Messiah, what chance did I have of getting into the Kingdom?

Well, it wasn't until I fully understood the reason why they were being cast aside that the light bulb finally went off, and my awakening began. While these people were claiming to do all of these things in the Name of the Messiah, they were defined as "lawless."

Again, the word "lawless" in the Greek is "anomia," which specifically means "without the Law" or "without the Torah." So, while these people may have been calling Him Lord, they were not following His instructions. The good fruit that the Messiah is looking for comes from living righteous lives in accordance with His Torah.

The actions that the "many" were referring to were not the fruits He was looking for. So now we see at the end of the age, many will stand before the Messiah and call Him their Lord, but He says He never knew them. In other words, He was not in a Covenant relationship with them.

At that point, it hit me like a ton of bricks. This group of "many" people had to constitute Christians. They were the only ones who could fit the description of a people who think they are serving the Messiah, but are not obeying the Torah. It all comes down to obedience. Those who refuse to obey will be rejected, because they are lawless.

Of course, the ultimate question is: How could this

happen? How could many Christians wrongly believe that they know the Master, and are serving Him. After all – Didn't Jesus start the Christian religion?

Well, that is where so much of the deception originates. As it turns out, Christianity is actually an invention of the Roman Empire – not Yahushua. Yahushua did not come to start a new religion, or establish a new entity called The Church. He made it very clear that He came for the Lost Sheep of the House of Yisrael.[24]

The problem is that very few people recognize that fact, or understand who constitutes the House of Yisrael. That will be examined further in this book.

After decades of persecution throughout the Roman Empire, those who followed Yahushua continued to grow in numbers. Eventually, it became politically expedient to tolerate and accept them, and ultimately control them.

Through Emperor Constantine, and the various counsels held throughout his reign, the Christian religion was molded and defined to become a separate religion from the faith of Yisrael, and the Covenant described in the Scriptures. During the reign of Emperor Theodosius I, Christianity became the official state religion of the Roman Empire through the Edict of Thessalonica in 380 AD.

Christianity, as it turns out, was not the result of a Roman Emperor converting to Christianity, but rather the Roman Empire fashioning a new religion by merging elements of sun worship and Yahushua. Yahushua was rebranded as Iesus, strangely resembling Dionysus, the son of Zeus, along with a variety of sun gods who all happened to be born on December 25th.[25]

---

[24] "But He answered and said, I was not sent except to the lost sheep of the House of Yisrael." Matthew 15:24

[25] The reason for this is because the winter solstice used to land on December 25. Due to the procession of the equinoxes, the winter solstice now occurs on December 21. Since the winter solstice is the day with the least amount of daylight, it is associated with the death and rebirth of the sun. Those involved in sun worship therefore revere this date. This is just one example of the Christian religion incorporating aspects of sun worship.

Now this book is not intended to detail all of the pagan influences in Christianity. There are plenty of other books focused specifically on that subject.[26]

If you are unaware of the fact that Christianity is filled with pagan influences, then I suggest you put this book down and read up on that issue. This book is for those who have already come to that understanding – those who have had their own awakening.

It doesn't take much investigating to discover that Christianity uses the Scriptures as a façade. The religion itself is actually blended with Babylonian sun worship. The religion was created by Rome, hundreds of years after the death and resurrection of the Messiah. Without a doubt, Christianity distorts the true identity and message of Yahushua the Messiah.

Because of its pagan roots, those who follow Christian traditions end up bearing pagan fruits. That is the reason why many who think they are serving the Messiah may end up being rejected by Him. They have followed the traditions of a religion, rather than the actual words of Yahushua.

It is an understatement to say that this was an eye-opening experience when I finally saw this deception with clarity. It forced me to strip away all of my inherited traditions and go back to the beginning. The Prophet Jeremiah actually referred to a time when the people of Elohim would stumble and forget Him – they would stray from "the ancient paths."[27]

I started to trace my faith back to its' ancient roots, and I began to look for those ancient paths. My quest led me back to a man named Abram. Tradition holds that Abram too had an awakening before he began his journey out of Babylon.

---

[26] For a more detailed focus on the pagan roots of the Christian religion see *The Two Babylons* by Alexander Hislop and *Come out of Her My People* by C.J. Koster. Also, the Walk in the Light Series books entitled *Restoration, Pagan Holidays* and *The Final Shofar*, written by Todd D. Bennett, deal with the issue.

[27] Jeremiah 18:15

We read in the Book of Yasher[28] the following account when he viewed his father's idols and recognized their futility:

"*[30] And Abram viewed them, and behold they had neither voice nor hearing, nor did one of them stretch forth his hand to the meat to eat. [31] And in the evening of that day in that house Abram was clothed with the spirit of Elohim. [32] And he called out and said, Woe unto my father and this wicked generation, whose hearts are all inclined to vanity, who serve these idols of wood and stone which can neither eat, smell, hear nor speak, who have mouths without speech, eyes without sight, ears without hearing, hands without feeling, and legs which cannot move; like them are those that made them and that trust in them. [33] And when Abram saw all these things his anger was kindled against his father, and he hastened and took a hatchet in his hand, and came unto the chamber of the gods, and he broke all his father's gods.*" Yasher 11:30-33*

The Scriptures foretold that we would also have a similar experience. "*[19] O YHWH, my strength and my fortress, my refuge in the day of affliction, the Nations shall come to You from the ends of the earth and say, Surely our fathers have inherited lies, worthlessness and unprofitable things. [20] Will a man make gods for himself, which are not gods? [21] Therefore behold, I will this once cause them to know, I will cause them to know My hand and My might; and they shall know that My Name is YHWH.*" Jeremiah 16:19-21

You see, that is what Babylon does – it makes gods for

---

[28] The Book of Yasher is not considered to be canonized Scriptures, although we must remember that it was the Catholic Church that actually completed the canonization process. There are many extra-Biblical texts that we know were read and utilized by Yisraelites. In fact, the Book of Yasher is mentioned two times in the Scriptures at Joshua 10:13 and 2 Samuel 1:18. Whether the Book of Yasher that we now have available is the same as the one referred to in the Scriptures is the subject of some debate. Nevertheless, there is value in examining these texts and weighing their content accordingly. This issue is discussed in greater detail in the Walk in the Light series book titled *The Scriptures*.

us that do not represent YHWH. Only when we understand that YHWH alone is "the Most High Elohim"[29] can we make the important distinction from the gods (elohim) of Babylon.

Abram was called out of Babylon, and was separated from the Nations. Through his life, and journey of faith, we are given a vivid picture of the ancient path that leads to YHWH, and that directs us back to the Garden, where we can commune with YHWH Elohim.

When the people of Babel were divided into various languages and nations, YHWH chose Abram and his seed as a Covenant people who would be His portion, and His inheritance.[30] Abram was called a Hebrew because He "crossed over" from Babylon to the Promised Land.

Over the centuries, mankind has attempted to reunite and rebuild Babylon – a unified economic, political and religious system. We can see these attempts through organizations such as the United Nations, the World Bank, the Roman Catholic Church, and a plethora of others with a "globalist" agenda.

As western culture becomes more prevalent, we are currently witnessing a revival of a Babylonian society that permeates much of the world. Because most of us have been immersed in it our entire lives, it seems normal.

Just like Abram, I discovered that I too was living in Babylon, and I was being called out. I recognized that I needed to leave Babylon.

---

[29] See Genesis 14:18-22; Numbers 24:16; Deuteronomy 32:8. It is important to understand that the Hebrew words "el" and "elohim" can be ascribed to powerful spiritual beings and the term is not exclusive to the Creator, called "God" in the English Bible.
[30] Deuteronomy 32:7-12

2

The Journey Begins

There is an old saying that every journey begins with the first step, and our journey out of Babylon is no exception. It is important to understand exactly what Babylon is, in order to know what you are leaving. Only then can you properly fix upon your destination, determine your course, and truly begin your journey.

I regularly encounter people who think they are detached from Babylon, when they are actually fully immersed and connected to it. I am convinced that this is the most significant event in a person's awakening - fully understanding Babylon, and recognizing it's influence upon their lives.

Now we know from history that ancient Babylon was ruled by Nimrod. We read about it in the text of Genesis where it describes the Tower of Babel event.[31]

It was a time after the great judgment of the flood, when people came together in complete rebellion against YHWH Elohim. Prior to that time there were no nations and Nimrod was building a kingdom - the first recorded kingdom in the Scriptures.

This is highly significant, because Adam was essentially created to be the king of the planet. He was the representative of YHWH, and His heavenly Kingdom. Adam was supposed to rule from Eden. Because of the sin of the man and the woman, they were cast out. Mankind was displaced,

---

[31] Genesis 10:8-12 and Genesis 11:1-9

and all of creation fell into chaos.

The Fallen Angels, known as the Watchers, infected the planet with their own hybrid species that warred against mankind. By the time we read about Noah, things had gotten to the point where all flesh was corrupted.[32]

Noah and his family were set apart and preserved, along with the animals in the ark, to repopulate the corrupted planet after the flood.

This was an incredible time in the history of the planet that is mostly remembered in myths and legends. There are only hints in the Scriptures when we read about the time when *"there were giants (Nephilim) on the earth in those days, and also afterward, when the sons of Elohim came in to the daughters of men and they bore children to them. Those were the mighty men who were of old, men of renown."* Genesis 6:4

The text of I Enoch,[33] known as *The Book of the Watchers*, provides greater detail as to how this all came about. It was essentially a worldwide takeover by the Fallen Angels and their hybrid offspring. This is where we get legends such as Atlantis, a city that literally "sunk in the sea" when the waters of the flood covered the earth to quench the rebellion.

You would think that a worldwide flood would settle the issue once and for all, but history is replete with men and spiritual beings collaborating to rebel against YHWH.

That was the foundation for the one named Nimrod. He was a son of Cush, and therefore the great grandson of Noah, although there was something different about Nimrod. The Scriptures record that Cush was a son of Ham and *"the sons of Cush were Seba, Havilah, Sabtah, Raamah and Sabtechah . . ."*[34] There is no mention of Nimrod.

---

[32] Genesis 6:12

[33] I Enoch is another one of those extra-Biblical texts, like Yasher. It was not written by the Enoch that we read about in Genesis 5. In fact, it was written by various people and I do not agree with some of the contents, such as the Book of Luminaries which advocates a solar calendar. Nevertheless, I find it helpful to fill in some of the gaps that are not included in the Scriptures.

[34] Genesis 10:7

Only after the five sons of Cush are listed in Genesis is Nimrod mentioned in Genesis 10:8, with the following commentary: "*Cush begot Nimrod; he began to be a mighty one on the earth.*"

Some texts describe Nimrod as a "mighty hunter," and it is not always clear what that means. Targum[35] Jonathan provides: "*And Cush begat Nimrod: he began to be mighty in sin, and to rebel before YHWH in the earth.*" There is no doubt that Nimrod was categorized as a "gibbor" (גבר), which is the same description given to the giants, the Nephilim.[36]

Babylon was the first recorded kingdom set up by a mighty one, and it stood in direct opposition to YHWH. Nimrod was the king of this kingdom that spanned the entire region of Mesopotamia.

This is where we find the origins of Babylonian sun worship, including the Babylonian trinity of Nimrod, Semaramis and Tammuz. Babylon represented a unified political, economic and religious system wholly opposed to YHWH.

In fact, another way of translating Genesis 10:10 would be to describe Nimrod as "*a mighty one in the face of YHWH.*"[37] YHWH does not take kindly to other mighty ones being worshipped by His creation - be they gods, men or demi-gods (Nephilim).

This first kingdom is best known for the judgment rendered upon it at the infamous Tower of Babel. That structure was described in Genesis 11:4: "*And they said, 'Come, let us build ourselves a city, and a tower whose top is in the heavens;*

---

[35] The Targums are Aramaic Translations of various Scriptural texts. They sometimes shed light into how the ancient translators interpreted certain passages through the explanations, expansions and paraphrasing found within them. As with all extra-Scriptural texts, the reader should use caution and reject anything that contradicts the Scriptures.

[36] "*There were Nephilim on the earth in those days, and also afterward, when the sons of Elohim came in to the daughters of men and they bore children to them. Those were the mighty men (gibborim) who were of old, men of renown.*" Genesis 6:4

[37] That type of language often refers to something opposed to YHWH. We clearly see this as an important issue as it is dealt with in the First Commandment. "*² I am YHWH your Elohim, who brought you out of the land of Egypt, out of the house of bondage. ³ You shall have no other gods in My face.*" Exodus 20:2-3

let us make a name for ourselves, lest we be scattered abroad over the face of the whole earth.'"

The plan was to build a city, and a tower, to expand the kingdom. The tower was supposed to reach into the heavens, but the passage is not so clear as to the purpose. It does seem evident that they were already fearing being scattered so the tower was meant to prevent that from happening.

We know from subsequent passages that they were indeed punished by being scattered around the planet, and the languages confused.[38]

The Targums actually provide some interesting clarity as follows: *"And they said, Come, we will build us a city and a tower, and the head of it shall come to the summit of the heavens; and we will make us (an image for) worship on the top of it, and put a sword in his hand to act against the array of war, before that we be scattered on the face of the earth."*[39]

This seems to reinforce the fact that it was rebellion against YHWH, and involved counterfeit worship "in the face" of YHWH – literally at His doorstep.

So Babylon represents man unified against YHWH. A system of government where man ignores the laws, the authority, the economics . . . the kingdom of YHWH. It is a kingdom of man set up in opposition to the Kingdom of YHWH.

As mentioned previously, Adam was supposed to oversee the Kingdom of YHWH here on Earth. The Garden of Eden represented the "headquarters" of that Kingdom. Adam was supposed to be both King and High Priest - establishing and administering the rule of YHWH on the planet.[40] After the flood we saw Noah in that role, mediating

---

[38] Some believe that this event is also when the continents were divided. According to Genesis 10:25 *"To Eber were born two sons: the name of one was Peleg, for in his days the earth was divided, and his brother's name was Joktan."*

[39] Targum Jonathan Genesis 11:4

[40] The Order of Melchizedek has been a mystery to many but it is really not that complicated. We read in Psa. 110:4 *"YHWH has sworn and will not relent, "You are a priest forever according to the order of Melchizedek."* The Order of Melchizedek is the Priesthood of the Firstborn. This was the essence of the Cain and Abel incident. Cain, as the firstborn, failed in his priestly

a covenant between YHWH and all of creation.[41]

While Babylon was a kingdom established in direct defiance to the rule of YHWH, we know that the plan for the Tower of Babel was thwarted. The one language that existed at the time was confused. The people were scattered and divided into nations with different languages.

That was not the end of Babylon though. Over time we have seen kingdoms rise, and attempt to take over the world and unify mankind once again.

We are given a description in Daniel concerning the progression of those empires into one image, with Babylon as its head. That Babylon was a "new and improved" form of Babylon, different from the one established by Nimrod.

Here is a description of that image provided by Daniel: *"[31] You, O king, were watching; and behold, a great image! This great image, whose splendor was excellent, stood before you; and its form was awesome. [32] This image's head was of fine gold, its chest and arms of silver, its belly and thighs of bronze, [33] its legs of iron, its feet partly of iron and partly of clay."* Daniel 2:31-33

This image describes world empires that trace from Babylon to Persia, to Greece and to Rome. The Roman Empire split in two. The legs and feet trace down through history to where we find ourselves today in the feet and toes of that image.

Most people reading this book are living in the midst of a Babylonian styled culture, dominated and influenced by the United States of America. While it is called a Christian nation, it is really just a revival of Babylon, because Christianity was a religion invented by the Roman Empire, hundreds of years after the death and resurrection of the Messiah.[42]

Part of the awakening process involves recognizing

---

duties.

[41] See Genesis 6:18 and Genesis 9:9-15

[42] For more information on the development of Christianity it is recommended to read the Walk in the Light Series book entitled *Restoration*.

Christianity, Western culture and the push toward global governance are all simply a continuation of Babylon. This modern and evolved Babylon will be judged, and we are given a specific warning to *"Come out of her My people, lest you share in her sins, and lest you receive her plagues."*[43]

Of course, this sounds like language from the Exodus - and it is. If you are part of "His People," then you need to separate from this man-centered system.

Once we recognize and understand the Babylonian system that we are immersed in, we must first decide whether or not we actually want to leave. The allure of Babylon is strong and it is meant to enslave us. Most are addicted to the conveniences and amenities that Babylon has to offer. The riches, the power and the pleasures are seductive.

One description of the allure of Babylon provides the following: *"For all the nations have drunk of the wine of the wrath of her fornication, the kings of the earth have committed fornication with her, and the merchants of the earth have become rich through the abundance of her luxury."* Revelation 18:3

The Scriptures are clear that Babylon will be judged again, and the question is whether you will be separated from Babylon or whether you will be judged with Babylon. The plan of YHWH is always to separate the righteous from the wicked. We saw a vivid example of that with Lot in Sodom, and also Yisrael while Egypt was being plagued.

Clearly, we all need to come out of Babylon and be set apart. The question that many have is where to begin? Thankfully, we were already given a roadmap through the Scriptures. You see, at Babel, a decision was made my YHWH to give mankind over to other elohim - Sons of Elohim to be exact.[44]

---

[43] Revelation 18:4
[44] Remember that according to Genesis 6:4, some of the Sons of Elohim were the ones who mated with the daughters of men and produced "giants" (Nephilim). After the Babel event here is what occurred *"When the Most High divided their inheritance to the nations, when He separated the sons of Adam, He set the boundaries of the peoples according to the number of the Sons of Elohim."* Deuteronomy 32:8 So the people were divided into nations and subjugated under the

YHWH would choose one man named Abram, along with Abram's descendants to re-establish His Kingdom on earth. He would make Covenant with this man and his seed after leading him out of Babylon to a new land – the Promised Land. This is where our journey begins, patterned through the life of Abram and his seed.

The Scriptures describe our journey of faith as our "walk with Elohim." Jeremiah talks about the "ancient paths," and Messiah Yahushua referred to it as "the narrow way that leads to life."

There is an actual path that we are supposed to follow, and that ancient path was literally walked out by Abram. His life was a pattern and a prophecy – a guide for future generations.

The Babylon in Abram's day was a unified kingdom ruled by Nimrod. The Babylon we must contend with is much more sophisticated and harder to recognize. Currently it is subtle and pervasive, but in the future it will likely become more apparent as the enslavement and control over mankind strengthens.

Interestingly, it was Terah who first brought Abram out of the heart of Babylon – from a place known as Ur of the Chaldeans. "*³¹ And Terah took his son Abram and his grandson Lot, the son of Haran, and his daughter-in-law Sarai, his son Abram's wife, and they went out with them from Ur of the Chaldeans to go to the land of Canaan; and they came to Haran and dwelt there. ³² So the days of Terah were two hundred and five years, and Terah died in Haran.*" Genesis 11:31-32

So, Terah actually started to lead his family out of Babylon, and they were on their way to Canaan. He never made it out though. For some reason they got waylaid in Haran. Haran is a very fertile area, on the Northern border of Nimrod's kingdom that reached to Nineveh, Rehoboth Ir, Calah and Resen.[45] It was renowned as a center for moon

---

authority of Sons of Elohim.
[45] See Genesis 10:11

worship, and contained the Temple of Sin, the Akkadian moon god.

Terah never actually crossed over the Euphrates into the Land of Canaan. He made it to the edge, but stopped short. Now there are various reasons why they might have stopped. Maybe Terah was tired from the journey from Ur. Maybe he started having doubts if the move was a good idea. Maybe he couldn't leave the land where his son named Haran had previously died.[46]

Another reason might have been the fact that the Land of Canaan was reportedly full of giants. Maybe people told him he was crazy to cross over the Euphrates and enter into that savage land. Maybe he feared for the life of his son Abram.

It is possible that Terah continued to serve the gods of Babylon.[47] It may just be that he was comfortable in Haran and satisfied just to stay there. For whatever reason, the Scriptures record that *"they came to Haran and dwelt there."* He didn't finish the journey. Obviously, there is a lesson there for all of us.

While in Haran, Terah's son Abram was visited by Elohim and given a great promise.

> *"[1] Now YHWH said to Abram, 'Get out of your country and your kindred and your father's house to the land that I will show you. [2] And I will make of you a great nation, and I will bless you and make your name great, so that you will be a blessing. [3] I will bless those who bless you, and him who dishonors you I will curse, and in you all the families of the earth shall be blessed."* Genesis 12:1-3

Now YHWH was calling Abram out of the first

---

[46] *"This is the genealogy of Terah: Terah begot Abram, Nahor, and Haran. Haran begot Lot. [28] And Haran died before his father Terah in his native land, in Ur of the Chaldeans."* Genesis 11:27

[47] *"And Joshua said to all the people, Thus says YHWH Elohim of Yisrael: 'Your fathers, including Terah, the father of Abraham and the father of Nahor, dwelt on the other side of the River in old times; and they served other gods.'"* Joshua 24:2

recorded kingdom, and promising to make him into a great nation. It would be through this nation that YHWH would restore His Kingdom and unite a people from the nations created at Babel. This is the "Big Picture" that so many people fail to understand from the Scriptures.

Abram and his descendants would be used to accomplish the ultimate plan of YHWH. It involved the "families" that were divided and scattered into nations. That is the meaning of the phrase "*And in you all the families of the earth shall be blessed.*"

Abram's response appears to have been immediate and swift. "*⁴ So Abram departed as YHWH had spoken to him, and Lot went with him. And Abram was seventy-five years old when he departed from Haran. ⁵ Then Abram took Sarai his wife and Lot his brother's son, and all their possessions that they had gathered, and the people whom they had acquired in Haran, and they departed to go to the land of Canaan. So they came to the land of Canaan.*" Genesis 12:4-5

Abram received instructions, and he obeyed. It appears that they had established a life and accumulated wealth. He also had a family support structure in Haran. So the task of detaching and leaving may have gotten even harder. He knew that strangers and giants were in front of him, but he was given a promise. He believed, and he obeyed.

This is true faith, and faith involves action. Our actions demonstrate our faith. That is what James was emphasizing when he made the following statement:

> "*¹⁸ But someone will say, 'You have faith, and I have works.' Show me your faith without your works, and I will show you my faith by my works. ¹⁹ You believe that there is one Elohim. You do well. Even the demons believe - and tremble! ²⁰ But do you want to know, O foolish man, that faith without works is dead? ²¹ Was not Abraham our father justified by works when he offered Isaac his son on*

the altar? ²² Do you see that faith was working together with his works, and by works faith was made perfect? ²³ And the Scripture was fulfilled which says, 'Abraham believed Elohim, and it was accounted to him for righteousness.' And he was called the friend of Elohim. ²⁴ You see then that a man is justified by works, and not by faith only."
James 2:18

It is interesting that James refers to Abraham. Obviously, Abraham was the new name given to Abram after he entered into the Covenant of Circumcision.[48] The point is that it was the actions of the man that set him apart, and his actions were a demonstration of his faith. If he didn't cross over the Euphrates and enter into the Land of Canaan, he would have ended up like his father Terah.

So, leaving Babylon is often a test of our faith, and interestingly, it's not just about moving to a different place. Terah moved his family from Ur to Haran, but he never really left Babylon. Haran was a major trading city located on the road from Nineveh to Carchemish. The culture was the same, the economic system was the same, the gods were the same. It was still Babylon.

I see people making geographic moves to "safe zones" or places of refuge, but many are often still intimately connected to the economic system and societal structure of western Babylonian culture. They are in the same position as Terah in Haran. They are still trusting in Babylon.

Interestingly, the Hebrew word "haran" (חרן) means: "burned, hot or parched." It is a spiritually dry place. We are not supposed to settle there if we want to completely follow YHWH.

We all need to learn to completely detach from Babylon, and it is not easy. We clearly need YHWH's help

---

[48] Genesis 17:5

and guidance in order to do it. Like Abram, we must exercise obedience, and that involves faith. In order to have faith we must know and trust YHWH – the One we serve.

YHWH appeared to Abram in Haran, and Abram obeyed. He didn't go to a place of refuge. YHWH directed him into a land filled with giants.

Once he entered into the Land, YHWH appeared to him again. "⁶ *Abram passed through the land to the place of Shechem, as far as the terebinth tree of Moreh. And the Canaanites were then in the land.* ⁷ *Then YHWH appeared to Abram and said, 'To your descendants I will give this land.' And there he built an altar to YHWH, who had appeared to him.*" Genesis 12:6-7

This is notable, because YHWH appeared and confirmed His promise after Abram fulfilled the mandate to move. It was then that Abram built an altar to YHWH in the midst of the land of the Canaanites.

He didn't do it in secret either. This was not some random tree in a remote place. It is commonly understood that the Terebinth Tree of Moreh was a spiritual center in the Land of Canaan. So he publicly identified and worshipped the Elohim that he served. He didn't join in with the Canaanite worship of Baal and attend their Temple services. He remained set apart.

This is the start of many people's journey out of Babylon. They need to "build an altar to YHWH" so to speak. They need to specifically identify the Elohim they serve – by Name.

This process involves leaving "Haran." They need to step outside of their inherited Babylonian religious construct that celebrates Babylonian sun rites, such as Christmas and Easter. Calling upon the Name of YHWH, believing the promises, and obeying are critical steps in the journey out of Babylon.

Sometimes people wonder why YHWH is not appearing to them. It may be that they are stuck in Haran and He will, once they cross over to the other side and start to demonstrate their faith. Some people try to stay in their church, thinking that they can help reveal truth to others – that is Haran. Once we discern Babylon in our lives and around us, we then need to determine the direction out, and move in that direction.

This is the part of the journey that hinders many, because it is a narrow path that often involves leaving the comforts of Babylon. Those who shed their inherited religious system often enter into a wilderness experience. They are in unknown territory which can involve conflict with family and friends.

The important thing is to cross over. In order to get to Shechem, Abraham had to "cross over" the Great Euphrates to exit Babylon. There were no bridges. He needed to take the plunge and get wet. He then had to pass through the wilderness to a land filled with giants. Finally, he had to cross over again. This time he had to immerse into the Jordan to enter into the land of Promise.

Remember this process, because it is the same journey that Yisrael took when they left Egypt. They had to first cross the Red Sea during the exodus. They were led by Moses, who represented the Torah. They then had to journey through the wilderness, and were confronted by giants.

That generation failed, just as Terah had apparently failed. The next generation then crossed over the Jordan and finally entered the Land of Promise led by Yahushua (Joshua). Can you see the repeating pattern?

Our journey is the same as our ancient predecessors, only we walk it out in modern times. We follow the same ancient path, only now we have Yahushua the Messiah to lead us through the wilderness. Our journey is a Covenant journey, and we can only find our way if we understand the ancient Covenant.

3

Understanding the Covenant

In this book we will be examining a progression of steps to help us leave Babylon. We mentioned that Babylon consists not only of false religious systems, but also the cultures that we live in that mold us and shape the way we think and act.

As a result, some of the steps in leaving Babylon will involve changing the way we think, and the way that we act. The changes in behavior are intended to place us on a different path. Leaving Babylon involves plotting a new course. We change our focus, and direction. Our actions help to remind us, and keep us attuned to the Kingdom of Elohim.

It is important to point out that this journey is both a physical, and a spiritual journey. Our actions are an outward expression of the changes that are happening inside of us. Physical acts alone have no effect if our hearts are not circumcised.

This is the trap that some people get stuck in when they leave Babylon. They stop celebrating pagan holidays and pagan traditions, but then end up falling into a new set of customs and traditions. They think that just because they are changing their behavior, that is enough. What they fail to realize is that the behavior changes are meant to transform our lives.

This was the problem that Yahushua had with the Pharisees. They looked good on the outside, but they were unclean on the inside.[49] As a result, their form of righteousness was not sufficient to get them into the Kingdom. Modern day Judaism derives directly from the Pharisaic sect, so we are not looking to Judaism when we consider how to be obedient – we look to Yahushua.

The Kingdom of Heaven is not flesh and blood. Yahushua specifically said *"For indeed, the Kingdom of Elohim is within you."* Luke 17:21 In Chapter 11, we will be looking closer at that Kingdom, because it is important for us to focus on the Kingdom, and recognize that as our reality if we are in the Covenant.

Yahushua came preaching that the Kingdom of Heaven was drawing near. Satan had tried to offer Him the kingdoms of the earth, but He refused that offer. Instead, He proceeded to take it by force. By casting out demons, and freeing people from infirmities He was manifesting the Kingdom. He was making a frontal assault against the kingdom of darkness, while training up disciples, and ushering in the Kingdom.

His actions were calculated and intentional, with purpose. For instance, Luke describes a series of events that provide an incredible emphasis on the Kingdom, and a pattern for how He would bring about the Kingdom.

We all know that Yahushua began with 12 disciples representing the 12 Tribes of Yisrael. He gave them power and authority, and sent them to preach the Kingdom.

"1 Then He called His twelve disciples together and gave them power and authority over all demons, and to cure diseases. 2 He sent them to preach the Kingdom of Elohim and to heal the sick. 3 And He said to them, 'Take nothing for the journey, neither staffs nor bag nor bread nor money; and do not have two tunics apiece.'" Luke 9:1

The text informs us that they went out preaching the

---

[49] *"25 Woe to you, scribes and Pharisees, hypocrites! For you cleanse the outside of the cup and dish, but inside they are full of extortion and self-indulgence. 26 Blind Pharisee, first cleanse the inside of the cup and dish, that the outside of them may be clean also. 27 Woe to you, scribes and Pharisees, hypocrites! For you are like whitewashed tombs which indeed appear beautiful outwardly, but inside are full of dead men's bones and all uncleanness. 28 Even so you also outwardly appear righteous to men, but inside you are full of hypocrisy and lawlessness."* Matthew 23:25-28

Kingdom, and healing. When they returned a large multitude of around 5,000 men found them as they were at a deserted place near Bethsaida. The crowds were hungry so Yahushua had them divide up into groups of 50, and He fed them all with five loaves and two fish.

After they all ate and were filled there were twelve baskets of food left over.[50] The emphasis on twelve cannot be ignored.

He then asked His disciples who the crowds said that He was and they responded – John the Baptist, Elijah or one of the prophets of old risen again. This clearly reveals that the people believed in the resurrection. Yahushua then asked who His disciples said that He was and Peter responded - "The Messiah of Elohim."

He commanded them not to tell anyone, because He first needed to be rejected by the elders, the priests, and scribes - then killed and raised on the third day.

After eight days He took Peter, James and John up onto the mountain to pray. An incredible event occurred on the mountain, referred to as "The Mount of Transfiguration."[51] The appearance of His face was altered, and His robe became white and glistening. Moses and Elijah appeared to Him, and spoke of His upcoming death.

From that point He set His face to go to Jerusalem, and continually taught the message of the Kingdom. All of His actions and teachings were about the Kingdom, and while on the way we read about Him sending out another group of disciples – this time seventy.

"¹ After these things the Master appointed seventy others also, and sent them two by two before His face into every city and place where He Himself was about to go. ² Then He said to them, 'The harvest truly is great, but the laborers are few; therefore pray

---

[50] Luke 9:10-17
[51] While tradition places the Mount of Transfiguration as Mount Tabor, it should be noted that the largest Mountain in the area is Mount Hermon, the location where the 200 fallen angels descended according to 1 Enoch. It may be that Yahushua was at the same place, which may be a star gate of some sort, as He prepared to rectify the sins of the past that began there.

the Master of the harvest to send out laborers into His harvest.'" Luke 10:1-2

He sent them ahead with a specific mission and message - *" . . . heal the sick there, and say to them, 'The Kingdom of Elohim has come near to you.'"* Luke 10:9

Of course, the number seventy is no coincidence. Seventy represents the number of people groups that descended from Noah.[52] These are the people who ended up in Nimrod's kingdom, and were later disbursed at Babel. That is why the number seventy represents the Nations.

So, Yahushua was emphasizing that Yisrael was first in the process of restoration. Yisrael would then be used to restore the nations to YHWH. This is critical to understand if you want to participate in the process of restoring creation.

When the seventy returned they gave a great report. *"Then the seventy returned with joy, saying, 'Master, even the demons are subject to us in Your Name.'"* Luke 10:17

This was very prophetic as it correlates to when Yisrael became complete in the Covenant Land with 12 Tribes, and then later when Yisrael went into Egypt with 70 beings as we read in Genesis 46:27: *". . . all the persons of the house of Jacob who went to Egypt were seventy."*

So, we see the fulfillment of 12 Tribes becoming a "people" in Egypt. Yahushua was showing that was how He was going to rebuild the Kingdom through the Renewed Covenant that would include the Nations.[53]

Remember that Yisrael – the nation of priests was circumcised to bear the outward sign of the Covenant, and then participated in the Covenant meal – The Passover. Those protected by the blood of the lamb were delivered out of Egypt. The twelve tribes of Yisrael came out with a mixed multitude representing the seventy Nations.

---

[52] Genesis 10 provides the genealogy of Noah and his descendants, often referred to as "The Table of Nations."

[53] *"Indeed He says, 'It is too small a thing that You should be My Servant to raise up the tribes of Jacob, and to restore the preserved ones of Yisrael; I will also give You as a light to the Gentiles, that You should be My salvation to the ends of the earth.'"* Isaiah 49:6

"A mixed multitude went up with them also, and flocks and herds - a great deal of livestock." Exodus 12:38

The mixed multitude was "grafted in," and included within the tribes. This combined group of Covenant People is known as Yisrael. They were then brought to Mount Sinai where they entered into a covenant relationship with the King of the Universe. This covenant event was essentially a wedding.

According to tradition, the event at Sinai occurred at the Appointed Time of Shavuot, often referred to as Pentecost. Of course, we know from the text of Acts that it was on Shavuot when *"there were dwelling in Jerusalem Yahudim, devout men, from every nation under heaven."* Acts 2:5

The Spirit was poured out as "tongues of fire," and all of these "devout men" were amazed. *"⁷ Then they were all amazed and marveled, saying to one another, Look, are not all these who speak Galileans? ⁸ And how is it that we hear, each in our own language in which we were born?"* Acts 2:7-8

So, the patterns of Shavuot hearken to a reversal of Babel through the Covenant. The Nations will be restored to YHWH through Yisrael, but first Yisrael must be restored. We know that at Sinai, the wedding ceremony between YHWH and Yisrael did not go well. While Mosheh was on the mountain receiving the Tablets, the people below were committing idolatry with Egyptian gods – originally deriving from Babylon.[54]

The Covenant was renewed, and the next generation eventually entered the Promised Land. Sadly, their descendants fell away from the Covenant. They were divided into two Kingdoms, punished, separated, and then scattered into the Nations. So, the divided Kingdom of Yisrael must be restored through the Covenant. Through that process, the Nations will be restored as well.

---

[54] We can assume that the golden calf represented Apis, the pre-eminent Egyptian bull deity considered to be the offspring of the cow goddess Hathor. Apis was also associated with Osiris, and later transformed into the Hellenistic-Egyptian god Serapis.

It is an incredible plan of restoration through the Covenant that seemed to constantly fall into ruin, but each failure of the Covenant people was another step in the process leading to the Messiah, Who would then fulfill the Covenant and restore all things.

Everything Yahushua did was focused on restoring the Kingdom, and that process of restoration would flow through the Covenant that originated with Abraham and Sarah. Previously we looked at the promises to Abraham and Sarah concerning the fact the Kings and Nations would come from them. Once again that places the emphasis on the Covenant, and on the Kingdom.

We are now going to examine the question: "Just exactly what is the Covenant, and why do we need it?"

Aside from understanding that we are sinners, and we need a savior, Christians generally do not understand the Covenant within its' proper context.

While most recognize that Yahushua came establishing a "New" Covenant at the "Last Supper," they typically do not know the source or terms of the Covenant. They are also under the misconception that Yahushua was doing something brand new and completely different. He was not.

Rather, He was renewing the broken Covenant, and fulfilling the promises provided through the life of Abraham through Mosheh and the prophets who all foretold that the Covenant would be renewed and fulfilled through the Promised Son.

I am trained to be a lawyer, and whenever a client comes into my office with a contract issue, the first thing that I say to them is "let me see the contract." The contract is where all of the rights, duties, obligations, privileges and punishments are to be found – at least in a well drafted contract.

A covenant is actually a higher form of agreement than a contract. It establishes a more intimate relationship than a contract. It is a relationship more likened to a treaty, or a marriage. The damages associated with breaking a covenant often go beyond monetary. Sometimes they are life and death, as we see in ancient blood covenants.

Therefore, every person should have the Covenant explained to them <u>before</u> they make a decision to follow the Messiah. That was the primary issue in Acts 15 as the early assembly was contemplating what to do with Gentiles (those from outside Yisrael - ie. the Nations), who were turning to YHWH.

Some people were claiming that you needed to be circumcised first, in order to be saved. James realized that most pagans didn't know the Covenant. He did not want to "trouble them" by overwhelming them as they began their new walk with Elohim. Therefore, he gave them some basic requirements to get "cleaned up" from their pagan ways. That way they could enter the set apart assembly on the Sabbath, and hear Moses being read - the Torah.[55]

This process would allow them to hear and learn the Covenant path spelled out through the Torah. After hearing the "full gospel" provided through the Torah, the Prophets and the Writings, they could then make an "educated" or "informed" decision.

Of course, this is similar to what happened with Yisrael after they were delivered from Egypt. They were explained the terms of the Covenant. They were then given the option to enter into the Covenant, or not. What an amazing Elohim YHWH is. He did not ask them to make a decision while they were slaves. Otherwise, they would have been under duress.

Instead, He first freed them, and destroyed Pharaoh and his army. Only then, when Yisrael was freed from

---

[55] *"18 Known to Elohim from eternity are all His works. 19 Therefore I judge that we should not trouble those from among the Nations who are turning to Elohim, 20 but that we write to them to abstain from things polluted by idols, from sexual immorality, from things strangled, and from blood. 21 For Moses has had throughout many generations those who preach him in every city, being read in the synagogues every Sabbath." Acts 15:18-21*

bondage, did He give them a choice to make. They were not under duress at that point – they could receive the free gift of deliverance.

This is the grace that Christians so frequently speak of, yet fail to understand. Just because Yisrael was delivered from bondage by the grace of Elohim does not mean that they were free to do whatever they wanted to do. If they wanted to enter into the fullness of the Covenant, they needed to agree to the terms and obey those terms – the Torah. If they wanted to enter into a relationship with YHWH, it had to be on His terms.

While in Egypt, the Hebrews already knew about the Covenant. They were circumcising their children according to the command given to Abraham. That is why circumcision was required before the Passover.

With converts turning to Messiah, the circumstances were different. They were not born into the Covenant. They were born in the Nations. They would therefore only take the sign of the Covenant after fully entering into the Covenant.

As a result, every Christian born in the Nations should be taught the Covenant before they ever decide to repent. In Hebrew, the word for "repent" literally means "turn."

It is impossible to repent when you don't even know what you are turning from, and what you are turning to. The Torah defines sin and righteousness.

Sin is lawlessness, and lawless means to live without the Torah – without the instructions.[56] Righteousness involves following the instructions.[57]

Therefore, repentance involves turning away from sin and turning toward righteousness. You cannot truly repent without knowing the Torah. And the Torah is an integral part of the Covenant. We need to know and understand the terms of the Covenant before we can partake in the Covenant.

---

[56] *"Whoever commits sin also commits lawlessness, and sin is lawlessness."* 1 John 3:4
[57] *"My tongue shall speak of Your word, for all Your commandments are righteousness."* Psalm 119:172

But before we look at the Covenant itself, lets first examine the question: Why do we need the Covenant? As already mentioned, a covenant establishes a relationship, and it sets terms and conditions for that relationship. From the very beginning we can see that YHWH was establishing a Covenant with His Creation.

The first word in the Scriptures is B'resheet (בראשית). B'resheet begins with a "bet" (ב). Remember that each Hebrew character is a pictograph that represents something. The "bet" (ב) represents a house. Here is a depiction of the "bet" (𐤁) in Ancient Hebrew.[58]

Here is what B'resheet looks like in the ancient script – 𐤕𐤉𐤔𐤀𐤓𐤁. It also contains the word "brit" (𐤕𐤉𐤓𐤁) – which literally means "cutting," and is the word for Covenant.

In fact, the word B'resheet (𐤕𐤉𐤔𐤀𐤓𐤁) is literally "brit" (𐤕𐤉𐤓𐤁) - Covenant - surrounding the word "esh" (𐤔𐤀) – which means "fire."

Look closely and you can see the message embedded in B'resheet – the first word of the Scriptures. From the very beginning, we see the emphasis on a "house," and a "covenant of fire."

We know that a relationship was established in Eden, and it was a covenant relationship. Eden was paradise. It was the Kingdom of Elohim on Earth. Adam was charged with guarding, protecting and tending paradise. His position and presence in the Kingdom was conditioned upon His obedience.

He disobeyed and the relationship with the Creator was broken because of disobedience. As a result, he was expelled from the Garden, and separated from the source of life. From that point on, sin entered Creation and eventually

---

[58] The Hebrew language has changed over the centuries form Paleo to Ancient to Modern Hebrew. The current Modern Hebrew language is sometimes referred to as Chaldean flame letters that came out of the Babylonian exile of the House of Yahudah. So the modern Hebrew Script is not the same language used by the United Kingdom of Yisrael. As we move toward a restoration of the Covenant, that will likely include a restoration of the language as we read about in Zephaniah. *"For then I will restore to the peoples a pure language, that they all may call on the name of YHWH, to serve Him with one accord."* Zephaniah 3:9 For a more thorough discussion of the ancient Hebrew see the Walk I the Light series entitled *The Scriptures.*

all flesh became corrupted – except for one family.

"*12 So Elohim looked upon the earth, and indeed it was corrupt; for all flesh had corrupted their way on the earth. 13 And Elohim said to Noah, The end of all flesh has come before Me, for the earth is filled with violence through them; and behold, I will destroy them with the earth.*" Genesis 6:12-13

This corruption resulted from the rebellious Sons of Elohim. "*1 Now it came to pass, when men began to multiply on the face of the earth, and daughters were born to them, 2 that the Sons of Elohim saw the daughters of men, that they were beautiful; and they took wives for themselves of all whom they chose.*" Genesis 6:1-2

We are provided great detail about this corruption in the text of I Enoch.[59] Things got perpetually worse on Earth as these Sons of Elohim took over the planet. They established their own kingdom when Adam and his offspring were supposed to establish the Kingdom of Elohim.

Eventually, YHWH would not tolerate the corruption, and it appears that He waited as long as possible. Mankind was on the brink of extinction, as Noah and his family were the last remaining undefiled people who followed YHWH. In order to preserve His creation, YHWH took those remaining beings and placed them into an ark to protect them from judgment.

He then proceeded to cleanse the planet from the defilement of the rebellious Sons of Elohim when the planet was flooded. But that did not end the corruption, as we read: "*There were giants on the earth in those days, and also afterward, when the Sons of Elohim came in to the daughters of men and they bore children to them. Those were the mighty men who were of old, men of renown.*" Genesis 6:4

After the flood, we then read how Nimrod "*began to be*

---

[59] I Enoch is a text that has taken on increasing importance as people become aware of the information contained therein. It is not considered to be "canonized" text by the Catholic and Protestant Churches although it is considered to be Scripture by the Ethiopian assemblies and was certainly revered in New Testament times. It is actually divided into five sections or books, and it is important to carefully handle these varying texts since certain portions are dated differently and some even appear to contradict the Torah (ie. The Astronomical Book).

a mighty one on Earth." Genesis 10:8 The word "mighty one" is gibbor (גִּבּוֹר) – a word often associated with giants, and the Nephilim.

We know that Babylon, under Nimrod, is where mankind defiantly opposed YHWH. As a result, YHWH decided to confuse their plans. This was not just a confusion of language. The people were scattered abroad the face of the earth.

"*⁸ So YHWH scattered them abroad from there over the face of all the earth, and they ceased building the city. ⁹ Therefore its name is called Babel, because there YHWH confused the language of all the earth; and from there YHWH scattered them abroad over the face of all the earth.*" Genesis 11:8-9

This event had profound effects. Not only were people scattered according to geography and language; they were divided into Nations, and assigned Sons of Elohim over them.

We read about that in Deuteronomy 32:7-8 as follows: "*⁷ Remember the days of old, consider the years of many generations. Ask your father, and he will show you; your elders, and they will tell you: ⁸ When the Most High divided their inheritance to the nations, when He separated the sons of Adam, He set the boundaries of the peoples according to the number of the Sons of Elohim.*"[60]

This occurred at Babel. In fact, the Book of Jasher actually provides some additional insight into this event. Here is what that text has to say: "*And Elohim said to the seventy angels who stood foremost before Him, to those who were near to Him, saying, Come let us descend and confuse their tongues, that one man shall not understand the language of his neighbor, and they did so unto them.*" Jasher 9:32[61]

So, we can see that a transfer of oversight occurred

---

[60] Some Bibles provide "according to the number of the sons of Yisrael" instead of "according to the number of the sons of Elohim." First of all, using Yisrael makes no sense, since Yisrael did not even exist at the time. More importantly, the use of Sons of Elohim was confirmed through the discovery of the Dead Sea Scrolls.

[61] The Book of Jasher (Yasher), better referred to as The Book of the Upright or The Book of the Just Man, is another one of those texts like I Enoch. It is not considered to be Christian Canon, but it was nevertheless used by Believers and Yisraelites, and even mentioned in Joshua 10:13 and 2 Samuel 1:18.

when the people were divided into the seventy nations – *"according to the number of the Sons of Elohim."*

Immediately after this event the Scriptures then draw our attention to Abram. They describe ten generations from Shem to Abram, and the focus turns to a covenant made between YHWH and Abram. The purpose of that Covenant would be to heal the relationship between the Nations and YHWH, and provide a way for them to be restored to His Kingdom.

This is where we begin to examine the next question: What is the Covenant?

Instead of the Nations, YHWH chose Abram and his seed to restore creation through a renewed Covenant with a man. You see, all Covenants between man and YHWH are for the same purpose – to populate the Kingdom of YHWH. It was through the life of Abram, renamed Abraham, that we see the pattern for the Covenant.

The life of Abraham was a picture of the Covenant, but that pattern was not limited to him and his wife – it extended through his children. The entire pattern of the Covenant was revealed through the lives of Abraham, Isaac and Jacob.

Through those three lives we see how YHWH would rebuild his Kingdom, beginning with the uncircumcised Abram. That is why YHWH is referred to as the Elohim of Abraham, Isaac and Jacob. Through these three generations we can see that the Covenant would be established, elevated and renewed through generations.

It is a Covenant of the firstborn, and sometimes that Covenant is taken by force. *"And from the days of John the Immerser until now the Kingdom of Heaven suffers violence, and the violent take it by force."* Matthew 11:12

This text alludes to those who break forth, and have a zeal for the Kingdom. The picture that we are supposed to see here is a flock of sheep being released from their pen, and let loose to pasture. As the shepherd begins to open the gate they surge, lunge, and leap to get out and be free.

That is what we saw through the life of Jacob who was the second son, but obtained the firstborn status. He was later transformed into Yisrael. He took it by force. In fact, that is why the name Yisrael was given to him.[62]

The renewals and continuation of the Covenant through the generations reveal the path to becoming Sons of Elohim, through the Assembly of Yisrael. The generations of 1) Abraham, 2) Isaac and 3) Jacob reveal the pattern from 1) Adam to 2) Yahushua to the fulfillment of 3) Yisrael - a kingdom of firstborn Sons of Elohim.

When focusing on Abram we see that the Covenant pattern only passed to the next generation when he left Egypt, was circumcised and his seed passed through the cutting of the Covenant into Sarah. That is when the promised son named Isaac was conceived. He was then circumcised on the eighth day, which is an integral part of the Covenant of circumcision.

Isaac then had to wait in the Promised Land until his servant went and retrieved his bride, and brought her to him. Isaac's seed then passed through the cutting of the eighth day. That seed from the promised son could then result in Jacob, who would be transformed into Yisrael.

When we understand the Covenant in its proper context, according to the pattern revealed through Abraham and his seed, we then can better understand subjects such as circumcision. We no longer get confused with doctrines such as replacement theology, which teaches that the Church replaced Yisrael. Yisrael was and remains the Assembly of the Firstborn. The Church is a fiction of the Christian religion.

Remember that Jacob left the Promised Land to find a bride. In the midst of his journey to find a bride, he was transformed into a tribe. He eventually returned to the Covenant Land, and only then was he renamed Yisrael – when he returned with his wives and family.

He later left the Promised Land and went to Egypt

---

[62] Genesis 32:28

because of his favored son – the beloved son Joseph. He died in Egypt, yet his bones were brought back to the promised land. He was buried with his fathers in Kiryat Arba, which is Hebron. While in Egypt his descendants increased into a great people. They became a Nation, and were delivered by YHWH precisely on time as promised to Abram when the Covenant was originally established.

Here is that promise:

"13 Then He said to Abram: 'Know certainly that your descendants will be strangers in a land that is not theirs, and will serve them, and they will afflict them four hundred years. 14 And also the nation whom they serve I will judge; afterward they shall come out with great possessions. 15 Now as for you, you shall go to your fathers in peace; you shall be buried at a good old age. 16 But in the fourth generation they shall return here, for the iniquity of the Amorites is not yet complete.' 17 And it came to pass, when the sun went down and it was dark, that behold, there appeared a smoking oven and a burning torch that passed between those pieces. 18 On the same day YHWH made a covenant with Abram, saying: 'To your descendants I have given this land, from the river of Egypt to the great river, the River Euphrates - 19 the Kenites, the Kenezzites, the Kadmonites, 20 the Hittites, the Perizzites, the Rephaim, 21 the Amorites, the Canaanites, the Girgashites, and the Jebusites.'" Genesis 15:13-20

After the allotted time had passed, the descendants of Abraham were delivered from Egypt. They dwelled in the wilderness for 40 years, because that generation failed to trust and obey. Again, this emphasizes the generational aspect of the Covenant.[63]

The next generation eventually entered the Promised

---

[63] Forty years was generally the time span associated with a generation.

Land under the leadership of Joshua (Yahushua)[64] who established the pattern for the Messiah. He began as the servant of Moses, and became the leader of Yisrael. He led them through the waters of the Jordan as a corporate immersion. He circumcised them at Gilgal, and then led them into possession of the Promised Land.

Yisrael was ultimately divided and exiled due to their disobedience, but the promise of Messiah is that He will, once again, gather Jacob and restore Yisrael to the Covenant and to the Land. This is the Covenant and the Kingdom that we belong to, if we follow Yahushua the Messiah.

The Messiah is the fulfillment of the Covenant, and this is what many Christians fail to recognize. Isaiah made that fact very clear when he spoke of Messiah the Servant.

"*6 I, YHWH, have called You in righteousness, and will hold Your hand; I will keep You and give You as a Covenant to the people, as a light to the Nations, 7 To open blind eyes, to bring out prisoners from the prison, those who sit in darkness from the prison house.*" Isaiah 42:6-7

The Messiah came according the Covenant of the Elohim of Abraham, Isaac and Jacob – the Covenant that culminates with Yisrael. Yahushua is the Covenant yet sadly, Christians who proclaim to follow Him separate themselves from the Covenant.

This is the basis for the Good News, often referred as "The Gospel," that Christianity places at the heart of their belief system. Sadly, the Christian understanding of the Gospel is often outside of the Covenant, because they mistakenly believe that Yahushua abolished the Covenant when He actually renewed it.

If you take away the Covenant made with Abraham, Isaac and Jacob – there is no other covenant established by YHWH. You are then left with what we see today in Christianity - a lawless religion built upon traditions, and false

---

[64] The familiar English version, as well as the Hebrew name are shown to distinguish the patriarch from the Messiah.

doctrines. It is a religion outside the Covenant.

Indeed, while most Christians believe that the Church is the Bride, they fail to understand that Yisrael provided the pattern for the Bride - as well as the patterns of renewal promised to the Bride. If you want to be restored through the renewed Covenant you do not want to be separated from Yisrael. Rather, you want to be joined with, and grafted into Yisrael. If you want to be part of the Bride, you must be part of Yisrael.

Recall the pattern of Sinai. Yisrael was the Bride. While Moses was on the mountain, Yisrael fell away from the Covenant. That is why Moses broke the Tablets, but that was not the end. YHWH provided "grace" and "forgiveness" by allowing the Covenant to be renewed.

Moses was told to cut new tablets, and YHWH wrote the same Commandment on those new tablets. This was symbolic of the circumcision of the flesh versus the circumcision of the heart foretold by Moses.

"And YHWH your Elohim will circumcise your heart and the heart of your descendants, to love YHWH your Elohim with all your heart and with all your soul, that you may live." Deuteronomy 30:6

In fact, Yisrael was promised another like Moses. *"I will raise up for them a Prophet like you from among their brethren, and will put My words in His mouth, and He shall speak to them all that I command Him."* Deuteronomy 18:18

This promise was referring to the Messiah - the One who would renew the Covenant, just as Moses had renewed the Covenant. Only this time, the Messiah would not be writing the Commandments on tablets of stone.

We read about this process through Ezekiel. *"I will give you a new heart and put a new spirit within you; I will take the heart of stone out of your flesh and give you a heart of flesh."* Ezekiel 36:26

We also read about the renewed Covenant through the prophet Jeremiah. *"³¹ Behold, the days are coming, says YHWH, when I will make a renewed covenant with the House of Yisrael and* with the House of Yahudah - [32] *not according to the covenant that I made with their fathers in the day that I took them by the hand to lead them out of the land of Egypt, My Covenant which they broke, though I was a Husband to them, says YHWH.* [33] *But this is the Covenant that I will make with the House of Yisrael after those days, says YHWH: I will put My Torah in their minds, and write it on their hearts; and I will be their Elohim, and they shall be My people."* Jeremiah 31:31-33

Notice that the Torah is the focus of the Renewed Covenant made with the House of Yisrael and the House of Yahudah. It is written in their minds, and on their hearts. No more will the Torah be etched on tablets of stone. The Torah will be placed upon the circumcised hearts of those within the Renewed Covenant – the whole House of Yisrael.

This is why Yahushua proclaimed that He came for the lost sheep of the House of Yisrael,[65] and this is why He renewed the Covenant at a Passover meal including twelve disciples, representing the Bride Yisrael.

The circumcised always represented the righteous, and the Covenant of Circumcision is the Covenant of blood referred to in the Scriptures. It was initiated through the spilling of blood through circumcision, and fulfilled by the blood of the Messiah.

The uncircumcised always represented the "godless," and the "lawless" – those outside of the Covenant. So, the Covenant renewed by the Messiah includes those whose hearts have been circumcised. They have voluntarily entered into the Covenant and agree to the terms of the Covenant – the Torah.

Many of us have been taught that it is a "old" and outdated covenant located within the Old Testament. When we see the fallacy of those labels, we can then examine the Covenant from a fresh perspective, understanding that the journey out of Babylon is found on the Covenant path that

---

[65] Matthew 10:6 and 15:24

typically begins by going straight into the wilderness.

4

Finding Rest in the Wilderness

Just as the Yisraelites needed to go directly from Egypt into the wilderness, so too, many of us need to experience the wilderness. Remember that Egypt was just a different form of Babylon. It was a kingdom and culture that worshipped the sun. They esteemed the same gods of Babylon, just with different names. They worshipped numerous gods, including the pagan trinity of Osiris, Isis and Horus.[66]

Many people who have undergone an awakening concerning the Babylonian influences in Christianity find themselves in a wilderness experience of their own. While their faith is firmly grounded in the Messiah, they recognize that Christianity is not properly representing Yahushua, or His teachings. They are no longer identifying with Christianity, which is a man-made religion deriving from the Roman Empire.[67]

Some look to Judaism, but soon recognize it as another man-made religion. In fact, it traces directly back to the Pharisaic sect, which Yahushua opposed and openly confronted on many occasions. I warn people not to look to Judaism for guidance, because it is no different than asking a Pharisee about Yahushua. It carries the same anti-Messiah spirit that Yahushua was constantly confronting, and it is a

---

[66] This Egyptian - Father, Mother, Son trinity mirrors the Father, Mother, Son trinity of Babylon – Nimrod, Semmaramus, Tammuz.
[67] The origins of Christianity are discussed in the Walk in the Light book titled *Restoration*. It is essential to understand that Christianity was not a new religion created by Yahushua, separate and apart from the covenant faith of Yisrael. Rather, it was a religion created in and through the Roman Empire hundreds of years after His death and resurrection.

dead end for anyone interested in following Yahushua.

Ultimately, the wilderness experience is something that everyone must undergo to fully join the Set Apart Assembly of Yisrael.

In the wilderness, people discover that they have inherited paradigms about Yisrael, the Church and the Jewish people that have caused confusion about the true identity of those in Covenant with YHWH.

Both Christianity and Judaism claim to represent the faith of Yisrael, but they do not. While Christianity holds to a belief in the Messiah at the core – they do not represent His Name or His teachings properly and within their proper context of the Covenant.

Judaism purports to obey the Torah, but they have actually built "a fence around the Torah" through their so-called "oral torah." As a result, they do not accurately teach the Torah. In fact, they are actually violating the Torah by adding to the Commandments.[68]

Many people are beginning to recognize the need to understand both the Torah and the Messiah, because they are not mutually exclusive. You cannot have one without the other. In fact, Yahushua in the flesh was a fulfillment of the written Torah and the Prophets. He was the Torah in the flesh. That is why He is called "The Word."

Neither religion accurately teaches this truth. As a result, it becomes difficult for those seeking truth to remain in a formal religious system. Now I know from experience that many Christians who are awakened try to stay in Church. Most are excited to share what they have learned. They think that if they can just tell their Pastor, and others in the church, they too will get excited and receive the truth.

I can tell you that it rarely happens that way. Sadly, many end up receiving the "right foot of fellowship," because people usually do not want to change. Tradition often trumps

---

[68] "You shall not add to the word which I command you, nor take from it, that you may keep the commandments of YHWH your Elohim which I command you." Deuteronomy 4:2

the truth when it comes to organized religion. Even if they don't get asked to leave, it becomes increasingly difficult to continue to fellowship in a church that rejects the Torah.

This is especially true when the church does not keep the Scriptural Appointed Times, but rather participates in Babylonian derived festivals such as Christmas and Easter. We cannot, and should not, be unified or connected with these practices in any way.

As time goes on it becomes more and more apparent how little you have in common with the Christian religion, due to the extensive pagan infiltration of the religion. The only real connection is the Messiah, but Christianity applies a pagan name, and lawless teachings to their Christ named Jesus.

As a result, that final connection is eventually severed. So, most end up leaving the Church one way or another. This is actually a necessary step in the journey, because organized religion is in integral part of Babylon.

As we have discussed, Christianity contains a lot of Babylon, and we are warned to: "*⁴ . . . come out of her, My people, lest you share in her sins, and lest you receive of her plagues. ⁵ For her sins have reached to heaven, and Elohim has remembered her iniquities.*" Revelation 18:4-5

Of course, this passage is referencing Babylon, which began with Nimrod and then flowed through to Nebuchadnezzar. In Daniel we are provided with an interpretation of a dream given to Nebuchadnezzar concerning the latter days.[69]

Nebuchadnezzar was shown a vision of a great image described as awesome. "*³² This image's head was of fine gold, its chest and arms of silver, its belly and thighs of bronze, ³³ its legs of iron, its feet partly of iron and partly of clay.*" Daniel 2:32-33

This great image represented a succession of kingdoms that would continue until their ultimate destruction by a

---

[69] Daniel 2:28

- 48 -

"stone" (aben) cut without hands. These kingdoms were all part of the same image that included Nebuchadnezzar as the head of gold.

We currently see the final phase of the image – the feet "partly of iron and partly of clay" that derives from Rome. But remember, you identify a person by their face, not their feet. So this beast is still Babylon.

Babylon has now flourished into a world economic, political and religious structure that is set up in opposition, and defiance to Elohim. Christianity, which is the official religion of the Roman Empire, has become an integral part of that system.

Again, Rome is commonly understood to be the legs of iron on the image. Make no mistake, the Pope still represents western Christianity from Rome, and he is tirelessly working to get the eastern Church, Protestants, and all religions under one global umbrella, connected with the environmental movement.[70]

Christianity generally teaches that Jesus abolished the Torah, and that the Torah puts us under bondage. This is exactly the opposite of what Yahushua taught. So, Christianity generally stands in opposition to Elohim. That is why is a good thing to separate and learn to be set apart from Babylon, and the religion of Babylon.

The question for many is "What now?" Most instinctively seek to find another fellowship, congregation, assembly or organization. That makes sense since they are hungry and thirsty. Having been tossed into the wilderness, they want out. They are looking for an oasis where they can find something to quench their thirst.

I offer a word of caution. The oasis you are seeking may not be another group, and such a move can pose its own set of risks. Sometimes you end up jumping into a religion, or sect, with its own new set of issues.

---

[70] See papal encyclical letter titled Laudato Si' issued by Pope Francis on May 24, 2015, which was the Roman Catholic reckoning of Pentecost.

Generally, Elohim is calling you out so that you can spend some time with Him in the wilderness. The important thing is not necessarily to escape the wilderness. Rather, it may be necessary to recognize this as a time in the wilderness, and focus on what you need to learn from it.

Sometimes you need to get away from the noise, the clamor, and the opinions of others. It may be time to simply get to know Elohim. Look at it as an introduction to your Elohim, Whose true nature and identity have been hidden from you while you were immersed in Babylon.

This is, after all, the pattern established in the Scriptures, and you are privileged if you are being led on this journey. Abram had to leave Babylon, and Yisrael had to leave Egypt. They had to separate from their cultures that followed false religious systems.

They needed to spend time in the wilderness to learn to be set apart, and to become people of the Covenant. It is there where they learned to hear His voice, and follow His ways.

Yisrael was tested in the wilderness, and one of the first Commandments in the wilderness after they left Egypt and crossed the Red Sea involved the Sabbath.[71]

"⁴ Then YHWH said to Moses, Behold, I will rain bread from heaven for you. And the people shall go out and gather a certain quota every day, that I may test them, whether they will walk in My Torah or not. ⁵ And it shall be on the sixth day that they shall prepare what they bring in, and it shall be twice as much as they gather daily." Exodus 16:4-5

It is interesting that the Sabbath was connected to a test concerning the manna. YHWH was feeding His people, and giving them rest. These were some amazing gifts for a bunch of former slaves who had to learn to rest. These two gifts were a test of obedience. At the heart of the matter was whether they had faith. If they walked in obedience to the instructions,

---

[71] The first test after they crossed the Red Sea involved the bitter waters of Marah. YHWH then led them to a literal oasis called Elim. After that He provided them with manna.

that would be a physical expression of their belief.

Many people say that they believe in YHWH. The true test of faith occurs in the wilderness. Remember the example of Terah? He didn't end up leaving Babylon. He didn't fully detach, and that may have been a test of his faith.

YHWH helped Yisrael have faith by protecting the firstborn in every house covered by the blood, and then by parting the Red Sea. He led them and nudged them along with Pharaoh and his army at their heels. They didn't have much of a choice in the matter if they wanted to stay alive. YHWH then brought them into an environment where survival was very difficult. They had little choice but to trust Him.

Instead of having to work to survive in the wilderness, YHWH gave them rest. So following the pattern of Yisrael, observing the Sabbath is one of the most important things that we can do after leaving Babylon.

Therefore, before you get in a hurry to leave the wilderness and join a new group, I would encourage you to start to observe the Sabbath, and get to know the One Who created the Sabbath. Use this time to rest, and learn to recognize His voice in the quiet of "ha'midbar" (the wilderness).[72]

As you draw close to Him, He will draw close to you. It is during this time that we learn to follow Him, and trust in His provision. As we walk in obedience, we demonstrate that we are His people, and He is our Elohim.[73] We then need to understand how to become part of the Assembly of Yisrael by bearing the sign of Yisrael, which is the Sabbath.

"*16* *Therefore the children of Yisrael shall keep the*

---

[72] The Hebrew word "midbar" (מדבר) means: "wilderness." The Torah text commonly called "Numbers" is actually "B'midbar" (במדבר), which means: "in the wilderness." Interestingly, it contains the Hebrew word "debar" (דבר), which literally means "word." The Hebrew "mem" (מ) represents water. So in the quiet expanse of the wilderness, we can hear His word and be washed by the water of His word.

[73] This is language found repeatedly throughout the Scriptures to describe those in a Covenant relationship with YHWH – "You will be My People and I will be your Elohim."

Sabbath, to observe the Sabbath throughout their generations as a perpetual covenant. [17] It is a sign between Me and the children of Yisrael forever; for in six days YHWH made the heavens and the earth, and on the seventh day He rested and was refreshed." Exodus 31:16-17

So, by observing the seventh day Sabbath you are bearing the Sign of the Covenant. It demonstrates the El that you serve – the One Who Created the Heavens and the Earth, and then rested on the seventh day.

The Christian religion is a religion rooted in the Roman Empire – one of the Empires that constitutes the image of the Beast whose head is Babylon. The religion of Rome has been advanced through the Catholic Church, which has developed a religious system in opposition to the Covenant Assembly of Yisrael.

In fact, the Christian religion claims to be "Spiritual Israel," essentially attempting to replace the Torah Keeping Assembly of Yisrael.[74]

As a result, the Catholic Church instituted a new sabbath. They established Sunday as the Christian sabbath, instead of the seventh-day Sabbath prescribed by YHWH. They did this as a mark of the Church's authority.[75] So even the Catholic Church understands that the Sabbath is a "sign or a mark." Sadly, they fail to acknowledge and observe the true Sabbath that acts as a sign for the real people of Yisrael.

The Hebrew word for "sign" is "owt" (אות), and it also means "mark." It is something visible that people can see. So, while the rest of the world is running around doing their

---

[74] We actually observe something similar occurring in the physical realm as a group called "The Jewish People" attempts to lay claim to the title, and the Land, allotted to the obedient Covenant Assembly of Yisrael. This has created utter confusion for people desiring to follow YHWH Elohim. More on the subject of Yisrael in Chapter 18.

[75] Nowhere do the Scriptures provide the right or ability for any individual or organization to change the Commandments of Elohim. In fact, YHWH says that He does not change. (Malachi 3:6) He also specifically Commands us not to add to or take away from the Words that He commanded. (Deuteronomy 4:2)

pleasure as you are home resting, it is a visible sign that you belong to Yisrael and are in Covenant with the Elohim of Yisrael.

It is a weekly Appointed Time when you synchronize your life with the Creator, and His Kingdom. In fact, it is the first of the Appointed Times. *"¹ And YHWH spoke to Moses, saying, ² Speak to the children of Yisrael, and say to them: The Feasts of YHWH, which you shall proclaim to be set apart convocations (miqra qadosh), these are My Feasts. ³ Six days shall work be done, but the seventh day is a Sabbath of solemn rest, a set apart convocation (miqra qadosh). You shall do no work on it; it is the Sabbath of YHWH in all your dwellings. ⁴ These are the feasts of YHWH, set apart convocations (miqra qadosh) which you shall proclaim at their appointed times."* Leviticus 23:1-4

Notice that the command concerning the Sabbath is in verse 3, and it is bracketed by verses 2 and 4. It is separated from the other Appointed Times, known as "moadim." The Sabbath is a weekly "moed," while the other "moadim" occur annually.[76]

The annual moadim are tied to specific months and days. The count for the Sabbath actually began at the first week of Creation. The Sabbath is only tied to a seven-day count that started in Genesis 1.

It is a weekly appointment that operates separately from the annual Appointed Times that are tied to both months and days, and therefore determined by the sun and the moon. There are some people who come out of Babylon, and they are so concerned about getting rid of errors and lies that they end up running into a whole new set of doctrines.

Some people are struggling with what is called "the lunar sabbath." They attempt to link the weekly Sabbath with the Lunar cycle, which really is quite chaotic and confusing. It has absolutely no basis in Scriptures, and has no support in history. There is no way that you can combine the seven-day

---

[76] The Hebrew word "moadim" (מוֹעֲדִים) is plural, and means "Appointed Times." The singular form is "moed" (מוֹעֵד).

Sabbath cycle with the moon, that has an average cycle of 29.53 days.[77]

We first read about the Sabbath during Creation week as follows:

> "[1] Thus the heavens and the earth, and all the host of them, were finished. [2] And on the seventh day Elohim ended His work which He had done, and He rested on the seventh day from all His work which He had done. [3] Then Elohim blessed the seventh day and sanctified it, because in it He rested from all His work which Elohim had created and made." Genesis 2:1-3

This was the climax and culmination of creation, and it demarcated the reckoning of time known as the week. Creation started with the creation of a day, which begins in the evening and continues through to the following evening.

Some are being lured into a "boker to boker" or "sunrise to sunset" reckoning of a day, but again, this is not supported by the Scriptures.[78]

The Hebrews reckoned a day from evening to evening, and that concept is clearly confirmed throughout creation week. This was the calendar in existence at the time of Yahushua, and He never said anything against it. By all accounts He was operating under the same calendar as Yisrael.

The reckoning known as a year was mentioned in the middle of the week, on the fourth day.[79]

---

[77] I talk about it more in the Time and the Calendar video series as well as the Walk in the Light series book entitled *The Sabbath*, but there is no sense spending a lot of time trying to disprove a negative.

[78] This issue is discussed further in my YouTube teaching titled "*Understanding a Hebrew Day*" as well as the Walk in the Light series book titled *Appointed Times*.

[79] Genesis 1:14 provides that the two great lights, the sun and the moon, are for "*signs and moadim and for days and years.*" Notice that weeks are not mentioned here, because they only rely on the passage of days. There is also no mention of a month, but since the annual Appointed Times are designated to occur in certain months, we can discern that the moon is for months. That is confirmed in Psalm 104:19, which specifically states "*He made the moon for Appointed Times (moadim).*"

The Sabbath occurs every seventh day, beginning after sunset at what we would call Friday evening on the Gregorian calendar. What makes the Sabbath so special, and so unique, is the fact that it occurs every seven days. There was no mention of the moon determining the first Sabbath. In fact, the moon was not mentioned until day four.

So, the week count was not tied to the moon, although the annual Appointed Times - the moadim - are determined by the sun and the moon. We can see this through Genesis 1:14 and Leviticus 23:4. We will discuss the importance of the annual Appointed Times in a future chapter.[80]

The Seventh Day Sabbath is so special and important that it is the 4th Commandment given from Mount Sinai:

> "[8] Remember the Sabbath day, to keep it holy (set apart). [9] Six days you shall labor and do all your work, [10] but the seventh day is the Sabbath of YHWH your Elohim. In it you shall do no work: you, nor your son, nor your daughter, nor your male servant, nor your female servant, nor your cattle, nor your stranger who is within your gates. [11] For in six days YHWH made the heavens and the earth, the sea, and all that is in them, and rested the seventh day. Therefore, YHWH blessed the Sabbath day and hallowed it." Exodus 20:8-11

Notice again the emphasis on the seventh day, because it is only tied to the week count that began at creation. Our primary understanding is that it is holy - set apart - from all other days. It is not to be common and therefore no work is to be done.

The Hebrew word for "work" is "mel-aw-kaw" (מלאכה), and it is generally associated with manual labor, industry, and business – things that are common, and could be

---

80 The Appointed Times are discussed further in Chapter 16. They are also the subject of the Walk in the Light series book entitled *Appointed Times*.

done on the other six days. This was interpreted in Amos and Nehemiah to include shopping, trading and the like. Of course, the "mel-aw-kaw" that Elohim rested from was "creation" itself.

This leads to the questions that I get all the time – "Is this work or not?" Can I do this or should I do that? Many people want a list, but they are missing the point of the exercise.

When asked those questions, I typically refer people to the Commandments. The Scriptures provide only seven Commandments, and we already mentioned 6 of them.

1) Remember (zikrone) the Sabbath. (Exodus 20:8)
2) Keep it Set Apart. (Exodus 20:8)
3) Work for six days. (Exodus 20:9 and Leviticus 23:3)
4) You do no work on the seventh day. The seventh day is the Sabbath. (Exodus 20:10 and Leviticus 23:3)
5) Do not make others work on the Sabbath. (Exodus 20:10)[81]
6) Rest on the Seventh Day. (Leviticus 23:3)

The Scriptures provide one other specific prohibition concerning the Sabbath.

7) *"You shall kindle no fire throughout your dwellings on the Sabbath day."* Exodus 35:3

This final command is generally associated with cooking. We already saw how the Sabbath was linked with the manna, and preparing food. This specific commandment is also a subject of controversy. Does turning on a light, or turning on the ignition of a car, involve kindling a fire?

While the Commandments are simple, there are many questions that people have when applying them to their lives.

---

[81] The Commands in Exodus 20:10 would appear to encompass the general prohibition against commerce found in Nehemiah 10:31 and 13:15-21.

After all, we want to do it right. This is the reason why many get lured into looking to Judaism for answers to the myriad of questions that arise concerning obeying the Commandments.

The religion of Judaism has what they call an "oral torah," consisting of hundreds of rules and regulations concerning the Sabbath. That is part of the reason why I warn people about turning to Judaism for answers. Through their oral torah they have actually added to the Torah.

The process of determining what is permissible, and what is not permissible according to the Torah is called "binding and loosing."[82] We read about this in Matthew 16, when Yahushua warned His disciples about "the leaven of the Pharisees and the Sadducees."

The leaven was their doctrine.[83] They thought they had the power to interpret the Torah through binding and loosing. In other words – what can be done, and what cannot be done.

Yahushua had already declared that He was the Master of the Sabbath when they challenged Him on what could be done on the Sabbath. We specifically read about that in Matthew 12.

Yahushua was declaring that He had the authority to "bind and loose" – not the Pharisees and Sadducees, and He conferred that authority on His disciples.

"And I will give you the keys of the kingdom of heaven, and whatever you bind on earth will be bound in heaven, and whatever you loose on earth will be loosed in heaven." Matthew 16:19

The Pharisees and the Sadducees thought they had the power, but Yahushua gave it to His disciples. So, we don't look to Rabbinic Judaism for guidance with Torah observance. That involves mixing the leaven of the Pharisees, and that is the ultimate lesson of the Feast of Unleavened Bread – the first Feast that the Yisraelites celebrated during their exodus from

---

[82] This is discussed in our YouTube teaching called "The Gates of Hell."
[83] "Then they understood that He did not tell them to beware of the leaven of bread, but of the doctrine of the Pharisees and Sadducees." Matthew 16:12

Egypt.[84]

Yahushua sent the Spirit to help us, and we now have the ability to determine these issues.[85] The set apart Spirit (Ruach ha'qodesh) was sent to help us walk in the ways of the Torah. It is sad to see people quench the Spirit, and look to the Pharisees instead of the Helper.

Many Christians are taught to believe that the Spirit was sent so they could perform miracles and exercise spiritual gifts. Clearly, that thinking is backwards, as we can see from the stark warning given by Yahushua in Matthew 7:21-23.[86]

Of course, the Sabbath was given so we can rest in the quiet of the day, and focus on Him. That is how we learn to hear His voice and follow His Ways. That is how we know Him and He knows us.

This leads to another question: Do we just stay in our homes and rest on the Sabbath, or do we also fellowship on the Sabbath? The answer really depends upon your circumstances. Factors such as the distance involved in getting to a fellowship must be considered.[87]

This deals with two specific commands, both found in Leviticus 23. *"Six days shall work be done, but the seventh day is a Sabbath of solemn rest, a miqra qadosh. You shall do no work on it; it is the Sabbath of YHWH in all your dwellings."* Leviticus 23:3

The Sabbath is set apart – "qodesh." In fact, it is called a "qadosh miqra" - set apart rehearsal. It is to occur "in all your dwellings."

---

[84] The Feast of Unleavened Bread is one of the Appointed Times, also known as "moadim," that will be discussed further in Chapter 16. The moadim are also discussed in depth in the Walk in the Light series book titled *Appointed Times*.

[85] See John 14:26, 15:26 and 16:7.

[86] *"21 Not everyone who says to Me, 'Lord, Lord,' shall enter the kingdom of heaven, but he who does the will of My Father in heaven. 22 Many will say to Me in that day, 'Lord, Lord, have we not prophesied in Your name, cast out demons in Your name, and done many wonders in Your name?' 23 And then I will declare to them, 'I never knew you; depart from Me, you who practice lawlessness!'"* Notice that it is the many who appear to be manifesting the gifts who are told to depart. The emphasis is on the fact that they were "lawless." They were not following the Commandments. So, we should be seeking strength and guidance from the Spirit to obey, prior to trying to prophesy, cast out demons, or perform miracles.

[87] Rabbinic Judaism has actually decided that you can only walk 2,000 cubits on the Sabbath. That is an obvious example of adding to the Torah.

So, the Sabbath is a set apart "rehearsal" or "gathering" in our dwellings. The Hebrew word for "dwelling" is "moshab" (מושב), which generally refers to a persons' settlement, neighborhood, or community. It literally means: "place."

Many people ask if there is a specific distance that they can travel. While there is no specific number of steps or distance found in the Torah, we see a reference to a Sabbath Day's journey in Acts 1:12

"Then they returned to Jerusalem from the mount called Olivet, which is near Jerusalem, a Sabbath day's journey away." Acts 1:12 In this instance we know that Bethpage, on the Mount of Olives, was actually considered to be on the border of the city limits of Jerusalem.

That is why the Mount of Olives is mentioned. They walked to "the border" of their "moshab," which was Jerusalem. So, the Sabbath day journey was within their "dwelling." The point was that if you were leaving your "community" it likely involved travel, which required exertion, and that was not restful. The point of the rehearsal it to learn to set the day apart and rest.

Of course, modern means of travel rarely require exertion and moshabs, especially in urban areas can be rather large. So, as a general rule, if gathering involves work and effort and travel beyond your "moshab" you may want to consider remaining in your dwelling place – your community.

Before you start travelling long distances on the Sabbath just to fellowship, you may want to examine your motivation, and pray to YHWH for guidance. Maybe it's just not time for you yet. Maybe you just need to spend some alone time with YHWH. Maybe you are the beginning of a new community. Maybe the "qadosh miqra" (the set apart rehearsal) will occur in your own home.

These are all considerations that you should prayerfully consider, with the guidance of the "set apart spirit" (Ruach ha'qodesh). After all, as we saw, the set apart Spirit is "the Helper," and our guide in the matters of being set apart.[88]

This leads me to the final piece of advice. When considering the Sabbath. There is a possible 8th Commandment that provides insight into the mystery of the final Appointed Time, known as "the eighth day" – Shemini Atzeret.[89]

It involves "calling the Sabbath a delight," and it is described in Isaiah as follows:

> "[13] If you turn away your foot from the Sabbath, from doing your pleasure on My holy (set apart) day, and call the Sabbath a delight, The holy (set apart) day of YHWH honorable, and shall honor Him, not doing your own ways, nor finding your own pleasure, nor speaking your own words, [14] Then you shall delight yourself in YHWH; and I will cause you to ride on the high hills of the earth, and feed you with the heritage of Jacob your father. The mouth of YHWH has spoken." Isaiah 58:13-14

So that's the ultimate goal! When your Sabbath experience transcends from a list of do's and don'ts, and becomes a delight. When you truly delight in YHWH, and His Shabbat, you will ride on the high hills of the earth. That is what you would refer to as "fulfilling" the Sabbath Command.

Notice the emphasis on the fact that this is a "holy" (set apart) day, and it belongs to YHWH. It is supposed to be different from all other days, because He set it apart from the first week of creation. He invites us to meet with Him, and be set apart as He is set apart.[90]

---

[88] See John 14:1, 14:26, 15:26, 16:7

[89] Leviticus 23:36

[90] In Leviticus 19:1-2 the idea of being set apart is directly linked with the Sabbath."[1] *And YHWH spoke to Moses, saying,* [2] *'Speak to all the congregation of the children of Israel, and say to them: You shall be set apart, for I YHWH your Elohim am set apart.* [3] *Every one of you shall revere his mother and his father, and keep My Sabbaths: I am YHWH your Elohim."*

Most of us raised in Christianity were given little to no instruction concerning what it means to be set apart. Those who have rejected the Torah because they are supposedly "under grace" do not recognize the distinctions set forth in the Torah.

For instance, there were times when people were instructed to remove their sandals, because they were standing on "holy ground."[91] The Priests and Levites would perform their duties in the Temple in bare feet because it was "holy."

Also, recall the regulations for the Levites, and how they were to conduct themselves in and around the Temple? Aside from being barefoot, they needed to learn how to dress, and act in the presence of a "Holy" Elohim. Those seemingly old and mundane rules for priests are highly significant for anyone who desires to dwell with YHWH.

As a result, anyone called to be "born again" should be keenly aware of these matters, if they expect the "Holy" (Set Apart) Spirit to dwell within their physical bodies.

Christianity has had a tendency to spiritualize everything and ignore these fundamental teachings, because they erroneously believe it was all done away with. Sadly, they reject the Torah, and this is really the purpose of the Torah - to teach us the distinctions required to live set apart lives. These distinctions begin with the physical, and transcend into the spiritual.

As we read from Isaiah, that is what the Shabbat is supposed to teach us on a weekly basis, as we prepare ourselves for life in the Kingdom of Elohim. It begins in the physical realm, every seventh day, in our dwelling places. It guides us into the deeper spiritual meaning, and prepares us for life in our future spiritual home.

As a result, keeping the Sabbath is a major step in the journey out of Babylon. It gives us much needed rest for the journey, and keeps us set apart, so that we can remain on the

---

[91] Exodus 3:5 and Joshua 5:15

path that leads us home.

5

Learning to be Set Apart

We have examined how observing the Sabbath is a big step in the journey out of Babylon. While Rabbinic Judaism, in the tradition of the Pharisees, has developed a plethora of man-made rules and regulations regarding the Sabbath as part of their oral torah,[92] there are probably only 7 discernible Commandments concerning the Sabbath with a fulfillment revealed through Isaiah.

The Sabbath is an important step in leaving Babylon, because it involves obeying a Commandment that has been altered and changed in the Christian religion. While the Creator established the seventh day as the Sabbath, Christianity has declared the first day (Sunday) to be its sabbath.

In fact, Christianity considers it to be the "mark of authority" of the Catholic Church. They claim to have the power to change the Commandments.[93]

Now many Protestant Christians might "protest," claiming that they do not belong to the Catholic Church. Regardless of your denomination, you are still subject to the Catholic Church if you identify with their Sunday sabbath. You display its mark.

It doesn't take much digging to prove this. So by observing the Seventh Day Sabbath instead of Sunday you are

---

[92] Rabbinic Judaism has developed what is known as "The 39 Melakhot" which provide categories of activities prohibited on the Sabbath. Each of those 39 categories then contain various actions and activities claimed to be prohibited.

[93] This issue is discussed in greater detail in the Walk in the Light series book entitled *The Sabbath*.

rejecting the mark of authority of the Church.

It is a major shift in becoming set apart from the Church. As a result of this change, most people will think you are Jewish, because Judaism purports to keep the Sabbath although it does not.

The religion of Judaism has added to the simple Commandments through its laws and traditions. While they might hit the right day, they have turned the day of rest into a heavy burden. That is why we must avoid following those traditions, in order to ensure that we are set apart from Judaism.

There are other Commandments that are intended to help us be set apart from the world. One particular Commandment that is closely connected with the Sabbath is found in Numbers 15:38 - *"Speak to the children of Yisrael, and tell them to make tassels on the corners of their garments throughout their generations, and to put a cord of blue on the tassel of each corner."*

You might be asking – How does a Commandment concerning clothing relate to the Sabbath? The answer is clear when we look at the passage in context. Immediately preceding the Commandments concerning wearing "tassels" we read the following account:

> "*32 While the children of Yisrael were in the wilderness, they found a man gathering sticks on the Sabbath day. 33 And those who found him gathering sticks brought him to Moses and Aaron and to all the congregation. 34 They put him in custody, because it had not been made clear what should be done to him. 35 And YHWH said to Moses, 'The man shall be put to death; all the congregation shall stone him with stones outside the camp.' 36 And all the congregation brought him outside the camp and stoned him to death with stones, as YHWH commanded Moses.*" Numbers 15:32-36

To some, this seems like an over reaction – stoning him for picking up sticks? Well, it demonstrates the significance of the Sabbath. It is supposed to a sign. If a member of the congregation is defiantly profaning the Commandment, and the sign, then they cannot be a part of the congregation.

Yisraelites are supposed to be revealing their loving and merciful Elohim by the way they present His sign of the Sabbath. If they do exactly what YHWH forbids, it is like a slap in the face to Him. They are rejecting His gift of rest.

This should make Christians take pause before they flippantly say that "the Sabbath was changed to Sunday" or that "every day is the Sabbath." It wasn't changed by YHWH, and obviously, every day is not a day that we rest from our labors. That contradicts the specific Commandment to work six days.[94]

Immediately after this stoning event, the text then describes the Commandment to wear "tassels" with a thread of blue. After the Command, the text reveals the purpose. *"And it shall be a tassel for you to look at and remember all the Commandments of YHWH, to do them, not to follow after your own heart and your own eyes, which you are inclined to whore after."* Numbers 15:39

The word for "tassels" is "tzitzit" (ציצת) in Hebrew, and it means "a lock or a fringe." It is the plural of "tseets" (ציץ) which means: "flower" or "wing."

So the Commandment actually reads as follows:

> *"[38] Speak to the children of Yisrael: Tell them to make tzitzit on the corners of their garments throughout their generations, and to put a blue thread in the tzitzit of the corners. [39] And you shall have the tzitzit, that you may look upon it and remember all the Commandments of YHWH and*

---

*do them, and that you may not follow the harlotry
to which your own heart and your own eyes are
inclined, [40] and that you may remember and do all
My Commandments, and be set apart for your
Elohim. [41] I am YHWH your Elohim, who
brought you out of the land of Egypt, to be your
Elohim: I am YHWH your Elohim."* Numbers
15:38-41

The Commandment to wear the tzitzit with the thread
of blue is so that we can look upon it, and remember the
Commandments. It is a constant visual reminder to help us be
set apart. It is very significant to point out that the
Commandment ends with the First Commandment of the Ten
Commandments from Sinai. *"I am YHWH your Elohim, who
brought you out of the land of Egypt."* Exodus 20:2

It is as if YHWH Elohim was stating that you are
going to put on the tzitzit, and start at the beginning. We also
read a similar Command in Deuteronomy 22:12: *"You shall
make yourself tassels on the four corners of the garment with which
you cover yourself."*

It helps us to better understand the purpose by placing
this passage in context as well. The preceding
Commandments provide the following: *"[10] You shall not plow
with an ox and a donkey together. [11] You shall not wear cloth of wool
and linen mixed together."* Deuteronomy 22:10-11

So, we see that the context leading up to the
Commandment concerning "tassels" involves a prohibition
against mixing. The Torah is, after all, instructions in
righteousness. Those instructions provide distinctions. They
help us distinguish between right and wrong, clean and
unclean, wickedness and righteousness. The instructions show
us how to be set apart. Being set apart and living a set apart life
involves learning these distinctions and acting upon them.

The prohibition against mixing carries into many areas
of our lives. Interestingly, in Deuteronomy 22:12 the text does

not use the word tzitzit. Instead, the word translated as "tassels" is "gadolym" (גְּדֹלִים) in the Hebrew. It is the plural form of "gadol" (גָּדֹל). Gadol literally means "to grow up," "to become great," "magnified," or "high." It is used to describe the "High" Priest – Cohen Gadol.

So, by wearing tzitzit, we are essentially elevating our clothing through the tzitzit. They transform our regular attire into priestly garments. Again, this helps us to be set apart as priests. After all, the Torah specifically provides: "*And you shall be to Me a Kingdom of Priests and a Holy (set apart) Nation. These are the words which you shall speak to the children of Yisrael.*" Exodus 19:6

Both Numbers and Deuteronomy provide that the tzitzit are to be worn on the four "corners" of our garments and the Hebrew word for "corner" is "kanaph" (כָּנָף).

This reminds us of a powerful prophecy concerning a sign of the Messiah found in Malachi as follows: "*But to you who fear My Name the Sun of Righteousness shall arise with healing in His wings (כָּנָף); and you shall go out and grow fat like stall-fed calves.*" Malachi 4:2

Here the Hebrew word for "wings" is the Hebrew word "kanaph" (כָּנָף). Kanaph means – "a border, a corner, a wing of a garment." The connection with tzitzit is obvious. So, this prophecy is telling us that the Sun of Righteousness – the Messiah - will come with healing in His tzitzit.

We know this was exactly the case with Yahushua. In fact, it was an evidence that He is the Messiah. We read about a woman with a flow of blood touching the "hem" of His garment and being healed. "*And suddenly, a woman who had a flow of blood for twelve years came from behind and touched the hem (κρασπέδου) of His garment.*" Matthew 9:20

In the Greek we read the word "krespedon" (κρασπέδου), which means means "a fringe or tassel." Clearly it is referring to the "kanaph" of the garment, and the tzitzit worn by Yahushua. I doubt that many Christians understand that Yahushua wore tzitzit. I never did.

There were many more who were healed as we read further in Matthew. "*34 When they had crossed over, they came to the land of Gennesaret. 35 And when the men of that place recognized Him, they sent out into all that surrounding region, brought to Him all who were sick, 36 and begged Him that they might only touch the hem (κρασπέδου) of His garment. And as many as touched it were made perfectly well.*" Matthew 14:34-36

It appears that this was something that occurred regularly. That is likely why the woman with the flow of blood knew to do it. We read the following in Mark: "*Wherever He entered, into villages, cities, or the country, they laid the sick in the marketplaces, and begged Him that they might just touch the hem (κρασπέδου) of His garment. And as many as touched Him were made well.*" Mark 6:56

In all of these passages, the hem of His garment was the kanaph - His tzitzit. Notice in Mark that "*wherever He entered*" they did this. So it was happening all of the time. Yahushua was obeying the Commandment, and wearing tzitzit. People were healed by taking hold of His tzitzit. The message was that there is healing through the Commandments. That is how our relationship with YHWH is healed – when we follow Yahushua, and obey the Commandments.[95]

In fact, this is also a fulfillment of another prophecy found in Zechariah. "*Thus says YHWH of hosts: In those days ten men from every language of the nations shall grasp the kanaph of a Yahudi man, saying, 'Let us go with you, for we have heard that is with you.'*" Zechariah 8:23

This passage is typically poorly translated, and understood. First of all, many translations have "robe," "sleeve," or "garment" instead of "kanaph." So, it is unclear

---

[95] It is worth pointing out that the first Command given by YHWH after Yisrael left Egypt through the waters of the Red Sea involved obedience and healing. "*26 . . . If you diligently heed the voice of YHWH your Elohim and do what is right in His sight, give ear to His Commandments and keep all His statutes, I will put none of the diseases on you which I have brought on the Egyptians. For I am YHWH who heals you.*" Exodus 15:26

what the people are grabbing, or why they are grabbing it. Almost all translations describe a "Jewish man." That has led people to flock to Orthodox Rabbis in order to learn the Torah within the context of Judaism, but that is not what the text is saying.

The Yahudi man was Yahushua from the Tribe of Yahudah. The ten men represent the lost sheep of the House of Yisrael scattered among the Nations. So, this passage is telling of a time when the tribes would learn the Torah from the Messiah. If that is what you are doing now, you are living out a prophecy. Isn't that incredible?

That leads to the question of how to obey the Command. People wear the tzitzit in different ways. Some wear their tzitzit on a prayer shawl that they don while praying.[96] Some wear a tallit katan, which is a four-cornered undergarment worn all the time. Still others attach them to four belt loops on their pants, representing their four corners.

The question also arises as to how the tzitzit should be tied. That is another one of those areas where Judaism has developed numerous rules and regulations that belie the fact that this is actually a very simple Command. We tie a blue thread on the corners of our garments. Do we add white or other colors, or do we tie in a certain configuration? My response is: What does the Torah tell us?

After all, we are not intended to be a congregation of drones. We are made in the image of YHWH, and therefore we have been endowed with creative instincts and abilities. Organized religion always attempts to create uniformity and that is one of the dangers in looking to Judaism.

Certain Rabbis prescribe certain methods of tying the tzitzit. As a result, the way you tie your tzitzit can reflect the traditions of a certain Rabbi, or sect of Judaism.[97] So you may

---

[96] The prayer shawl is a Jewish tradition, and I do not believe that it sufficiently fulfills the Commandment.

[97] I often wear tzitzit that denote the Name of YHWH by tying the blue thread in accordance to the Gematria value of the corresponding letters of the Name. We sell tzitzit of this sort on our website www.shemayisrael.net

be sending a message to other people that you are not intending to convey.

I often get asked whether only men are commanded to wear the tzitzit, or whether women may also wear them. When we look at the Commandment in Numbers 15:38 we read: "*Speak to the children of Yisrael.*" In the Hebrew the word for children is "beni" (בני) which literally means "sons," but it is often translated as "children."

The priestly function falls upon the male, so clearly men are required to wear the tzitzit as the priests of the house. There is certainly no restriction against women wearing tzitzit on their clothing. Again, the purpose to look upon and remember the Commandments is to help us be set apart. Women need to obey and be set apart, so they can certainly wear the reminder on their four cornered garments as well.

Not only are the tzitzit a constant reminder of the Commandments and our need to be set apart, they are also a sign of our being set apart – just like the Sabbath is a sign. They represent and demonstrate that we diligently obey the Commandments in the Torah over the traditions of men.

Very interestingly, many years ago when I first started walking out the Torah, I was intrigued that Orthodox Jews wore tzitzit that did not contain a blue thread. After questioning someone I discovered that it had to do with their tradition concerning the source of the blue.

The Hebrew word for "blue" in Numbers 15:38 is "techelet" (תכלת). We first read of this in Exodus 25:4 when it refers to the gifts of "blue," purple and scarlet thread, fine linen and goat's hair for the tabernacle - among other things. It is repeatedly mentioned as being used in the Tabernacle.

It was also used for the garments for the High Priest. "[1] *Of the blue* (תכלת), *purple, and scarlet thread they made garments of ministry, for ministering in the holy place, and made the holy garments for Aaron, as YHWH had commanded Moses.* [2] *He made the ephod of gold, blue* (תכלת), *purple, and scarlet thread, and of fine woven linen.* [3] *And they beat the gold into thin sheets and cut it into threads, to work it in with the blue (תכלת), purple, and scarlet thread, and the fine linen, into artistic designs."* Exodus 39:1-3

The word "techelet" is generally associated with a very rich blue, violet color. The Orthodox Jews have a tradition that the source of the "techelet" color was from a sea snail[98] that became extinct, so they simply stopped using the color. After finding that this sea snail was actually not extinct – some began to wear the blue thread again, but most continue to wear all white.

The Jewish tradition involving an unclean gastropod mollusk created a dilemma. Even with the discovery of the snail, and an opportunity to put some color in their tzitzit, the majority choose their tradition, and wear only white tzitzit.

It is really quite incredible since the Command specifically requires color. This is a good example of why we cannot submit to the Pharisees in our "halakah" – our walk.

They often place their traditions and their oral torah above the simple and specific Commandments of Elohim. In fact, Yahushua actually commented on the Pharisees missing the point of wearing the tzitzit. *"But all their works they do to be seen by men. They make their phylacteries broad and enlarge the borders (kraspedon) of their garments."* Matthew 23:5

You see, it is always important to remember the purpose of the Commandment. The act of wearing tzitzit is meaningless if we forget the purpose. Instead of using the tzitzit to remember the Commandments and be set apart, they were using them as a status symbol. They missed the point entirely.

Many make the same mistake concerning the blue, or lack thereof. They get so caught up with their tradition regarding the source of the color that they end up forgetting, or ignoring, the actual color that is a commandment, and a sign.

So, we have to make sure that when we begin this

---

[98] Murex trunculus

journey of being set apart we stay focused on the goal, and not get distracted. We started with the simplicity of the Sabbath and we now see that being set apart is not confined to a once a week exercise. The Sabbath is actually the preparation point for a week of being set apart.

Being set apart is something that we are thinking about and doing constantly. It permeates every part of our lives - even down to what we wear.

If we truly follow the Master, then we should be wearing our tzitzit as priests in the Order of Melchizedek.[99] This is, after all, our calling.

In Luke we read an account of when Yahushua was in the Nazareth Synagogue on the Sabbath. He was handed the Isaiah scroll and read the following: "[8] *The Spirit of YHWH is upon Me, because He has anointed Me to preach the gospel to the poor; He has sent Me to heal the brokenhearted, to proclaim liberty to the captives and recovery of sight to the blind, To set at liberty those who are oppressed;* [19] *To proclaim the acceptable year of YHWH.*" Luke 4:18-19

This event occurred right at the beginning of His ministry, and He was quoting from Isaiah 61. One cannot ignore all the allusions to the Jubilee Year that we see in that passage through the use of the words "liberty" and the "the acceptable year of YHWH."[100] Interestingly, Yahushua stopped and stated: "*Today this Scripture is fulfilled in your hearing.*" Luke 4:21

The implication is that it was a Jubilee Year. If that portion of Isaiah was fulfilled at that time, then we anticipate the fulfillment of the rest of the passage, which speaks of a future return and restoration. A great promise is given to the

---

[99] The Melchizedek priesthood is one of the great mysteries of the Scriptures that saw a fulfillment and revelation through the Messiah. The Melchizedek will be discussed further in the next chapter.

[100] The Jubilee year occurs every 50 years and is described in Leviticus which describes in part: "*And you shall consecrate the fiftieth year, and proclaim liberty throughout all the land to all its inhabitants. It shall be a Jubilee for you; and each of you shall return to his possession, and each of you shall return to his family.*" Leviticus 25:10

people. *"But you shall be named the priests of YHWH, they shall call you the servants of our Elohim." Isaiah 61:6*

Later in Isaiah we read of a new heaven and a new earth, and there will be priests chosen to serve in the House of YHWH.

> *"'20 Then they shall bring all your brethren for an offering to YHWH out of all Nations, on horses and in chariots and in litters, on mules and on camels, to My Holy (set apart) mountain Jerusalem,' says YHWH, 'as the children of Yisrael bring an offering in a clean vessel into the house of YHWH. 21 And I will also take some of them for priests, for Levites,' says YHWH. 22 'For as the new heavens and the new earth which I will make shall remain before Me,' says YHWH, 'So shall your descendants and your name remain. 23 And it shall come to pass that from one New Moon to another, and from one Sabbath to another, all flesh shall come to worship before Me,' says YHWH." Isaiah 66:20-23*

Yahushua came as a High Priest preparing a priesthood to dwell in the House of YHWH. So as we follow Him and walk as He walked, we also wear what He wore. We clothe ourselves with His righteousness, and as we put on the tzitzit each day, we are reminded to be set apart. We learn to be set apart so that we can learn to be priests.

6

Learning to Be Priests

In the last chapter we talked about being set apart, and the Commandment to wear tzitzit. The point is not to just wear the tzitzit, although that involves an initial act of obedience. Ultimately, we wear the tzitzit to remind us to obey all the Commandments that apply to us.

We also discussed how the tzitzit are referred to as "gadolym" (גְּדִלִים) in Deuteronomy 22:12, which demonstrates that they are meant to elevate our purpose when we wear them. They are to remind us that we are part of Yisrael – a nation of priests. So when we don the tzitzit every day, we are supposed to conduct ourselves as priests. With that understanding we should consider what it means to be a priest.

The term "priest" carries various connotations depending upon your religious upbringing or background. The primary religion that contains priests is the Roman Catholic Church. Christianity also has Reverends, Pastors, Ministers and Monks, while Judaism has Rabbis.

All of these modern religious positions establish a buffer between the "lay-people" and the "professionals." As a result, the thought of a so-called "lay-person" acting and functioning as a priest without going to seminary or being ordained is a foreign concept to most.

In order to properly understand the function of a priest, it is vital to look to the Scriptures. The Hebrew word for priest is "cohen" (כֹּהֵן), and it refers to one who mediates or officiates in a "religious" capacity. The first time we read the word "cohen" in the Scriptures is in the story of Abram.

"*[18] Then Melchi-tzedek king of Salem brought out bread and wine; he was the priest (כהן) of El Most High. [19] And he blessed him and said: 'Blessed be Abram of El Most High, Possessor of heaven and earth; [20] And blessed be E Most High, Who has delivered your enemies into your hand.' And he gave him a tithe of all.*" Genesis 14:18-20

So, the first specific mention of a priest in the Scriptures is "melchi-tzedek" (melchizedek) which is a combination of two Semitic words "melech" (king) and "tzedek" (righteous). This is also the first mention of the "tithe" (ma'ah'sir).

Interestingly, there are some who try to separate the Melchizedek from the Covenant, but it is not possible.[101] We see Abram tithing before the Commandment was ever given to Yisrael, and we see priests before there was ever a man or tribe named Levi.

It is important to understand that the Torah instructions were in existence from the beginning. The Torah is built into the very fabric of Creation. With that understanding, when we look back to the Garden we see that Adam was supposed to act as a High Priest. When we view the Garden as the dwelling place of Elohim on Earth, it helps us better comprehend what was going on.

The Garden of Eden was literally the House of Elohim on Earth. The Hebrew word for "garden" is "gan" (גן), and it means a "protected place." Anyone who has grown a garden knows that it requires nurturing and protection. Adam was charged to "tend and to keep it" according to Genesis 2:15.

The word "tend" is "abad" (עבד) in Hebrew. It means "to labor, to serve," and it can even mean "worshipper."[102] If we break down this word "abad" (𐤏𐤁𐤃) looking at the Ancient Hebrew script we see "ayin" (𐤏), which represents an "eye." We also see "bet" (𐤁), which represents a "house," and "dalet" (𐤃) which represents the "door." Adam was commissioned to

---

[101] See the article entitled The Melchizedek deception on the shemayisrael.net website.
[102] Hebrew Strong's Dictionary number 5647

watch the house door, or rather "guard the gate."

Indeed, the other word used to describe his function to "keep" the garden is "shamar" (שָׁמַר), and it specifically means "to protect and to guard." It is often used to refer to a "watchman."[103]

So, Adam was a worshipper, and a watchman. He was placed in a specific location to perform a specific service. If he diligently performed those duties, YHWH Elohim would visit and commune with him.[104] He could remain there, and have access to the Tree of Life.

Of course, Eden (עֵדֶן) literally means "paradise," because mankind was supposed to have direct access to the Creator and live forever. If we break down this word "Eden" (ᴎᴗ☉), looking at the Ancient Hebrew pictographs, we see "ayin" (☉) which, again, represents an "eye." We also see "dalet" (ᴗ), which represents a "door," and "nun" (ᴎ) which represents the "life." So, Eden literally means: "see the door to life."

Adam knew the instructions and because of his disobedience he was cast out of Eden and denied re-entry.

> "[21] Also for Adam and his wife YHWH Elohim made tunics of skin, and clothed them. [22] Then YHWH Elohim said, 'Behold, the man has become like one of Us, to know good and evil. And now, lest he put out his hand and take also of the tree of life, and eat, and live forever' [23] therefore YHWH Elohim sent him out of the garden of Eden to till the ground from which he was taken. [24] So He drove out the man; and He placed cherubim at the east of the Garden of Eden, and a flaming sword which turned every way, to guard the way to the tree of life."
> Genesis 3:21-24

---

[103] Hebrew Strong's Dictionary number 8104
[104] See Genesis 3:8

It is important to consider what it meant for YHWH to make "tunics of skin" for the man and the woman. First of all, something obviously had to die. Blood had to be shed. So, a slaughtering occurred and man was clothed with the dead skins. He was covered by death.

The word for tunic is "katanote" (כתנות). It is the same word later used to describe the "tunic" that Jacob made for Joseph,[105] and the "tunic" that the High Priest would wear during his service. While a tunic can also carry the general meaning of a piece of clothing – one cannot ignore the powerful connection.

Man had a problem called death, and he was required to wear a reminder of death as a covering (kippurim). YHWH revealed that He was ultimately the One Who was the High Priest. He would provide atonement (kippurim), and we see that further elucidated through the life of Abram, later renamed Abraham.

The first time that we read the name Abram (אברם) in the Scriptures, it is affixed to the alep taw (את) as את-אברם. The name Abram actually contains a powerful message. The first two letters form the word "ab" (אב), which means "father" in Hebrew. The first and the last letters form the word "am" (אם), which means "a people." Located within the people (אם) we see the word "bar" (בר), which means "son."

So, through this father would come a son, that would turn into a people. This is the pattern provided through the Scriptures pointing to the ultimate fulfillment through our Heavenly Father, and His only begotten Son.

In order for Abram to fulfill his destiny, he needed to leave Babylon. It was only when he finally crossed over and entered into the Land of Canaan that YHWH could fulfill the promises, and cut covenant with him.

The word for covenant in Hebrew is "brit" (ברית), and

---

[105] The only difference is the missing "waw" (ו), which represents a "peg." In the case of Joseph we read "et-katanote" (את-כתנת), which provides tremendous Messianic hints. See Genesis 37-23, 31 and 32.

it literally means "cutting." The blood covenant involves cutting, and that results in the shedding of blood. Through the life of this man we see a series of cuttings after he entered the Land, when his name was changed to Abraham, and when he offered up his promised son.[106]

Now throughout his covenant journey, Abraham clearly knew the Torah, and he obeyed the Torah before it was given at Sinai. *"In your seed all the nations of the earth shall be blessed, because you have obeyed My voice."* Genesis 22:18 In fact, we are told that the blessings promised to his descendants were the result of his obedience to YHWH.

When YHWH appeared to Isaac He told him: *"³ Dwell in this land, and I will be with you and bless you; for to you and your descendants I give all these lands, and I will perform the oath which I swore to Abraham your father. ⁴ And I will make your descendants multiply as the stars of heaven; I will give to your descendants all these lands; and in your seed all the nations of the earth shall be blessed; ⁵ because Abraham obeyed My voice and kept My charge, My Commandments, My statutes, and My Torah."* Genesis 26:3-6

Abraham obeyed the Commandments, and the Torah. So don't let anyone deceive you into thinking that obedience is not significant. The focus of Abraham's life was the fact that he obeyed - even to the point of offering up his promised son. His obedience was proof of his belief, and therefore YHWH *"accounted it to him for righteousness."* Genesis 15:6

The concept of righteousness is often lost in western religions that tend to relegate this subject into the abstract realm. Things such as "holiness" and "righteousness" seem out of reach for most - lost in the ethereal. To a Hebrew, thinking with a eastern mindset, these things are down to earth and practical. We will discuss this in more detail later in Chapter 12.

For the time being, it is important to recognize that righteousness is very much connected to obedience. We read

---

[106] The significance of the different Covenants in the life of Abraham are discussed in the Walk in the Light series book entitled *Covenants*.

in Psalm 119:173: *"For all Your Commandments are righteousness."*

Psalm 132:9 proclaims: *"Let Your priests be clothed with righteousness."* Just as the tunic made for Adam was a remembrance of his disobedience, the pure linen tunics of the priests were supposed to remind them of obedience.

It could be said that the culmination of Abraham's faith, and the ultimate test of his belief, involved his promised son Yitshaq (Isaac), described as his "only son."[107]

An important pattern of the Mechi-tzedek Priesthood was focused on the firstborn, and we see a prophetic pattern of that priesthood through the initial meal with Abram. Here it is again. *"¹⁸ Then Melchizedek king of Salem brought out bread and wine; he was the priest of El Most High. ¹⁹ And he blessed him and said: 'Blessed be Abram of El Most High, Possessor of heaven and earth; ²⁰ And blessed be El Most High, Who has delivered your enemies into your hand.' And he gave him a tithe of all."* Genesis 14:18-20

This occurred after Abram had defeated Chedorlaomer, a giant king that Nimrod was unable to defeat. It had to be an amazing battle. That victory resulted in the rescue of Lot, and the return of possessions of other kings in the region.

As a result, Abram ended up dining with a King – the King of Salem, which is Jerusalem. This King was Melchi-Tzedek, which literally means My King is Righteous, or King of Righteousness.

At that point Abram had a promise of a child and land, but he had not seen either of those promises fulfilled. Immediately after receiving the blessing from Melchizedek, we read the following account.

"¹ After these things the word of YHWH came to Abram in a vision, saying, 'Do not be afraid, Abram. I am your shield, your exceedingly great

---

[107] Genesis 22:2

reward.' ² But Abram said, 'Master YHWH, what will You give me, seeing I go childless, and the heir of my house is Eliezer of Damascus?' ³ Then Abram said, 'Look, You have given me no offspring; indeed one born in my house is my heir!' ⁴ And behold, the word of YHWH came to him, saying, 'This one shall not be your heir, but one who will come from your own body shall be your heir.' ⁵ Then He brought him outside and said, 'Look now toward heaven, and count the stars if you are able to number them.' And He said to him, 'So shall your descendants be.' ⁶ And he believed in YHWH, and He accounted it to him for righteousness." Genesis 15:1-6

That promise, confirmed by the Word of YHWH, was later fulfilled. Abram received a name change when he entered into the Covenant of Circumcision. Thereafter, his seed passed through the cutting into Sarah, who bore the promised son Isaac. The promise then passed to Jacob who was later renamed Yisrael when he returned to the Land through the same way taken by Abram.

In fact, it is interesting to note that all of the Covenant patriarchs found their wives in Babylon. Abram brought Sarai out with him. Abraham then sent his servant Eliezer to Haran (Padan Aram) to find a wife for Isaac. Jacob later left the Land and journeyed to Haran (Padan Aram) to find a wife and ended up returning with a family.[108]

This line of seed from Abraham carried the firstborn status and culminated in a people who would represent the firstborn, or firstfruits of a redeemed mankind. We specifically read about that status when YHWH called Moses to deliver Yisrael from Egypt.

"²² Then you shall say to Pharaoh, Thus says YHWH:

---

[108] This is an amazing pattern when we consider the fact that Yahushua is calling His Bride out of Babylon.

Yisrael is My son, My firstborn. ²³ So I say to you, let My son go that he may serve Me. But if you refuse to let him go, indeed I will kill your son, your firstborn." Exodus 4:22-23

After the Passover, when the firstborn of Yisrael were protected by the blood of the lamb, and the firstborn of Egypt were killed, we read: *"And it came to pass, when Pharaoh was stubborn about letting us go, that YHWH killed all the firstborn in the land of Egypt, both the firstborn of man and the firstborn of beast. Therefore, I sacrifice to YHWH all males that open the womb, but all the firstborn of my sons I redeem."* Exodus 13:15

That is why we read in Exodus *"Consecrate to Me all the firstborn, whatever opens the womb among the children of Yisrael, both of man and beast; it is Mine."* Exodus 13:2

When we look even closer at Kol Yisrael (all Yisrael) we see that Joseph and his firstborn, Ephraim, carry the status of firstborn. This was evident from the special "tunic of many colors" given to Joseph.

It was a "et-katanot" (את-כתנת). A garment of royal status. It set him apart from his brothers, and it was also the garment that was torn and bloodied by his brothers as proof of his supposed death. We know that Joseph did not die, but was elevated to the right hand of Pharaoh, just as Yahushua was resurrected and went to the right hand of the Father. What an amazing pattern of the Messiah.

Later in Jeremiah we read about the restoration of the lost sheep of the House of Yisrael (Joseph)[109] through the Messiah.

"They shall come with weeping, and with supplications I will lead them. I will cause them to walk by the rivers of waters, in a straight way in which they shall not stumble; For I am a Father to Yisrael, and Ephraim is My firstborn." Jeremiah 31:9

In royal families, the firstborn ascend to the throne. The same holds true in the Kingdom of Elohim. That is why

---

[109] Joseph ended up being the leading Tribe of the Ten Northern Tribes. Therefore, the Ten "lost tribes" are often collectively referred to as the House of Yisrael, Joseph, or his son Ephraim, who was elevated to first-born status by Yisrael. See Genesis 48:1-20.

we read in Exodus 19:6 *"And you shall be to Me a Kingdom of Priests and a Set Apart Nation."* And then later, *"²¹ YHWH said to Moses, Go down and warn the people, lest they break through to gaze at YHWH, and many of them perish. ²² Also let the priests who come near YHWH consecrate themselves, lest YHWH break out against them."* Exodus 19:21

While Yisrael was called to be a nation of priests, it appears that there were already priests among the people.[110] We see the same distinction made in the following passage: *"Then YHWH said to him, 'Away! Get down and then come up, you and Aaron with you. But do not let the priests and the people break through to come up to YHWH, lest He break out against them."* Exodus 19:24[111]

These statements concerning priests were made before the Ten Commandments were spoken by YHWH, and written on tablets of stone. It was before the incident of the golden calf, and before the Levites were chosen. So, there were priests of Yisrael before the wedding ceremony between YHWH and Yisrael occurred at Sinai.

Indeed, the Yisraelites were supposed to give all of their firstborn to YHWH, the firstborn of their animals, their crops and their sons.[112] Those firstborn sons were to act as priests, because Yisrael was originally a Nation of Priests operating under the Melchizedek Order.

Only after the incident of the golden calf were the Levites chosen as priests. We read that in Exodus 32. *"²⁸ So the sons of Levi did according to the word of Moses. And about three thousand men of the people fell that day. ²⁹ Then Moses said, Consecrate yourselves today to YHWH, that He may bestow on you a blessing this day, for every man has opposed his son and his brother."* Exodus 32:28-29

---

[110] Some might believe that the "priests" being referred to in this passage are Aaron and his sons, although Moses is not given any specific command concerning their service until Exodus 27 and 28. In that context Aaron and his sons are chosen to act in the House of Elohim.
[111] Even though Aaron is mentioned here in this passage, there are other priests being mentioned.
[112] Exodus 22:29

As a result of their actions, the sons of Levi would represent all of the firstborn of Yisrael, and therefore, they would act as priests. *"Then the priests, the sons of Levi, shall come near, for YHWH your Elohim has chosen them to minister to Him and to bless in the Name of YHWH; by their word every controversy and every assault shall be settled."* Deuteronomy 21:5

So, the sons of Levi acted as priests on behalf of all the firstborn of Yisrael. This would continue until the Messiah atoned for the sins of Yisrael, and restored the Melchizedek priesthood.

Despite this change in priesthood – all of Yisrael was still supposed to be a "holy nation" as we read in Leviticus. *"Speak to all the congregation of the children of Yisrael, and say to them: 'You shall be holy (qadoshim), for I YHWH your Elohim am holy (gadosh).'"* Leviticus 19:2

As mentioned previously, the English word "holy" can be rather abstract. Like with the word "righteous," it almost seems out of reach for us, especially since it has been drilled into us that we are "sinners."

In the Hebrew we read "qadosh" (קָדוֹשׁ), which means "set apart." Of course, this is at the heart of our discussion – becoming set apart from Babylon, which represents a kingdom juxtaposed against to the Kingdom of Elohim.

It is the same word used when referring to the firstborn priests "consecrating" themselves. *"Also let the priests who come near YHWH consecrate (qadosh) themselves, lest YHWH break out against them."* Exodus 19:22

So being "qadosh" describes our condition, and how we live our lives. We know that Yisrael failed to remain "qadosh." They failed to separate from the Nations. Instead, they mixed with the Nations, and fornicated with their gods – which is idolatry. We read the reason for their failure in Hoshea.

"My people are destroyed for lack of knowledge;
because you have rejected knowledge,
I reject you from being a priest to me.

And since you have forgotten the Torah of your Elohim,
I also will forget your children."
Hosea 4:6

The English does not fully convey the message in Hosea. The Hebrew word for "knowledge" is "dat" (דעת). In the text we actually read "ha'dat" (הדעת), better translated as "the knowledge" or "the understanding."

The understanding is clearly the Torah as can be discerned from the passage, as well as other Scriptures.

"The fear of YHWH is the beginning of wisdom; a good understanding have all those who do His Commandments.
His praise endures forever."
Psalm 111:10

"Give me understanding, and I shall keep Your Torah.
Indeed, I shall observe it with my whole heart."
Psalm 119:34

"Your hands have made me and fashioned me. Give me understanding, that I may learn Your Commandments."
Psalm 119:73

"Through Your precepts I get understanding.
Therefore, I hate every false way."
Psalm 119:104

I hope that you get the point. Yisrael failed to act as a Kingdom of Priests, because they rejected, and then forgot, the Torah. They were ultimately punished, but Moses and the Prophets provided the promise that Yisrael would be regathered, and restored to the Covenant.

We have already talked about how we are currently witnessing people from around the world waking up and identifying with Yisrael. Many coming from a Christian background have spent most of their lives identifying with an entity called "The Church." They have been taught to believe that the Church has somehow replaced the Covenant Assembly of Yisrael, even though that is found nowhere in the Scriptures.

As with many misconceptions and misunderstandings, language and communication has a lot to do with the problem. The Hebrew Scriptures describe Yisrael as a "set apart assembly" by using the word "qahal" (קָהָל). The equivalent word in the Greek language is "ekklesia" (ἐκκλησία). Regrettably, when Greek texts are translated into English, the word "church" is used to describe the "ekklesia," instead of the word "assembly."

As a result, people read about "Yisrael" as the assembly in the Old Testament, and "The Church" as the assembly in the New Testament. Even though the underlying words in the Hebrew and Greek mean the same thing, the translation creates the appearance of two different entities. The Church of the New Testament appears to have replaced the Yisrael of the Old Testament.

This has powerful implications, because the word "church" derives from the word "circe." No doubt the word means "a circle." The word "church" was used in the New Testament because places of worship among the German and Celtic nations were always circular.[113]

Indeed, "Kirke" also known as "Circe" is the name of a pagan Greek goddess. She is considered to be the daughter of the sun god Helios.

Attempting to identify the Set Apart Assembly with a word that has such pagan connections is clear error. On the other hand, it accurately applies to the Christian assembly from the Roman Catholic religion that traces straight back to

---

[113] Witness the circular Stonehenge and Globeki Tepi along with other ancient stone megaliths throughout the earth.

Babylonian sun worship.[114]

The Church identifies and relates to Babylon - not Yisrael. As a result, anyone identifying with Yisrael should not want to identify with the Church. The chosen people are not confined to genetic Jews, or the religious system they were raised within.

They should not carry labels such as Judaism, Messianic Judaism, Christianity, Hebrew Christians, or the Church. They all send mixed and inaccurate messages. The true identity of those who are in a covenant relationship with YHWH is Yisrael. Yisrael consists of the chosen people who are new creations – genetically grafted into the family of Elohim through the blood of the Messiah.

This is crystal clear in the Scriptures, but clouded by tradition. Read how Peter describes the assembly: *"But you are a chosen generation, a royal priesthood, a Holy (set apart) Nation, a people for His own people, that you may proclaim the praises of Him who called you out of darkness into His marvelous light."* 1 Peter 2:9

When referring to this "chosen generation" the word for "generation" is "genos" (γένος). It means: "offspring", "races," "family," or "stock." This is where we get "genetics" and the word "genome."

The point is that YHWH Elohim is building a family to fill His House, and Yisrael is that family. We see this message built into the first character of the Torah. The word Beresheet (בראשית) not only begins with a "bet" (ב), which represents a house; it also includes the word for "house" – "beit" (בית).

So, let me be very clear. This is not about the Jews being a chosen race or special, because they have better genes as some incorrectly promote. First of all, we are talking about Abraham, and the seed of Abraham. His seed were not the greatest, but rather the least in numbers. And they were only

---

[114] I have seen a theory that the Tabernacle was a circular tent, and that the Assembly of Yisrael camped in the wilderness in a circle, like the Mazzaroth. That would still not justify replacing the identity of the Assembly of Yisrael with a different title.

special if they were in Covenant with Elohim, and obeyed His Commandments.

That is made clear by the following passage:

"⁶ *For you are a holy (set apart) people to YHWH your Elohim; YHWH your Elohim has chosen you to be a people for Himself, a special treasure above all the peoples on the face of the earth. ⁷ YHWH did not set His love on you nor choose you because you were more in number than any other people, for you were the least of all peoples; ⁸ but because YHWH loves you, and because He would keep the oath which He swore to your fathers, YHWH has brought you out with a mighty hand, and redeemed you from the house of bondage, from the hand of Pharaoh king of Egypt. ⁹ 'Therefore know that YHWH your Elohim, He is Elohim, the faithful Elohim Who keeps covenant and mercy for a thousand generations with those who love Him and keep His Commandments; ¹⁰ and He repays those who hate Him to their face, to destroy them. He will not be slack with him who hates Him; He will repay him to his face. ¹¹ Therefore you shall keep the Commandment, the statutes, and the judgments which I command you today, to observe them.'"*
Deuteronomy 7:6-11

This is exactly the same group that Peter was referring to. A people called out of darkness, and into the light. Through the light of life provided by the Messiah, all are able to join this set apart family. These are all descriptions of Yisrael. They are supposed to be "holy," which means: "set apart."

And what are they to do? The word "proclaim" is "exagello" (ἐξαγγέλλω) in the Greek. It literally means "to publish" the praises and excellencies of Elohim. We do this through our words and deeds.

As priests, we are supposed to be separated from the world (Babylon), and living within the boundaries of the Covenant by obeying His Commandments.

This leads us straight back to the Fourth Commandment concerning the Name of YHWH. That Commandment is often translated as *"you shall not take the Name of YHWH your Elohim in vain."* Exodus 20:7

Westerners often translate "take" to involve "speaking" the Name flippantly, but in Hebrew we read "tasha" (תשא). It means "to lift" and "to carry." So it is an action word. Remember that the High Priest literally wore a crown of gold on his forehead bearing the Name of YHWH. He carried and displayed the Name of YHWH.[115]

This is an extremely significant distinction, and that is the message being translated though what is commonly called "The Priestly Blessing."

"[22] And YHWH spoke to Moses, saying: [23] Speak to Aaron and his sons, saying, This is the way you shall bless the children of Yisrael. Say to them: [24] 'YHWH bless you and keep you; [25] YHWH make His face shine upon you, and be gracious to you; [26] YHWH lift up His countenance upon you, and give you peace.' [27] So they shall put My Name on the children of Yisrael, and I will bless them." Numbers 6:22-27

The High Priest was supposed to put the Name of YHWH on the children of Yisrael so that they could carry the Name as well. By doing so, they were all supposed to represent YHWH through their words and deeds.

Yahushua came as the High Priest according to the Order of Melchizedek. He literally carries the Name of YHWH. The Name Yahushua means "YHWH saves" or "YHWH is salvation."

We carry the Name by shining as a light to the nations, which brings glory to that Name. Yahushua stated: *"[14] You are the light of the world. A city that is set on a hill cannot be hidden. [15]*

---

[115] See Exodus 28:36-38

Nor do they light a lamp and put it under a basket, but on a lampstand, and it gives light to all who are in the house. [16] Let your light so shine before men, that they may see your good works and glorify your Father in heaven." Matthew 5:14-16

We glorify the Father through our works, by bearing fruit. Indeed, carrying the Name of YHWH involves bearing fruit, otherwise you bring the Name to naught.

This was made clear by Yahushua when He referred to Himself as the Vine. *"[5] I am the vine, you are the branches. He who abides in Me, and I in him, bears much fruit; for without Me you can do nothing. [6] If anyone does not abide in Me, he is cast out as a branch and is withered; and they gather them and throw them into the fire, and they are burned. [7] If you abide in Me, and My words abide in you, you will ask what you desire, and it shall be done for you. [8] By this My Father is glorified, that you bear much fruit; so you will be My disciples. [9] As the Father loved Me, I also have loved you; abide in My love. [10] If you keep My Commandments, you will abide in My love, just as I have kept My Father's Commandments and abide in His love."* John 15:9

So, if you bring the Name to naught, you are not bearing any fruit, and you will get cut off. We need to be connected with the Vine, and obey the Commandments as He instructed us so that we can bear much fruit and bring glory to the Name of YHWH through our obedience. That is how we live as priests - by carrying the Name and message of YHWH to the Nations through our lives.

That gives an entirely new understanding from the one many of us were taught in Sunday School. Once you understand your role and purpose within the Covenant, it then becomes apparent that the instructions provided to the Nation of Priests are applicable to you. They are instructions for righteous living – living set apart. Being set apart doesn't just involve one day of the week. It involves how we live our lives day by day – moment by moment.

The Creator gave us an instruction manual – known as

the Torah.[116] Many Christians fail to understand this. They call the Torah - "The Law." As a result, they believe that obeying the Torah puts a person "under the Law," which results in bondage. This is absolutely false.

The Torah was a wedding gift to the Bride Yisrael. It showed her how to be "holy," so she could dwell in the presence of a "holy" Elohim. We are supposed to obey, but be careful not to add to it or take away from it.

"You shall not add to the word which I Command you, nor take from it, that you may keep (shamar) the Commandments of YHWH your Elohim which I command you."
Deuteronomy 4:2

"Whatever I command you, be careful to observe it; you shall not add to it nor take away from it."
Deuteronomy 12:32

That is what the Pharisees and Sadducees did, and that is why Yahushua was always challenging and confronting them. The Sadducees ended up going extinct, and the Pharisees ended up creating their own religion known as Rabbinic Judaism.

With that understanding let's see what the Torah says about being "holy" – set apart. Interestingly, the first time the Torah specifically directs Yisrael to be holy (set apart), it involves food.

"And you shall be holy (set apart) men to Me: you shall not eat meat torn by beasts in the field; you shall throw it to the dogs."
Exodus 22:31

---

[116] It is important to distinguish the instructions from the Scroll or Codex that contains the instructions. The Torah goes beyond ink on parchment or animal skin. The Word of Elohim is alive. When spoken and lived, it has power. Some people turn scrolls and books into idols. That is a mistake, and misses the point.

We also read in Leviticus another Commandment connecting what we eat and being set apart. *"⁴⁴ For I am YHWH your Elohim. You shall therefore consecrate yourselves, and you shall be holy (qadoshim) for I am holy (qadosh). Neither shall you defile yourselves with any creeping thing that creeps on the earth. ⁴⁵ For I am YHWH who brings you up out of the land of Egypt, to be your Elohim. You shall therefore be holy (qadoshim), for I am holy (qadosh)."* Leviticus 11:44-45

So, there is a close connection between being holy (set apart), and what we eat. In fact, diet was at the heart of the sin in the Garden. Remember, the first recorded Commandment in the Scriptures involved fruit.

"¹⁶ And YHWH Elohim commanded the man, saying, Of every tree of the garden you may freely eat; ¹⁷ but of the tree of the knowledge of good and evil you shall not eat, for in the day that you eat of it you shall surely die." Genesis 2:16-17

This was done purposefully by the Creator. Since we all typically eat every day, throughout the day, it is an opportunity to remind us to be set apart every time we eat.

As with the Sabbath, we see death associated with disobedience.[117] The Torah shows us the difference between clean and unclean, righteousness and wickedness. We are supposed to learn these distinctions, and act accordingly. Not just in what we eat and what we wear, but in all of our conduct.

Interestingly, in the very center of the Torah, known as "the heart of the Torah"[118] we are given instructions concerning a variety of issues involving how we should live. Of course, it is no coincidence that the heart of the Torah is found in the heart of the book of Leviticus – the book named for priests.

YHWH wants us to be like Him. That is the purpose of our entire existence, and that is the pattern provided through family. Parents are supposed to guide and direct their

---

[117] Partaking from the Tree of the Knowledge of Good and Evil (i.e. All Knowledge), probably involved more than simply eating a piece of fruit. Nevertheless, the principle is there.
[118] Leviticus 19 and 20

children, and prepare them to succeed in life.

Priests learn to conduct themselves in the presence of a set apart Elohim. They then teach others how to live in the House of Elohim. We can see that the Tabernacle was a picture of a future fulfillment of that House, when Elohim would dwell within us. If our bodies represent the dwelling place for the Set Apart Spirit (Ruach ha'Qodesh), then these vessels should be set apart.

In the House of Elohim blood was spilled, and only specific animals could be offered. We were also given Commandments concerning what goes into our bodily "temples." There is nothing about the shed blood of Yahushua, or the forgiveness and cleansing it provides, that changes these distinctions.

YHWH has specifically provided us with the rules of His House, which are the rules of His Kingdom. Yisrael failed and was expelled from the Land, just as the man and the woman were expelled from the Garden. It is the same pattern and punishments, because the Commandments have not changed.

The punishments were the result of disobedience, when the Commandments and distinctions were not observed. Yahushua shed His blood and died to provide a way back in.

Incredibly, Christians now act like these distinctions, and Commandments no longer matter. As a result, they are disqualified from being priests. If they continue in their lawlessness, they will not be part of the Holy Nation – the Kingdom of Yisrael.

Yahushua was very clear concerning the Torah. *"17 Do not think that I came to destroy the Torah or the Prophets. I did not come to destroy but to fulfill. 18 For assuredly, I say to you, till heaven and earth pass away, one jot or one tittle will by no means pass from the Torah till all is fulfilled."* Matthew 5:17-18

He also said: *"If you love Me you keep My*

Commandments."[119] Recall that the word "keep" is "shamar" (שָׁמַר) in Hebrew, and it means – "to guard" and "to protect." Remember Adam was a worshiper and a watchman. He was commanded to "shamar" the Garden.[120] Yisrael was later commanded to "shamar" (guard) the Commandments.

If we are part of the Assembly of Yisrael we must make sure to guard, and keep the Commandments. This includes the dietary instructions, if expect to be be Priests.

Now it is also important to understand the role of the priests. Before there was a King, the Priests were the ones who guided the people like shepherds over the flock of Yisrael. They were not just in Jerusalem serving in the Temple. They lived among the people, and taught them the ways. They also led the people into battle. So, they were servants, teachers and warriors.

Yahushua came first as a servant, teaching the Torah. He will return as a warrior. In fact, Yahushua will return as King and High Priest – The Melchizedek. So, Yahushua is looking for Sons of Elohim to serve Him and reign with Him in a royal priesthood. But there will be no lawless priests in the Kingdom.

The prophets described a time after His return when people would declare: *"Come, and let us go up to the Mountain of YHWH, to the House of the Elohim of Jacob; He will teach us His ways, and we shall walk in His paths. For out of Zion (Tzyon) shall go forth the Torah, and the word of YHWH from Jerusalem."* Isaiah 2:3

The priests will be the ones serving at the Mountain of YHWH learning, and then teaching the Torah. If you want to rule and reign in the Kingdom you need to know and obey the Commandments. The Commandments are not too difficult.[121]

The Messiah will be returning for a Bride who will

---

[119] John 14:15
[120] *"Then YHWH Elohim took the man and put him in the Garden of Eden to tend and keep (shamar) it."* Genesis 2:15
[121] *"For this commandment which I command you today is not too difficult for you, nor is it far off."* Deuteronomy 30:11

serve as priests with Him. There will be a Great Wedding Feast. We need to wear garments appropriate for a wedding, and conduct ourselves appropriately. That is why we continue our rehearsals for the Appointed Times.

YHWH is concerned about all aspects of our lives, including our diet. I can assure you that the dietary instructions will be in full force and effect at the Marriage Supper of the Lamb.[122]

When we were in Babylon we were taught that we could eat whatever we wanted, but that was a lie. Those who believe that lie are subjected to all of the sicknesses and diseases of Egypt – this was a curse for disobedience. There are also blessings associated with obedience.

Remember the first Commandment given to Yisrael after the bitter waters of Marah. "If you diligently heed the voice of YHWH your Elohim and do what is right in His sight, give ear to His commandments and keep all His statutes, I will put none of the diseases on you which I have brought on the Egyptians. For I am YHWH who heals you." Exodus 15:26

So, we see that there is healing associated with obedience. We specifically saw this from the example of people taking hold of the tzitzit of the Messiah. The tzitzit represent the Commandments.

As we continue our discussion, we will see that there are many other blessings associated with obedience. And of course, that was the point from the very beginning.

As long as mankind obeyed the Commandments they could dwell in the presence of Elohim in Eden, and Eden means paradise. The Covenant and the instructions of the Covenant were intended to be a blessing – not a curse.

Sadly, Babylonian religions teach that the Torah is a curse, and they lead people into separation and destruction. As you leave Babylon, walk in truth, and live set apart lives it will become increasingly clear that the dietary instructions are an

---

[122] Revelation 19:9

important part of that process.

Start out by reading Leviticus 11 and Deuteronomy 14. You are probably already following most of the instructions. Remember that the priests served in the House of YHWH. They kept the fire burning, they filled the lamps with oil and they kept food on the table. You want to eat and conduct yourself in a manner that is consistent with living in the House of YHWH.

Once we are set apart and walking the righteous path many then ask "How can we be priests without a Temple?"

We are in an everlasting priesthood - a priesthood that existed before there was sin, and the need for the shedding of blood on an altar. Long before there was a Temple and a Levitic priesthood, there was the Melchizedek Priesthood. The Temple merely provides a pattern for us, and the slaughterings and offerings represent our service.

The Psalms actually show the way into the House now that the blood of the Lamb has made our priestly robes white.[123] *"Enter into His gates with thanksgiving, and into His courts with praise. Be thankful to Him, and bless His Name."* Psalm 100:4

While we remain in the physical realm, our voices transcend into the spiritual realm. Here is an account of the dynamics that are occurring in the Heavenly Throne room.

"³ Then another messenger, having a golden censer, came and stood at the altar. He was given much incense, that he should offer it with the prayers of all the set apart ones upon the golden altar, which was before the throne. ⁴ And the smoke of the incense, with the prayers of the set apart ones, ascended before Elohim from the messenger's hand." Revelation 8:3

The word "prayer" is "proseuche" (προσευχη) in Greek. It means "prayer, supplication, worship." So, there is a functioning Temple service going on right now in the Heavens, and we can participate in it,[124] if we are among the set apart ones.

---

[123] Revelation 7:14
[124] See also Revelation 5:8

The realization that we are actually functioning in an eternal Heavenly Kingdom now, while still here on Earth, is not always easy to grasp, but it is critical to understand. We can actually begin our service immediately, and start ministering in the heavenly realm.

This is what Daniel was doing when he was captive in Babylon. The Temple in Jerusalem had been destroyed, but he had seen the Heavenly Service. He understood what was going on in the spiritual realm as he had already witnessed the coronation of the Messiah in the Heavenly Court.[125]

He was offering up prayers for himself, the people of Yisrael and presenting his supplication before YHWH Elohim for the set apart Mountain of Elohim *"at the time of the evening offering."*[126] So, Daniel was ministering as a priest while in exile, and it was at one of these times of prayer that Gabriel appeared to him concerning the Seventy Weeks.[127]

We know that the incense offering was made every evening and every morning, at the time of the evening and morning slaughterings.[128] They weren't using clocks like we do today. They were using the sun. This will be important to understand when we review the Creator's Calendar in a future chapter.

Daniel's prayers and supplications were offered up as incense to the Heavenly Throne Room and they were heard. Of course, this event involving Daniel and Gabriel should immediately make us think about the event described in Luke 1, after the Temple was rebuilt.

Gabriel appeared at the right side of the altar of incense when Zachariah the Priest was making the incense offering "at the hour of incense."[129] Gabriel told him about the son who

---

[125] Daniel 7:9-14
[126] Daniel 9:21
[127] See Daniel 9:24-27
[128] *"7 Aaron shall burn on it sweet incense every morning; when he tends the lamps, he shall burn incense on it. 8 And when Aaron lights the lamps at twilight, he shall burn incense on it, a perpetual incense before YHWH throughout your generations."* Exodus 30:7-8
[129] See Luke 1:8-12

would be born to him and his wife, often referred to as John the Baptist.

So, it is clear then that we can serve as priests whether there is a Temple or not. The point was always that our service is rendered unto the Heavenly Throne Room. The Earthly Temple was just a model to teach us this truth.

Once we enter His gates and His Courts to serve, do we offer a sacrifice? Yes. The sacrifices of joy and praise. *"And now my head shall be lifted up above my enemies all around me. Therefore, I will offer sacrifices of joy in His tabernacle; I will sing, yes, I will sing praises to YHWH."* Psalm 27:6

Jeremiah repeatedly speaks of bringing *"sacrifices of praise to the House of YHWH."* (see Jeremiah 17:26, 33:11) While the "sacrifice" of praise is inferred in the English, Hosea is clear on this point when he offers up a prescription for repentance. *"¹ Return Yisrael to YHWH your Elohim, for you have stumbled because of your iniquity; ² Take words with you, and return to YHWH. Say to Him, 'Take away all iniquity; receive us graciously, for we will offer the sacrifices of our lips.'"* Hosea 14:1-2

The phrase "sacrifices of our lips" is literally "bulls of our lips." In Hebrew we read "parim" (פרים) which refers to "young bulls" of the type that would be offered up for sin.[130]

The author of Hebrews also makes reference to the fruit of our lips.[131] *"Therefore by Him let us continually offer the sacrifice of praise to Elohim, that is, the fruit of our lips, giving thanks to His Name."* Hebrews 13:15

Indeed, the Psalms provide that *"the sacrifices of Elohim are a broken spirit – a broken spirit and a contrite heart."* Psalm 51:17 Blood sacrifices were not in the original plan, and only became a requirement when sin entered creation.

With thanksgiving, through praise and by blessing His

---

[130] Leviticus 4:1-3

[131] This would be a good point to mention the power of sound and the spoken word. Remember that Elohim made everything through sound – His spoken word. We are made in the image of Elohim and thus have power through speech. It has been said that the power of life and death rests with the tongue and a powerful argument can be made to support that position. As priests we should learn to utter our thanks and praise, not in silence, but through our speech.

Name, we serve Him with our lives. It is impossible to truly do this without knowing His Name.

Sadly, most Christians have completely failed to understand the purpose and function of those who follow the Messiah. They have been taught very poorly and, as a result, most are lawless and disqualified from serving as priests.[132]

We are not called to be like the Levitic priests. Rather, we are called to enter into an eternal priesthood by our eternal High Priest – Yahushua a priest forever according to the Order of Melchizedek.[133] This eternal priesthood was mentioned in the Psalms.

> "YHWH has sworn and will not relent,
> 'You are a priest forever according to
> the order of Melchizedek.'"
> Psalms 110:4

Peter clearly explains the restoration and fulfillment of the promise that Yisrael would become a nation of priests through the Renewed Covenant.

> "[4] Coming to Him as to a living stone, rejected indeed by men, but chosen by Elohim and precious, [5] you also, as living stones, are being built up a spiritual house, a holy priesthood, to offer up spiritual sacrifices acceptable to Elohim through Messiah Yahushua. [6] Therefore it is also contained in the Scripture, 'Behold, I lay in Zion (Tzyon) a chief cornerstone, elect, precious, and he who believes on Him will by no means be put to shame.' [7] Therefore, to you who believe, He is precious;

---

[132] It is this moment of rejection that we read about in Matthew. "[21] Not everyone who says to Me, 'Lord, Lord,' shall enter the kingdom of heaven, but he who does the will of My Father in heaven. [22] Many will say to Me in that day, "Lord, Lord, have we not prophesied in Your Name, cast out demons in Your Name, and done many wonders in Your Name? [23] And then I will declare to them, 'I never knew you; depart from Me, you who practice lawlessness!'" Matthew 7:21-23

[133] For a discussion on the difference between the Aaronic Priesthood consisting of the Tribe of Levi and the Melchizedek Priesthood, see Hebrews Chapter 7.

but to those who are disobedient, 'The stone which the builders rejected has become the chief cornerstone,' [8] *and 'A stone of stumbling and a rock of offense.' They stumble, being disobedient to the word, to which they also were appointed.* [9] *But you are a chosen generation, a royal priesthood, a Holy Nation, His own special people, that you may proclaim the praises of Him who called you out of darkness into His marvelous light;* [10] *who once were not a people but are now the people of Elohim, who had not obtained mercy but now have obtained mercy."* 1 Peter 2:4-10

We present ourselves as a living sacrifice,[134] following the example of our High Priest. That is our service within the House. Only the High Priest and his sons served in the House full-time.[135]

As previously mentioned, the Levites lived among the people and would also be responsible for teaching and shepherding the Yisraelites in the ways of the Torah.

The lost sheep of the House of Yisrael have been scattered throughout the world. That is why Yahushua commissioned His disciples, as Priests according to the Order of Melchizedek, to go into the nations and proclaim the Good News.

He called them and said: *"Follow Me, and I will make you fishers of men."*[136] He trained them to be fishers of men to fulfill the Prophecy of Jeremiah 16:16 that proclaimed: *"Behold I will send for many fishermen, says YHWH, and they shall fish them . . ."*

His final recorded instruction, as depicted in the New King James Version, was to *"Go into all the world and preach the Gospel to every creature."* Mark 16:15

---

[134] *"I beseech you therefore, brethren, by the mercies of Elohim, that you present your bodies a living sacrifice, holy (set apart), acceptable to Elohim, which is your reasonable service."* Romans 12:1

[135] And again, I would be remiss if I did not point out how Peter juxtaposes the chosen ones against the disobedient.

[136] Matthew 4:19

The Gospel is the focus of our service as Priests to the Nations. It is also supposed to be the Christian message to the world.

We have already discussed various problems with Christian doctrine. In order to fully understand where things went wrong with the Christian religion it is critical to go understand the Gospel as described in the Scriptures.

7

Understanding the Gospel

So far in this book we have been exploring the process of becoming set apart from pagan religious and cultural influences, and walking the path established by the Creator as detailed in the Scriptures. Part of that process involves understanding the Covenant as it relates to the Christian Gospel that originally set many of us on this path.

Most Christians either learned about the Gospel growing up in a church, or they converted to Christianity after hearing the Gospel. In either case, the Gospel is at the heart of the Christian message.

In the last chapter we looked at the final instruction given by Yahushua to "*Go into all the world and preach the Gospel to every creature.*" Mark 16:15

While it appears that the primary message of the Messiah is the Gospel, the word "gospel" is not necessarily the most appropriate term to describe it. You see, the Greek word translated as "gospel" is "euaggelion" (εὐαγγέλιον), and it literally means "good message" or "good news."

The English word "gospel" actually has possible pagan origins. It derives from the Old English word "godspell" and the Germanic "gottspel," which actually can refer to a "divine spell."

The Hebrew word "basar" (בשׂר) is the equivalent of the Greek "euaggelion" (εὐαγγέλιον), and they both refer to proclaiming "a good message." We see an example of the usage in Luke 4:18 when Yahushua read from the Prophet Isaiah and stated: "*The Spirit of Master YHWH is upon Me, because*

YHWH has anointed Me to preach good news (בשׂר) to the poor." Isaiah 61:1

In the Luke 4:18 rendering we see the word "euaggelizo" (εὐαγγελίζω). In other words, Yahushua came to "evangelize," which is the same as "basar." As a result, when we refer to the Good News of Messiah, we would be better off using the Hebrew word "basar" (בשׂר) or "basorah" (בשׂרה), rather than the English word "gospel."

So, the Gospel of Jesus Christ promoted by Christianity should actually be the Besorah of Yahushua ha'Moshiach, but it is not. In fact, it is easy to see that they are very different messages.

The traditional "Gospel of Jesus Christ" teaches that Jesus died for your sins. In order to be saved you simply need to believe, confess that you are a sinner, repent, and ask Jesus into your heart.

Sadly, this formula utterly fails to provide a definition of sin, making repentance a somewhat abstract concept along with the related notions of belief, faith, grace and salvation.

The Christian Gospel also fails to place the Messiah in the proper prophetic and Scriptural context within the Covenant made with Abraham, Isaac and Jacob, later renamed Yisrael. It teaches that Christians constitute a group of people in a New Covenant, and they are collectively referred to as "The Church." This new assembly of people called "The Church" is supposedly different from the Set Apart Covenant Assembly of Yisrael.

In fact, Christianity generally teaches that Jesus abolished the Law and replaced it with a brand-new Covenant. The basis for this is the erroneous belief that the Law puts us in bondage, and "we cannot possibly obey the Law."[137]

---

[137] Essentially, Christianity is teaching that the God of the Old Testament is a sadistic God, placing burdens and expectations on His people that they could never obey. This comes straight from the teachings of Marcion. Marcion of Sinope lived between 85 CE and 160 CE. He was the Bishop of a heretical religious sect referred to as the Marcionites. He taught a dualist belief system that the god of the Old Testament was a separate and distinct god from the New Testament. As a result, he emphasized various texts over the Old Testament and

The Covenant, as previously discussed, defines a relationship with our Creator. It is the process by which YHWH is expanding and filling His Heavenly Kingdom. He is actually birthing a royal family to fill His Kingdom through that Covenant relationship.

It is important to understand that man was originally created to be in the Kingdom - in the Family of Elohim. He was originally created in the "image" of Elohim. The English word "image" is "tselem" (צֶלֶם) in Hebrew. It can mean "a resemblance, an illusion or a representative figure."

So, man was supposed to be the physical representative of Elohim on planet Earth. He was supposed to establish the Kingdom of Elohim on this Earth. Thus, the assignment previously discussed to "tend" and "watch" the Garden.

The first man was called Adam (אדם). Adam actually means "red" and it contains the word "dam" (דם), which means "blood." Of course, we all know that blood is red. So, we see an emphasis on blood and red with this man made in the image of Elohim

If you look at the light spectrum you see red as the highest color in the rainbow. It is the highest in the heavens - closest to Elohim. It also has the lowest frequency and the longest wavelength of the visible colors of light.[138]

This special Creation, literally called "soil man,"[139] was placed in paradise, and given instructions on how to function in an Earthly Kingdom. He was representing Elohim and His Kingdom which is operating in the heavenly realm.

---

essentially threw out the foundation of the faith. Because of the destructive nature of his false teachings, many attribute the decision to develop the canon of the New Testament to Marcion. The development of the canon of the New Testament was an attempt to solidify orthodox doctrine and agree upon texts that supported that doctrine. Prior to that time, various letters and Gospels were circulating amongst the Assemblies, and were not necessarily treated as Scriptures.

[138] It is helpful to understand that creation was made through frequency and light. Elohim uttered sound vibrations to create light vibrations that resulted in this physical existence. An interesting discussion on the issue can be found in *The Rainbow Language* written by David Matthews.

[139] This definition is used in the Transparent English Version of Genesis, written by James D. Tabor. It is a faithful rendering of the Hebrew word.

There is a throne-room in the heavens with elders, "angels," and incredible creatures. In the Heavenly Court, decisions are made, judgments are being rendered and then dispatched. These heavenly activities connect with, and impact the Kingdom here on Earth.[140]

While some are cognizant of this reality, most people live their lives completely oblivious to this functioning eternal Kingdom – both in the Heavens and here on Earth. As a result, much of the world population is simply consumed with the day to day problems and concerns of Babylon.

They spend their entire existence completely oblivious to the operation of these two kingdoms, and with no clue how they fit within one of them. They have been born outside the Kingdom of Elohim, and few ever become aware of the way back in. Religions are very good at insuring that they never do.

Adam was made in the image of Elohim, and given an important role in the Kingdom. Sadly, he and Hawah[141] were deceived. They rebelled by disobeying the instructions and were cast out of the Garden - out of the Kingdom.

After the expulsion from the Garden, we read that their son Seth was born in the image and likeness of Adam, not Elohim. "*And Adam lived one hundred and thirty years, and begot a son in his own likeness, after his image, and named him Seth.*" Genesis 5:3

So, while Adam was originally made to be a part of this Kingdom, made in the image of Elohim; from Seth onward we see men and women born in the image of Adam in His fallen state, outside of Paradise.[142]

In fact, it was at the birth of Seth that we are first provided an age for Adam, because his years were now numbered. He was supposed to live forever in the Kingdom, but once outside He was dying every day.

---

[140] The subject of the Kingdom will be discussed further in Chapter 11.

[141] Hawah (חוה) is the actual Hebrew name of the first woman often called Eve.

[142] So where does that leave Cain and Abel? Many believe that both were conceived in the Garden, and were the result of the "forbidden fruit" incident. That event is further discussed in the Walk in the Light Series book entitled *The Messiah*.

We are now all born in these temporal containers of flesh and blood with skin that gets worn out and wrinkled with age. We have organs that slow down, and ultimately cease to function. That is the direct result of sin and death that came through disobedience.

As long as the man and the woman were in the Garden, they had access to the Tree of Life. They could live forever. Outside of the Garden, separated from Elohim, there was death.

Now there is tradition that the man and the woman were originally beings of light. And again, it is interesting that Adam was named after a color – red, which is a frequency of light. The menorah, which is symbolic of the seven Spirits of YHWH,[143] emanates seven lights that correlate to the seven colors of the rainbow.

The Scriptures detail how the Menorah is constructed to represent an Almond Tree, which many believe was representative of the Tree of Life.[144] The word for Almond Tree is "luz," and that word "luz" actually means "light" in certain languages.[145]

Light is often associated with the force of life that separates us from death. In Job 33:29-30 we read *"[29] Behold, Elohim works all these things, twice, in fact, three times with a man, [30] To bring back his soul from the pit, that he may be enlightened with the light of life."*

In the Psalms we read: *"For You have delivered my soul from death. Have You not kept my feet from falling, that I may walk before Elohim in the light of the living?"* Psalm 56:13

That light of life was actually the first thing spoken into Creation on day one. *"[3] Then Elohim said, Let there be light; and there was light. [4] And Elohim saw את-the light, that it was good; and Elohim divided the light from the darkness."* Genesis 1:3-4

---

[143] See Isaiah 11:2; Revelation 1:4, 3:1, 4:5 and 5:6
[144] Exodus 25:33-34
[145] Luz is the Latin root for light. Interestingly, the place called Beit El (House of Elohim) was formerly called "Luz". See Genesis 28:19 and 35:6

Many associate this with the light of the sun, but the sun wasn't created until day four.

This is better understood when we associate light with life and death with darkness. Notice that the light was specifically called good, and it was directly connected with the aleph taw (את) – the Word that represents the Messiah.

Of course, in John we read the following:

> "*¹ In the beginning was the Word, and the Word was with Elohim and the Word was Elohim. ² He was in the beginning with Elohim. ³ All things were made through Him, and without Him nothing was made that was made. ⁴ In Him was life, and the life was the light of men. ⁵ And the light shines in the darkness, and the darkness did not comprehend it.*"
> John 1:1-5

That is why we need to be born again – or reborn into new vessels where we can fully function in the Kingdom of light. That is what Yahushua meant when He said: "*Most assuredly, I say to you, unless one is born again, he cannot see the Kingdom of Elohim.*" John 3:3 We cannot survive in these frail and dying containers of flesh,

We were given a glimpse of those new bodies on the Mount of Transfiguration which likely occurred on Mount Hermon – a gateway used by the Fallen Angels when they corrupted the planet. We read in the text of Luke that "*As He prayed, the appearance of His face was altered, and His robe became white and glistening.*" Luke 9:29

Yahushua also specifically stated: "*I am the light of the world. He who follows Me shall not walk in darkness, but have the light of life.*" John 8:12

So, man lost that light and was left in darkness after the fall. We already mentioned the corruption of the Nephilim that resulted in the flood. The fallen ones were essentially trying to take over creation, and establish their own kingdom of darkness. We see traces of that ancient "Old World Order" everywhere.

Archaeologists have documented and uncovered countless remains of their monolithic structures throughout the planet that survived the flood. Many try to attribute these archeological sites to aliens, because they are so hard to explain if you do not recognize this struggle that has been going on since the Garden.

After Adam and Hawah broke the Covenant and were expelled from the Garden, the fallen ones continued their efforts to establish their kingdom. At the same time, YHWH has been focused on calling a family out of the darkness, and into His Kingdom of Light.

That effort has occurred through a process of covenants. The purpose of those covenants is to re-establish the relationship with YHWH, and restore the original bond that existed between Elohim and man in the Garden.

We are not talking about an old covenant versus a new and different covenant, as many incorrectly believe. It is all one covenant process occurring through the ages to draw mankind back to his Creator. This Covenant relationship has simply been offered through a series of progressions, and renewals.

We saw a cleansing and renewal through the flood during the life of Noah. Then, after the Tower of Babel and the scattering of the peoples across the face of the Earth, we saw Elohim choosing to work with one man – Abram.

Abram was called out of Babylon and into a Covenant relationship. Just as we saw the plan set forth from the word B'resheet – in the beginning; so too, we see the plan presented through the name of this man.

Remember that the first time we read about Abram we were told: "Now Terah lived seventy years, and begot Abram, Nahor, and Haran." Genesis 11:26 We already spoke about the fact that the number seventy represents "the nations" in the last chapter so we can discern that this man will have an impact upon the nations.

In fact, the text later provides: *"In your seed all the nations of the earth shall be blessed, because you have obeyed My voice."* Genesis 22:18 Notice the fact that obedience was directly tied to the promised blessings.

It is worth examining the name of Abram again. Remember that the aleph taw (את) is affixed to his name, and the first time his name is mentioned in the Hebrew Scriptures we read "et-Abram" (את-אברם). Now this is not unique to Abram, but it points to his significance in the Covenant plan. Again, the "et" is aleph taw (את) which points to the Messiah – the Word that was in the beginning creating.

The name Abram (אברם) consists of four consonants aleph (א), bet (ב), resh (ר), and mem (ם). Abram begins with aleph bet – ab (אב), which means "father." Next we see bet resh which spells "bar" (בר), and means "son."

The first and last letters spell aleph mem – "am" (אם). The Hebrew word "am," also pronounced "em," means "mother." But, there is also an instance where it refers to the chosen people prophetically through Yisrael.

We see the entire concept of a family built into the name of Abram, and it points to a chosen people – am – usually ayin mem (עם), but when referring to the creation of Yisrael spelled aleph mem (אם).

So a family, and a people, will come from a father and a mother through a son out of the Nations. Of course, that "son" ultimately points to "the only begotten Son," better referred to as "the unique Son" – Yahushua the Messiah. It would also progress through the sons of Abram, after he was circumcised.

This is critical to understand - Abram was first uncircumcised when he was chosen. He was part of the Nations. He later "crossed over" into the Land of Promise, which represents immersion, also known as "baptism."

He entered into a land filled with giants, and it was there where he then entered into a blood covenant. The unique thing about that covenant is the fact that YHWH was the only party that passed through the pieces, and took on the punishment of death. Abram was placed in a deep sleep during that process.[146]

Later, Abram was given a new name – Abraham. It was then that he shed his own blood through the Covenant of Circumcision. His wife named Sarai was given a new name as well – Sarah. From that point on the Covenant would progress from Isaac to Jacob until we see Jacob being given a new name – Yisrael.

The Covenant that began with Abram later culminated with Yisrael. We know that this name was given to Jacob after he wrestled with a mysterious man – who many believe was Yahushua.

The definition of his new name is given in the text of Genesis 32:28. "*And He said, Your name shall no longer be called Jacob, but אם-Yisrael; for you have struggled with Elohim and with men, and have prevailed.*"

Now this is where we see the fulfillment of the promise given through the name of Abram. Remember that when referring to a people the word "am" (עם) is typically spelled ayin (ע) mem (ם), but in this text we see "am" (אם) spelled aleph (א) mem (ם), when Yisrael is used the first time.

In this text we read: "*Your name shall no longer be called Jacob, but אם-Yisrael; for you have struggled (שׂרית) with עם-Elohim and with עם-men, and have prevailed.*"

As with many instance of Hebrew naming, the definition is provided with the name. The fact that Jacob "struggled" is a key component of the name. Remember that Jacob struggled with his brother in the womb.[147]

The word in the text translated as struggled is "saritah"

---

[146] The blood Covenant event hearkens back to the time described in Genesis 2:21 when Adam was placed into a "deep sleep" as Hawah was taken from his body. The connection was not a coincidence as YHWH was in the process of birthing a bride for Himself through the Covenant. I believe that Yahushua was represented by the "smoking oven and burning torch" that passed through the cuttings, before He took on flesh. (see Genesis 15:17-18)

[147] Genesis 25:22

(שָׂרִית), from the root "sarah" (שָׂרָה). The name is literally "yisar-el." It begins with "yud" (י), "sin" (שׂ), "resh" (ר) – "yisar" (יִשַׂר). Abram's wife was originally Sari (שָׂרִי). Spelled "sin" (שׂ), "resh" (ר), "yud" (י), it shares the same root as "struggle," because she struggled to have a son.

Her name was changed to "Sarah," which means "princess." Interestingly, the root of both her names was "sar" (שַׂר), which means "prince." So, along with struggling, the focus is clearly on royalty.

The first part of the name Yisrael refers to princes and princesses struggling, and the last part - "el" refers to Elohim.

Yisrael would become a people, and ultimately that people group would come from the Nations through the Covenant promised to Abram, who was called out of Babylon.

Yisrael is the royal family of Elohim that will populate the Kingdom through their struggle with the Nations to hold on to that firstborn status.

Yisrael represents the Kingdom established through the Covenant. That Covenant was elevated even further when Yisrael was delivered from their bondage in Egypt. They were brought to Mount Sinai where Yisrael then entered into a marriage Covenant at the Mountain of Elohim.

They were delivered from Egypt with a mixed multitude of people. That was a fulfillment of the pattern established by Abram when he left Egypt centuries earlier. He left Egypt when Pharaoh released his bride from captivity, after being plagued.[148] Through that process he also brought with him Hagar (הגר), whose name literally means: "the stranger."[149]

Yisrael's deliverance from Egypt was also prophetic of a future time when Yisrael will be gathered from all the Nations, and the Bride will be brought to a great mountain to marry the Lamb. We read about that in Revelation 21.[150]

---

[148] See Genesis 12:1-13:2 and Genesis 16:1-3
[149] The letter "hey" (ה) means "the" while "gimel resh" (גר) means "stranger or foreigner."
[150] "' Now I saw a new heaven and a new earth, for the first heaven and the first earth had passed away.

A problem occurred when those who left Egypt and entered into the Covenant at Mount Sinai actually broke that Covenant by worshipping a false god. It is critical to understand that YHWH intended to dwell with these people, but their sin caused a separation. While YHWH agreed to renew the Covenant through Moses as a mediator, the relationship would not exist as intended.

Just as Moses was a mediator, the Levites would also act as mediators, because YHWH would live in a House separated from the people. This was not a return to the Garden, but the relationship and the Covenant continued to point a way back.

Now, we know that 40 years passed until the next generation could enter into the Promised Land. This was because the generation that left Egypt refused to trust and obey. After they finally entered into the Land, Yisrael would continually struggle to live righteously.

They would constantly fall away, and follow after the gods of the nations. They repeatedly failed to remain faithful to YHWH as His inheritance

When they fell away, He sent judges to unite them and deliver them. While YHWH was supposed to be their King they wanted to be like other nations – they wanted a man to be their king.

This was displeasing to YHWH as we read about in 1 Samuel 12. Nevertheless, YHWH granted their request. They were given a king, but that did not help much. The people still ended up falling away and being punished. This was because mortal kings are imperfect, and many of them failed to lead Yisrael on the righteous path.

As it turns out the first King Saul was unable to properly lead the people in obedience, so he was replaced by

---

Also there was no more sea. ² Then I, John, saw the holy city, New Jerusalem, coming down out of heaven from Elohim, prepared as a bride adorned for her husband. ³ And I heard a loud voice from heaven saying, "Behold, the tabernacle of Elohim is with men, and He will dwell with them, and they shall be His people. Elohim Himself will be with them and be their Elohim." Revelation 21:1-3

David. David followed YHWH and united the twelve Tribes into one Kingdom, but that was short lived. While his son Solomon was wise, he strayed from the precepts of YHWH and committed abominations with other gods.[151]

This resulted in YHWH tearing apart his Kingdom. Yisrael was ultimately divided into two separate kingdoms. The Northern Tribes were called the House of Yisrael and the Southern Tribes were called the House of Yahudah (Judah).

As we stated before, Yisrael was supposed to be a "holy nation" and a kingdom of priests.[152] The point was that all the nations of the earth would be blessed by the example set by Yisrael. Yisrael was supposed to shine as a light, and draw the nations to Elohim.

Instead, they were drawn away from YHWH to the gods of the other Nations. YHWH decided that if they wanted the gods of the Nations then He would give them up to the Nations. He viewed Yisrael as an adulterous bride.

So, this Bride of YHWH was first divided, and then each House went on to fall into a pattern of adultery. The Northern Tribes were literally divorced by YHWH, and then conquered and completely removed from the Land by the Assyrians.

> "Then I saw that for all the causes for which backsliding Yisrael had committed adultery, **I had put her away and given her a certificate of divorce;** yet her treacherous sister Yahudah did not fear, but went and played the harlot also." Jeremiah 3:8

The Southern Tribes were just as wicked, but for the sake of David and his house they were not immediately divorced. Nevertheless, the House of Yahudah was ultimately punished. They were conquered by Nebuchadnezzar, and some were exiled to Babylon while a remnant remained in the

---

[151] 1 Kings 11:1-13
[152] Exodus 19:6 and 1 Peter 2:9

Land. They were exiled for seventy years, and it should be clear by now that seventy was not just some random number. It had a meaning and was sending a message.

After the seventy year Babylonian exile, some of the Yahudim returned, as recorded in Ezra and Nehemiah. It was not a complete restoration and there was no legitimate king until Yahushua was born. That brief and unstable period allowed a way for the Messiah to come through Yahudah, and restore the severed relationship with both House of the divided Kingdom the renewed Covenant.

The Prophets promised that the divided Kingdom would once again be restored and reunited, but that would require a wedding for the House of Yisrael who was divorced.

In the last chapter we mentioned Hosea, who declared that the people were destroyed for lack of "the knowledge." He was a very interesting prophet who, through his life, demonstrated the heart wrenching position Yisrael had created for YHWH.

Hosea was instructed to marry a whore and live with her as a husband while she continued to be unfaithful to him. They had children who were named to represent that deteriorating relationship between YHWH, and His Bride.

Thankfully, Hosea also prophesied about the restoration of the relationship. It would occur through the promise of the children of Yisrael becoming Sons of the Living El – Sons of YHWH.

"*10 Yet the number of the children of Yisrael shall be as the sand of the sea, which cannot be measured or numbered. And it shall come to pass in the place where it was said to them, 'You are not My people,' There it shall be said to them, 'You are sons of the living El.' 11 Then the children of Yahudah and the children of Yisrael shall be gathered together, and appoint for themselves One Head; and they shall come up out of the land, for great will be the day of Jezreel!"* Hosea 1:10-11[53]

---

[53] What many people fail to understand is that "Sons of Elohim" are actually a unique category of heavenly beings in the Kingdom of Elohim.

Another prophet, Ezekiel, provided a powerful prophecy about the whole house of Yisrael being gathered, and resurrected from the Valley of the Dry Bones.[154] He went on to prophesy about two sticks coming together through one King.

> "[15] *Again the word of YHWH came to me, saying,* [16] *As for you, son of man, take a stick for yourself and write on it: 'For Yahudah and for the children of Yisrael, his companions.' Then take another stick and write on it, 'For Joseph, the stick of Ephraim, and for all the House of Yisrael, his companions.'* [17] *Then join them one to another for yourself into one stick, and they will become one in your hand.* [18] *And when the children of your people speak to you, saying, Will you not show us what you mean by these?* [19] *say to them, Thus says Adonai YHWH: Surely I will take the stick of Joseph, which is in the hand of Ephraim, and the tribes of Yisrael, his companions; and I will join them with it, with the stick of Yahudah, and make them one stick, and they will be one in My hand.* [20] *And the sticks on which you write will be in your hand before their eyes.* [21] *Then say to them, Thus says Adonai YHWH: Surely I will take the children of Yisrael from among the nations, wherever they have gone, and will gather them from every side and bring them into their own land;* [22] *and I will make them one nation in the land, on the mountains of Yisrael; and One King shall be King over them all; they shall no longer be two nations, nor shall they ever be divided into two kingdoms again.* [23] *They shall not defile themselves anymore with their idols, nor with their detestable things, nor with any of their transgressions; but I will deliver them from all their dwelling places in*

---

[154] Ezekiel 37:1-14

which they have sinned, and will cleanse them. Then they shall be My people, and I will be their Elohim. [24] David My servant shall be king over them, and they shall all have One Shepherd; they shall also walk in My judgments and observe My statutes, and do them. [25] Then they shall dwell in the Land that I have given to Jacob My servant, where your fathers dwelt; and they shall dwell there, they, their children, and their children's children, forever; and My servant David shall be their prince forever. [26] Moreover I will make a Covenant of Peace with them, and it shall be an everlasting Covenant with them; I will establish them and multiply them, and I will set My sanctuary in their midst forevermore. [27] My tabernacle also shall be with them; indeed I will be their Elohim, and they shall be My people. [28] The nations also will know that I, YHWH, sanctify Yisrael, when My sanctuary is in their midst forevermore." Ezekiel 37:15-28

There are many similar promises found throughout the Prophets. This was Good News to a divided, exiled and divorced people. In fact, this was the Good News that Yisrael was anticipating through their Shepherd King – the Messiah. It was Good News according to the Covenant, and it was Good News for the Kingdom of Yisrael.

Finally, it was Good News for the Nations who would be offered an opportunity to join this Royal Family and enter into the Kingdom of Elohim through Yisrael. By doing so they could become Sons of the Living Elohim – Sons of YHWH.

This is the context for the Good News – referred to as "the Gospels" by Christians. And this leads us back to our discussion concerning the progression of the Covenant.

Elohim doesn't replace His Covenant with brand new covenants. Instead, He elevates them, and makes them greater until they reach their final fulfillment through a restoration of

Eden. That is why Yahushua specifically stated: *"Do not think that I came to destroy the Torah or the Prophets. I did not come to destroy but to fulfill."* Matthew 5:17

Yahushua did not come to destroy the Covenant with Yisrael – He came to fulfill the prophecies concerning the Covenant with Yisrael, and He came exactly as prophesied in Daniel.

Daniel was visited by the messenger Gabriel, and provided a timeline of seventy weeks. Again, the number seventy was not random, and sixty-nine of those weeks would lead up to the Messiah.

"Know therefore and understand, that from the going forth of the command to restore and build Jerusalem until Messiah the Prince, there shall be seven weeks and sixty-two weeks."
Daniel 9:25

Yahushua the Messiah came exactly as described when we understand that those weeks are prophetic years. He was thereafter cut off exactly as prophesied in Daniel 9:26.

"And after the sixty-two weeks Messiah shall be cut off, but not for Himself."
Daniel 9:26

Daniel 9:27 then proceeds to state that: *"He shall make a firm covenant with many for one week: and in the midst of the week he shall cause the sacrifice and the offering to cease; and on the wing of abominations [shall come] one who makes desolate; and even to the full end, and that determined, shall [wrath] be poured out on the desolate."* Daniel 9:27 (HNV)

Many people have been deceived into thinking that this final week in the seventy week prophecy was somehow put off into the future, and that the one making the covenant is the anti-christ.

This understanding is a seriously flawed, and has

people looking for a variety of future events that simply do not have to happen. We will discuss that further in Chapter 21 when we talk about *Understanding Prophecy*.

The important thing to understand here is that the final week in the prophecy was referring to the work of the Messiah. The Hebrew word translated as "firm" is a derivative of "gibor," which means to "strengthen, to elevate, to make great."

That is exactly what was needed. The House of Yisrael was in exile, and needed to be restored into the Covenant that they had broken. The restoration was not going to occur through the Temple sacrificial system involving the shedding of the blood of animals. Remember that the Covenant made with Abram required the death of the "one" who passed through the cuttings.

Yahushua was the only One who could pay the price. He was the substitute, and He needed to die. His death and resurrection also resolved a dilemma created by the divorce and harlotry of Yisrael.

You see, according to the Torah, Yisrael could not be remarried to her Husband. Here is the specific Commandment.

> *"¹ When a man takes a wife and marries her, and it happens that she finds no favor in his eyes because he has found some uncleanness in her, and he writes her a certificate of divorce, puts it in her hand, and sends her out of his house, ² when she has departed from his house, and goes and becomes another man's wife, ³ if the latter husband detests her and writes her a certificate of divorce, puts it in her hand, and sends her out of his house, or if the latter husband dies who took her as his wife, ⁴ then her former husband who divorced her must not take her back to be his wife after she has been defiled; for that is an abomination before YHWH, and you shall not bring sin on the land which*

YHWH your Elohim is giving you as an inheritance."
Deuteronomy 24:1-4

This is an amazingly mysterious and prophetic
Commandment that most people simply gloss over, but it is
an incredible test for the Messiah. While mainstream Judaism
is looking for a Messiah to come and conquer the enemies of
the Jews and build a Third Temple, that expectation is
insufficient.

Yisrael is divorced from YHWH. She whored after
other gods. While she desires to reconcile and remarry
YHWH, this Commandment stands in the way.

It would seem that Yisrael is precluded from
remarriage, but Yahushua satisfied the penalty. As the
representative of YHWH, He died and was resurrected, thus
allowing Him to lay claim to Yisrael, and take her as His
Bride.

That is the wedding being referred to all throughout the
New Testament texts, not a wedding between Jesus and the
Christian Church. Yahushua did not come to start the
Christian religion, He came to fulfill the requirement
necessary to renew the broken Covenant, and restore the
Kingdom of Yisrael.

He came to seek out the lost sheep of the House of
Yisrael who had been divorced and scattered. His life was a
marriage proposal. His death and resurrection allowed for the
House of Yisrael to be remarried through the Covenant, as the
Bride of the Lamb.[155]

This is why He stated to the Yahudim: *"And other sheep
I have which are not of this fold; them also I must bring, and they*

---

[155] This is why the first recorded miracle was at a wedding. In John 2:1-12 we read about turning
water into wine, using the same stone vessels that would have held the waters of purification
for the bride. The event occurred in Cana, which derives from the Hebrew Qana. It means:
"acquired." Yahushua was revealing that He had come to "acquire" a bride for Himself.
Remember that at the Last Supper (Last Passover) He declared that the wine symbolized His
blood. By turning water into wine, He revealed that He would cleanse and acquire a bride
through His blood.

will hear My voice; and there will be one flock and one shepherd."
John 10:16

He was telling the House of Yahudah that He came for the House of Yisrael, as the Shepherd described by Ezekiel. In fact, He specifically stated "*I was not sent except to the lost sheep of the House of Yisrael.*" Matthew 15:24

This is why He spent so much time speaking parables about wedding feasts and the Kingdom of Elohim. He was searching for His Bride to join Him in His House to rule in His Kingdom. He would restore all Yisrael through this process.

That's why He chose twelve disciples and then seventy, as we discussed previously. Through Yisrael the Nations would be gathered into the Kingdom – just as we saw from Abram.

The invitation to join the family is a free gift. That is the "grace" provided by the Messiah. But those who desire to be in this Covenant must obey the conditions of the Covenant that establish the relationship. That is why He also spent so much time explaining the Torah, and rebuking the Pharisees for adding to the Torah and taking away from the Torah.

The instructions were never meant to be difficult.

"For this Commandment which I command you today is not too difficult for you, nor is it far off."
Deuteronomy 30:11

"For this is the love of Elohim, that we keep His commandments. And His Commandments are not burdensome."
1 John 5:3

Yahushua said: "*28 Come to Me, all you who labor and are heavy laden, and I will give you rest. 29 Take My yoke upon you and learn from Me, for I am gentle and lowly in heart, and you will find rest for your souls. 30 For My yoke is easy and My burden is light.*"
Matthew 11:28-30

A yoke is what guides us, and directs our path. He was referring to His Instructions - the Torah. Those instructions lead us on the righteous path. In fact, we express our love through our obedience. Yahushua specifically stated: *"If you love Me, keep My Commandments."* John 14:15

Now, with the proper context of the Good News of the Covenant we can easily discern who gets into the Covenant. Remember the promise in Ezekiel 37? *"David My servant shall be King over them, and they shall all have One Shepherd; they shall also walk in My judgments and observe My statutes, and do them."* Ezekiel 37:24

Also, do you remember the promise of the renewed Covenant promised through Jeremiah? *"[31] Behold, the days are coming, says YHWH, when I will make a renewed Covenant with the House of Yisrael and with the House of Yahudah - [32] not according to the covenant that I made with their fathers in the day that I took them by the hand to lead them out of the land of Egypt, My covenant which they broke, though I was a Husband to them, says YHWH. [33] But this is the Covenant that I will make with the House of Yisrael after those days, says YHWH: I will put My Torah in their minds, and write it on their hearts; and I will be their Elohim, and they shall be My people. [34] No more shall every man teach his neighbor, and every man his brother, saying, Know YHWH, for they all shall know Me, from the least of them to the greatest of them, says YHWH. For I will forgive their iniquity, and their sin I will remember no more."* Jeremiah 31:31-34

While many English Bibles provide for a "New Covenant," the Hebrew points to a "renewal."[156] Of course, the Covenant is renewed with the party to the Covenant - Yisrael. And this renewal is focused on obedience to the Torah.

The New Testament texts provide genealogies of Yahushua that detail how He came from the lineage of David.

---

[156] The Hebrew word translated as "new" is "hadash" (חדש), which shares the same root as "hodesh" (חדש) used to describe the renewed moon. Now we know that when we see the first sliver of the moon it is not a brand new moon. It is the same moon, simply renewed through light.

They provide this information so we know for certain that He qualifies to be the Messiah – the One described in Hosea 1 and Ezekiel 37:24.

He specifically came and renewed the Covenant at Passover.[157]

"For this is My blood of the renewed Covenant, which is shed for many for the remission of sins."
Matthew 26:28

"And He said to them, This is My blood of the renewed Covenant, which is shed for many."
Mark 14:24

"Likewise, He also took the cup after supper, saying, This cup is the renewed Covenant in My blood, which is shed for you."
Luke 22:20

It was new in the sense that it was established through His blood. It was renewed, because it involved the same parties. Notice that the renewal was performed with the twelve disciples – representing "kol Yisrael." Only this time, instead of the blood of lambs to save them from death, it would be the blood of the Lamb of Elohim.

Yahushua Himself was ultimately the fulfillment of the Covenant that would redeem His Bride – Yisrael. We specifically see this from the description of the Bride in the text of Revelation.

"9 Then one of the seven angels who had the seven bowls filled with the seven last plagues came to me and talked with me, saying, 'Come, I will show you the bride, the Lamb's wife.' 10 And he carried me away in the Spirit to a great and high mountain, and

---

[157] The Greek word kainos (καινῆς) also means renewed.

showed me the great city, the set apart Jerusalem,
descending out of heaven from Elohim, ¹¹ having the
glory of Elohim. Her light was like a most precious
stone, like a jasper stone, clear as crystal. ¹² Also she
had a great and high wall with twelve gates, and
twelve angels at the gates, and names written on
them, which are the names of the twelve tribes of the
children of Yisrael: ¹³ three gates on the east, three
gates on the north, three gates on the south, and three
gates on the west." Revelation 21:9-13

The Renewed Jerusalem is all about Yisrael. Only
those in the Covenant Assembly can enter in, and it is through
the gates where the Tree of Life is located. We also read:
"Blessed are those who do His Commandments, that they may have
the right to the Tree of Life, and may enter through the gates into the
city." Revelation 22:14

Only the obedient are getting into the City, and the
City represents the fulfillment of the Covenant with Yisrael.
You cannot separate Yisrael from the Covenant, and the only
way you enter into the Kingdom is through Yisrael.

It's that simple! And it is literally "crystal clear."

This is the Good News, and it is where Christianity
goes awry. Most Christians fail to understand the Good News
within the context of the Covenant. Instead of placing the
Messiah within the Covenant, they teach that Jesus came to
start a new covenant with "The Church," and that "The
Church" replaced Yisrael. This new covenant resulted in a
new group of people called Christians, and a new religion
called Christianity. This is simply not true, and it is not
Scriptural.

YHWH never gave up on mankind, He never gave up
on the Nations, and He never gave up on Yisrael. He simply
chose to refine His Covenant, and redeem all creation through
Yisrael. Yisrael is the conduit for the Nations to come into the

Covenant. Yisrael represents His Kingdom here on Earth.[158]

So, the Good News is that the Messiah came according to the promises that the Covenant would be renewed and the Kingdom of Yisrael would be reunited and restored to the Land. That is the "Full Gospel."

He came preaching that the Kingdom was at hand and He spent time teaching and preaching the "Good News of the Kingdom."

"And Yahushua went about all Galilee, teaching in their synagogues, preaching the Good News of the Kingdom, and healing all kinds of sickness and all kinds of disease among the people."
Matthew 4:23

"Then Yahushua went about all the cities and villages, teaching in their synagogues, preaching the Good News of the Kingdom, and healing every sickness and every disease among the people."
Matthew 9:35

Notice that the Good News of the Kingdom was accompanied with signs of healing – life. That is the goal - to bring the Kingdom to Earth and heal all of Creation. Sin resulted in death and prevented the Kingdom from expanding out of the Garden to the entire planet. Restoring the Kingdom by "healing the Nations" is the solution.[159]

That is why Yahushua taught His disciples to pray *"Your Kingdom come, Your will be done on Earth as it is in Heaven."* Matthew 6:10 and Luke 11:2

He began His mission by warning people to repent in preparation for the Kingdom.[160] The Kingdom is a message for all the Nations, but it starts with Yisrael and then goes forth to the Nations.

---

[158] Just to be clear, we are not talking about the Zionist Jewish State. When we refer to Yisrael, we are talking about a people brought into the Covenant renewed by Yahushua.
[159] Revelation 22:2
[160] Matthew 4:17

The Good News is a message for a divided creation to return, and be reunited and restored with the Creator. It is an invitation back to the Garden. Admission is free for those who are willing to obey the rules of the Kingdom – the Torah. That is the message of grace that is so often misunderstood and distorted by the Christian religion.

All the nations can now gain access to the Kingdom thanks to the atoning and healing work of the Messiah.

> *"And this Good News of the Kingdom*
> *will be preached in all the world*
> *as a witness to all the Nations,*
> *and then the end will come."*
> Matthew 24:14

That is exactly what the disciples of Yahushua were doing after He was resurrected and ascended – telling people about the Good News of the Messiah.

We read an example of this with Philip. *"But when they believed Philip as he preached the things concerning the Kingdom of Elohim and the Name of Yahushua Messiah, both men and women were immersed."* Acts 8:12

Philip was preaching the Kingdom and the Name of Yahushua. He was identifying Yahushua as the promised King of the Kingdom that is coming to Earth.

Again, it is a simple message. If only Christianity had adopted the message of Philip, rather than the confusing message interpreted and transmitted from Paul's letters.

The Messiah is still fulfilling this great promise, and we look forward to His future coming and gathering of Yisrael. That process will include those who call upon His Name, and obey His voice. The Good News is that the Kingdom is being established and restored by the Son of David – King Messiah.

The blood of Messiah provides the way for all of the Nations to be blessed, because all of fallen mankind can partake in the Good News and join with Yisrael. Yahushua made the way for everyone to enter into the Kingdom, but we need to obey the rules of the Kingdom if we want to dwell in the Kingdom.

The Torah provides us with those guidelines, and instructions. Sadly, this is not necessarily the Good News that has been presented through Christianity. In fact, it is almost the opposite.

Christianity teaches that Jesus came and fulfilled the Law, and in doing so, He abolished the Law. They teach that He replaced the Law with grace, and freed us from the bondage of the Law. That message makes no sense, and is completely opposed to the Covenant path that requires obedience.

We don't want to be freed from the Torah. We want to take up His yoke, and let the Torah lead us to life, once we have received atonement through His blood. That process frees us from the curse, and the penalty that comes from disobedience.

If you want to be one of the Sons of Elohim, living and serving in the Kingdom, then you had better start learning and doing His instructions. Take up his yoke, and start walking like a child of Elohim.

So, it is clear that our journey is not just about leaving Babylon, it is about entering the Kingdom through the Covenant. And this is exactly what Yahushua meant when He said *"the Kingdom of Heaven draws near."*

Much of the Christian Gospel is simply backwards, and it is definitely incomplete. It is not actually Good News, because it is directing people away from the Covenant and down a path that leads to lawlessness, death and destruction.

The actual Good News is that the Covenant is available for all the Nations. Yisrael and Yahudah failed in their role as priests. They failed to point the Nations to YHWH. Instead, they followed after the pagan gods that the Nations worshipped.

Yahushua came and fulfilled their mission.[161] He did what Yisrael failed to do. That is why He renewed the Covenant through His blood. He is the Lamb of Elohim that we rely upon to cover us from the wrath of YHWH.

The Good News is that we can all join into the Covenant journey blazed by Abram. We can all come out of Babylon and become Hebrews.

This is evident from the proclamation made by Peter on Shavuot (Pentecost) – *"Repent, and let every one of you be immersed in the Name of Yahushua ha'Maschiach for the remission of sins; and you shall receive the gift of the Set Apart Spirit (Ruach ha'Kodesh)."* Acts 2:38

The immersion is what ties us back to Abram, and Yisrael. There were no bridges on the Euphrates River, and the Jordan River. Our predecessors got wet when they "crossed over" on the Covenant journey. We must pass through the waters when leaving Babylon, just like Yisrael passed through the waters when leaving Egypt.

Our immersion is the beginning of that journey. Getting wet symbolizes washing away the Babylonian residue that we left behind. It cleanses us and prepares us to walk on the straight and narrow path of righteousness. It prepares us to dwell with a set apart Elohim. It is an ancient practice that connects us to this ancient journey.

Just as the priests would mikveh (immerse) before entering the Temple, all people would do the same, in preparation for their meeting with Elohim. It was therefore very appropriate that immersion (baptism) remained a part of repentance. It was included in the process of meeting with YHWH through the death and resurrection of the Son.

Once we understand the true Good News referred to as

---

[161] When Yahushua washed the feet of His disciples at His last Passover, He was demonstrating that His disciples needed to be priests. The priests served in bare feet in the Temple, and needed to wash their feet because they were on set-apart ground. Priests were servants of YHWH and the people, acting as intermediaries. Yahushua was a High Priest according to the priestly order of Melchizedek, and His disciples serve in that Order. (Hebrews 6:20)

the Gospel, it is then important to focus on obedience.

8

Focusing on Obedience

By now, it should be clear that the Christian Gospel is supposed to be the Good News that Yahushua came to renew the broken Covenant, and restore the Kingdom of Elohim on Earth through Yisrael. Instead, it generally ignores the Covenant and calls it "old." The Christian religion then directs people on a path that actually contradicts the teachings and purpose of the Messiah.

Once you recognize this fact, along with the need to separate from that belief system, you then need to identify with the Covenant Assembly of Yisrael. That is not to be confused with the religion of Judaism, or the modern State of Israel.[162] The Covenant Assembly is not a religious institution, or a governmental entity authorized by the United Nations.

Yisrael was chosen by YHWH to represent Him, and His Kingdom, here on earth. Yisrael was called to be a nation of priests. Because of the sin of the golden calf, the priestly function was transferred from the firstborn of all the tribes to one tribe - Levi.

The Levites functioned as representatives of the firstborn in the House of Elohim. They did not just serve in the Temple in Jerusalem. They lived throughout the Land, disbursed among the tribes, and they were supposed to teach the people the ways of righteousness. These substitute

---

[162] Many Christians as well as those in the Hebrew Roots Movement and Messianic Judaism fail to understand the modern State of Israel, as opposed to the Covenant Assembly of Yisrael. They consider the "Jewish People" and the State of Yisrael to constitute the Assembly of Yisrael. That confusion will lead many astray as the future unfolds. This issue is discussed in more detail in Chapter 18 entitled *Understanding Yisrael*.

"firstborn" could enter the House of YHWH, and would prepare the others by teaching them how to be set apart. This was a pattern that would see a future fulfillment through the Messiah, and the Melchizedek Priesthood.[163]

The entire Nation of Yisrael was supposed to shine as a light to the nations around them. In fact, Yisrael was supposed to teach the nations of the Earth about the Kingdom of YHWH, and reveal how it operates. Yisrael was supposed to represent the heavenly Kingdom of YHWH in this physical existence.

Both Yisrael and the priesthood failed in their responsibilities. Instead of shining as a light and drawing the nations to YHWH, the people of Yisrael were drawn to the false gods of the nations that surrounded them and the people that lived amongst them. The problem was that they never fully expelled the Canaanites from the Covenant Land as YHWH commanded. They never completely set apart to Covenant Land.

Yisrael was specifically provided with the following instruction:

> "¹ When YHWH your Elohim brings you into the land which you go to possess, and has cast out many nations before you, the Hittites and the Girgashites and the Amorites and the Canaanites and the Perizzites and the Hivites and the Jebusites, seven nations greater and mightier than you, ² and when YHWH your Elohim delivers them over to you, you shall conquer them and utterly destroy them. You shall make no covenant with them nor show mercy to them. ³ Nor shall you make marriages with them. You shall not give your daughter to their son, nor take their daughter for your son. ⁴ For they will turn

---

[163] The Melchizedek Priesthood represents the original priesthood of the firstborn. Adam originally functioned in this role on behalf of mankind. This was altered at Sinai, and will be restored through the Messiah.

your sons away from following Me, to serve other
gods; so the anger of YHWH will be aroused
against you and destroy you suddenly. [5] But thus you
shall deal with them: you shall destroy their altars,
and break down their sacred pillars, and cut down
their wooden images, and burn their carved images
with fire. [6] For you are a holy (set apart) people to
YHWH your Elohim; YHWH your Elohim has
chosen you to be a people for Himself, a special
treasure above all the peoples on the face of the
earth." Deuteronomy 7:1-6

The bottom line was "no mixing" with the inhabitants of the Land. Sadly, Yisrael failed to "guard" the Land, just as Adam failed to "guard" the Garden. As a result, Yisrael was led astray from the Commandments. Yisrael disobeyed and was divided, punished, and exiled – just like Adam and Hawah.

The Messiah came as the Second Adam to restore the Melchizedek priesthood within Yisrael and be that light to the Nations as prophesied by Isaiah.

"[6] I, YHWH, have called You in righteousness,
and will hold Your hand; I will keep You and give You as a
Covenant to the people (עַם), as a light to the Nations (גּוֹיִם). [7] To
open blind eyes, to bring out prisoners from the prison, those who sit
in darkness from the prison house."
Isaiah 42:6-7

Yahushua identified Himself with the prophecy by proclaiming: "*I am the light of the world.*" John 8:12 Of course, the text of John had already connected Yahushua with the very light imparted into Creation at the beginning.[164]

The prophecy in Isaiah 42 is really interesting, because

---

[164] John 1:1-9 as it relates to Genesis 1:1-5. When Elohim saw the light, that light was connected to the Aleph Taw (את) and described as "good."

the distinction between the two groups of people is not so obvious in the English. What we see in the Hebrew is that the Messiah will be a Covenant for the people – "am" (עַם) Yisrael, and a light to the Nations – "goyim" (גּוֹיִם).

As previously explained, a covenant is "brit" (בְּרִית) in Hebrew, and it often refers to the actual slaughtering of a blood sacrifice. So, Messiah would be the substance and offering of the Covenant between YHWH and Yisrael. This is how He would function as the Passover Lamb – the Lamb of Elohim whose blood protected the firstborn from death.

Isaiah further provides: *"Indeed He says, It is too small a thing that You should be My Servant to raise up the tribes of Jacob, and to restore the preserved ones of Yisrael; I will also give You as a light to the Nations (גּוֹיִם), that You should be My salvation to the ends of the earth."* Isaiah 49:6

Yahushua began His service by calling out twelve of His "people" (עַם) - representing a restored Yisrael. He trained those disciples in the Galilee region, which was known as the "Galilee of the Nations." (Isaiah 9:1)

The word "galilee" means "turning, folding, revolving," and that aptly describes the region in the north of the Promised Land. The word "nations" is "goyim" (גּוֹיִם) in Hebrew. It is sometimes translated as Gentiles, and refers to those who are not in covenant with YHWH.

The reason it was called the Galilee of the Nations is because it was an international crossroads geographically. This was also originally the Land of the Northern Tribes that had been taken captive by the Assyrians. Those tribes were scattered to the four corners of the Earth, and replaced by peoples from the Nations.

Later, the Phoenicians moved into the region and then left after Alexander Janeaus required their conversion. Eventually, Herod transplanted Yahudim from Judea. This region was constantly turning over, like a revolving door for the inhabitants.

The Galilee represented the mixing of the Nations.

Yahushua came as a Covenant and a Light to the Nations, exactly as described in Isaiah. That is why Yahushua stated "*I am the light of the world. He who follows Me shall not walk in darkness, but have the light of life.*" John 8:12 (see also John 9:5)

So those who follow Yahushua the Messiah join into Yisrael through the renewed Covenant. They are now priests in the Order of Melchizedek – the restored priesthood of the firstborn. As priests, we are supposed to shine the light to the world.

Because Yisrael was punished and mixed in with the nations, a person's genetic lineage, or ethnic identity, is not the critical factor. What is important is whether they have been washed clean, and transformed into a new creation by the blood of the Messiah.

That is the process referred to as being "born again," and that is how we get into the Kingdom.[165]

Yahushua is the son of Elohim. He holds the firstborn status, and all authority in Heaven and Earth has been given to Him. He holds the keys to death and Sheol.[166] If we are covered by His blood, then we expect to be resurrected into His eternal priesthood.

Until then, while in these temporal bodies, we are rehearsing and serving with the promise that we too carry the firstborn status in the Kingdom, and can serve as priests in the Order of Melchizedek.

The genetic make-up you were born with is not the distinguishing factor. The question is whether the Torah has been written on your heart and placed in your mind through the renewed Covenant prophesied by Jeremiah.

Here it is again:

"*31 Behold, the days are coming, says YHWH, when*

---

[165] "Yahushua answered and said to him, 'Most assuredly, I say to you, unless one is born again, he cannot see the kingdom of Elohim.'" John 3:3

[166] "And Yahushua came and spoke to them, saying, 'All authority has been given to Me in heaven and on earth.'" Matthew 28:18 See also Revelation 1:18

I will make a renewed Covenant with the House of Yisrael and with the House of Yahudah - [32] *not according to the Covenant that I made with their fathers in the day that I took them by the hand to lead them out of the land of Egypt, My Covenant which they broke, though I was a husband to them, says YHWH.* [33] *But this is the Covenant that I will make with the house of Yisrael after those days, says YHWH: I will put My Torah in their minds, and write it on their hearts; and I will be their Elohim, and they shall be My people.* [34] *No more shall every man teach his neighbor, and every man his brother, saying, Know* את-*YHWH, for they all shall know Me, from the least of them to the greatest of them, says YHWH. For I will forgive their iniquity, and their sin I will remember no more."* Jeremiah 31:31-34

This is the Covenant promise that Yahushua renewed at the Last Passover, before He was crucified. He did not discard or replace the former Covenant. He renewed and elevated the Covenant that had been broken. This renewed Covenant involves the <u>much needed</u> forgiveness of sins that man required since being cast out of the Garden. The blood of animals had pointed to the need since the sin in the Garden. But that blood never provided forgiveness, only a temporary covering (kippurim).

The renewed Covenant also involves "knowing" את-YHWH. The word "knowledge" is "yada" (ידע) in Hebrew. It often implies an intimate relationship - face to face. We can discern that Jeremiah 31:34 contains a powerful reference to the Messiah that can only be seen in the Hebrew text. Remember that the aleph taw (את) – is "The Word" referenced in John 1.

"[1] In the beginning was the Word, and the Word was with Elohim, and the Word was Elohim. [2] *He was in the beginning with Elohim.* [3]*

All things were made through Him, and without Him nothing was made that was made."
John 1:1-3

This points to a significant connection between the Messiah and language. We will be discussing that further when we examine the importance of the Hebrew language in a future chapter. From the Hebrew text of Jeremiah we can see that our knowledge of YHWH comes through the Messiah.

The reason that the Torah is put in our minds, and written on our hearts, is so that we won't forget it - so we can obey. Therefore, it is obedience to the Commandments that is the distinguishing factor, not whether you can trace your genes to the tribe of Yahudah, or one of the other eleven tribes.

A critical part of being a priest is learning how to be set apart through obedience. *"But this is what I commanded them, saying, 'Obey My voice, and I will be your Elohim, and you shall be My people. And walk in all the ways that I have commanded you, that it may be well with you.'"* Jeremiah 7:23

We also read how Hosea specifically addressed the issue.

"My people are destroyed for lack of the knowledge. Because you have rejected the knowledge, I also will reject you from being priest for Me. Because you have forgotten the Torah of your Elohim, I also will forget your children."
Hosea 4:6

We need the Torah in our minds so we know what to do, and we need it in our hearts so that we actually do the Commandments. As priests we need both, and the distinguishing part of a priest is his service to Elohim.

Yahushua vividly demonstrated that by the fact that He was the Son of Elohim, but He also was the suffering Servant who laid down His life for His people. While He deserved the highest, He assumed the lowest and gave His life for His service.

This raises an important issue. When some people realize that they have been lied to, they set off on a quest for knowledge. They spend so much time getting the knowledge in their minds, that they forget about their hearts. This can be a real test. In have seen individuals who end up falling away from the Messiah by chasing after rabbinic Judaism and Kabbalistic teachings in their insatiable quest to acquire more knowledge.

Some spend all of their time running after every crazy lie or deception that they hear about on the internet. The enemy has laid out bait to snare people, and there are landmines all alongside the straight path of truth. It is critical to stay focused on Yahushua, our High Priest, as we learn and serve within the renewed Covenant. That is why the Torah provides us with reminders to do the Commandments.

We have mentioned the importance of setting apart the Sabbath, wearing of tzitzit to remind us of the Commandments, and we even spoke about the dietary instructions.

Since most of us eat three meals a day this is something that we need to address regularly. While in the past, people would generally consume their meals in their homes, today we live in a very mobile society, and that is not always the case.

Nevertheless, there is another very practical Commandment concerning setting apart our homes that we read about in one of the most important Commandments known as the Shema.[167]

It is known as "The Shema" because it it begins with the Hebrew word "shema" (שמע) which means: "hear and obey."

"*4 Shema Yisrael: YHWH our Elohim, YHWH is one! 5 You shall love YHWH your Elohim with all your heart, with all*

---

[167] When asked which was the greatest Commandment, Yahushua recited The Shema (see Mark 12:29).

your soul, and with all your strength. ⁶ And these words which I command you today shall be in your heart. ⁷ You shall teach them diligently to your children, and shall talk of them when you sit in your house, when you walk by the way, when you lie down, and when you rise up. ⁸ You shall bind them as a sign on your hand, and they shall be as frontlets between your eyes. ⁹ You shall write them on the doorposts of your house and on your gates." Deuteronomy 6:4-9

We read a similar Commandment in Deuteronomy 11:18-21 as follows: "*¹⁸ Therefore you shall lay up these words of mine in your heart and in your soul, and bind them as a sign on your hand, and they shall be as frontlets between your eyes. ¹⁹ You shall teach them to your children, speaking of them when you sit in your house, when you walk by the way, when you lie down, and when you rise up. ²⁰ And you shall write them on the doorposts of your house and on your gates, ²¹ that your days and the days of your children may be multiplied in the land of which YHWH swore to your fathers to give them, like the days of the heavens above the earth.*"

The doorposts are the "mezuzot" – the same mezuzot where the blood of the Passover lamb was to be placed according to Exodus 12:7. Of course, this is no coincidence. There is a direct relationship between the terms of the Covenant, and the blood of the Covenant.

There is no specific way to observe this Commandment. Some put scrolls of Scriptures in tubes that are affixed to the doorposts. Some place written plaques. Some actually inscribe the words on the doorposts.

How you do it is not as important as why you do it. Like the tzitzit, the "mezuzah" is a physical act that we perform, because they both remind us of the Commandments - the tzitzit on our bodies, and the mezuzah on our homes. The mezuzah announces to the world: "In this home the rules of the Kingdom apply." "Within these gates the Torah rules."

This actually takes us back to the Sabbath Commandment. "*⁸ Remember the Sabbath day, to keep it set apart. ⁹ Six days you shall labor and do all your work, ¹⁰ but the seventh day is the Sabbath of YHWH your Elohim. In it you shall do no work:*

you, nor your son, nor your daughter, nor your male servant, nor your female servant, nor your cattle, nor your stranger who is within your gates. " For in six days YHWH made the heavens and the earth, the sea, and all that is in them, and rested the seventh day. Therefore, YHWH blessed the Sabbath day and set it apart." Exodus 20:8-11

This is all about being set apart. It applies to those within our gates – those who we have control over. I believe that however you choose to display the mezuzah, it should be something that people can actually read.

Up to this point, I have recommended some basic Commandments to get you focused, and headed in the right direction. They are very practical Commandments that show the importance of obedience. I did this because most of us have come out of Christianity, a religion that talks about obedience, but actually promotes lawlessness through the abstract doctrine of grace.[168] While most Christians would agree that we need to obey God, they do not even follow the Ten Commandments.

The early Assembly dealt with a similar situation when they were faced with Gentiles joining the Assembly. You see, most of the early followers of Yahushua were Yisraelites, born and raised with a knowledge of the Torah. The ones who believed from the Nations (i.e. Gentiles) needed to build a foundation for their faith. They needed to catch up, so to speak.

It was determined that these "pagans" needed an "Introduction to Torah" course, and that is what we read about in chapter 15 of the Book of Acts.

---

[168] The word "grace" actually refers to "thanks." When people "say grace" before or after a meal, they are giving thanks for the food. The Scriptures also refer to "mercy" and "favor". The true understanding of grace should be that we have been shown mercy and favor from Elohim, Who provided His Son to die for our sins. We give thanks for this incredible act of mercy that saved us from the penalty of our sins. Our response should be to endeavor NOT to sin any longer, yet the Christian doctrine of grace advocates that the Torah has been abolished and replaced by grace, whatever that means. It is an incongruous argument that sounds good, but makes no sense when presented in the context of the Scriptures and the Covenant. As a result, this Christian notion of grace has led many down a path of lawlessness that leads to destruction. This subject is described in detail in the Walk in the Light series book titled *The Law and Grace.*

In that portion we read about a decision that was made by James[169] concerning how to instruct new converts concerning the Covenant walk.

The issue is described in Acts 15:5 as follows *"But some of the sect of the Pharisees who believed rose up, saying, 'It is necessary to circumcise them, and to command them to keep the Torah of Moses.'"*

Now the fact that the Pharisees raised the question is significant. The Pharisees had developed an extensive tradition concerning circumcision and conversion. These were Pharisees who expressed belief in Yahushua, but they still carried their Pharisaic traditions.

Circumcision was and remains a very controversial issue, which we will deal with in more detail in a later discussion. For now, we will simply consider the issue at Acts 15 - "Do they need to be circumcised in order to be saved?" Keeping the Torah of Moses was a given.

Now their concept of being "saved" was not necessarily the same "salvation" that is understood by modern Christians. The Jerusalem Assembly was dealing with people coming out of paganism, and into the Covenant faith through Yahushua. That involved not just a prayer or confession, but a change in behavior. That is the essence of repentance - turning away from lawlessness, and then walking in righteousness.

The Torah of Moses provided the instructions in righteousness, but in many ways it was foreign to them. The pagans grew up worshipping pagan gods. That worship involved going to pagan temples, and sacrificing to those gods. It also involved eating meat sacrificed to those idols, along with certain sexual rites - depending on the god.

For those turning to YHWH, the immediate question was "What did they need to do in order to be redeemed - to

---

[169] James was the brother of Yahushua. His actual name was Jacob (Yaacob). His name was changed in honor of King James and that is a simple example of how many of our English translations of the Scriptures have issues that need to be corrected. It is simply astounding to see certain Christians pegged as "King James only" who essentially idolize a fantastic but flawed text.

become part of Yisrael?"

When asked about eternal life, He always directed people to the Commandments first.[170] He didn't force people through a conversion process before He would teach and minister to them.

That is why James (Yaakob), the chief authority figure, moved slowly. The point was not to burden them with knowing all of the Torah and being circumcised in order to enter into the Assembly. They needed to first learn about the Covenant before they could bear the sign of the Covenant. But in order to begin the process they needed to immediately separate from their pagan worship.

James (Yaakob) decided as follows: *"[18] Known to Elohim from eternity are all His works. [19] Therefore I judge that we should not trouble those from among the Gentiles who are turning to Elohim, [20] but that we write to them to abstain from things polluted by idols, from sexual immorality, from things strangled, and from blood. [21] For Moses has had throughout many generations those who preach him in every city, being read in the synagogues every Sabbath."* Acts 15:18

These were not Gentiles converting to a religion. They were foreigners "turning to Elohim." It involved the Nations joining Yisrael, exactly according to the original plan. That was what Yisrael was supposed to be doing all along.

The way you "turn" to Elohim is through "repentance." Repentance involves turning from our own wicked ways and turning to the Elohim of Abraham, Issac and Jacob – the Elohim of Yisrael. We turn to Him through our actions and obedience.

So, the pattern was similar to what is being presented in this book. The goal was to get them cleaned up from the filth of Roman religion, and learn to be set apart. That way,

---

[170] See Matthew 19, Mark 10 and Luke 18. In John Yahushua states that whoever believes in Him shall have everlasting life. The point is not that anyone who believes in Him as a historical figure gets a free ticket to heaven. The object lesson was referring to the serpent in the wilderness. In other words, anyone who follows the instructions, looks to Him and places their faith in Him will be saved. This obviously involved heeding His words and following His instructions.

they could join the assembly, and participate with other set apart people. Quite simply – "Don't be polluted by idolatry, sexual immorality and change your diet."

The overriding theme was that they start going to the Synagogue,[171] because that was where the Torah Scrolls were located, and that was where Moses (Torah) was read. They could learn the Torah – every Sabbath. This was not a formula to guarantee their personal salvation. Rather, it was guidance to get them on the Covenant path that ultimately leads to salvation.

As they heard the Torah being read week after week they could begin to walk out the faith. Circumcision could come when they were fully prepared to enter in to the Covenant.

After all, the primary Commandment concerning circumcision was to circumcise all males on the eighth day.[172] That obviously was not the case with these Gentiles turning to YHWH. Therefore, the only time restriction was that they be circumcised before they participated in Passover.

"And when a stranger dwells with you and wants to keep the Passover to YHWH, let all his males be circumcised, and then let him come near and keep it; and he shall be as a native of the Land. For no uncircumcised person shall eat it." Exodus 12:48

Clearly, they were supposed to obey the Commandments, although obedience is a process, and James was not going to subscribe to some burdensome Pharisaic conversion process. He provided a formula for them to start getting set apart, so they could be in the Assembly and hear the Torah.

Every Christian convert should go through a similar

---

[171] It is important to understand that the Synagogue was more like a community center or a school in that day. The focus of religious life at that time was the Temple in Jerusalem. That began to change, especially after the destruction of the Temple and the formation of the religion of Judaism by the Pharisees. Now we see Synagogues called Temples and they function as religious buildings, just like a Church in Christianity or a Mosque in Islam. This was not the case when the events of Acts 15 occurred.

[172] Genesis 17:12 and Leviticus 12:3

process, but they do not. They might be told to obey the Ten Commandments, but even then, they are not told the Name of YHWH, and they are probably told that the Sabbath was changed. So, they don't even keep those Commandments.

Because Bibles are readily available they are usually provided with some reading materials, and often recommended to start with the Gospel of John. They will be told to attend a church on Sunday, where they will likely be taught that more than half of the Bible does not apply to them, because they are under grace.

We already discussed that priests must learn to be set apart and that process is the result of our obedience. Samuel declared: *"to obey is better than sacrifice, and to heed than the fat of the rams."* 1 Samuel 15:22

Incredibly, YHWH does not desire our obedience to make our lives difficult or to laden us with heavy burdens. Rather, He wants us to obey so that He can bless us.

Read the great promises associated with obedience.

"¹ Now it shall come to pass, when all these things come upon you, the blessing and the curse which I have set before you, and you call them to mind among all the nations where YHWH your Elohim drives you, ² and you return to YHWH your Elohim and obey His voice, according to all that I command you today, you and your children, with all your heart and with all your soul, ³ that YHWH your Elohim will bring you back from captivity, and have compassion on you, and gather you again from all the nations where YHWH your Elohim has scattered you. ⁴ If any of you are driven out to the farthest parts under heaven, from there YHWH your Elohim will gather you, and from there He will bring you. ⁵ Then YHWH your Elohim will bring you to the land which your fathers possessed, and you shall possess it. He will prosper you and multiply you more than your fathers. ⁶ And YHWH your Elohim will circumcise your heart and the heart of your descendants, to love YHWH your Elohim with all your heart and with all your soul, that you may live. ⁷ Also YHWH your Elohim will put all these curses on your enemies and on those who hate you, who persecuted you. ⁸ And you will again obey the

voice of YHWH and do all His Commandments which I command you today. ⁹ YHWH your Elohim will make you abound in all the work of your hand, in the fruit of your body, in the increase of your livestock, and in the produce of your land for good. For YHWH will again rejoice over you for good as He rejoiced over your fathers, ¹⁰ if you obey the voice of YHWH your Elohim, to keep His Commandments and His statutes which are written in this Scroll of the Torah, and if you turn to YHWH your Elohim with all your heart and with all your soul." Deuteronomy 30:1-10

Did you notice that the circumcision YHWH truly desires is the circumcision of our hearts? Why? So that we can love YHWH Elohim with all our hearts and soul (nefesh), so we can live. That is the Shema, and that is the way to salvation.

I am repeatedly hearing the statement from the Torah community that obedience is not a salvation issue. This seems to be the new mantra that Hebrew Roots folks are using to make Torah observance more palatable to Christians.

I am concerned that this may be misleading to some, and I feel compelled to point out that obedience, as taught by the Messiah, is central to our Covenant walk.

Remember that disobedience is the reason why mankind was expelled from the Garden of Eden. The Garden represented the Kingdom of Elohim on Earth, and it was governed by His Torah. It was mankind's failure to follow the rules of the Kingdom that resulted in their being expelled.

Through the mercy of Elohim, He established a Covenant that would make a way for us to return through the Covenant Assembly of Yisrael. Central to that Covenant is the Torah.

As a result, obedience to the Torah is nothing to be ashamed of, and certainly not to be diminished. Interestingly, but for the religion of Christianity, this would not even be a discussion.

In the past, when a stranger joined with Yisrael they were not typically concerned with a guarantee of going to heaven. They wanted to follow the Elohim of Yisrael. Therefore, they would agree to obey Him and worship Him as instructed in the Torah. Their actions of obedience to the Torah revealed that they served Elohim, and not some other pagan god. It was their actions that defined their status, and their relationship with Elohim.

Sadly, Christianity has become so fixated on salvation that they often neglect the path that gets you there - which is the Covenant. It has become a religion so motivated on what a person can get for themselves (salvation) that the entire Covenant gets turned upside down and inside out. They want the desert before the meal, but salvation is the end of the journey, not the beginning.

We are supposed to give first and receive later – that is the pattern of the Messiah. He gave His life and trusted the Father to resurrect Him from the dead. We give our lives and our service to Elohim, and place our faith and trust in Him. We rely on His love and mercy to take care of us now, and after we die. In the meantime, we live our lives in accordance with His instructions. When we enter into the Covenant we place our faith and trust in Yahushua's blood, that was shed in fulfillment of the Covenant.

Many modern Christians evangelize by posing the standard question: "What must I do to be saved?" Again, the focus is not "What can I do for God" or "What does God want from me," but rather "What can I get from God." This is a symptom of our society and culture, and it results in a predictable response from the modern Christian religion.

The answer is often a simple and fast multi-step formula and prayer for achieving salvation. Once the prayer is uttered, it is claimed that the person is instantly saved. Sometimes they only have to raise a hand, or go to the front of the church in order to get saved. Easy-peasy.

This is simply not Scriptural, and sadly it appears that this mentality has steeped into the Hebrew Roots community, which consists of many people who have left the Christian

Church. They have been so beaten up by the doctrine of grace that they are almost afraid to speak about the absolute need to follow the Law – the Torah.

I would like to encourage my brethren that you do not need to make excuses, or diminish your obedience, by stating that it is not about salvation. If our Messiah had followed that belief and lived a life contrary to the Torah, He would have disqualified Himself from that position. He needed to be set apart, and live perfect according to the Torah in order to be the unblemished Lamb of Elohim. He repeatedly told people to follow Him. In other words, walk the way that He walked, and live the way that He lived.

We have all been tarnished by sin. Thus, we need the washing of His blood to cleanse us. Once clean we need to remain set apart, and walk the perfect path that has been revealed to us.

We are to follow the path blazed by the Messiah, which involves obedience. That is specifically why, when Yahushua was asked what a man must do to inherit eternal life, He responded " . . . *if you want to enter into life, keep the Commandments.*" Matthew 19:17

He then went on to say: "*If you want to be perfect, go, sell what you have and give to the poor, and you will have treasure in heaven; and come, follow Me.*" Matthew 19:21 Yahushua was always encouraging people to go beyond the letter of the Torah, and find the heart of the Torah. Of course, that is the goal – circumcised hearts.

He tells us to enter by the narrow gate "*because narrow is the gate and difficult is the way which leads to life, and there are few who find it.*" Matthew 7:14

In fact, He went on to state: "²⁴ *Strive to enter through the narrow gate, for many, I say to you, will seek to enter and will not be able. ²⁵ When once the Master of the house has risen up and shut the door, and you begin to stand outside and knock at the door, saying, 'Lord, Lord, open for us,' and He will answer and say to you, 'I do not know you, where you are from,' ²⁶ then you will begin to say, 'We ate and drank in Your presence, and You taught in our streets.' ²⁷ But He will say, 'I tell you I do not know you, where you are from. Depart from Me, all you workers of iniquity.'"* Luke 13:24-27

This is a powerful word. He met with these people. He ate with them, and taught them. Yet He proclaims: "*I do not know you.*"

He does not know them, because they are not in a Covenant relationship with Him. We know this because He calls them "*workers of iniquity.*" That is a term equated with lawlessness. In other words, they refuse to follow the Commandments. Sadly, you won't hear this message being preached from many Christian pulpits.

The path to life is narrow, difficult and few will find it. Let those words sink in for a minute.

When we talk about obedience being about blessings and disobedience being about curses, we need to follow these statements to their natural conclusion. While our actions certainly have immediate and tangible consequences in the flesh, they also have eternal consequences. Your actions reveal your heart, and if you want to obey then you are expressing your love for the Master. To the contrary, if you do not want to obey or refuse to obey, then you are expressing your lack of love.

That is why Yahushua said: "*If you love Me, keep My Commandments.*" John 14:15 Obedience is how we express our love, and obedience to the Torah is how we live righteously. It is the righteous who inherit eternal life. And the righteous are defined by the way they live their lives, not because of a simple confession of faith, or act that they did in the past. In fact, it is the workers of iniquity - those who refuse to obey - who are the cursed, rejected and sent away to be punished. (Matthew 25:41-46)

This is pretty serious. I am not being "religiously correct," because Yahushua was not "religiously correct." He offended many with the truth, because the truth does not usually fit within people's religious paradigms. Yahushua was trying to save people by getting them on the right path so that they could receive the forgiveness that He provides through the Covenant.

Ultimately, Yahushua will judge all, because He has inherited the Earth. Thankfully, He has provided us with His standard of judgment in the Scriptures, so there will be no surprises. He told us how He would judge the wicked and the righteous, and it always came down to how they lived their lives.

Incredibly, in Matthew 7:21-23 it sounds as though He was specifically trying to warn the future Christians when He said: "*²¹ Not everyone who says to Me, 'Lord, Lord,' shall enter the kingdom of heaven, but he who does the will of My Father in heaven. ²² Many will say to Me in that day, 'Lord, Lord, have we not prophesied in Your name, cast out demons in Your name, and done many wonders in Your name?' ²³ And then I will declare to them, 'I never knew you; depart from Me, you who practice lawlessness!'*"

The word "lawless" specifically means: "without the Torah." So you might want to rethink the notion that obedience is not a salvation issue. Salvation to me is whether I get into the Kingdom - back into the Garden where I can partake of the Tree of Life. That is where we have eternal life.

Once again, the Scriptures are clear on this point: "*¹⁴ Blessed are those who do His Commandments, that they may have the right to the Tree of Life, and may enter through the gates into the city. ¹⁵ But outside are dogs and sorcerers and sexually immoral and murderers and idolaters, and whoever loves and practices a lie.*" Revelation 22:14-15

The notion that Yahushua abolished the Torah is an obvious lie. Could it be the new lie that "obedience to the Torah is not a salvation issue?" Yahushua was the Torah in the flesh. He taught the true Torah. He lived, died and was resurrected because of the Torah. Therefore, if you reject the Torah then you are rejecting the Messiah and His message.

The Messiah was very clear about this. We also need to be clear about it, so we don't mislead anyone. Our message must be honest and truthful. Yahushua had many people turn away because they found His message to be too hard. We must be prepared for the same response to our message. It will probably not appeal to the masses.

It is by the shed blood of Yahushua, the prophesied Lamb of Elohim, that we can enter through the door that leads to life. We also receive forgiveness through that blood when we sin and repent, but it is all within the context of the Covenant. We are sending a false and mixed message if we attract people to the Torah, and tell them that it is only about being blessed in the here and now - essentially making it optional.

The Torah is the rule of the Kingdom. It needs to be practiced, rehearsed, lived and perfected by those who desire to receive salvation after they die (or if they happen to be alive when the Messiah sends out His messengers to gather the elect).

Yahushua proclaimed "*Repent for the Kingdom of Heaven is at hand.*" That should be our message as well, and obedience is implicit in the act of repentance.

I would therefore suggest if you are in the Covenant renewed by Yahushua, that you delight in the Torah. Boldly proclaim the need to obey the Torah for all those who follow Messiah. Anything less is a disservice to Yahushua, His Message and the Covenant that leads to salvation.

9

Understanding Salvation

In the last chapter we talked about obedience, and our need to obey. It is a undisputed fact that our journey out of Babylon places us on a path of obedience. In fact, it is our obedience that keeps us on the straight and narrow path that leads to life.

We looked at the Commandment of the mezuzah, and then examined Acts 15, when the salvation of the Gentiles was discussed by the early Assembly in Jerusalem. That text brought us back full circle to the Sabbath as part of the pattern, and a waypoint on the path to salvation.

So, obedience is connected to salvation, it always was. If you want to be part of the Covenant Assembly, you must observe "the rules of the house" so to speak. In this case, "the house" was originally represented by the Garden of Eden – Paradise.

The goal is to return to Paradise through the Covenant, and we gain entry to the House by the shed blood the Lamb of Elohim – Yahushua the Messiah.

Once in the House we need to live a life of obedience, which is the opposite of lawlessness. This is an important distinction that many find confusing due to the distorted doctrine of grace.[173]

---

[173] The word grace simply means "thanks". In some modern Christian denominations it has been confused with the Hebrew concept of "favor" and "mercy." It is often used to promote the idea that we play no part in the salvation process. We are simply saved by "grace" alone. This is a distortion of Ephesians 2:8 which states: "*8 For by grace you have been saved through faith, and that not of yourselves; it is the gift of Elohim, 9 not of works, lest anyone should boast.*" The idea being expressed here is that no one can earn their salvation through their works. We all

You see, we cannot get past the threshold, the door, without the shed blood of the Lamb of Elohim – Yahushua. That is the lesson of Passover.

The shed blood of Yahushua was a free gift available to anyone. But do not forget that the mezuzah is also on the door where the blood was placed. So while the blood protects the inhabitants, they are also expected to be obedient.

The blood was required because of our disobedience. It provides forgiveness from our sins, which is the same thing as disobedience. Once in the House, we now need to stop sinning and obey the Commandments. Why would Yahushua die for our sins just so that we can keep on sinning? It really makes no sense whatsoever.

The only understanding that makes sense is that we need atonement to wash us clean from the filth of our sins. Once we get clean, we must stay clean by avoiding sin. We avoid sinning through obeying the Commandments, because the Commandments define the path of righteousness.

This leads us to some common questions such as: 1) How many are there? 2) Which ones do we obey? and 3) Can we even obey?

That is why we have the tzitzit, so when we wear them, we remember the Commandments. The Commandments were formally given to Yisrael at Sinai, and Sinai is a good place to consider salvation. That was the place where Yisrael was brought after being set free from slavery.

That process of deliverance from slavery was coupled with salvation for those who were covered by the blood of the lamb at Passover. The firstborn of Yisrael who obeyed the Commandments were literally "saved" from death. All the

---

need to be washed clean by the shed blood of Yahushua, which is a free gift from Elohim. The portion that most ignore is the statement that we are "saved by faith." You see "faith" is what we believe and it should be evident through our actions – our "works." So while we are not saved by our works, our works reveal our faith. Remember that Abram believed in YHWH "and He accounted it to him for righteousness." Genesis 15:4. See also James 2 and Hebrews 11. For a detailed discussion on this subject see the Walk in the Light series entitled The Law and Grace.

Yisraelites were saved from the final seven judgments rendered upon Egypt.

When they were brought to Sinai, they were given Commandments through the very voice of Elohim. When YHWH was formalizing His relationship with the Bride, Yisrael, He spoke the Ten Words, also known as the Ten Commandments. Those Commandments begin with establishing the nature of the relationship.

> *"¹ And Elohim spoke all these words, saying,*
> *² I am YHWH Eloheycha (your Elohim), who brought you out of*
> *the land of Egypt, out of the house of bondage.*
> *³ You shall have no other gods (elohim) before me."*
> Exodus 20:1-3

He identified Himself by Name. He stated that He was YHWH their Elohim. He was the One Who delivered them from Egypt. He moved them out of Pharaoh's house and was going to bring them to His House, but it needed to be an exclusive relationship. They were not supposed to be mixing with any other gods – that would be idolatry.

The reason for this is because YHWH was making a proposal to Yisrael who would become His Bride. The Yisraelites were to be clean - without spot or blemish. They were to present themselves like virgins, untainted by relationships with other gods.

This is often missed by Christians who believe that "The Church" is "the Bride of Christ." What they fail to understand is that Yisrael is the Bride. She entered into a Marriage Covenant at Sinai, although she fell into idolatry in the midst of the ceremony with the golden calf debacle.[174]

The episode involving the golden calf was a turning point for Yisrael. While they were in Egypt celebrating the

---

[174] Just as Adam failed, so did Yisrael. And just as YHWH did not give up on mankind, He did not give up on His Bride. Even though she was unfaithful, YHWH still made a way for her to return through the Covenant renewed by His Son.

Passover, the firstborn males were the priests for their households. They represented their families as Melchizedek priests. That was the same priestly line that derived from Adam, as the firstborn of creation.

The firstborn would have been the ones conducting the sacrifices on behalf of their house. They were the ones protected by the blood of the Passover Lamb.

The emphasis on the firstborn was specific and intentional. These people were entering into a Covenant relationship with YHWH, and Yisrael was supposed to be the firstborn son of YHWH.

> *"Then you shall say to Pharaoh,*
> *Thus says YHWH:*
> *'Yisrael is My son, My firstborn.'"*
> Exodus 4:22

Immediately prior to the giving of the Ten Commandments YHWH made clear the purpose of His taking these people as a Bride.

> *"⁵ Now therefore, if you will indeed obey My voice and keep My covenant, then you shall be a special treasure to Me above all people; for all the earth is Mine. ⁶ And you shall be to Me a Kingdom of Priests and a Set Apart Nation.' These are the words which you shall speak to the children of Yisrael."*
> Exodus 19:5-6

The children of Yisrael were to be priests – cohenim. They were to be a "holy" (set apart) nation. They were supposed to teach the Nations how to worship YHWH. Instead they attempted to worship YHWH like the nations worship their gods.

> *"¹ Now when the people saw that Moses delayed coming down from the mountain, the people gathered*

together to Aaron, and said to him, Come, make us gods that shall go before us; for as for this Moses, the man who brought us up out of the land of Egypt, we do not know what has become of him. ² And Aaron said to them, Break off the golden earrings which are in the ears of your wives, your sons, and your daughters, and bring them to me. ³ So all the people broke off the golden earrings which were in their ears, and brought them to Aaron. ⁴ And he received the gold from their hand, and he fashioned it with an engraving tool, and made a molded calf. Then they said, This is your god, O Yisrael, that brought you out of the land of Egypt! ⁵ So when Aaron saw it, he built an altar before it. And Aaron made a proclamation and said, 'Tomorrow is a feast to YHWH.' ⁶ Then they rose early on the next day, offered burnt offerings, and brought peace offerings; and the people sat down to eat and drink, and rose up to play." Exodus 32:1-6

As the Bride of YHWH, Yisrael was expected to conduct herself as a faithful wife. When she committed idolatry with the golden calf, it was an act of adultery. She was an unfaithful Bride from the start.

That event resulted in the Levites being chosen to act as "mediators" and "intercessors" between YHWH and the other Tribes. The Levites would be given charge over the House, and only the line of Aharon would be "priests" (cohenim) who could enter into the House.

The rest of the Bride, Yisrael, could only visit the House. She could not enter into the presence of her Husband. She definitely could not enter into the Bridal Chamber, represented by the "Holy of Holies."

This was not an ideal relationship. Yisrael was supposed to abide by the rules of the House, and keep the House in order. That role was now delegated to the Levites, but the remaining tribes were still charged with being a nation of "cohenim." That was the responsibility she was given over the Covenant Land – the Promised Land.

Just as Adam and Hawah were placed in the Garden and charged to "tend and watch"[175] over it, Yisrael was given the same charge over the Promised Land.

Adam was given specific instructions, and part of "tending" and "watching" was to maintain the sanctity and purity of the Garden. He was to be a King and Priest of the Planet – the Melchizedek Priest. The Garden was like the House, and the rest of the planet was the estate.

We know that he lost his privileges due to disobedience. That led to a corruption of creation that ultimately led to the flood, and a reset through Noah and his family.

Mankind later rebelled against YHWH at Babel, and they were divided and separated. Abraham was chosen to be the conduit to draw the Nations back to YHWH, and restore the planet. As with Adam, it started in the Garden, represented by the Covenant Land.

While the Levites represented the people as priests in the House of Elohim, all of Yisrael was intended to be priests throughout the Land. They were supposed to learn how to be priests to the Nations.

The entire process of delivering Yisrael out of Egypt was to provide a pattern for salvation. The firstborn were saved from the wrath poured out upon the Egyptians, and Yisrael was thereafter delivered from bondage.

They were "saved" because they obeyed the Commandments, and followed the instructions regarding the Passover. Failure to obey would result in death of the firstborn. So, salvation was intimately connected with obedience, and Yahushua came to teach, fulfill and point the way.

While His service was focused on love, that love was demonstrated by obedience. He made that very clear in the

---

[175] Genesis 2:15

following statements.

> *"If you love Me, keep My Commandments."*
> John 14:15

> *"He who has My Commandments and keeps them, it is he who loves Me. And he who loves Me will be loved by My Father, and I will love him and manifest Myself to him."*
> John 14:21

> *"If you keep My Commandments,*
> *you will abide in My love,*
> *just as I have kept My Father's Commandments*
> *and abide in His love."*
> John 15:10

There is no getting around the fact that obedience is an evidence of our love. It is the outward expression of our inner belief.

The problem is that many going down this ancient path have been scarred by the Christian doctrine of grace. While they correctly understand that Yahushua died and shed His blood for the forgiveness of sins, they fail to understand that forgiveness is not the same thing as salvation.

Forgiveness is for past conduct, while salvation is something that occurs after forgiveness is rendered. None of this is a decision that we make, by the way. The very Name of Messiah reminds us that "Yah is our salvation," and "Yah saves His people."

I grew up my entire life hearing about people making a "decision" for Christ, or a "decision" to receive forgiveness that resulted in salvation. It all sounds very lofty and spiritual, but it is incorrect.

Salvation is not our decision, rather it is a decision that the Master makes. Christianity teaches that a prayer or a confession leads to immediate salvation, but the Scriptures provide that salvation comes at the end.

We are ultimately saved when the King grants us entry into His Kingdom, and access to the Tree of Life. That is the only way that we obtain eternal life. Up to that point, we are not yet saved.

The decision that we ultimately make is to repent, and repentance involves action. When we repent, we turn away from lawlessness, which is disobedience. We then keep turning toward YHWH until we are directly aligned with Him, and His righteous path.

In the past, when a stranger joined with Yisrael they were not typically concerned with a guarantee of going to heaven. They simply desired to follow the Elohim of Yisrael, and enjoy the blessings of being in a Covenant relationship with YHWH.

There were no guarantees of "eternal security" if they simply raised their hand or said a prayer. These are Christian fabrications.

A person joining with Yisrael would agree to obey YHWH, and worship Him in the manner prescribed in the Torah. Their actions of obedience to the Torah revealed that they served Elohim, and not some other pagan god. It was their actions that defined their status, and their relationship with Elohim.

Sadly, Christianity has become so fixated on instant gratification that they created a formula for salvation that does not include obedience. In doing so, they neglect the path that gets you there, which is the Covenant.

Entrance to the Kingdom through obedience is the path to salvation. This is evident from the text of Revelation:

"Blessed are those who do His commandments,
that they may have the right to the Tree of Life,
and may enter through the gates into the City."
Revelation 22:14

I think it is fair to say that if you get into the Kingdom, and have access to the Tree of Life, you will have eternal life. That is when you are ultimately saved. Salvation is equivalent to eternal life, and access to the Tree of Life is only for those who "do the Commandments."

Yahushua hit this head on when He was asked the question: "What shall I do to inherit eternal life?" He did not tell the person to raise his hand, or say a prayer. He told him to look to the Torah, and keep the Commandments.

Here is the account from Luke.

> "[25] And behold, a certain lawyer stood up and tested Him, saying, 'Teacher, what shall I do to inherit eternal life?' [26] He said to him, 'What is written in the Torah? What is your reading of it?' [27] So he answered and said, 'You shall love YHWH your Elohim with all your heart, with all your soul, with all your strength, and with all your mind, and your neighbor as yourself.' [28] And He said to him, 'You have answered rightly; do this and you will live.' [29] But he, wanting to justify himself, said to Yahushua, 'And who is my neighbor?' [30] Then Yahushua answered and said: 'A certain man went down from Jerusalem to Jericho, and fell among thieves, who stripped him of his clothing, wounded him, and departed, leaving him half dead. [31] Now by chance a certain priest came down that road. And when he saw him, he passed by on the other side. [32] Likewise a Levite, when he arrived at the place, came and looked, and passed by on the other side. [33] But a certain Samaritan, as he journeyed, came where he was. And when he saw him, he had compassion. [34] So he went to him and bandaged his wounds, pouring on oil and wine; and he set him on his own animal, brought him to an inn, and took care of him. [35] On the next day, when he departed, he took out two denarii, gave them to the innkeeper, and said to him, Take care of him; and whatever more you

spend, when I come again, I will repay you. *36 So which of these three do you think was neighbor to him who fell among the thieves?' 37 And he said, 'He who showed mercy on him.' Then Yahushua said to him, 'Go and do likewise.'"* Luke 10:25-37

So the man answered his own question by quoting Deuteronomy 6:4 and Leviticus 19:18. Yahushua said he was correct, and then went on to teach what it meant to *"love your neighbor as yourself."*

He was not changing the Torah or abolishing the Torah. His teaching was revealing how to fulfill the Torah.[176] It is a very high standard, and shows us the limits of selfless love that comes from a circumcised heart.

There was another incident in Mark when someone asked Yahushua the same question: "What shall I do to inherit eternal life?"

"17 Now as He was going out on the road, one came running, knelt before Him, and asked Him, Good Teacher, what shall I do that I may inherit eternal life? 18 So Yahushua said to him, Why do you call Me good? No one is good but One, that is, Elohim. 19 You know the Commandments: Do not commit adultery, Do not murder, Do not steal, Do not bear false witness, Do not defraud, Honor your father and your mother. 20 And he answered and said to Him, Teacher, all these things I have kept from my youth. 21 Then Yahushua, looking at him, loved him, and said to him, One thing you lack: Go your way, sell whatever you have and give to the poor, and you will have treasure in heaven; and come, take up the cross, and follow Me." Mark 10:17-21

Here Yahushua told the man to obey the Commandments. While the man may have been keeping "the letter of the Torah" he was holding back. He had made an idol out of his riches, and could not let go. While Yahushua loved

---

[176] This is precisely what Yahushua meant when he said: *"17 Do not think that I came to destroy the Torah or the Prophets. I did not come to destroy but to fulfill. 18 For assuredly, I say to you, till heaven and earth pass away, one jot or one tittle will by no means pass from the Torah till all is fulfilled."* Matthew 5:17-18.

the man, the man could not truly love Him in return. The passage ends with the man becoming sad and going away sorrowful, for he had great possessions.

You cannot love YHWH with all heart and your neighbor as yourself, if you are not willing to give up all of your material wealth and belongings. That is a test of your love, and that is why Yahushua later said: *"How hard it is for those who have riches to enter the Kingdom of Elohim!"* Mark 10:23

Again, the man had riches so that he could help the poor, but the man could not let go of them.

Yahushua made it very clear, right before His last Passover and crucifixion that He would be separating the sheep from the goats and would be granting entrance to the Kingdom based upon how they treated the poor.

"³¹ When the Son of Man comes in His glory, and all the set apart messengers with Him, then He will sit on the throne of His glory. ³² All the Nations will be gathered before Him, and He will separate them one from another, as a shepherd divides his sheep from the goats. ³³ And He will set the sheep on His right hand, but the goats on the left. ³⁴ Then the King will say to those on His right hand, 'Come, you blessed of My Father, inherit the Kingdom prepared for you from the foundation of the world: ³⁵ for I was hungry and you gave Me food; I was thirsty and you gave Me drink; I was a stranger and you took Me in; ³⁶ I was naked and you clothed Me; I was sick and you visited Me; I was in prison and you came to Me.' ³⁷ Then the righteous will answer Him, saying, 'Lord, when did we see You hungry and feed You, or thirsty and give You drink? ³⁸ When did we see You a stranger and take You in, or naked and clothe You? ³⁹ Or when did we see You sick, or in prison, and come to You?' ⁴⁰ And the King will answer and say to them, 'Assuredly, I say to you, inasmuch as you did it to one of the least of these My

brethren, you did it to Me.' [41] Then He will also say to those on the left hand, 'Depart from Me, you cursed, into the everlasting fire prepared for the devil and his angels: [42] for I was hungry and you gave Me no food; I was thirsty and you gave Me no drink; [43] I was a stranger and you did not take Me in, naked and you did not clothe Me, sick and in prison and you did not visit Me.' [44] Then they also will answer Him, saying, 'Lord, when did we see You hungry or thirsty or a stranger or naked or sick or in prison, and did not minister to You?' [45] Then He will answer them, saying, 'Assuredly, I say to you, inasmuch as you did not do it to one of the least of these, you did not do it to Me.' [46] And these will go away into everlasting punishment, but the righteous into eternal life." Matthew 25:31-46

Did you notice that they all called Him Lord? They all thought they had a relationship with Him. They all thought they were part of His flock, but He separated them because of their actions.

Can you see that Yahushua is holding His sheep to the high standard of obedience that He taught regarding loving your neighbor?

He was regularly instructing people to go beyond the "letter of the Law" to the "heart of the Torah." The goats were trying to make excuses that they didn't see Him. While they may have been circumcised in the flesh, their hearts were clearly not circumcised. Salvation requires a circumcised heart.

I addressed this issue in depth in my book titled *Salvation: The Covenant Journey*. But it should be clear just from these few examples that our obedience is a critical component of our salvation, and disobedience is never acceptable for someone who wants to be saved, and inherit eternal life.

Sadly, most Christians have been taught the exact opposite. They believe that they are saved instantaneously, and that they are going to heaven no matter what they do thereafter. Doing good works is a plus, but optional.

As a result, many are simply biding their time until they get raptured.[177] They have not been instructed how to "love YHWH" and "love their neighbor" so they are unprepared to live in the Kingdom. Therefore, they will not be getting in to the Kingdom.

Sadly, there will be many goats who have been terribly deceived and they won't figure it out until it is too late. They think that they have a relationship with Yahushua, but they are not known by Him because they do not keep the Commandments.

Here is the warning provided by Yahushua:

"*[21] Not everyone who says to Me, 'Lord, Lord,' shall enter the kingdom of heaven, but he who does the will of My Father in heaven. [22] Many will say to Me in that day, "Lord, Lord, have we not prophesied in Your name, cast out demons in Your name, and done many wonders in Your name?' [23] And then I will declare to them, "I never knew you; depart from Me, you who practice lawlessness!"* Matthew 7:21-23

This used to send chills up my spine, because I didn't even feel worthy enough to fall into this group of "many" who were doing all sorts of spiritual things. If they couldn't get in, how could I ever possibly get in?

I finally discovered the key. While they may have been doing "spiritual" things, they were lawless. They were not following the Torah. I grew up in the Christian religion which held up these spiritual "gifts" as the hallmark of a person's rank and authority. That is a lie and a deception.

Eventually, it became clear to me that this group of "many" deceived people were actually Christians. They are

---

[177] While there will clearly be a gathering of the remnant of Yisrael in the future, that does not equate to the Christian understanding of the rapture, which is essentially viewed as an escape from tribulation.

the only ones who think they have a relationship with the Messiah, yet call on the wrong name and reject the Commandments.

Many Christians are "lawless," and "many" will be in for a big surprise when they don't get raptured, and when they are denied access to the Kingdom.

Therefore, as we continue on the path out of Babylon it is imperative that we understand how to live in the Kingdom, by learning how to become Kingdom minded.

10

Becoming Kingdom Minded

So far, we have spent a lot of time discussing the concept of being set apart, and obedient to the Commandments. Some of these changes and adjustments to our lives are easy, and some are a little more difficult.

Changing your dietary habits may prove a bit daunting at first, but it is fairly straightforward. For most people, switching the focus from Sunday to Saturday is not really a problem, unless it conflicts with work, or sporting events. Wearing tzitzit, and placing the Word on our doorposts is definitely new, but we can understand that they are intended to remind us that we are in a different Kingdom, with instructions and Commandments that guide us in our homes and our daily lives.

These are all adjustments that we gradually make as we study and apply the Torah to our lives. In an upcoming chapter we will be discussing some of the pagan holidays imbedded in our religion and our culture. That is when things start to get really interesting. We are not simply talking about tweaking our daily habits, our weekly routines, or personal beliefs and doctrines. Rather, it can create a seismic cultural shift.

Up to this point we have primarily considered Babylon in the context of a false religious system, but it is much more than that. In fact, Babylon permeates almost every area of our lives. It is our entire western culture, which has blended pagan elements into our everyday lives. In order to leave Babylon, we need to recognize all of these areas of influence.

The reality is that in America we are still under Rome, which is just another part of Babylon. For instance, we do not reckon time the way the Scriptures instruct in Genesis 1:14. Rather, we determine time according to the Gregorian calendar developed in 1582, and named after Pope Gregory XIII. This was a modification of the Roman Julian calendar, named after Julius Caesar.

The Roman calendar is based upon the solar cycle, and it traces all the way back to Babylonian sun worship. It is a pagan sun calendar where every day of the week is attributed to a "Host of Heaven."

The seven heavenly bodies that were visible with the naked eye were worshipped by the ancients, and we see this clearly reflected in the names of the week.

Day	Name	Celestial Body
1	Sun Day	Sun
2	Monday (Moon Day)	Moon
3	Tuesday (Tiw's Day)	Mars
4	Wednesday (Wooden's Day)	Mercury
5	Thursday (Thor's Day)	Jupiter
6	Friday (Frigg's Day)	Venus
7	Saturday (Saturn's Day)	Saturn

So, you can see the pagan origins involving the blending and adaptation of certain Roman and Teutonic deities, influencing our weekly cycle. Ultimately, they all trace back to Babylon.

We can see the same thing with our reckoning of the months, as many are linked with Roman deities and celebrations. For instance, January is named after the Roman god Janus. February is named after the god Februus and Februarius, the Roman festival of general expiation and purification. March is named after the Roman god Mars. April is Aphrodite's month. May is named after the Greek goddess Maia, and the Roman goddess Maesta. June is named after the Roman goddess Juno.

From this point forward we see something interesting.

July, which is currently the seventh month, was originally called Quintilis, meaning the fifth month. It was later renamed in honor of the Roman Emperor Julius Caesar. August, which is currently the eighth month, was originally called Sextillis, meaning the sixth month. It was later renamed after the Roman Emperor Augustus Caesar.

After these two months renamed after Roman emperors, we see the original numbering of the months continue, although they do not coincide with their current designations.

For instance, September means "seven" (septum), but it is currently described as month nine. October means "eight" (octum), but is currently described as month ten. November means "nine" (novum), but is currently described as month eleven. December means "ten" (decum), but is currently described as month twelve.

Through the deviation in the numbers of the months, we can see a hint of a more ancient calendar. We will examine that ancient calendar, the Creator's Calendar, in Chapter 15.

For now, the point is simply that we have been immersed in a very ancient pagan system that impacts every aspect of our existence – even the way we tell time. It is a system deriving from Babylon, and it operates contrary to the will, and the prescribed ways of YHWH. Those in Babylon are not reckoning time as the Creator commands, so they are typically out of synch with Him and His time.[178]

Our entire system of telling time is rooted in pagan Babylonian sun worship. This not only effects the religious holidays that we celebrate, but our every day lives. Sadly, the religion that most of us have been raised in has not revealed this information to us. Instead, it teaches us to adapt to Babylon, rather than being set apart from Babylon.

As previously noted, the Christian religion is actually

---

[178] This has a profound impact on those who seek to understand Bible prophecy because in order to understand the future you need to understand how YHWH reckons time - not Babylon.

the product of Rome so, of course, it uses Rome's timing. This begs the question of what kingdom the Christian religion is promoting – Babylon or the Kingdom of Elohim? When you start digging down, it becomes clear that it is corralling many well-intentioned people away from YHWH.

We have already seen that the Christian Gospel, and understanding of salvation, does not prepare people for the true message of the Messiah – which is the Kingdom of Heaven.

The modern understanding of salvation promoted by many Christian denominations is actually the result of a society that wants "drive-thru" service with instant gratification and answers to life. The notion of simply saying a prayer to obtain salvation and "eternal security"[179] fits nicely into a Babylonian culture. So, Christianity seems to be adapting to Babylon, not setting itself apart from Babylon.

The minor lifestyle changes that we have already discussed are intended to get us headed in the right direction, as we journey out of Babylon. The point of resting on the Sabbath, wearing tzitzit, placing a mezuzah on your doorpost and changing your diet are specifically focused on obedience, and being set apart.

To truly walk with Elohim, we need to understand our purpose and our identity. We are, after all, supposed to be "a kingdom of priests and a set apart nation." Exodus 19:6

We have talked about learning to be priests, and it is critical to understand that we are called to be priests in a functioning Kingdom. That is our new purpose and focus.

---

[179] Eternal security is the teaching that essentially promotes the notion of "once saved always saved." In other words, if you said the prayer of salvation which resulted in a person becoming saves, no matter the person does after that moment does not affect the person's salvation. This specifically flies in the face of what Peter taught. *"[20] For if, after they have escaped the pollutions of the world through the knowledge of the Master and Savior Yahushua Messiah, they are again entangled in them and overcome, the latter end is worse for them than the beginning. [21] For it would have been better for them not to have known the way of righteousness, than having known it, to turn from the holy commandment delivered to them. [22] But it has happened to them according to the true proverb: 'A dog returns to his own vomit,' and, 'a sow, having washed, to her wallowing in the mire.'"* 2 Peter 2:20-22

YHWH does not save His people so they can float on clouds and strum harps.

Remember that Babylon was a kingdom established by Nimrod in opposition to YHWH. After that kingdom was divided, YHWH chose Abram and his seed to restore His Kingdom to this Earth - as it is in heaven.

When I grew up as a Christian, I was never instructed that I was supposed to be a priest in any kingdom. I never understood that I had a purpose beyond being saved, and spreading the Gospel. The Gospel that I was taught to spread was found in John 3:16 - *"For God so loved the world that He gave His only begotten Son that whoever believes in Him should not perish but have everlasting life."*

The focus was on getting people saved, not populating the Kingdom of YHWH with priests equipped to serve in that Kingdom. Get the person to say the prayer, give them a Bible and tell them to attend church on Sunday. Check that box and move on to the next lost soul.

That was the goal of Christian evangelism. Beyond that, life for most converts went on as usual. There was little to no teaching regarding the Priesthood, or the Kingdom.

If the Christian religion started focusing on quality rather than quantity things would be much different. They forget the words of Yahushua that *"many are called, but few are chosen."* Matthew 22:14

In fact, Yahushua repeatedly pointed out that His Father's Kingdom is very selective, and there are few who will be getting in. We will continue to talk about this because it stands in stark contrast to the popular, all-inclusive message currently being promoted by Christianity. That message places the emphasis on love, but not on obedience and righteous living as prescribed by the Scriptures.

Growing up in Christianity, I was not prepared to live as a priest in a Kingdom and a Holy Nation. I was never even taught the definition of sin, righteousness or "holiness."[180] Rather, being an American citizen, my religion essentially instructed me how to live as a Christian within the American system, and it was really a seamless fit.

As far as I could tell, the Democratic system along with the focus on life, liberty and the pursuit of happiness was perfectly consistent with Christianity. This was especially true in light of the fact that America was a "Christian Nation."[181]

Since America was a Christian Nation, then pursuing the American Dream seemed like the natural thing to do in order to lead a full Christian life. So, pursuing a higher education, finding a career and accumulating wealth became the driving force in my life. That was the paradigm for life that I was presented with. As I later discovered, it was very different from the instructions of the Messiah.

While much of my life was focused on my daily needs, and planning for the future, my Messiah specifically stated: *"[19] Do not lay up for yourselves treasures on earth, where moth and rust destroy and where thieves break in and steal; [20] but lay up for yourselves treasures in heaven, where neither moth nor rust destroys and where thieves do not break in and steal. [21] For where your treasure is, there your heart will be also."* Matthew 6:19-21

Well, isn't that exactly what the American dream consists of - acquiring wealth, property and saving for retirement? Isn't it all about being a consumer in the capitalistic system that supports the U.S. economy?

It gets even more serious. Yahushua went on to state: *"[31] Therefore do not worry, saying, 'What shall we eat?' or 'What shall we drink?' or 'What shall we wear?' [32] For after all these things the Nations seek. For your heavenly Father knows that you need all these things. [33] But seek first the Kingdom of Elohim and His*

---

[180] These concepts are critical to living and serving in the Kingdom. They are found through the Torah and the Commandments which many in Christianity say have been abolished, or "nailed to the cross." For a detailed discussion of the application and relevance of the Torah see the Walk in the Light series book entitled *The Law and Grace*.

[181] There is a common mantra that America is, or at least was, a Christian nation.

righteousness, and all these things shall be added to you. [34] Therefore do not worry about tomorrow, for tomorrow will worry about its own things. Sufficient for the day is its own trouble." Matthew 6:31-34

Did you notice the difference between "the Nations," and the Kingdom of Elohim? It seems that the Nations are involved in things quite opposite from the Kingdom of Elohim. As a result, we do not want to fall into the category of the Nations.

Now I had read both of these passages repeatedly throughout my life, but I never seemed to think that it applied directly to me. After all, I was just following the American Dream. Well, as it turns out, the American Dream essentially involves building your own kingdom in the Nations, not necessarily the Kingdom of YHWH.

In my case, it diverted most of my time and energy to selfish endeavors that I eventually realized were in many ways diametrically opposed to my purpose of being a priest in the Kingdom. Now I am not making some blanket statement that wealth is evil, but there was a reason why Yahushua said: *"For it is easier for a camel to go through the eye of a needle than for a rich man to enter the Kingdom of Elohim."* Luke 18:25[182]

Remember when a rich man came to Yahushua and asked Him what he needed to do to inherit eternal life? Yahushua told him to obey the Commandments. He then instructed the rich man as follows: *"Sell all that you have and distribute to the poor, and you will have treasure in heaven; and come, follow Me."* Luke 18:22

Yahushua knew that the man's wealth had him trapped. Imaging getting a personal invitation from the Messiah to follow Him? What a privilege and what an honor. Yet the man was actually a slave to his wealth. He was not free to follow Yahushua. What a pity.

---

[182] Many people struggle with this verse and apply various interpretations to the text. The thought of a camel fitting through the eye of a needle seems impossible. Some believe that the eye of the needle is referring to a small gate in a city used at night to limit ingress and egress. It is very likely that the word "camel" is the Hebrew word "gamel" which means "cable or cord". This seems to be consistent with the meaning – its difficult, but not impossible.

These are just a sample of the comments Yahushua made concerning wealth. It is also helpful to look at how people lived when Yahushua was making these statements.

Of course, the lifestyle of John the Immerser, is well known to most. The Scriptures tell us that *"John himself was clothed in camel's hair, with a leather belt around his waist; and his food was locusts and wild honey."* Matthew 3:4

When commenting on John, Yahushua said *"For I say to you, among those born of women there is not a greater prophet than John the Immerser; but he who is least in the Kingdom of Elohim is greater than he."* Luke 7:28

Consider the life of Yahushua, the Son of Elohim, the Messiah, and the King the Yahudim. He described His existence as follows: *"Foxes have holes and birds of the air have nests, but the Son of Man has nowhere to lay His head."* Matthew 8:20

Both John and Yahushua lived with little to no possessions. The first word we read from John is "repent," which means to turn. *"¹ In those days John the Immerser came preaching in the wilderness of Judea, ² and saying, 'Repent, for the Kingdom of Heaven is at hand!'"* Matthew 3:1-2

Yahushua came with the exact same message. After John was placed in prison we read: *"From that time Yahushua began to preach and to say, 'Repent, for the Kingdom of Heaven is at hand.'"* Matthew 4:17

Yahushua picked up where John left off, and the consistent message was to repent, and focus on the coming Kingdom. In fact, the point was really that the Kingdom had arrived. The phrase "at hand" meant that it was in reach – it was here!

The message was intended to wake people up, and get them focused on the Kingdom of YHWH. So, they lived a very simple life here on Earth. Their message was about the Kingdom, and getting people to focus on the Kingdom.

Now, the Yisraelites in that day were somewhat familiar with a kingdom, although they were living in a divided nation, under a heretical king, subject to the Roman Empire. This was very different than the united Kingdom ruled by David.

In fact, David was really the only righteous King to rule over a united Kingdom of Yisrael. His son Shlomo,[183] despite all of his wisdom, fell into horrible sin. That resulted in the subsequent split of the Kingdom into two Houses – two Kingdoms.

So, the message of the Kingdom was a welcome one for those living in the days of John and Yahushua. They longed for a righteous king to come and rule over a restored and reunited Kingdom of Yisrael.

We still await that promise today, and the message of the Kingdom is even more imminent as we await the return of the King to establish the Kingdom here on Earth. Sadly, we are immersed in a much more pervasive form of Babylon than those alive during the days of Yahushua and John.

The Babylon system that we live within is suffocating most of the world. We actually read about a final judgment on this system, and a warning to the people of Elohim concerning that judgment in the Book of Revelation.

> *"² And he cried mightily with a loud voice, saying, "Babylon the great is fallen, is fallen, and has become a dwelling place of demons, a prison for every foul spirit, and a cage for every unclean and hated bird! ³ For all the nations have drunk of the wine of the wrath of her fornication, the kings of the earth have committed fornication with her, and the merchants of the earth have become rich through the abundance of her luxury. ⁴ And I heard another voice from heaven saying, Come out of her, My people, lest you share in her sins, and lest you receive of her plagues. ⁵ For her sins have reached to heaven, and*

---

[183] Shlomo (שלמה) is the actual transliteration of the Hebrew name often referred to as Solomon in English.

Elohim has remembered her iniquities. ⁶ Render to
her just as she rendered to you, and repay her double
according to her works; in the cup which she has
mixed, mix double for her. ⁷ In the measure that she
glorified herself and lived luxuriously, in the same
measure give her torment and sorrow; for she says
in her heart, 'I sit as queen, and am no widow, and
will not see sorrow.' ⁸ Therefore her plagues will
come in one day - death and mourning and famine.
And she will be utterly burned with fire, for strong
is YHWH Elohim who judges her." Revelation
18:2-8[184]

Notice the warning – *"Come out of her My people."* The
phrase "My People" is Covenant language. It specifically
refers to those in Covenant with YHWH. The reason for the
separation is so that we don't get mixed in with Babylon or
share in her sins. Those sins will result in judgment upon her
that are described as plagues.

Of course, this should remind us of when Yisrael was
in Egypt. Even though they were slaves, they were separated
from the Egyptians. That meant they did not have to share in
all the plagues upon Egypt that culminated with the Passover,
and the death of the firstborn.

Prior to that Passover and Exodus from Egypt,
YHWH recalibrated their reckoning of time and the calendar.
"¹ Now YHWH spoke to Moses and Aaron in the land of Egypt,
saying, ² This month shall be your beginning of months; it shall be the
first month of the year to you." Exodus 12:1-2

Remember that they were living in Egypt, a culture
centered on Babylonian derived sun worship. The Yisraelites
were immersed in a form of Babylon, and needed to get back

---

¹⁸⁴ Now those who argue that Revelation was written in 65 CE would naturally look at this as
a warning regarding the impending judgment upon Jerusalem, especially since it is later
referred to as a city in verse 10. That may very well be the case, but the principle is the same
and also clearly has application to the current Babylon that covers the entire world.

into synchronicity with the time of the Kingdom.

They were on their way to a wedding ceremony at Mount Sinai and, as the Bride, she needed to arrive, get cleaned up and ready herself for the scheduled appointment - the wedding date on YHWH's calendar. We find His calendar, and His schedule of events, provided through the Appointed Times.[185]

They are the pattern and the roadmap for separation and we will be talking more in depth about them in Chapter 16. They are important appointments and one of the keys to the Appointed Times is observing them at precisely the right time. We can see from the Scriptures that timing is very important.

The point is that if you are operating on Babylon's calendar you are going to miss the Appointments of YHWH. You won't be ready like the five foolish virgins described by Yahushua.[186]

For now, it is important to recognize that you cannot even keep the Appointed Times unless you know how to tell time. YHWH does not operate on Babylon's clock, or calendar. He has His own method of determining time, and His Appointed Times as described in Genesis 1:14 which states, in part, *"let them be for signs and seasons (Appointed Times), and for days and years."*[187]

We will also discuss the Creator's Calendar in Chapter 15. As we saw with the names of the week days and the names of the months, the calendar is just one aspect of our lives where we need to distinguish between the ways of Babylon and the ways of Elohim.

Christianity does not follow the calendar of the

---

[185] The Appointed Times are primarily found in Leviticus 23. They are discussed in Chapter 16 of this book. For a detailed analysis of the Appointed Times see the Walk in the Light Series book entitled *Appointed Times*.

[186] See Matthew 25:1-13

[187] The word often translated as "seasons" is "moadim" (מוֹעֲדִים) in Hebrew. The word "seasons" often makes us think of spring, summer, fall and winter. That is not what "moadim" (מוֹעֲדִים) refers to. The Hebrew word "moadim" (מוֹעֲדִים) specifically refers to the Appointed Times of YHWH.

Creator, and does not keep His Appointments. Rather, it observes the pagan holy days of Babylon, such as Easter and Christmas. It has adapted these pagan holidays into times of celebration that have focused on the consumption of presents and candy. That works well in a society focused on the pursuit of happiness and self-gratification. The simple fact is that YHWH does not tell us to celebrate these dates.

As with the Christian notion of salvation, these practices completely contradict the teachings of Yahushua Who said *"If anyone desires to come after Me, let him deny himself, and take up his stake, and follow Me."*[188]

Christians in Babylon have gotten so accustomed to the pleasures of life that they have completely lost touch with the concept of denying themselves. They won't even deny themselves the taste of ham, bacon or shrimp when the Scriptures clearly forbid eating such things.[189]

People have lost sight of the fact that their Scriptures point to a covenant that leads into the Kingdom – a different kingdom than the one that they currently live in. Sadly, they are ignoring those Scriptures, and simply adapting a religion that suits their own personal needs and desires. It has nothing to do with denying yourself.

Believe me, this is not the faith walked and taught by the Messiah, and His disciples. Rather, it is the natural evolution of a man-made religion that was mixed with sun worship, and created by the Roman Empire.

So, we actually have the culture impacting the religion, and it doesn't stop with salvation or holidays. When I was working on the Leaving Babylon video series, I happened to be walking near Harvard University, and passed by the Old Cambridge Baptist Church. Founded in 1844, it is a very old and traditional looking church, but what stood out to me were

---

[188] Matthew 16:24, Mark 8:34, Luke 9:23
[189] For an in-depth discussion of the Scriptural dietary instruction and their application to all people see the Walk in the Light series book titled *Kosher*. The Scriptures clearly define those things that are food and can be eaten. They also specify what is not food, and should not be eaten.

the flags and signs in the front of the church.

There were a number of signs placed in the front lawn stating such things as "Black Lives Matter," "Blessed Ramadan," "LGBTQIA lives are sacred," and "Trans Lives are Beautiful," along with many others.

The church also flew the six colored "rainbow" flag that does not accurately represent the seven-colored rainbow in the Scriptures. The seven-colored rainbow is built into creation, and is a sign of the Covenant made between YHWH and creation. The six-colored rainbow is profaned by mankind, and is an attempt to alter and distort the sign of the Covenant. It represents lifestyles and conduct that directly contravene the order built into Creation.

Now anyone who knows the Scriptures can recognize that these political, religious, social and sexual movements do not comport with the ways of YHWH. This demonstrates how many Christian Churches are being influenced by their culture, instead of the other way around. It is a good example of the pervasive power of culture and tradition.

As I write this book, the "United" Methodist Church was on the verge of dividing due to the disagreement on the trans-gender issue. It is incredible that an issue so clearly defined within the order of creation can be such a controversial issue, especially for a group that claims to believe the Scriptures.

This demonstrates the failure of the Christian religion to properly and steadfastly represent the Creator. These people do not see any problem calling themselves Christians, and displaying signs that are opposed to the Commandments contained in the Scriptures upon which they supposedly base their faith.

In fact, if you go to the website of the Old Cambridge Baptist Church they have actually adopted the downward pointing triangle, and six colored flag as a symbol. They state: "Since 1983, we have celebrated the gift of LGBTQ lives and all that they add to the rich tapestry of the congregation's life together, welcoming LGBTQ people into every facet of church life."

Lofty and eloquent words, no doubt, but completely remiss of any Scriptural support. This is how far some elements of Christianity have strayed from the basic tenets found in the Scriptures. They need their eyes to be opened concerning these glaring contradictions.

In fact, this is what we all need. We need the eyes of our understanding to be opened, and we must wake up to the reality that we are living in the matrix of Babylon. Many who profess to follow the Messiah are actually the daughters of Babylon, and Christianity is the religious portion of "Mystery Babylon."[190]

So, the journey out of Babylon is not just about switching churches, resting, or gathering on a different day of the week. It is about detaching from a fraudulent and corrupted religious system that purports to follow Elohim, but has prostituted herself. Actions speak louder than words and Christianity, as a whole, has become a lawless religion, a rebellious and unfaithful whore masquerading as the "Bride of Christ."

Therefore, we must become Kingdom minded if we are to come completely out of Babylon. We must fully immerse ourselves into the Kingdom of Elohim. If we are citizens of the Commonwealth of Yisrael, then the Covenant terms - the Commandments - should permeate every area of our lives.

While it is easy to see the errors and influences of Babylon in the Old Cambridge Baptist Church, discerning Babylon in our individual lives is not always that easy. It runs deep and much of it involves things that aren't so obvious if we have been raised in Babylon.

Of course, in order to identify Babylon's influence, you first need to recognize what Babylon is. We already discussed

---

[190] Mystery Babylon is the title given in the text of revelation to the system that we now recognize as the false religious systems that derive from the sun worshipping origins of Babylon.

the origin of Babylon. It was a system set up in opposition to YHWH. This is where we see mankind establishing a civilization opposed to the ways of Elohim.

Prior to the flood in Noah's time a paternal society existed, with Adam as the father and High Priest over mankind. Adam taught the ways of YHWH, and we see a righteous line flowing through to Noah.

The Nephilim corrupted the planet, which resulted in the flood. Then, after the flood, we read about Nimrod and his kingdom making a name for themselves. *"And they said, 'Come, let us build ourselves a city, and a tower whose top is in the heavens; let us make a name for ourselves, lest we be scattered abroad over the face of the whole earth.'"* Genesis 11:4

This was an act of defiance against YHWH, and an attempt to remove the Creator from creation. Instead of living for Elohim and directing their time, energy and attention toward His service, they were going to live for themselves. Instead of uplifting the Name of YHWH, they were going to make a name for themselves. Mankind's attention was turned from the Creator to the creation

Now we know that at Babel mankind was disbursed, and the language of man was confused. There were no Nations prior to this event – only clans. It was at Babel where Nations were created and divided.

In order for creation to be restored, the Nations must return to YHWH. The New Testament Scriptures speak of Mystery Babylon as something in the future. Those of us who have woken from our slumber see it for what it is.

I grew up in a culture that instilled in me the virtues of life, liberty and the pursuit of happiness - emphasis on the pursuit of happiness. It had nothing to do with denying myself, and everything to do with acquiring wealth and seeking pleasure. My culture impressed upon me the fact that I had rights, and that I was supposed to use those rights to pursue my own personal goals.

Those born into Babylonian cultures are actually living

in and amongst the Nations that were divided after the Tower of Babel incident. Remember that was when the rebellious kingdom of Nimrod was divided into separate Nations, and each one of those Nations was placed under one of the sons of Elohim - not under YHWH.[191]

Those Nations now seek our time, attention, money, devotion and allegiance. That is why we pledge allegiance to the flag of the United States of America. We take oaths and learn to be good citizens. We are encouraged to take pride in our country, and express patriotism. These actions and ideas are all contrary to our lives in the Kingdom of Elohim.

As citizens of the Kingdom of Elohim how can we pledge allegiance to a flag of a nation that is different from the banner of Yisrael? To the contrary, the prophets repeatedly speak of a day when the Nations shall be drawn to a banner raised up by the Hand of YHWH.

Here is one reference to that event: *"[26] He will lift up a banner to the Nations from afar, and will whistle to them from the end of the earth; surely they shall come with speed, swiftly. [27] No one will be weary or stumble among them, no one will slumber or sleep; nor will the belt on their loins be loosed, nor the strap of their sandals be broken."* Isaiah 5:26-27

This is referring to a future Exodus when the people of Elohim will once again be delivered and restored to Him, but I was never taught to be ready for such an event.[192] Instead, I was taught to plant stakes, settle in and build a future for myself and my family. I was raised in an era of greed and gain, and I attended a Christian denomination that promoted that same paradigm.

---

[191] *"[7] Remember the days of old, consider the years of many generations. Ask your father, and he will show you; Your elders, and they will tell you: [8] When the Most High divided their inheritance to the nations, when He separated the sons of Adam, He set the boundaries of the peoples, according to the number of the Sons of Elohim."* Deuteronomy 32:7-8

[192] Anyone familiar with the Passover should recognize that this passage is likely a reference to a future Passover and a future Exodus when the people will be gathered out of the nations of the earth that all derive from Babylon. Remember the Commandment for the Exodus? *"And thus you shall eat it: with a belt on your waist, your sandals on your feet, and your staff in your hand. So you shall eat it in haste. It is YHWH's Passover."* Exodus 12:11

While I lived in a Federal Republic – the United States of America – I was told that I lived in a democracy. I was steeped in the tradition that the will of the majority was the ultimate and best form of government. The tenets of democracy were promoted with religious zeal as if the majority opinion was that of the greatest wisdom. Ultimately, democracy really amounts to "mob rules." That is not how YHWH administers His Kingdom.

The church I attended was essentially a religious democracy with the congregation determining what doctrine and truth they wanted to hear. It had a constitution, and the majority voted in the pastor, and fired the pastor. They had a building and a budget, and all members had a vote. It was essentially a religious system that mirrored the political system of the country. Democracy was the norm, and as far as I was concerned it was Biblical.

I was instilled with the notion that my "normal" life was essentially ordained by God, and the American Dream was the ultimate fulfillment of a divinely orchestrated democratic society.

As a result, I was never prepared to live and serve in a Kingdom. In fact, America was established due to a rebellion from an oppressive monarch. The goal was to get out of the kingdom, and stay out of the kingdom. So, the American ideals of liberty and freedom are actually juxtaposed against the notion of being subject to a king.

The American Dream that I was taught consisted of doing well in high school, going to college, getting a good job, making a lot of money, buying a house, starting a family, driving a new car, eating out at restaurants, going on nice vacations and enjoying life to the fullest.

That was part of the definition of success, and it involved investing most of your money and accumulating wealth. If done properly, your life would crescendo with a comfortable retirement when you could cease from your labors and enjoy the "Golden Years" before you die.

This paradigm of reality is deeply flawed, but this was the pattern of a normal life that I was presented with through my culture. It completely dictated the way that I thought, lived and even worshipped Elohim.

Most of us have been steeped in this cultural, political and religious mindset - or something very similar. When you step back and examine it in light of the Scriptures and teachings of Yahushua, it becomes clear that it is actually very much opposed to the ways of Elohim.

Sadly, this demonstrates the power of tradition and belief. Most of us were convinced that this is the way we are supposed to live. I believe it may be one of the greatest deceptions perpetrated upon mankind.

As we saw with the concept of salvation, many have been led to believe that all they have to do is say a quick prayer, or raise their hand and voila! - they are saved for eternity no matter how they live their lives. Likewise, many have been led down the path of a self-centered, lawless[193] existence, and had it presented as normal - even successful.

Here is how the Scriptures direct us to success. *"This Scroll of the Torah shall not depart from your mouth, but you shall meditate in it day and night, that you may observe to do according to all that is written in it. For then you will make your way prosperous, and then you will have good success."* Joshua 1:8

In the Hebrew text, the word translated as "success" is "sakal" (שׂכל), and is more akin to "insight, wisdom and understanding."

Real success is found through the Covenant, and in the Kingdom. It is found in our knowing, understanding and walking in the ways of YHWH. So, we need to be translated from our Babylonian instilled kingdom of self into the Kingdom of Elohim. This is a huge paradigm shift for many.

---

[193] Lawlessness is simply defined as "without the Torah." Yahushua specifically stated that He will reject many lawless people, despite the fact that they call Him Lord and believed that they served Him. We must obey and serve on His terms, not on our terms or the terms of any man-made religion. See Matthew 7:21-23

Remember the first words of John and Yahushua - *"Repent, for the Kingdom of Heaven is at hand."* The two are intimately related - 1) Repentance, and 2) The Kingdom. These really sum up the true concept of salvation that we were discussing in the previous chapter.

Eternal life is only found by being in His presence, which involves being in His Kingdom. We are saved when we escape the curse of death, and enter into life. You don't make a decision to "receive Jesus," and then do what you want. Instead, the path to salvation means that you repent – you turn away from your lawlessness, and turn toward Elohim and the ways of His Kingdom.

When you repent, you turn your back on Babylon and turn toward YHWH. You don't just look at Him after you turn. You walk on His path, and follow His ways.

Remember, that this is all about a return to Eden – Paradise. Mankind was expelled from the Garden due to disobedience. Therefore, obedience is clearly required for any kind of return. That is what repentance is about. In Hebrew, it is known as "teshuva," which describes the act of turning and living righteously.

Most of us have been involved in a cultural indoctrination that has us focused on ourselves from our youth. We like to get presents on Christmas, and on our birthdays. We are supposed to look good and feel good. We are encouraged to pursue self-improvement – to get an education, find a career and climb the ladder of success so we can make money. After all, money leads to happiness. Right?

We are also taught to plan and prepare for every contingency. We have insurance for anything that can go wrong. The objective is to control our destinies, and remove all uncertainty without God. We don't need faith, just a good doctor, health insurance and a retirement plan.

There is little to no room for faith in Elohim, and people are certainly not encouraged to live by faith – that would be irresponsible. Instead, we are supposed to plan for all of the "what ifs" that might happen in life.

One of the major "what ifs" involves health. America is a sickly and diseased society, and continually getting worse. The Scriptures reveal that this is a curse on those who disobey Him. If a people obey Him, He promises to heal them of their sicknesses. If they disobey Him, He says He will curse them.[194] The curses are meant to get people's attention, so they repent and turn back to Him.

Instead of acknowledging and heeding these very specific promises, America has chosen to go a different route. Instead of faith in Elohim, America has decided to place faith in the medical profession, hospitals, pharmaceutical drugs, and the health insurance industry. Obviously, this is not working, although it is highly profitable.

What America really needs to do is repent. Instead, everyone is instructed to get health insurance, as if an insurance company can provide them with health and healing. So, money that could go into the work of the Kingdom of YHWH is supporting a corrupt and flawed Babylonian system that essentially excludes faith in Elohim.

Much of the problem lies with the fact that people are living in rebellion. Then when they get sick, their natural tendency is to run to the pharmacy for medicine, or run to the doctor or hospital for a solution. People rarely trust in Elohim for healing. Faith and prayer are typically only a last resort - when all else fails. At that point, they might go to a healing crusade looking for a miracle, but most trust the advice of their doctor to the very end.[195]

The Babylonian mindset has it all backwards. It excludes Elohim, or relegates man's ways to the forefront and discards or disregards Elohim all together. Instead of trusting Elohim for our daily bread and living by faith, we are taught

---

[194] Exodus 23:25, Deuteronomy 7:15, Deuteronomy 28:59-61
[195] I cannot count how many people I have witnessed undergo chemotherapy and other radical treatments that are actually killing them, because they place blind faith in their doctor. If people would only express that level of faith in Elohim they would see miracles in their lives.

to plan out the rest of our lives.[196] Instead of believing and trusting the promises of blessings for obedience we are taught to seek the blessings without the obedience.

Babylon wants all the good without God. As a result, the society in which we live removes Elohim from most of our daily decisions or concerns. It removes all reason for faith and trust in Elohim. Sadly, this thinking has affected even those who profess and desire to follow Elohim.

Many of us have inherited these cultural traditions that actually run deeper and more powerful than the religious traditions of our faith.

Aside from our desire to insure for every contingency and engineer our futures, most Americans have embedded within them the concepts of capitalism, free-markets, constitutional rights, individual freedoms and personal liberties, along with the drive for personal wealth acquisition and success which permeates everything we do.

It affects our attitudes, our world-view, our politics and daily decision-making. It even impacts the religion or the faith that we profess. There can be no doubt that American Christianity has adapted to the culture within which it has thrived.

The message that is being preached often involves success, prosperity, feeling good and enjoying every day life - etcetera and so forth. All you have to do is turn on the television and watch pastors of "mega churches" to see that they are dressing, speaking and teaching in a way that appeals to modern culture - a culture that elevates people because of their wealth, fame and abilities.

We even have television shows that help mold and select the next American Idol. They don't even pretend that this is not about idolatry - they admit it. Society then directs their worship, adoration and money to these idols and enriches them.

---

[196] We are specifically told that "the just shall live by faith" (Hebrews 10:38), and of course, faith was the hallmark of Abraham who left Babylon in faith, trusting in the promises of Elohim.

We make idols out of actors, musicians, athletes and now Christian teachers and preachers with "successful" ministries. Success in the Christian realm is often determined by the size of the church, the number of congregants or likes on a Facebook page. How about a TV ministry? That is the ultimate, and it all mimics the success of the world.

Just as people fill mega churches to hear their favorite preacher, they also fill stadiums to watch sports and cheer on their idols. They fill concert halls to watch and applaud music idols, and flock to theaters to watch their favorite movie "stars."[197]

We like to be entertained just as the Babylonians, the Greeks and the Romans. This is very similar to the culture that Yahushua came and taught in - yet He remained set apart.

This is an important part of returning to our Hebrew Roots – Leaving Babylonian culture. If you look at the geography of the Galilee it is amazing to examine where Yahushua walked and taught. He was surrounded by the Decapolis cities – which were all pagan.

Yahushua lived in Nazareth, very close to Sepphoris, the provincial capital of the Galilee. Sepphoris contained many of the pagan elements of the Decapolis cities. Tiberias was also where the Greek and Roman influenced Yahudim, often referred to as Herodians, lived.

We do not read about Yahushua going to these places and teaching. He spent a lot of time in the northwest corner of the Kinneret,[198] which contained "orthodox" communities such as Capernaum, Korazim and Bethsaida. He went into the Galilee of the Nations[199] preaching the good news of the Kingdom.

Therefore, discovering your Hebrew roots through Yahushua does not necessarily involve simply changing your

---

[197] Interestingly, the Sons of Elohim are referred to as "stars" and the worship of the fallen Sons of Elohim is at the heart of sun worship and Babylonian religions. (See Job 38:7 and Genesis 6)
[198] Kinneret is the name of the lake often referred to as The Sea of Galilee.
[199] Isaiah 9:1

habits or routines, as we discussed previously. Leaving Babylon involves a complete paradigm shift in the way that you think and live, as well as a separation from Babylon.

In order to do this, it is important to recognize and understand those cultural norms that we have embedded deep within us. Some extend down to the core of our beings. We need to identify the things that define us and form the environment that we live in, because they establish the framework for our existence. Unless we perform a diligent search, we don't necessarily even recognize these Babylonian influences that have become a part of us.

So many people have desires, and they don't even realize that they have been placed there by their culture. They have been programmed by external forces. Do you want a Ferrari or a Rolex because you need one, or because you have been taught to lust for these beautiful shiny material objects?

We live in a culture where people are obsessed by personal appearance from their hairstyle, to their make-up, to their clothes, to the way they smell. They are consumed by the accessories of life that they use and wear such as watches, cell phones, and even the earbuds.

These are all treated as status symbols, and people place incredible value on these name brand items. People are so concerned with the outside when they really should be focusing on the inside.

Yahushua said it best when He rebuked the Pharisees *"[25] Woe to you, scribes and Pharisees, hypocrites! For you cleanse the outside of the cup and dish, but inside they are full of extortion and self-indulgence. [26] Blind Pharisee, first cleanse the inside of the cup and dish, that the outside of them may be clean also. [27] Woe to you, scribes and Pharisees, hypocrites! For you are like whitewashed tombs which indeed appear beautiful outwardly, but inside are full of dead men's bones and all uncleanness. [28] Even so you also outwardly appear righteous to men, but inside you are full of hypocrisy and lawlessness."* Matthew 23:25-28

Whenever I go to a big city it grieves me to see all the

glamorous people walking down the streets wearing and flaunting their fortunes and just passing by poverty-stricken people on the streets as if they didn't even exist. There is something fundamentally wrong with our society when we get to the point where people can walk by others, and just ignore their plight.

This is one of the effects of living in Babylon. Your wealth determines your status and position, and because it is all about self – there is no obligation to give. Many need to heed the words of Yahushua to the Assembly of Laodicea.

"*17 Because you say, 'I am rich, have become wealthy, and have need of nothing' - and do not know that you are wretched, miserable, poor, blind, and naked - 18 I counsel you to buy from Me gold refined in the fire, that you may be rich; and white garments, that you may be clothed, that the shame of your nakedness may not be revealed; and anoint your eyes with eye salve, that you may see. 19 As many as I love, I rebuke and chasten. Therefore be zealous and repent.*" Revelation 3:17-19

Notice again how Yahushua emphasized repentance. In the Kingdom of Elohim – we are commanded to give to the poor. You cannot ignore the poor, but in Babylon it's your right. You don't have to let go of your stuff if you don't want to.

Now I'm not about to critique our entire culture, and I'm painting with a broad brush. There are certainly a lot of well-meaning people who are giving and selfless, but that is typically in spite of Babylon, not because of Babylon.

For the most part Babylon teaches people to love the world, and the things of the world. This stands in stark contrast to the admonition found in the Scriptures. "*15 Do not love the world or the things in the world. If anyone loves the world, the love of the Father is not in him. 16 For all that is in the world - the lust of the flesh, the lust of the eyes, and the pride of life - is not of the Father but is of the world. 17 And the world is passing away, and the lust of it; but he who does the will of Elohim abides forever.*" 1 John 2:15-17

Isn't this the exact opposite of Babylon? Indeed, "the world" is another term for Babylon. Rather than esteeming the idols and heroes of Babylon, I recommend looking at the life that Yahushua led, and ask yourself if you are prepared to truly follow Him.

If He passed by you now would you be able to drop your nets and follow Him, or are you too caught up in yourself to give up what you have? This is important to ask yourself because Yahushua is calling all of us to follow Him – not just twelve disciples almost 2,000 years ago.

Read what Yahushua said was required of anyone who wanted to follow Him.

"^{24} . . . If anyone desires to come after Me, let him deny himself, and take up his stake, and follow Me. ^{25} For whoever desires to save his life will lose it, but whoever loses his life for My sake will find it. ^{26} For what profit is it to a man if he gains the whole world, and loses his own soul? Or what will a man give in exchange for his soul? ^{27} For the Son of Man will come in the glory of His Father with His angels, and then He will reward each according to his works." Matthew 16:24-27

Again, isn't this exactly the opposite of how we are taught to live? We are taught to try to save, protect and preserve our lives and comfortable existence at all cost. We are taught to seek gain and profit, but Yahushua tells us that is all pointless if we lose our souls. The true path involves denying ourselves and taking up our own execution stake, and following Him.

The problem is that it is not necessarily a convenient message for most, because it doesn't fit within their paradigm or their plans. Of course, this is nothing new. It has always been a difficult passage for people.

"^{18} And when Yahushua saw great multitudes about Him, He gave a command to depart to the other side. ^{19} Then a certain scribe came and said to Him, Teacher, I will follow You wherever You go. ^{20} And Yahushua said to him, 'Foxes have holes and birds of the air have nests, but the Son of Man has nowhere to lay His head.'

²¹ *Then another of His disciples said to Him, 'Master, let me first go and bury my father.' ²² But Yahushua said to him, 'Follow Me, and let the dead bury their own dead.' ²³ Now when He got into a boat, His disciples followed Him."* Matthew 8:18-23

Now mind you, He was only going to the other side of the Lake, and people were already making excuses. Imagine if He told them to go to the other side of the world. They were burdened by the affairs of the world. In contrast, He was the King and He didn't even have a home.

Now let's revisit what happened when He was asked about eternal life.

"¹⁷ Now as He was going out on the road, one came running, knelt before Him, and asked Him, 'Good Teacher, what shall I do that I may inherit eternal life?' ¹⁸ So Yahushua said to him, 'Why do you call Me good? No one is good but One, that is, Elohim. ¹⁹ You know the commandments: Do not commit adultery, Do not murder, Do not steal, Do not bear false witness, Do not defraud, Honor your father and your mother. ²⁰ And he answered and said to Him, Teacher, all these things I have kept from my youth. ²¹ Then Yahushua, looking at him, loved him, and said to him, One thing you lack: Go your way, sell whatever you have and give to the poor, and you will have treasure in heaven; and come, take up the cross, and follow Me. ²² But he was sad at this word, and went away sorrowful, for he had great possessions. ²³ Then Yahushua looked around and said to His disciples, How hard it is for those who have riches to enter the kingdom of Elohim! ²⁴ And the disciples were astonished at His words. But Yahushua answered again and said to them, Children, how hard it is for those who trust in riches to enter the Kingdom of Elohim! ²⁵ It is easier for a camel to go through the eye of a needle than for a

rich man to enter the Kingdom of Elohim." Mark
10:17-25

Here we see the Messiah stating that it is hard for those who have riches to enter into the Kingdom of Elohim. Nevertheless, that is exactly what people are taught to do. It is almost as if this culture is setting people up for failure in the Kingdom of Elohim, because having great wealth can create a problem if you are not willing to give it all up. This man went away sorrowful. He didn't follow Yahushua because of his riches.

How many people are in that same situation and don't even know it? How many Christians are living the American Dream, building a kingdom here on earth thinking it is perfectly normal?

Because of the allure of riches and their hinderance to following Him, Yahushua also specifically warned: *"¹⁹ Do not lay up for yourselves treasures on earth, where moth and rust destroy and where thieves break in and steal; ²⁰ but lay up for yourselves treasures in heaven, where neither moth nor rust destroys and where thieves do not break in and steal. ²¹ For where your treasure is, there your heart will be also."* Matthew 6:19-21

Did He really say that? It defies all modern convention and again, most prosperous cultures completely ignore this advice.

Yahushua elaborated even further by stating:

"²⁴ No one can serve two masters; for either he will hate the one and love the other, or else he will be loyal to the one and despise the other. You cannot serve Elohim and mammon. ²⁵ Therefore I say to you, do not worry about your life, what you will eat or what you will drink; nor about your body, what you will put on. Is not life more than food and the body more than clothing? ²⁶ Look at the birds of the air, for they neither sow nor reap nor gather into

barns; yet your heavenly Father feeds them. Are you not of more value than they? [27] Which of you by worrying can add one cubit to his stature? [28] So why do you worry about clothing? Consider the lilies of the field, how they grow: they neither toil nor spin; [29] and yet I say to you that even Solomon in all his glory was not arrayed like one of these. [30] Now if Elohim so clothes the grass of the field, which today is, and tomorrow is thrown into the oven, will He not much more clothe you, O you of little faith? [31] Therefore do not worry, saying, 'What shall we eat?' or 'What shall we drink?' or 'What shall we wear?' [32] For after all these things the Gentiles seek. For your heavenly Father knows that you need all these things. [33] __*But seek first the kingdom of Elohim and His righteousness, and all these things shall be added to you.*__ *[34] Therefore do not worry about tomorrow, for tomorrow will worry about its own things. Sufficient for the day is its own trouble."*
Matthew 6:24-34

Again, most of us live our lives in complete contradiction to these words, and we do the exact opposite because of the culture we were raised in. We constantly worry about tomorrow. In fact, we are taught to have a plan for every possible contingency, leaving little to no room for faith. We chase after careers to fund all of our plans, which turn us into slaves of Babylon instead of priests in the Kingdom of Elohim.

The Scriptures provide clear direction given by the Messiah to seek the Kingdom of Elohim first and everything you need will be provided. I read these words my entire life but they never penetrated, because I grew up in a culture and a religion that completely ignored those instructions and taught the exact opposite.

Seek yourself, your needs, your wants and your own priorities first and then fit all of that into the Kingdom if you can. Success is the mantra of the day and even if you're not successful you should "dress for success." So even if you're not rich you are supposed to look like it, act like it, and give the outward impression that you are a success. Fake it till you make it!

Did you notice when Yahushua said: *"For all these things the Gentiles seek?"* The word "Gentiles" refers to the "Nations" – those outside the Covenant path blazed by Abraham. While you may be sojourning within the Nations, you must remain set apart from their ways. At least those that conflict with the ways of YHWH.

Yahushua said, *"My Kingdom is not of this world. If My Kingdom were of this world, My servants would fight, so that I should not be delivered to the Yahudim; but now My Kingdom is not from here."* John 18:36

So, His Kingdom isn't even of this world that we live in. As a result, we really shouldn't be getting too settled in. This is especially true if we recognize that judgment is coming to Babylon, and we are warned to *"come out of her My people."*

We need to recognize this important distinction. We must detach from the kingdom of Babylon, and separate ourselves. Our land is not the country we were born and raised in, and our government is not dependent upon geography and national citizenship.

Our Kingdom is not of this world, yet most are completely dependent on Babylon for their very survival. They need to work to make money to buy all of the things that they want and need. This is the illusion and trap of Babylon.

Remember Revelation 18:3 referring to Babylon the Great? *"For all the Nations have drunk of the wine of the wrath of her fornication, the kings of the earth have committed fornication with her, and the merchants of the earth have become rich through the abundance of her luxury."*

We have been taught to be consumers – we work so that we can spend and consume and keep on consuming which keeps Babylon enriched. Most of us have no idea how to actually survive without Babylon. This is very different from the fathers of our faith.

Just as Abraham and the Patriarchs were sojourners and learned to rely on Elohim for their daily bread – we are supposed to do the same until the Messiah gathers us home. We are not supposed to be reliant on Babylon. That is why Yahushua taught His disciples to pray *"give us this day our daily bread."*[200]

If we follow Yahushua then, like Him, we are not of this world. The problem is that Babylon has taught us that we should be prudent investors, make long term plans and build our kingdoms in this world. We have been taught to be successful and make a name for ourselves – just like those in the rebellious kingdom of Babylon.

Most of us raised in western cultures have Babylon deeply ingrained within us, and while we may be kingdom minded, it is often the wrong kingdom that consumes our time and attention. As has been demonstrated, this goes beyond our religion and permeates into every area of our lives.

Yahushua taught His disciples to pray to the Father and ask *"Your Kingdom come, Your will be done on Earth as it is in Heaven."*[201] We should be praying this same prayer.

So, as we continue in this journey out of Babylon, we must examine all of our cultural influences that we have inherited, and make sure that our thoughts and actions align with the culture of the Kingdom of YHWH. Only then can we truly seek His Kingdom first, but in order to do that, we also need to understand the Kingdom.

---

[200] Matthew 6:11 and Luke 11:3
[201] Matthew 6:10 and Luke 11:2

II

Understanding the Kingdom

When a person hears the Good News of the Kingdom and repents, they are not instantly saved. Rather, they enter into a Covenant relationship with YHWH Elohim – King of the Universe. This new relationship is the beginning of the journey, and it is at the heart of leaving Babylon.

When you understand that your allegiance does not belong to a temporal kingdom of man, but rather an eternal Kingdom that encompasses the entire known universe and beyond, it should change the way that you think and act.

Now it is important to understand that the Kingdom of YHWH is like none that we witness in this world, or in history. The Kingdom is not a democracy, nor is it a constitutional monarchy.

YHWH is not a figurehead. He is described as El Shaddai - "El Almighty." He is the Most High Elohim.[202] Unlike many modern monarchs who reign, but do not rule – YHWH Elohim both rules and reigns over the universe, and all that exists.

Do you fully understand that truth? It is usually easier to process that mentally, and much more difficult to actually implement that reality into your day to day existence. That was the reason why YHWH chose Yisrael - to rehearse the

---

[202] As discussed previously, the Hebrew word "elohim" essentially means "powers." The term "el" can refer to any number of powerful spiritual beings, all of them have been created by YHWH. That is why He is referred to as "the Most High." He was not created and therefore is above all the rest. He does not die, although any of the created beings can die. That is the focus of the following passage: "⁶ I said, You are elohim, and all of you are sons of the Most High. ⁷ But you shall die like men, and fall like one of the princes. ⁸ Arise, O Elohim, judge the earth; for You shall inherit all nations." Psalm 82:6-8

Kingdom in real time here on Earth. Yisrael failed to reveal the Kingdom to the Nations, but that does not change the fact that the Kingdom is in operation.

No matter where you live and no matter what government's rule over the land that you live - YHWH's Kingdom is still fully functioning - whether you see it or not. Until we become Kingdom minded and until we fully understand the present reality of the Kingdom of Elohim, we will never completely leave Babylon.

As we have discussed, the kingdom of Nimrod was the first kingdom mentioned in the Scriptures. Previously, Adam was charged with establishing the Kingdom of YHWH on Earth, and Eden was the capital. That is why Adam was commanded to watch over it. He was supposed to keep the enemy out.

We know that the "nachash" (serpent or shining one) deceived mankind. He used stealth instead of force. You see, he understood the Kingdom of YHWH, and he knew the plan for creation. He understood that the way to defeat mankind was to get man to turn away from YHWH and His Kingdom.

The nachash knew that if he could get mankind to disobey, then mankind would be ejected from the Kingdom. The nachash could not physically remove man from the dwelling place prepared for him, but he could get man to change his own fate through his conduct.

This is the same thing that Balaam did when he advised Balak how to bring a curse upon the Yisraelites. Balak did not have to defeat the Yisraelites by force. Balaam taught Balak to simply entice the Yisraelites to stray from the Torah so that they would bring a curse upon themselves.[203]

Yahushua referred to that as "the Doctrine of Balaam" when speaking to the messenger of the assembly in Pergamos. *"But I have a few things against you, because you have there those who hold the Doctrine of Balaam, who taught Balak to put a*

---

[203] Numbers 31:16

stumbling block before the children of Yisrael, to eat things sacrificed to idols, and to commit sexual immorality." Revelation 2:14

Of course, we recognize that this is the most effective tactic of the enemy. Why start a fight when you can get them to bring a plague upon themselves?

That has been an effective strategy of the enemy throughout history. The enemy is currently perpetrating "the Doctrine of Balaam" through the Christian religion, repackaged and renamed as "The Doctrine of Grace."

This religious system draws people into an illusory state of existence and complacency with guarantees of salvation. Many popular Christian denominations provide the assurance that through their particular path people will some day enter into the Kingdom when they die. Sadly, it is a lie and the deceived will not get into the Kingdom because of their religious conduct.

The deception lies in the fact that while they may claim to believe in God, they fail to obey His Commandments – which constitute the rule of the Kingdom. They have disobeyed, thinking they are "under grace" when they have actually been under a curse.

Adam and Hawah were expelled from the Garden because they disobeyed. It is that simple. Their disobedience caused their separation from YHWH. Man could no longer dwell in the presence of Elohim if he would not obey the Instructions.

This is not a complicated concept, yet it has been extremely clouded by false teaching. YHWH gave us very simple, practical examples so that we can understand His ways.

He gives us a house so that we can practice dwelling in His House. Parents set standards for their children. They should let their children know what is acceptable conduct and what is prohibited. Disobedience involves punishment, while obedience leads to a peaceful existence. It's all a rehearsal for the Kingdom.

As an attorney, I deal with all sorts of issues that occur in the home, and I have met many parents who were forced to expel their children. While it pained them terribly, their children's conduct was so egregious and destructive that it was causing harm to the rest of the family.

Clearly, the age of the child is a significant factor. The older a child is, the more accountable they are for their behavior, and the less patience the parent has for rebellion and disobedience.

This is no different in the Kingdom of Elohim. YHWH is surely patient and long suffering with us all. But there is a point when "tough love" is the only answer. Even punishment is meant for our own good.

After the fall of man, the goal was to get back into the Garden, but it was going to take more than an altar call. The consequences of disobedience was severe, because of the responsibility given to Adam and Hawah.

The fall actually had tremendous consequences on all of Creation. Adam had opened the door to evil upon the Earth. He failed to watch over Creation. What resulted was an unstoppable incursion upon this planet by a class of beings called the Sons of Elohim. It resulted in a world takeover.

Here is a brief description of how it started in Genesis. "¹ Now it came to pass, when men began to multiply on the face of the earth, and daughters were born to them, ² that the Sons of Elohim saw the daughters of men, that they were beautiful; and they took wives for themselves of all whom they chose. ³ And YHWH said, 'My Spirit shall not strive with man forever, for he is indeed flesh; yet his days shall be one hundred and twenty years.' ⁴ There were Nephilim on the earth in those days, and also afterward, when the Sons of Elohim came in to the daughters of men and they bore children to them. Those were the mighty men who were of old, men of renown." Genesis 6:1-4

These Sons of Elohim, known as Beni ha'Elohim in Hebrew, were a class of supernatural beings that had direct access to the Throne Room.[204] We read about them in the Book of Job. They were present at creation *"When the morning stars sang together, and all the sons of Elohim shouted for joy . . ."* Job 36:7

The text in I Enoch provides further detail on this extra-terrestrial invasion. In that writing, the Sons of Elohim were referred to as "Watchers," and they were creating a hybrid genetic race of beings called Nephilim. It sounds like the plot from a fantasy fiction movie, but it actually happened.

The Scriptures described that all flesh was corrupted.

> *"[11] The Earth also was corrupt before Elohim, and the Earth was filled with violence. [12] So Elohim looked upon the Earth, and indeed it was corrupt; for all flesh had corrupted their way on the Earth. [13] And Elohim said to Noah, 'The end of all flesh has come before Me, for the Earth is filled with violence through them; and behold, I will destroy them with the Earth.'"* Genesis 6:11-13

So, the fallen Sons of Elohim were corrupting mankind, and men turned to wickedness. These "extra-terrestrial" entities were establishing their own race of beings, and creating their own kingdom in opposition to the Kingdom of Elohim.

The Sons of Elohim that had rebelled produced the sons of darkness, and it appeared that darkness was winning. In fact, it was headed toward an extinction level event for mankind, made in the image of Elohim, as the kingdom of darkness sought to achieve their "New World Order."

It seems that Noah and his family were the only ones left. Noah was described as pure and undefiled. He walked with Elohim, and his flesh was not corrupted. That is why he and his family were protected in an ark while the rest of creation was essentially washed clean.

---

[204] See Job 1:6 and 2:1

The flood event was literally a "Great Reset."[205] It was necessary to purify the planet. Otherwise, the forces of evil would have prevailed. YHWH hit the "self-destruct button," and protected eight people in an ark.

These eight people would begin again, and it is significant to note that eight represents "new beginnings." We see that number repeated through the Covenant. They were still tainted by the sin of Adam and Hawah though, and it did not take long for mankind to rebel. This time it occurred through the kingdom of Nimrod.

The Tower of Babel was a symbol of mankind's repeated rejection of YHWH. The people united against YHWH, and that resulted in punishment. Again, there is not much detail in the Scriptures, but this was an extraordinary event in history.

> "*1 Now the whole earth had one language and one speech. 2 And it came to pass, as they journeyed from the east, that they found a plain in the land of Shinar, and they dwelt there. 3 Then they said to one another, 'Come, let us make bricks and bake them thoroughly.' They had brick for stone, and they had asphalt for mortar. 4 And they said, 'Come, let us build ourselves a city, and a tower whose top is in the heavens; let us make a name for ourselves, lest we be scattered abroad over the face of the whole earth.' 5 But YHWH came down to see the city and the tower which the sons of men had built. 6 And YHWH said, 'Indeed the people are one and they all have one language, and this is what they begin to do; now nothing that they propose to do will be withheld from them. 7 Come, let Us go down and there confuse their language, that they may not*

---

[205] At the time I was writing this book, those advocating for a New World Order are calling for a Great Reset. It is important to note that Elohim is the only one qualified and empowered to perform such a thing. While the powers of darkness strive to advance their own goals and objectives, they are always playing into YHWH's ultimate plan.

understand one another's speech.' ⁸ So YHWH
scattered them abroad from there over the face of all
the earth, and they ceased building the city. ⁹
Therefore its name is called Babel, because there
YHWH confused the language of all the earth; and
from there YHWH scattered them abroad over the
face of all the earth." Genesis 11:1-9

Nine verses is all we get to describe this "earth shattering" event – literally. I say this because not only were people divided linguistically, this was also when the continents were physically separated. So, people were also divided geographically.

This is the first time that we read about "nations." Prior to that time there were simply clans all tracing back to Noah. Noah had made a Covenant with YHWH, but the people had broken that Covenant.

Does that mean that YHWH was finished with mankind? Certainly not. In fact, something very interesting happened when the Nations were created.

In the Dead Sea Scrolls and Septuagint translation of Deuteronomy 32 we read:

"⁷ Remember the days of old, consider the years of many
generations. Ask your father, and he will show you; your elders, and
they will tell you: ⁸ When the Most High divided their inheritance
to the nations, when He separated the sons of Adam, He set the
boundaries of the peoples according to the number of the Sons of
Elohim. ⁹ For YHWH's portion is His people;
Jacob is the place of His inheritance."
Deuteronomy 32:7-9[206]

---

[206] Some translations based upon the Masoretic text state that "He set the boundaries of the peoples according to the number of the Children of Yisrael." That does not make sense, since Yisrael was not even in existence at that time. The Septuagint and the Dead Sea Scrolls agree on the "Sons of Elohim" rendering.

We are supposed to remember "the days of old," which is the time before the flood. We have already talked about some Sons of Elohim who rebelled, and it appears that Elohim appointed certain Sons of Elohim to oversee the divided nations.

In fact, the Book of Jasher (Yasher) is quite specific on this point.[207] When YHWH said "Come let Us go down and confuse their language," He was talking to seventy beings – Sons of Elohim.

We read about that in the text of Jasher (Yasher). "And Elohim said to the seventy Sons of Elohim who stood foremost before Him, to those who were near to Him, saying, Come let us descend and confuse their tongues, that one man shall not understand the language of his neighbor, and they did so unto them." Yasher 9:32

That is why the number seventy is often attributed to represent "the Nations." While YHWH created Nations and set Sons of Elohim over them, it is important to understand that He chose Abram.

That is why the text immediately following the Tower of Babel traces the genealogy of Shem to Abram. YHWH chose Abram to rebuild and establish His Kingdom in the midst of the Nations.

Abram was chosen for a specific purpose. YHWH would work through a Covenant with this man, and his descendants, to restore the Nations back to Him. Through this process, YHWH would be replenishing His Kingdom with new "sons." This was confirmed by Yahushua when He was speaking about the resurrection.

> "34 Yahushua answered and said to them, 'The sons of this age marry and are given in marriage. 35 But those who are counted worthy to attain that age, and the

---

[207] While I do not treat the Book of Yasher as having the full weight and authority of Scripture, I find it interesting to provide some background information that sometimes proves helpful in understanding the full context of certain Scriptures.

*resurrection from the dead, neither marry nor are given
in marriage; ³⁶ nor can they die anymore, for they are
equal to the angels and are Sons of Elohim, being sons of
the resurrection."* Luke 20:34-36

Psalm 82 specifically addresses the Sons of Elohim in
the "congregation of the mighty." They became the "gods"
who failed to properly oversee the Nations. In this passage we
read about their ultimate judgment.

*"¹ Elohim stands in the congregation of the mighty; He
judges among the elohim. ² How long will you judge
unjustly, and show partiality to the wicked? Selah ³
Defend the poor and fatherless; Do justice to the
afflicted and needy. ⁴ Deliver the poor and needy; Free
them from the hand of the wicked. ⁵ They do not know,
nor do they understand; They walk about in darkness;
All the foundations of the earth are unstable. ⁶ I said,
You are elohim, and all of you are children of the Most
High. ⁷ But you shall die like men, and fall like one of
the princes. ⁸ Arise, O Elohim, judge the earth; for You
shall inherit all Nations."* Psalm 82:1-8

This passage is describing what is sometimes referred
to as "the Divine Council." The term "congregation of the
mighty" is literally "El council" (עדת-אל).

It is important to understand that the words "el" (god)
and "elohim" (gods) are not exclusively referring to YHWH.
In Hebrew, the words simply refer to a "mighty one" or
"power." The terms could be applied to a variety of spiritual
entities.

So, these "gods" were placed over the Nations, and we
can see where that led. That is why the Psalm concludes with
"arise Elohim" for you shall inherit the Nations. The Sons of
Elohim were given a job to do, and they failed. YHWH
Elohim had to get off the Throne, and do it Himself. That is

why He ended up sending His Son, so that He could ultimately inherit the Nations through the Covenant that flowed through Abram, and his seed.

The emphasis was upon the seed, because that is how YHWH would fulfill the Covenant. Remember the promise to Abraham during the Covenant of Circumcision.

> "⁵ No longer shall your name be called Abram, but your name shall be Abraham; for I have made you a father of many nations. ⁶ I will make you exceedingly fruitful; and I will make Nations of you, and kings shall come from you." Genesis 17:5-6

Also, consider the promise to Sarah involving the Covenant of Circumcision.

> "¹⁵ Then Elohim said to Abraham, 'As for Sarai your wife, you shall not call her name Sarai, but Sarah shall be her name. ¹⁶ And I will bless her and also give you a son by her; then I will bless her, and she shall be a mother of Nations; kings of peoples shall be from her." Genesis 17:15-16

So, we can see the restoration of the Kingdom on earth through Abraham, and his bride. That union resulted in a Kingdom. The Kingdom of Yisrael was supposed to represent the Kingdom of Elohim on Earth, and draw the Nations back to YHWH.

Yisrael was supposed to help restore mankind from the sin of Babel, and reunite the Nations back to YHWH. Instead, Yisrael was lured away from YHWH by the Nations.

As a result of the sin of Yisrael, the Kingdom was divided into two houses. The Scriptures describe the history of those two houses of Yisrael, and their different journeys away from YHWH. They also detail the unique and specific prophecies relating to Yisrael's return.

In order to properly understand Scriptural prophecy it is critical to grasp what happened to the Kingdom of Yisrael. This will be discussed further in the chapter titled Understanding Prophecy.[208]

The significance of the division of Yisrael is commonly referred to as "The Two House Doctrine." The problem is that once you put a label on something, it separates it from pure truth, and relegates it into an idea or a theory that can be criticized and debated.

This is what has been done with the so-called Two House movement. The notion of Two Houses is not simply a doctrine or belief. Rather, it is a historical fact, and the focus of much prophecy involving the restoration of creation. It is an integral part of Messiah's purpose, but amazingly it is something that often divides Hebrew Roots from Messianic Judaism. Christianity doesn't even teach the subject.

The division of the Kingdom of Yisrael into two separate houses is a large part of Scriptural history, and the uniting of the two houses is a major component of prophecy.

The restoration of the two houses is specifically described in Ezekiel 37, which talks about the breath of YHWH reviving the dry bones of the whole House of Yisrael, and the Two Sticks (Two Houses) being joined together in the Covenant Land and ruled by One King.

So, the earthly Kingdom expressed through Yisrael is still significant, but it must be in and through the context of the Covenant.

Jeremiah specifically prophesied: *"Behold, the days are coming, says YHWH, when I will make a renewed Covenant with the House of Yisrael and with the House of Yahudah."* Jeremiah 31:31

That renewed Covenant with the House of Yisrael and the House of Yahudah is centered around the Torah. The prophecy in Jeremiah went on to proclaim: *"But this is the*

---

[208] See Chapter 21

Covenant that I will make with the House of Yisrael after those days, says YHWH: I will put My Torah in their minds, and write it on their hearts; and I will be their Elohim, and they shall be My people." Jeremiah 31:33

We will discuss this renewed Covenant in more detail later on, along with a discussion exploring the identity of "My people." The Prophet Malachi specifically prophecies about the coming Messiah and exhorts us to *"remember the Torah of Moses"* Malachi 4:4

The problem is that many Christians believe that they are now "Spiritual Israel" while the "Jewish People" are still "Physical Israel." This has led to a plethora of problems that I discuss in my articles and books.[209]

Just because Christians refer to themselves as "The Church" does not mean that they are "Spiritual Israel," and just because a group of people call themselves "Jewish" does not mean that they are "Physical Israel" – even if they founded a Jewish State called Israel.

Recognizing these distinctions involving the identity of the House of Yisrael and the House of Yahudah is extremely important if you want to understand current events and the future prophetic plan of Elohim.

Many equate the Jewish people or the religion of Judaism with the House of Yahudah and even the House of Yisrael for that matter. This leads to massive confusion.

Yisrael and Yahudah are the two houses who are in the renewed Covenant, and that Covenant was renewed by the Messiah. Interestingly we see Christians claiming certain "rights" because of their belief in a messiah, while Jews, whether ethnic or religious, claim "rights" based upon their identification with ancient Yisrael.

So, clearly we see a parallel between the Christian and Jewish religions with the House of Yisrael and the House of Yahudah. Both claim to be in a relationship with Elohim, but

---

[209] The subject of the Jewish people and the modern State of Israel is discussed in detail in the book titled *The Israel Dilemma*, scheduled to be released after this book goes to print.

neither actually is, if they are not in the renewed Covenant. Only the Covenant defines who is in the Kingdom, not some title, label, or religious affiliation.

Let's say for arguments sake that the Jewish People are the descendants of the House of Yahudah. Even if that were the case, they are not exempt from the renewed Covenant simply because they think they are the "chosen people."

Likewise, Christians are not exempt from the Torah, because they believe in Jesus. Both people groups identify with a religious system, and neither of those groups fully embrace the renewed Covenant as described in Jeremiah.

Just as Joseph[210] needs to come out of Christianity, Yahudah has to come out of Judaism. Many are already undergoing this process.

This fact highlights a fundamental flaw that exists in Messianic Judaism, which attempts to combine aspects of the religion of Judaism with the Messiah.

It is critical to recognize that the religion of Judaism derives from the Pharisaic sect. It currently contains even more traditions, rules and regulations than it did when Yahushua rebuked the Pharisees in the New Testament Scriptures. Those who say that they follow Yahushua should never identify with this religion created by the Pharisees. The two walks are simply incompatible.

Interestingly, most who identify as Jewish do not actively participate in the religion of Judaism, and the religion of Judaism is fragmented into various "denominations" that follow different traditions and beliefs. They are lost sheep needing a shepherd, just like the lost sheep of the House of Yisrael.

So Joseph (the House of Yisrael) should not be joining with the religion of Judaism, just as Yahudah should not be

---

[210] Joseph was the "head" of Yisrael and the Tribe of Ephraim was treated as the "firstborn" due to the adoption ceremony performed by Yisrael in Genesis 48.

joining the religion of Christianity.[211]

Joseph and Yahudah should both be departing the man-made religions of Christianity and Judaism. Both Yisrael and Yahudah need to shed their pagan man-made religions and traditions and come together through the Messiah. Only through the Messiah can there be true unity.

Messianic Judaism involves the mixing of Pharisaic practices with belief in the Messiah. I have observed this result in division, and spiritual classifications such as "Jewish Believers" versus "Gentile Believer." This is not accurately presenting the message of the Kingdom, and it also results in fracturing the Covenant.

The word "Gentile" refers to "the Nations," or even "heathens." A Gentile is a stranger, or foreigner; someone outside the Covenant, and therefore outside of Yisrael. It is an oxymoron, and clear error, to use the term "Gentile Believer" when referring to someone in the Covenant. It is like calling someone a "righteous pagan." They are two contradicting terms. When you enter the Covenant, you shed the Gentile label and join Yisrael.

The Scriptures are very clear that there is to be One Torah for all. That is the entire point of Yisrael – to reflect the reign of the Heavenly Kingdom here on earth. *"One Torah shall be for the native-born and for the stranger who dwells among you."* Exodus 12:49

Yisrael was supposed to allow strangers to dwell with them, so they could learn the ways of YHWH. The same Torah would apply to all of them. The reason for this is because the Torah is the rule of the Kingdom.

The point is not to have just a privileged group in the Kingdom obeying the rule of the Kingdom. The point is for all mankind to join in the Covenant, and dwell in the Kingdom. We know that many reject the Kingdom. Nevertheless, the

---

[211] Organizations such as "Jews for Jesus" are actually attempting to draw people from the Pharisaic religion of Judaism into the lawless religion of Christianity. Out of the frying pan and into the fire.

invitation is open to all.

So, anyone who attempts to claim that the Torah is only for a select group of individuals completely fails to understand the Kingdom, and the Plan of Elohim.

All those in the Kingdom need to follow the same Torah. While Yisrael was supposed to demonstrate the Torah we know that they failed. In particular, the Levitic priesthood failed to teach the Torah to the people.

There are currently those stating that the Torah is for the Jews only, and that Gentiles only have to follow the Seven Noahide Laws.[212] There are also some who state that those who follow the Messiah Yahushua are under the Melchizedek Priesthood, and only follow certain Commandments found in the Book of the Covenant, which they say is different from the Torah.[213]

It is really a mass of confusion for those trying to follow YHWH. That is why it is important to focus on the Scriptures, and the teachings of Messiah Yahushua.

While the Spirit of YHWH unites the people of Yisrael, the enemy of Yisrael is constantly attempting to divide the people. It is a strategy straight from the Garden – divide and conquer. The man and the woman were divided by the nachash, and they both disobeyed. The Kingdom of Yisrael was divided, and both Houses ended up falling into sin and being ejected from the Covenant Land.

While the earthly representation of the Kingdom was divided and crumbling, the Prophet Isaiah was given a view into the Throne Room of YHWH - the Kingdom in the Heavens.

> *"[1] In the year that King Uzziah died, I saw את-Adonai sitting on a throne, high and lifted up, and the train of His robe filled the Temple. [2] Above it stood seraphim; each one had six wings: with two he covered his face,*

---

[212] The Noahide Laws are a rabbinic fabrication tracing back to Maimonides.
[213] Book of the Law and Book of the Covenant

*with two he covered his feet, and with two he flew. ³
And one cried to another and said: 'Holy, holy, holy is
YHWH of hosts; The whole earth is full of His
glory!' ⁴ And the posts of the door were shaken by the
voice of him who cried out, and the House was filled
with smoke. ⁵ So I said: Woe is me, for I am undone!
Because I am a man of unclean lips, and I dwell in the
midst of a people of unclean lips; For my eyes have seen
the King, YHWH of hosts. ⁶ Then one of the seraphim
flew to me, having in his hand a live coal which he had
taken with the tongs from the altar. ⁷ And he touched
my mouth with it, and said: 'Behold, this has touched
your lips; Your iniquity is taken away, and your sin
purged. ⁸ Also I heard the את-voice of Adonai, saying:
'את-Whom shall I send, and who will go for Us?' Then
I said, 'Here am I! Send me.'" Isaiah 6:1-8*

We are given a reference in time – the year Uzziah
died, which is understood to be around 740 BCE. This was
prior to the collapse of the Northern Kingdom, so there were
two different Kingdoms functioning in the Covenant Land at
that time.

The death of this interesting King was likely from the
leprosy inflicted upon him. Remember that Uzziah (עזיהו)[214]
was the King who tried to usurp the role of the priests by going
into the Temple, and attempting to burn incense before
YHWH.[215]

He was trespassing, as that was a place only for the set
apart Priests – not the King. The High Priest Azariah (עזריהו)[216]
withstood him, and told him to get out. During the
confrontation King Uzziah was stricken by leprosy. He was
cut off from the House of YHWH and Jerusalem for that

---

[214] Without the Masoretic vowel points, the pronunciation of this name more likely sounds
like Aza-Yahu.
[215] See 2 Chronicles 26:16-21
[216] Without the Masoretic vowel points the pronunciation of this name more likely sounds
like Azar-Yahu.

matter.

The play between their names is very interesting, and should have settled the issue itself. It's easier to see in the Hebrew than in the typical English transliterations. They essentially had the same name, except the name of the High Priest contained a "resh" (ר), which means "head."

So, while the King was the ruler over the people and the Land of the geographical Kingdom, the High Priest was the Head of the House – so to speak.

This is an important distinction as we continue to examine the Kingdom of YHWH and the House of YHWH. Remember that Yisrael originally did not have a king. After Moses and Joshua (Yahushua),[217] the High Priest was the one who was supposed to guide Yisrael. It was not until the corruption of the priesthood under Eli, during the life of Shemuel (Samuel), that the people cried out for a king.

YHWH was supposed to be their King, but the Yisraelites wanted a man to rule over them – like the other Nations. This is critical to understand. Yisrael was supposed to be a Kingdom of Priests, and a "holy" or "set apart" nation. They were described as "qadosh" (קדוש) in Hebrew.

They were supposed to stand in direct contrast to the other Nations. Instead, they wanted to be like the other nations. This demonstrated a failure in understanding their purpose within the Covenant. That is evidenced by the fact that they were separated from Elohim after the golden calf incident at Sinai.

While the people of Elohim lived in the Land with YHWH dwelling in the midst of them, they were nonetheless separated from Him.

Just as Adam and Hawah were expelled from the Garden, which was the House of Elohim, YHWH reversed

---

the process. Adam too was supposed to be a High Priest, not according to the Aharonic line. He was the High Priest according to the Melchizedek line. Melchizedek is two words "melchi" and "tzedek" which literally means "king-righteous."

It was actually defined as a unique priesthood in the Psalms.

> *"YHWH has sworn and will not relent,*
> *'You are a priest forever*
> *according to the order of Melchizedek.'"*
> Psalm 110:4

Uzziah was of the Davidic line. He was not permitted to function as a priest. The fact that the vision of Isaiah occurred in the year that Uzziah died was quite profound, because it is showing the Temple in the Heavens operating in full splendor.

This is one of the few places where we are given a description of a Heavenly creature that appears to be exclusively focused on the Throne Room. The Seraphim is described as having six wings, and two of those wings are used to fly.

Isaiah describes himself as "undone," because he is unclean, and in the Temple of all places! He certainly had Uzziah on his mind. Because of the location of his calling (i.e. the Temple), some speculate that he was a priest. Nevertheless, we see sin purged through this heavenly altar.

This was before Yahushua the Messiah. Of course, the Name Isaiah (Yeshayahu) means the same as Yahushua, only in reverse. Instead of Yahushua – "Yah saves," it is YeshaYahu – "salvation comes from Yah."

The seraphim are said to be the highest order of angelic beings and interestingly, they are not included in the pattern of the tabernacle. The seraphim are not mentioned by name, but they are physically described in the text of Revelation.

"[2] Immediately I was in the Spirit; and behold, a throne set in heaven, and One sat on the throne. [3] And He who sat there was like a jasper and a sardius stone in appearance; and there was a rainbow around the throne, in appearance like an emerald. [4] Around the throne were twenty-four thrones, and on the thrones I saw twenty-four elders sitting, clothed in white robes; and they had crowns of gold on their heads. [5] And from the throne proceeded lightnings, thunderings, and voices. Seven lamps of fire were burning before the throne, which are the seven Spirits of Elohim. [6] Before the throne there was a sea of glass, like crystal. And in the midst of the throne, and around the throne, were four living creatures full of eyes in front and in back. [7] The first living creature was like a lion, the second living creature like a calf, the third living creature had a face like a man, and the fourth living creature was like a flying eagle. [8] The four living creatures, each having six wings, were full of eyes around and within. And they do not rest day or night, saying: Qodesh, qodesh, qodesh, YHWH El Shaddai, Who was and Who is and Who is coming! [9] Whenever the living creatures give glory and honor and thanks to Him who sits on the throne, who lives forever and ever, [10] the twenty-four elders fall down before Him who sits on the throne and worship Him who lives forever and ever, and cast their crowns before the throne, saying: [11] You are worthy, O YHWH, To receive esteem and honor and power; For You created all things, and by Your will they exist and were created." Revelation 4:2-11

So, the Seraphim appear to be exclusively located in the Throne Room. They are different from the other winged beings called Cherubim.

Cherubim are described as having four wings, and they

were specifically incorporated into the design of the pattern of the Tabernacle. There were two cherubim atop of the Ark of the Covenant, and they are embroidered into the veil that separated the Holy of Holies – the most qodesh place where YHWH was enthroned.

The Prophet Ezekiel was also a priest, and he saw a vision of cherubim described as follows:

> "[4] And I looked, and, behold, a whirlwind came out of the north, a great cloud, and a fire infolding itself, and a brightness was about it, and out of the midst thereof as the colour of amber, out of the midst of the fire. [5] Also out of the midst thereof came the likeness of four living creatures. And this was their appearance; they had the likeness of a man. [6] And every one had four faces, and every one had four wings. [7] And their feet were straight feet; and the sole of their feet was like the sole of a calf's foot: and they sparkled like the colour of burnished brass. [8] And they had the hands of a man under their wings on their four sides; and they four had their faces and their wings. [9] Their wings were joined one to another; they turned not when they went; they went every one straight forward. [10] As for the likeness of their faces, they four had the face of a man, and the face of a lion, on the right side: and they four had the face of an ox on the left side; they four also had the face of an eagle. [11] Thus were their faces: and their wings were stretched upward; two wings of every one were joined one to another, and two covered their bodies. [12] And they went every one straight forward: whither the spirit was to go, they went; and they turned not when they went. [13] As for the likeness of the living creatures, their appearance was like burning coals of fire, and like the appearance of lamps: it went up and down among the living creatures; and the fire was

bright, and out of the fire went forth lightning. ^{14} *And the living creatures ran and returned as the appearance of a flash of lightning.*" Ezekiel 1:4-14

The point of all of this is to show that there is an amazing functioning Kingdom, filled with unique and intriguing creatures, probably more than we cannot even imagine.

Some of these amazing beings are fulfilling various roles in the Kingdom in and around the Throne Room. Others are dispatching information from the Throne. We read about the "messenger" Gabriel appearing to Daniel and Zachariah, the father of John the Immerser.

Some researchers have listed an hierarchy of nine angelic beings as follows: The First hierarchy contains Seraphim, Cherubim and Thrones. The Second hierarchy contains Dominions, Virtues and Powers. The Third and Final hierarchy contains Principalities, Archangels and Angels.

While man likes to build charts in two dimensions, I suspect that YHWH looks at these differently – from His unique perspective.

This list may not be accurate or complete for that matter, but is another reminder that the Kingdom of YHWH is vast and complex. The Scriptures merely scratch the surface, and our understanding is limited. We are on a "need to know basis." When people try to dabble into restricted areas, they often end up in trouble.

There is a special category of beings who appear before the Throne, but they are not there all the time. They are unique because of the familial relationship affixed to their description – the Sons of Elohim. The "Sons of Elohim" are a special category of powerful beings in the Kingdom.

The Scriptures actually describe them being present at Creation.

"⁴ Where wast thou when I laid the foundations of the earth? declare, if thou hast understanding. ⁵ Who hath laid the measures thereof, if thou knowest? or who hath stretched the line upon it? ⁶ Whereupon are the foundations thereof fastened? or who laid the corner stone thereof; ⁷ When the morning stars sang together, and all the sons of Elohim shouted for joy?"
Job 38:4-7

But wait! Isn't Yahushua the only begotten Son of Elohim? How can there be other Sons of Elohim? As mentioned previously, there is a Heavenly Court, sometimes referred to as The Divine Counsel,[218] that involves these Sons of Elohim.

We can see a hint of this in the passage previously quoted from Isaiah when the את-voice of Adonai asked "את-*Whom shall I send, and who will go for Us?*" Isaiah 6:8

Who is the "us" in this conversation? Some try to attribute this as proof of the Trinity, but that is simply not the case. The Trinity is a Babylonian derived concept incorporated into the Christian religion through the Roman Catholic Church at the Council of Nicaea.[219]

The passage is actually describing a conversation between YHWH, and the Sons of Elohim as we previously mentioned from the text of Yasher.

The Sons of Elohim may seem foreign to most Christians, but this is a subject mentioned throughout the Scriptures.

---

[218] Michael Heiser has done a comprehensive exposition on The Divine Council in his book titled *The Unseen Realm*.

[219] The Trinity is a concept that derives from Babylonian sun worship. Many Christians have grown up believing that that God is three separate persons – The Father, the Son and the Holy Spirit. The problem is that such a concept is not supported by the Scriptures. We will be discussing passages that describe YHWH as the Father Who sits on the Throne. We also see that Yahushua is the "only begotten" or "unique" Son of Elohim. YHWH is Spirit and the Prophet Isaiah describes Seven Spirits of Elohim (see Isaiah 11:2). The Seven Spirits of Elohim are also mentioned in Revelation 1:4r, 3:1, 4:4 and 5:5. So it is not accurate to attempt to describe the complex Most High Elohim in Babylonian Trinitarian terms.

Indeed, Job described the Sons of Elohim as presenting themselves before YHWH. *"Now there was a day when the sons of Elohim came to present themselves before YHWH, and Satan came also among them."* Job 1:6 (see also Job 2:1)

The Sons of Elohim are actually a classification of heavenly beings that reign with YHWH in His Kingdom, along with the other beings previously described. They are supposed to assist in the administration of the Kingdom, as a Royal Court.

As already mentioned, they were present at Creation. That would explain the account when Elohim declared *"Let Us make man in Our Image."*[220]

Indeed, we can discern from the Hebrew text that Yahushua, as the aleph taw (את) was present, and involved with Creation.[221] That is why He is described as "the only begotten Son," which is better understood as "the unique Son." He was destined to rule over this Planet.

Could it be that some other Sons of Elohim were jealous of the unique Son Yahushua? Were they jealous of His inheritance? Maybe they wanted to usurp His birthright? Indeed, there were attempts to corrupt it from the very beginning. The "nachash," described as a "serpent" seduced the man and the woman and corrupted them.

The Scriptures describe other Sons of Elohim who rebelled, and sought to establish their own kingdom here on Earth. They are specifically mentioned as being involved in the corruption of mankind that resulted in the flood.

> *"⁴ There were Nephilim in the earth in those days; and also after that, when the Sons of Elohim came in unto the daughters of men, and they bare children to them, the same became mighty men which were of old, men of renown. ⁵ And Elohim saw that the wickedness of man was great in the earth, and that every imagination*

---

[220] Genesis 1:26
[221] Genesis 1:1 in the Hebrew language contains the Aleph Taw (את) two times.

of the thoughts of his heart was only evil continually."
Genesis 6:4-5

The Book of I Enoch describes this event in much greater detail.[222] According to that text, there was a group of Sons of Elohim who made an agreement on Mount Hermon to rebel against the order of Creation established by YHWH.

The message from the beginning was that YHWH would build a House for His Son. These rebellious Sons of Elohim were trying to establish their own kingdom, and take over the House (i.e. – the planet). Since the unique Son Yahushua was destined to rule over Creation, it was His problem to fix.

We already mentioned that the Messenger Gabriel was dispatched to Daniel. He was responsible for providing the seventy week timeline in answer to Daniel's prayer concerning a return from the seventy year Babylonian exile.

Daniel was not only provided with information, He was also given visions. On one occasion, he was given a glimpse into the Heavenly Throne Room.

> *"⁹ I watched till thrones were put in place,*
> *and the Ancient of Days was seated;*
> *His garment was white as snow,*
> *and the hair of His head was like pure wool.*
> *His throne was a fiery flame, its wheels a burning fire;*
> *¹⁰ A fiery stream issued and came forth from before Him.*
> *A thousand thousands ministered to Him;*
> *Ten thousand times ten thousand stood before Him.*
> *The Court was seated, and the Scrolls were opened."*

---

[222] The text of I Enoch is divided into 6 different "books." They were written at different periods by different authors. It was not written by the Enoch of Genesis 5:24 *"And Enoch walked with Elohim; and he was not, for Elohim took him."* I find the first portion of the text known as The Book of Watchers to be particularly interesting as it elaborates more on the rebellion of the 200 Sons of Elohim who made a pact to rebel against Creation, and the rule against mixing "different kinds." I do not subscribe to the calendar portion because it describes a solar calendar that does not comply with the Torah.

Daniel 7:9-10

So, Daniel is describing a Heavenly Court centered around a Throne on wheels. This has been referred to as a "Chariot Throne," known as a "Merkabah" (מרכבה) in Hebrew. Notice that there are other thrones, besides the fiery Throne, and a myriad of participants, attendants and observers. This is an enormous event!

Further in the passage we are provided a description of a legal proceeding that occurred in the Throne Room, after the beast is destroyed and burned with fire.

"13 I was watching in the night visions, and behold, One like the Son of Man, Coming with the clouds of heaven! He came to the Ancient of Days, and they brought Him near before Him. 14 Then to Him was given dominion and glory and a Kingdom, that all peoples, Nations, and languages should serve Him. His dominion is an everlasting dominion, which shall not pass away, and His Kingdom the one which shall not be destroyed." Daniel 7:13-14

This is an incredible passage because it shows us when Yahushua, referred to as the Son of Man, receives His Kingdom. At this moment, the Messiah comes on the clouds to the Throne Room, and He is given dominion and rulership over a Kingdom.

We read about that Kingdom in similar account of the Heavenly Court found in the Book of Revelation.

"15 Then the seventh angel sounded: And there were loud voices in heaven, saying, 'The kingdoms of this world have become the Kingdoms of our Master and of His Messiah, and He shall reign forever and ever!' 16 And the twenty-four elders who sat before Elohim on their thrones fell on their faces and worshiped Elohim, 17 saying: We give You thanks, O YHWH El Shaddai, The One who is and who

*was and who is to come, because You have taken
Your great power and reigned. [18] The nations were
angry, and Your wrath has come, and the time of the
dead, that they should be judged, and that You
should reward Your servants the prophets and the
saints, and those who fear Your Name, small and
great, and should destroy those who destroy the
Earth. [19] Then the Temple of Elohim was opened in
heaven, and the ark of His Covenant was seen in
His Temple. And there were lightnings, noises,
thunderings, an earthquake, and great hail."*
Revelation 11:15-19

This is an interesting passage, because for much of my
life I was surrounded by people obsessed with finding the Ark
of the Covenant. The Ark represents the Throne of YHWH
here on Earth, and it is placed in His House. This passage says
that the Ark is in the Temple in Heaven, which makes sense
since YHWH allowed His Earthly dwelling place to be
destroyed.

I can understand an archaeologist's desire to find an
ancient artifact, but a follower of Yahushua must be careful
what motivates them on this issue. Is it so another Temple can
be built by the Jews? Is it so they can start up sacrifices again?

The question must then be asked: Why would someone
who follows Yahushua want the Pharisees to rebuild a Temple
that Yahushua called into judgment? I know people who are
actually interested in helping to fund the building of another
Temple.

This demonstrates to me that they really do not have a
proper understanding of what Yahushua did and taught.
Otherwise, why would a follower of Yahushua want to see a
system restored that ignores the Messiah, and His fulfillment?

Much of the confusion revolves around an incorrect
understanding of a prophecy found later in Daniel. We will
talk about that further in Chapter 21, when we discuss what is

commonly referred to as "Daniel's Seventy Week Prophecy." For now though, let us continue with our examination of the Kingdom.

All of the descriptions provided through Daniel and John, as well as other prophets such as Isaiah and Ezekiel, provide us with mere glimpses of moments revealing the machinations of an extraordinary Kingdom. This is the everlasting Kingdom that is functioning in the Heavenly realm now. It is a place we should all anticipate visiting in the future. It should be that real to us!

While men are often distracted and interested in establishing temporal Earthy kingdoms, if you follow Messiah, your interests should lie elsewhere.

You need to be praying for the Kingdom of Elohim to come "on earth as it is in the heavens."[223] That is the Kingdom we should be preparing for, if we are joined in Covenant with the One Who sits upon the Throne.

This is our reality, and the core of our faith - yet it is so foreign to many. The Kingdom has a King and a Court with multiple layers of powers and beings fulfilling various functions.

Power has been bestowed upon the Lamb, Who has been given this world. Our King is not like other Earthy kings. In fact, instead of flexing the incredible power and authority bestowed upon Him, He first chose to be a humble servant.

Yahushua provided the example by washing His disciples' feet. Imagine that! A king washing the feet of his subjects. He could wield incredible power, but He chose to be a servant.

Mind you, they weren't wearing nice shoes with socks. Their feet were likely pretty dirty after trekking about in sandals all day. We have often heard the phrase that actions speak louder than words. Well, Yahushua's actions shouted from the rooftops how we are supposed to operate in the

---

[223] Matthew 6:10 and Luke 11:12

Kingdom.

In the Kingdom, we must learn to be servants before we can rule as kings. Yahushua is our example and through His shed blood we can become priests and kings in the Kingdom.

Here is that promise that we see when given a glimpse of the Kingdom.

> "⁶ And I looked, and behold, in the midst of the throne and of the four living creatures, and in the midst of the elders, stood a Lamb as though it had been slain, having seven horns and seven eyes, which are the seven Spirits of Elohim sent out into all the earth. ⁷ Then He came and took the scroll out of the right hand of Him who sat on the throne. ⁸ Now when He had taken the scroll, the four living creatures and the twenty-four elders fell down before the Lamb, each having a harp, and golden bowls full of incense, which are the prayers of the saints. ⁹ And they sang a new song, saying: You are worthy to take the scroll, and to open its seals; for You were slain, and have redeemed us to Elohim by Your blood out of every tribe and tongue and people and nation, ¹⁰ And have made us kings and priests to our Elohim; and we shall reign on the earth."
> Revelation 5:6-10

We already discussed learning to be priests, and becoming Kingdom minded. This passage describes that people from out of every tribe and tongue and people and Nation will reign on the Earth.

That is a very different future than most Christians expect. So many think they going to heaven when they die. We will discuss this more in the chapter involving the Land Covenant. For now, it is clear that this reign on Earth is not centered around the Jewish people, but rather all those who are in the Covenant renewed by the blood of the Lamb.

It is important to understand that in order to live and operate in the Kingdom we must be walking on the Covenant path – a path blazed by Hebrews.

For most of us, the idea of becoming a Hebrew is, or was, a very foreign concept. The primary reason for this can be attributed to the difference between eastern and western thought and culture.

The Christian religion has been created and molded by western culture beginning with the Roman Empire, while the Covenant has been established and fulfilled in an eastern cultural environment from the beginning of time.

Those of us who have been born and raised in Babylon often have difficulty seeing that, because we don't think like easterners. We think like westerners.

Our Babylonian upbringing effects the way we think, the way we read and interpret the Scriptures, and the way we understand the Covenant.

That is something we will explore in the next chapter, when we examine Hebrew thought. In order to fully understand the Hebrew Scriptures, and the eastern blood Covenant, we need to learn how to think like easterners as we focus on becoming Hebrews.

12

Becoming a Hebrew

We have talked about the fact that the essence of the good news, often called the Gospel, involved the Messiah fulfilling and renewing a covenant. That Renewed Covenant was patterned around the life of the man named Abram, who was later renamed Abraham.

As we consider the notion of leaving Babylon, we also need to determine our destination. Otherwise, we might find ourselves permanently wandering in the wilderness, or worse yet, back in Babylon.

When Abram was told to leave Babylon, he had a destination - the land of Canaan. If we are to follow the pattern of Abram, then we too should be interested in the Covenant Land.

This is another one of the disconnects that exist between the Christian religion and the true scriptural faith. As we previously mentioned, Christianity has no definitive destination, except for heaven. In fact, most Christians believe that when someone dies, they go straight to heaven. That belief is not supported by the Scriptures.

While the notion of dead loved ones going to heaven may make grieving individuals feel better at funeral services, it simply is not correct. When a person dies, they go to Sheol until the resurrection. The goal is to be resurrected, and then ushered into the Kingdom after judgment.

While the Scriptures talk about the gathered elect meeting Yahushua in the clouds, our final habitation is not in the clouds. Our inheritance is the Kingdom that the Messiah will establish here on this Earth.

When in Covenant with the King, we are connected to a spiritual Kingdom that is being expanded on to this planet through the Messiah, along with those who are in Covenant with YHWH. That is why Adam was made from the "dust" of the Earth. He was intimately connected with this Creation.

He was provided land, and told: *"Be fruitful and multiply; fill the earth and subdue it; have dominion over the fish of the sea, over the birds of the air, and over every living thing that moves on the earth."* Genesis 1:28

This was the Kingdom mandate from the very beginning. The relationship between man and Elohim was severed due to the man's disobedience, and the plans for the Kingdom were delayed.

We previously discussed how the relationship with YHWH and man is being restored through the progressive Covenant relationship patterned through the life of Abraham and his descendants through to Yahushua.

Before he was called Abraham, we first read the promise to Abram:

> *"14 And YHWH said to Abram, after Lot had separated from him: 'Lift your eyes now and look from the place where you are - northward, southward, eastward, and westward; 15 for all the land which you see I give to you and your descendants forever. 16 And I will make your descendants as the dust of the Earth; so that if a man could number the dust of the Earth, then your descendants also could be numbered. 17 Arise, walk in the land through its length and its width, for I give it to you.'"* Genesis 13:14-17

So, we see that Abram was promised land, as well as numerous descendants who were compared to the dust of the Earth. This was a continuation of Adam's mandate. He was then told to walk that land.

Later with Jacob we read a similar promise:

"¹³ And behold, YHWH stood above it and said: I am the Elohim of Abraham your father and the Elohim of Isaac; the land on which you lie I will give to you and your descendants. ¹⁴ Also your descendants shall be as the dust of the Earth; you shall spread abroad to the west and the east, to the north and the south; and in you and in your seed all the families of the Earth shall be blessed. ¹⁵ Behold, I am with you and will keep you wherever you go, and will bring you back to this Land; for I will not leave you until I have done what I have spoken to you." Genesis 28:13-15

Again, notice how the Covenant people are likened to dust - combined with the promise of Land. Indeed, the Prophet Isaiah specifically provides a future prophecy concerning the people and the Land.

"You shall no longer be termed Forsaken,
nor shall your land any more be termed Desolate;
But you shall be called Hephzibah, and your land Beulah;
For YHWH delights in you and your land shall be married."
Isaiah 62:4

This prophecy brings us back to the beginning. It is a renewal, and a reset. It reveals how YHWH operates in cycles and patterns. Isaiah was referring to the Daughter of Zion (Tzyon) – those in a Covenant relationship with YHWH dwelling in Jerusalem.

Remember that Adam (אדם) is connected with the word for "ground" – "adamah" (אדמה). In fact, the first time that we read about the ground it is called "et-ha'adamah" (את-האדמה).²²⁴ Adam was taken from the dust of the Earth, and given land to care for.

---

²²⁴ The entire context for the mention of the ground was the fact that there was no "man" (אדם) to til "the ground" (את-האדמה). (see Genesis 2:5) The existence of the aleph taw (את) reveals that the Messiah will ultimately need to do the "heavy lifting."

Adam was connected to that land, and his relationship was likened to a marriage in the sense that he would watch over the Garden and tend to it so that it would bear fruit. He had to live a life of obedience for this relationship to work.

He was proven unfaithful. The man and the woman both failed. They were expelled and punished, along with the nachash – the serpent. Here is the punishment rendered upon the serpent after the rebellion in the Garden:

"So YHWH Elohim said to the serpent:
Because you have done this, you are cursed more than all cattle, and
more than every beast of the field;
On your belly you shall go,
and you shall eat dust all the days of your life."
Genesis 3:14

The man was rendered the following punishment:

"In the sweat of your face you shall eat bread
till you return to the ground,
for out of it you were taken;
for dust you are, and to dust you shall return."
Genesis 3:19

The punishments in the Garden included dust. While man was intended to live forever, now he would return to the dust – to sheol.[225] So, we see this cycle of a man's existence from the beginning

This would set in motion the cycles necessary to restore man to his Creator. These cycles are rehearsed through the annual cycles of the Appointed Times, which will be discussed in a future chapter. They were also patterned through the Covenant cycles lived out by Abram as he went through the transformation necessary to become Abraham.

---

[225] Sheol (שְׁאוֹל) is the Hebrew word that refers to the "grave" below the ground, not what we see above the ground.

This is all very consistent with eastern thought and action, which is cyclical in nature. And, of course, the eastern culture is one of covenants, while western culture is more about contracts.

As was mentioned in a previous chapter, contracts are typically focused on business or economics, while covenants go to deeper relationships that often deal with life and death issues. It is important to understand that different cultures have different ways of dealing with people, and viewing the world around them.

While eastern thinking is circular, western thinking is linear. While an eastern covenant typically progresses through time until the death of a party or even beyond, a typical western contract must have a definitive term – a beginning and an end. This thought process definitely impacts how cultures view relationships.

A covenant is a very eastern concept. The best example is probably seen through a marriage covenant. It is not focused on money, and benefiting the individual parties, but rather strengthening and building the mutual relationship. That relationship should deepen and mature with the passage of time. It is not static, and should not have a fixed time limit. It continues "till death do us part."

Sadly, many in western cultures look at a marriage as an economic contract that continues until the love is gone, or the partnership dissolves for some reason.

That is why so many marriages fail in the west – they view marriage as a contract – not a covenant. Contracts are meant to protect rights of individuals, and they are generally driven by selfishness – self-interest and self-preservation.

They are intended to benefit the individual parties, and provide damages in the event of a breach. Instead of a unified selfless interest, the parties often maintain a separation. "If you do your part then I'll do my part. Otherwise I'll sue you."

This approach is not compatible for a marriage, yet that is how many people view that relationship. Some people actually enter into "Pre-nuptial Agreements" that resolve matters ahead of time if the marriage fails. That's not a very positive outlook, nor is it a great beginning for a successful marriage.

So, covenants and contracts are very different ways of looking at relationships that impact the way we perceive our very existence. I hope you can see how our culture and thinking impact the way we look at the world around us, as well as our relationships.

That often carries over to religion. As a result, many people end up in a very selfish relationship with the Creator. In fact, evangelistic settings often promote the benefits of "accepting Jesus." People are tantalized by what blessings they can get from God. "What can I get out of this relationship?" Obviously, that is not a healthy attitude – definitely not what YHWH seeks from His Bride.

Another example of the differences between eastern and western thought can be seen in the Covenant promises that we just cited, where the descendants would be like "dust." Those passages also provided directions for the expansion of the Promised Land – the north, the south, the east and the west.

"¹⁴ And YHWH said to Abram, after Lot had separated from him: Lift your eyes now and look from the place where you are - northward, southward, eastward, and westward; ¹⁵ for all the land which you see I give to you and your descendants forever." Genesis 13:14-15

That promise was extended to Jacob at Beth El, which literally means "House of El." Here is the promise:

"Also your descendants shall be as the dust of the earth; you shall spread abroad to the west and the east, to the north and the south; and in you and in your seed all the families of the earth shall be blessed." Genesis 28:14

If you are a western thinker, your first instinct is to pull out a map. We envision a compass containing the four cardinal directions, along with specific lines and degrees. These are very artificial and abstract concepts that typify western thought and perspective. Now, there is nothing inherently wrong with these measurements, but an eastern thinker would view these directions in a much more concrete fashion, which is actually reflected in the Hebrew language.

In Hebrew, the word we translate as "north" is "tsephon" (צפן). Tsephon derived from Mount Zaphon on the northern edge of Syria. So, it was a large feature in the direction that we consider to be north.

The word for South is called "Negev" (נגב). Of course, the Negev is an expansive wilderness in the direction we consider to be south.

The word for East is called "Kedem" (קדם), linked with the color red (edom). This related geographically to the rising of the sun at dawn, or the red sandstone cliffs of the Land of Edom to the east - literally the Land of Red.

The word for West is called "Yam" (ים), meaning "sea." We can see the connection in Numbers 34:6:

"As for the western (yam) border,
you shall have the Great Sea (yam) for a border;
this shall be your western (yam) border."
Numbers 34:6

So, directions in the Scriptures, in line with the eastern mindset, were linked with real geographical places - not simply abstract points on a map, or directions on a compass. This is a very important distinction.

We also think of time differently. Westerners look to clocks, watches and devices to fragment time precisely, and tell them what time it is. The ancients did not delineate time in the same fashion.

That is why westerners often get annoyed when they travel to the east. While they might arrive right "on time" according to their watch, an easterner may arrive later, because they look at time differently. They aren't late in their eyes, because they do not view time the same.

Ancient easterners used the sun to determine the portions of the day, and the moon cycle to determine the months. Of course, that is how YHWH established time from the very beginning.

"¹⁴ Then Elohim said, Let there be lights in the firmament of the heavens to divide the day from the night; and let them be for signs and seasons (moadim), and for days and years; ¹⁵ and let them be for lights in the firmament of the heavens to give light on the earth; and it was so. ¹⁶ Then Elohim made two great lights: the greater light to rule the day, and the lesser light to rule the night. He made the stars also." Genesis 1:14-16

Aside from days and months, these two great lights also help us to determine years and "seasons." The word translated as "seasons" in most English Bibles is "moadim" (מוֹעֲדִים) in Hebrew.

A westerner generally reads Genesis 1:14 and thinks of winter, spring, summer and fall. An easterner understands these "moadim" to be "Appointed Times." Instead of vague seasons, the Appointed Times are specific, and scheduled times that YHWH establishes to meet with His people.

People typically make the mistake of referring to the Appointed Times as "Jewish Holidays." This is an error that stems from using the label "Jewish" to include all things Hebrew.

It is important to understand that the fathers of the Covenant - Abraham, Isaac and Jacob were not Jews, nor can they be described as Jewish. Abram was called a Hebrew.

"Then one who had escaped came and told Abram the

Hebrew, for he dwelt by the terebinth trees of Mamre the Amorite, brother of Eshcol and brother of Aner; and they were allies with Abram." Genesis 14:13

So, Abram, later named Abraham, was called a Hebrew, and all of his descendants were Hebrews. They were not Jewish – they were Hebrews. This is a very important distinction. Somehow, the term Jewish has been applied retroactively to many of the ancient patriarchs, which causes incredible confusion and perpetuates serious doctrinal errors.

The words "Jewish" and "Jew" derive from the name Judah (Yahudah) that was given by Leah to her son. We read the account in Genesis 29:35 when Leah said *"I will praise YHWH."*

In the Hebrew we read "aodah et-YHWH" (את-יהוה אודה). The root of the name derives from "yadah et-YHWH" which literally references "knowing" YHWH through the aleph taw (את). The name "Yahudah" (יהודה) was therefore ascribed to the child. It is literally the name YHWH with a dalet (ד) inserted.

The Hebrew letter "dalet" (ד) refers to a "door." So this tribe would be the "door" back to YHWH, and we know that Yahushua came from the tribe of Yahudah.

Yahudah was first a Hebrew name. The Hebrew word refers to an individual born to Leah and Jacob. Yahudah was one of the twelve tribes. Yahudah was also ascribed to the Southern Kingdom, after the Kingdom of Yisrael was divided into two houses. It encompassed the Land and Tribes of Benjamin and Yahudah.

Most of the Levites eventually joined the House of Yahudah, as did some from the Northern Tribes who refused to follow the abominations of Jeroboam. So Yahudah can be a mixture of individuals from all the tribes, focused on a specific geographical area in the Covenant Land.

The term "Jew" is clearly not inclusive of all the tribes of Yisrael, nor does it even include the Patriarchs of the

Covenant – Abraham, Isaac and Jacob. None of them were Jewish, and none of them followed the religion of Rabbinic Judaism.

They were Hebrews, and that is why we are not talking about "Jewish roots" in this discussion about leaving Babylon.

I remember when I began this Torah walk. There was generally talk about Messianic Judaism and Jewish Roots. That was very misleading because it often sent people down a path that involved Rabbinic and Pharisaic traditions. The problem is that the term Jewish can be applied to so many different possibilities.

Jewish Roots either means going back to the start of the Jewish religion after the destruction of the Temple in 70 CE, or it could refer to the start of the Southern Kingdom under Rehoboam, after the death of Solomon when the Kingdom of Yahudah began.

It might refer to the time when David began his reign over Yahudah, before he united the entire Kingdom. It might even refer to going back to the birth of the man named Yahudah. That's as far back as you can possibly go when examining "Jewish Roots."

Everything before that is Hebrew Roots when we are examining the Covenant made with Abraham, Isaac and Jacob. All of these men thought, acted and lived as easterners. The Scriptures were written in an eastern language by easterners, describing a journey of easterners as they walked out an eastern covenant with a Creator who comes out of the east – which we will examine in a bit

The word "Hebrew" is "eberi" (עברי) in the Hebrew language. It is spelled ayin (ע), bet (ב), resh (ר), yud (י). It derives from Eber (עבר).

The question is: Why was Abram identified with Eber when his father was Terah?

The reason is found in the Scriptures.

"To Eber were born two sons:

the name of one was Peleg,
for in his days the earth was divided;
and his brother's name was Joktan."
Genesis 10:25

The Nations were divided during the days of Peleg, and Peleg's father was Eber. His line stayed connected with the patriarchal line of Eber. While the languages were divided and the people scattered, Peleg and his line retained the Hebrew language and belief in YHWH. So the righteous line continued.[226]

We know that the generations passed as follows: Eber, Peleg, Ragau, Saruch, Nahor, Terah, Abram. They were all Hebrews through to Abraham, and beyond, including all the Tribes of Yisrael – Yahudah as well.

This is what his descendants were called in Egypt, even after Jacob was renamed Yisrael.

"Then they will heed your voice; and you shall come, you and the elders of Yisrael, to the king of Egypt; and you shall say to him, 'YHWH Elohim of the Hebrews has met with us; and now, please, let us go three days' journey into the wilderness, that we may sacrifice to YHWH our Elohim.'" Exodus 3:18

Did you catch that? YHWH Elohim of the Hebrews. This is a critical distinction, because many people try to portray YHWH as the Elohim of "the Jewish people." That is not accurate, because Hebrews and Jewish people are not mutually inclusive.

In fact, YHWH is repeatedly identified as the Elohim of the Hebrews.

"Then YHWH said to Moses, Rise early in the

---

[226] There are some who believe that the confusing of languages was a result of the geographical divisions. That it occurred over time.

morning and stand before Pharaoh, and say to him,
Thus says YHWH Elohi of the Hebrews: 'Let My
people go, that they may serve Me.'" Exodus 9:13

"So Moses and Aaron came in to Pharaoh and said to
him, Thus says YHWH Elohi of the Hebrews: How
long will you refuse to humble yourself before Me?
Let My people go, that they may serve Me." Exodus
10:3

Of course, this makes perfect sense when we recall that
YHWH divided the nations during the life of Peleg.

"7 Remember the days of old, consider the years of many
generations. Ask your father, and he will show you; your
elders, and they will tell you: 8 When the Most High
divided their inheritance to the nations, when He
separated the sons of Adam, He set the boundaries of the
peoples according to the number of the Sons of Elohim."
Deuteronomy 32:7-8

So, YHWH set Sons of Elohim over the nations, and
He chose the descendants of Eber - the Eberi clan, also known
as the Hebrews. The Hebrew line was never separated from
YHWH, and that is the conduit back to Him.

As we left off in the last chapter, in order to properly
walk out this Covenant path it is important to learn how to
think and live like a Hebrew.

The Hebrew mindset derives from an eastern culture.
It is well understood in scholarly circles that there are
powerful differences between eastern and western thought,
and we have already examined some examples.

A sentence in one of the letters from Paul aptly describe
this difference.

"For Jews request a sign,

and Greeks seek after wisdom."
1 Corinthians 1:22

The "Jews" he was referring to were eastern people originating from the Hebrews - Yahudim. The Gentiles were the Hellenized Greeks – western people from the Nations.

The eastern Yahudim looked for signs, because eastern thought is considered to be concrete. They wanted something real and tangible.

The Hellenized western thought process is considered to be abstract. They seek wisdom and knowledge. That is why Gnosticism flourished as the Greeks Hellenized the world and influenced Yahudim, and later Christian communities.

Now it is important to recognize that as Hebrews, we cannot be consumed with signs. Recall the words of Yahushua: *"This is an evil generation. It seeks a sign, and no sign will be given to it except the sign of Jonah the prophet. 30 For as Jonah became a sign to the Ninevites, so also the Son of Man will be to this generation."* Luke 11:29

The Yahudim had the Messiah walking and teaching amongst them, yet they still sought a sign.

On the other hand, the Scriptures made provision for signs from the very beginning. Genesis 1:14 specifically states: *"Elohim said, Let there be lights in the firmament of the heavens to divide the day from the night; and let them be for signs and moadim (Appointed Times), and for days and years."* Genesis 1:14

So, clearly we are to be looking at the heavenly lights for their intended signs. They help us tell time and properly keep the Moadim – the Appointed Times.

The Appointed Times are weekly, monthly and yearly times established by the Creator that every Hebrew should be observing. At the beginning of this book we talked about the weekly Sabbath. In a future chapter we will be discussing the annual Appointed Times. All of these cycles keep us focused on the Creator, and they are an important part of being Hebrew.

As mentioned already, western thought is considered to be linear, while eastern thought is cyclical or circular. Observing time in a cyclical fashion is very eastern, and involves the observations of markers such as the sun and the moon, along with their repeating and renewing cycles.

Westerners, on the other hand, typically count days and months on a fixed calendar, and perceive time from infinity past to infinity future. In fact, most of the western world follows a solar calendar that predetermines months and their duration, irrespective of the cycles of the moon.

This difference is not limited to time, as we already examined the difference in how directions are perceived. The differences in thought permeate all areas of life.

Of course, a cultures' way of thinking naturally gets transmitted into the spoken, and eventually written language. We can actually see a vivid example in how opposite eastern and western languages are by the way they are written. Many eastern languages are written from right to left. While many western languages are written from left to right.

Many written eastern languages derive from pictographs or hieroglyphs where the characters are a visual representation of something concrete. The character was understood to have a meaning, and when combined together they formed a related meaning.

Even when we trace a character's roots to an eastern language, it typically has no recognizable purpose in western language.

Take for instance the letter "A." It is the first letter of the English alphabet, and derives from the Greek letter "alpha" (A), which looks exactly the same as the English letter "A." In the English and in the Greek, there is no indication that it is a pictograph.

When we look back further into the eastern origins, we see that it has actually been turned sideways and later upside down. Here is the rendering of the "aleph" in ancient Hebrew - "𐤀." When we look back even further, we see the pictograph in the Paleo-Hebrew – "𒀀."

In the ancient language, it is very clear that the character represents an ox, or a bull. The character was meant to represent "strength" and "power." So, the ancient language expresses a clear message, and this amplifies as we combine the characters, and express their meanings in words.

This becomes clear when we expand our examination to the next character in the English language, the letter "B." The English letter "B" derives from the Greek letter "beta" (B). Again, the Greek and the English are the same. When we go back further into the eastern language we see the Hebrew "bet" (ב), which represents the floor plan of a house. The letter bet literally means "house."

When we combine the first two characters of the Hebrew aleph-bet (alphabet), we form the first possible word in the Hebrew language – "ab" (בא). When we look at the Hebrew characters we see "aleph" (א) which means: "strength," and "bet" (ב) which means "house." So, the word "ab" literally means "strength of the house," and "ab" is the Hebrew word for "father."

In the English language, the combination of the "A" and the "B" is meaningless. Characters only have meanings when combined into words, but you must know the definition of the word in order to discern the meaning.

This is a simple example that demonstrates how different western languages are from eastern languages. The western languages are upside down and backwards from ancient Scriptural language and thought.

When you understand the meaning of characters in a eastern language you can develop an understanding of the language easier. In western languages you have to simply memorize the combination of characters that form words. The characters and their combinations don't necessarily have any discernable relationship to the meaning of the words.

These are some simple examples to try to make the point, and demonstrate some of the differences. Just as many of the western cultures that make up Babylon are directly opposed to YHWH, even their languages and the way that they think and act are opposite.

So, as we journey out of Babylon we need to adjust the way that we think and perceive the world. This is not always an easy concept to grasp. We don't often examine the way we think, nor do we typically consider the notion that we think differently than other people . . . But it's true.

And if you were born in Babylon, I can pretty much assure you that you do not think the way that an ancient Hebrew thought.

Now remember that the Scriptures were written mostly by ancient Hebrews, about ancient Hebrews living in an ancient Hebrew culture, following an ancient Hebrew Covenant.

The Scriptures are not always literal. They need to be read and understood in their own context, culture and language. The authors of the Scriptural texts often employed what is known as "conceptual metaphor."

Conceptual metaphor refers to the way we use a concrete term or idea to communicate abstract ideas. For instance, consider the following passage.

"YHWH is my rock and my fortress and my deliverer;
My Elohim, my strength, in whom I will trust;
My shield and the horn of my salvation, my stronghold."
Psalm 18:2

Now obviously YHWH is not an actual rock, but the idea is to relate the fact that He is a solid, reliable, strong, powerful Elohim. YHWH is not an actual fortress or strong tower, but He provides refuge for His people. He is not a literal shield, but He protects us as a shield from enemy attacks.

YHWH is not an actual horn, which is "qeren," (קֶרֶן) in Hebrew. The "horn of salvation" is a reference to the practice of finding protection from death by taking hold of the horns of an altar.[227] So, just as people would cling to the horn of an altar to save their lives, we must cling to Him for salvation.

This is what John the Immerser's father prophesied when John was born, concerning the promise of a deliverer.

"[67] Now his father Zachariah was filled with the Holy (Set Apart) Spirit, and prophesied, saying: [68] Blessed is YHWH Elohim of Yisrael, For He has visited and redeemed His people, [69] And has raised up a horn of salvation for us in the house of His servant David." Luke 1:67-69

From this passage, we recognize that the Messiah would come from Yahudah, and we must cling to Him. All of these conceptual metaphors help us created beings understand the character, nature, function and purpose our existence within the framework of Creation.

We know that the Messiah came fulfilling many roles in the Covenant, and therefore various metaphors were used to describe Him aside from being a "horn of salvation."

The Messiah is described as the "Rosh Pina" (ראש פנה)– "the head stone or chief cornerstone."

> *"The stone which the builders rejected*
> *has become the chief cornerstone (rosh pina)."*
> Psalm 118:22

Rosh pina can also mean "head capstone." While I grew believing that the cornerstone was at the bottom of the building, the head stone of a pyramid is the capstone. Some believe that the pyramids were built by fallen Sons of Elohim or their offspring who were trying to duplicate here on Earth what they saw in the Heavens. We won't know for certain

---

[227] See 1 Kings 1:50

until we actually see the New Jerusalem, but it's definitely food for thought.

Indeed, we know that YHWH is the "head (rosh) of the house." His House is made of precious stones, and He has built the House for His Son. Remember the first word in the Scriptures - B'resheet (בראשית).

That single word is prefaced by the word for son – "bar" (בר), and it contains the word "rosh" (ראש) surrounded by the word for house – "beit" (בית).

So, right from the beginning we see a message built into the Hebrew language that sets the stage for all of creation in very concrete terms. That is why Yahushua described Himself as "the door" – representing the way into that House.

He described Himself as "the bread of life" which harkens to the manna in the wilderness. He provides food for the House.

He was described as the "Lamb of Elohim" – the one that covers and protects those in His House by His blood. That is the lesson that we learn from Passover.

These are all concrete descriptions to help us understand the role, purpose and function of the Messiah in ways that we can easily understand. Therefore, if we want to understand our Creator and the Messiah, we need to think like easterners.

As mentioned previously, YHWH actually identifies Himself with the east.

> "*¹ Afterward he brought me to the gate, the gate that faces toward the east. ² And behold, the glory of the Elohim of Yisrael came from the way of the east. His voice was like the sound of many waters; and the earth shone with His glory. ³ It was like the appearance of the vision which I saw - like the vision which I saw when I came to destroy the city. The visions were like the vision which I saw by the River Chebar; and I fell on my face. ⁴ And the glory of*

YHWH came into the Temple by way of the gate which faces toward the east. ⁵ The Spirit lifted me up and brought me into the inner court; and behold, the glory of YHWH filled the Temple. ⁶ Then I heard Him speaking to me from the Temple, while a man stood beside me. ⁷ And He said to me, Son of man, this is the place of My throne and the place of the soles of My feet, where I will dwell in the midst of the sons of Yisrael <u>forever</u>. No more shall the house of Yisrael defile My Set Apart Name, they nor their kings, by their harlotry or with the carcasses of their kings on their high places."
Ezekiel 43:1-7

Consider the first part of verse 7: *"And He said to me, Son of man, this is the place of My throne and the place of the soles of My feet, where I will dwell in the midst of the sons of Yisrael forever."*

The phrase "soles of my feet" is not literal, but is an eastern way of referring to ownership and control. This is what He means when He says the earth is His footstool.

"Thus says YHWH:
Heaven is My throne,
and Earth is My footstool.
Where is the House that you will build Me?
And where is the place of My rest?"
Isaiah 66:1

This is a very concrete way of showing that YHWH rules from the Heavens over the Earth. It is not stating that the Earth is shaped like a footstool - a flat platform atop of four large pillars.

We read Yahushua commenting on this in Matthew. *"³⁴ But I say to you, do not swear at all: neither by Heaven, for it is Elohim's throne; ³⁵ nor by the Earth, for it is His footstool; nor by*

Jerusalem, for it is the city of the great King." Matthew 5:34-35

Again, this is not about the Earth being a piece of furniture. It is about Elohim having absolute dominion and authority over the Earth, and showing the relative position of the Earth in His Kingdom.

The footstool at a king's throne represented his dominion and authority.

> *"YHWH said to my Adonai, sit at My right hand,*
> *till I make Your enemies Your footstool."*
> Psalm 110:1

This is referring to placing people at His feet. The footstool was before the throne, and it is where submission to the Sovereign took place.

> *"Exalt YHWH our Elohim,*
> *and worship at His footstool - He is set apart."*
> Psalm 99:5

> *"Let us go into His tabernacle;*
> *Let us worship at His footstool."*
> Psalm 132:7

So, the Earth being a footstool of Elohim is simply showing that He has dominion, and demands worship from this Creation. You cannot take this literally, because it was not meant to be taken literally.

The text of Ezekiel 43 also shows how Elohim identifies Himself with a direction - the east.

The east represents not only a direction, but also time. As the sun rises at the dawning of the day it marks the beginning of the light portion of a day. Just as the beginning of time began in darkness, so every day begins in the evening, and then light is brought forth in the morning.

We read in the first chapter of Genesis how Elohim

reckons time.

"14 Then Elohim said, Let there be lights in the firmament of the heavens to divide the day from the night; and let them be for signs and seasons, and for days and years; 15 and let them be for lights in the firmament of the heavens to give light on the earth; and it was so. 16 Then Elohim made two great lights: the greater light to rule the day, and the lesser light to rule the night. He made the stars also. 17 Elohim set them in the firmament of the heavens to give light on the earth, 18 and to rule over the day and over the night, and to divide the light from the darkness. And Elohim saw that it was good. 19 So the evening and the morning were the fourth day."
Genesis 1:14-19

Just as the notion of direction revolves around the Covenant Land, so does time.

Now, consider the first part of Ezekiel 43:7 again. *"And He said to me, Son of man, this is the place of My throne and the place of the soles of My feet, where I will dwell in the midst of the sons of Yisrael* <u>*forever*</u>.*"*

Notice the mention of time - "forever." The Hebrew word translated as "forever" in English is "olam" (עוֹלָם). Westerners think in terms of the abstract idea of eternity or infinity. This word is frequently translated as "forever," and in the English language it is misunderstood to mean a continual span of time that never ends.

It is different from an eastern perspective, which is more concrete. In the Hebrew mind "olam" is "what is at or beyond the horizon, a very distant time."

It simply means "long duration," "antiquity," and "futurity." It could also mean: "until the end of a period of time," and that period of time is determined by the context. Sometimes it is the length of a man's life, sometimes a number of generations, until a time of renewal or to the end of an age.

In fact "olam" could be translated "until the end of the age."

This is a good example of how translations from one language to another can impact the way we interpret the promises, and even how we look at the future.

Now let's take a specific example of how our understanding of Hebrew thought, or lack thereof, impacts our understanding of the future. When Yahushua predicted the destruction of the Temple shortly before His crucifixion, His disciples asked Him several questions.

The account is referred to as the Olivet Discourse, and it is recoded in Matthew 24, Mark 13 and Luke 21.[228]

Here are those questions as recorded in the text of Matthew 24:3 *"Tell us, when will these things be? And what will be the sign of Your coming, and of the end of the age?"*

There are actually three question here if you look closely, and a key to understanding Yahushua's answers is to determine what question He is answering.

"When will these things be?" refers to the destruction of the Temple. They apparently assumed that it would coincide with the coming of the Messiah and the end of the age, but these could all be three different events.

Many people make this same mistake, and that results in a skewed understanding of this prophecy. Yahushua gave a very detailed answer to their questions, and people often erroneously apply His answers to our future, instead of the disciple's future, which is our past.

One of the reasons is the reference to "the end of the age." Most westerners automatically assume that it refers to the end of time – i.e. the end.

As we just discussed, that is not necessarily the case. It could mean the end of the Temple period, or the end of the Kingdom of Yahudah that had previously returned from Babylonian exile. It could also mean the end of that current

---

[228] While it is assumed that the account in Luke 21 is the same as the one recorded in Matthew 24 and Mark 13, it is possible that was actually a different encounter that occurred exclusively in the Temple.

generation.

But wait. What about Yahushua's response? Surely He was talking about the end of time. Here is what He said: *"Immediately after the tribulation of those days the sun will be darkened, and the moon will not give its light; the stars will fall from heaven, and the powers of the heavens will be shaken."* Matthew 24:29

That definitely sounds like an apocalyptic event. The sun and the moon going dark, and stars falling from the sky. We have not seen this before, so it must mean the end of time. Right?

Well, to a western thinker it does, but not to an eastern thinker. Remember that the sun and the moon were established as visual markers for time, as we saw in Genesis 1:14-16. So referencing those bodies going dark can simply mean "times up." Stars can represent people as we saw in the promise to Abram and Isaac,[229] as well as in the dream of Joseph.[230]

Often, the sun, the moon and the stars represent the "hosts of Heaven."

"And take heed, lest you lift your eyes to heaven, and when you see the sun, the moon, and the stars, all the host of heaven, you feel driven to worship them and serve them, which YHWH your Elohim has given to all the peoples under the whole heaven as a heritage." Deuteronomy 4:19

The word for star is "kokav" (כוכב) in Hebrew. They are all named, and they are clearly connected with "powers"[231] – even the Sons of Elohim as we read in Job.

"⁶ To what were its foundations fastened? Or who laid its

---

[229] See Genesis 15:5, 22:17 and 26:4
[230] *"Then he dreamed still another dream and told it to his brothers, and said, "Look, I have dreamed another dream. And this time, the sun, the moon, and the eleven stars bowed down to me." Genesis 37:9*
[231] *"He counts the number of the stars; He calls them all by name." Psalm 147:4*

cornerstone, [7] When the morning stars sang together, and all the
Sons of Elohim shouted for joy?"
Job 38:6-7

So, these heavenly bodies are associated with the Hosts
of Heaven, and the Sons of Elohim. Remember Deuteronomy
32:7-8, when they were assigned over the Nations that were
established after the rebellion at the Tower of Babel?

"[7] Remember the days of old, consider the years of many
generations. Ask your father, and he will show you;
Your elders, and they will tell you: [8] When the Most
High divided their inheritance to the nations, when He
separated the sons of Adam, He set the boundaries of the
peoples according to the number of the sons of Elohim."
Deuteronomy 32:7-8

With the understanding that the sun, the moon, and the
stars are linked with time, as well as the Hosts of Heaven and
the Sons of Elohim that rule over the earth, we can begin to
understand that this is not necessarily referring to an actual
physical sign, but rather an overthrowing of powers.

Take for instance the prophecy in Isaiah that many link
with the fall of Lucifer, although Lucifer is not his actual
name.[232]

"[12] How you are fallen from heaven, O Hylel, son of the
morning! How you are cut down to the ground, you who weakened
the nations! [13] For you have said in your heart: I will ascend into
heaven, I will exalt my throne above the Stars of Elohim; I will also
sit on the mount of the congregation on the farthest sides of the north."
Isaiah 14:12-13

There are those "Stars of Elohim," and the mount of

---

[232] Lucifer is a Latin word inserted into the Latin Vulgate by Jerome when he translated from the Hebrew. The actual Hebrew word in "Hylel" (הילל).

the congregation is the same as "the congregation of El" that we read about in Psalm 82. In that Psalm we read about how the Sons of Elohim will be judged and "fall" as they lose their positions of power, and die like men.[233]

Did you notice the duration mentioned in the text – the farthest sides of the north?

So, this being named Hylel wanted to usurp YHWH, El Most High, and sit above the stars – the Sons of Elohim. Hylel is likened to a fallen star, because he lost his position.

Now can you see how stars falling can be describing powers in the heavenly realm being brought down? It does not necessarily mean a physical meteor shower, or asteroid assault.

Now consider as Isaiah prophesied about the downfall of Babylon at 13:9-10.

> "*⁹ Behold, the day of YHWH comes, cruel, with both wrath and fierce anger, to lay the land desolate; and He will destroy its sinners from it. ¹⁰ For the stars of heaven and their constellations will not give their light; The sun will be darkened in its going forth, and the moon will not cause its light to shine.*" Isaiah 13:9-10

This passage describes the judgment that came against Babylon. It is called "The Day of YHWH." This is an important point to understand. While most Christians think that there is a single "Day of the LORD" in the future at the end of days, there is not just one Day of YHWH in the future. Whenever YHWH renders punishment against a people or a kingdom it is known as the Day of YHWH.

Also, look at how the fall of Babylon is described – "*the stars of heaven and their constellations will not give their light; The sun will be darkened in its going forth, and the moon will not cause its light to shine.*" Are you beginning to see this as a Hebrew?

Now consider how Ezekiel describes the punishment

---

[233] Psalm 82:6-7

concerning Pharaoh and Egypt.

"When I put out your light,
I will cover the heavens, and make its stars dark;
I will cover the sun with a cloud,
and the moon shall not give her light."
Ezekiel 32:7

Again, this is the Hebrew way of describing the end of a kingdom, a nation or a ruler. In this case we are talking about the demise of Pharaoh, and his rule over Egypt. We are not talking about actual stars falling or disappearing, or the actual darkening of the heavenly bodies.

Now let's consider the Olivet Discourse as described in Matthew 24, and remember that the primary subject is the destruction of the Temple and Jerusalem. It was the same focus that Daniel had when he received the seventy week prophecy. These two events are intimately connected – like bookends for the restored House of Yahudah.

Yahushua was speaking to His disciples, and telling them what they could expect leading up to the destruction of Jerusalem and the Temple, which was the culmination or the end of **that** age.

In verses 9 through 28 Yahushua described the tribulation that would befall Jerusalem through the Roman invasion and destruction.

Many get confused because Yahushua mentioned the abomination event spoken of by Daniel. They have been erroneously taught that "the abomination of desolation" is something in our future.[234]

The argument then continues that since it is a future event from our generation, and since there is no Temple, we

---

[234] There was an "abomination of desolation" in Daniel that referred to the defilement by Antiochus IV Epiphanes around 167 BCE, and there was an "abomination of desolation" that referred to the destruction of the Temple and Jerusalem by the Romans in 70 CE. These were both future events for Daniel. In Yahushua's time, one had happened in the past, and one was anticipated in the future.

must rebuild the Temple, so that this event can occur in the future. I hope you can see what a slippery slope this is, and how error can compound upon error.

Yahushua specifically stated: *"Assuredly, I say to you, this generation will by no means pass away till all these things take place."* Matthew 24:34 He meant exactly what He said. He was referring to the generation that He was speaking to, not some generation thousands of years in the future.

So, all of what He is referring to is the destruction of Jerusalem, and the Temple by the Romans on 70 CE. What occurred during that event satisfies all of the things predicted by Yahushua. The destruction of Jerusalem and the Temple was the abomination of desolation spoken of by Daniel.

In fact, it was arguably the worst event of suffering and tribulation that Jerusalem had ever experienced. A careful reading of Josephus reveals that.[235]

Yahushua then states: *"Immediately after the tribulation of those days the sun will be darkened, and the moon will not give its light; the stars will fall from heaven, and the powers of the heavens will be shaken."* Matthew 24:29

Now interpret this as a Hebrew. We know that the stars are the powers of heaven – the Sons of Elohim. Yahushua was stating that after the tribulation that would befall the Yahudim (i.e. the judgment), there would be a disruption of the Kingdom of Yahudah that had been allowed to return from Babylonian exile.

It had been re-established by some Yahudim, under the supervision of the Medo-Persian Empire. It was then ruled by the Greeks, and the subsequent Seleucid Kingdom. It was briefly liberated by the Maccabees, then followed by Hasmonean rule. Finally, the Herodians, who were Edomites ruled over the land, under Roman occupation. There were various powers "over" Yahudah after their return from Babylon.

---

[235] See Flavius Josephus, *The Wars of the Jews*

So Yahushua was using Hebrew language to announce the end of a Kingdom. It would be "lights out" for the Kingdom of Yahudah after the tribulation of those days – which was the destruction of Jerusalem by the Romans. After the tribulation and judgment, it was all over.

Understanding that the stars represent powers makes sense of other passages like Revelation 2:1, 3:1 and 12:4. But they can also represent real heavenly bodies.

This is why there was an actual star, or heavenly body, used to announce the coming of the Messiah – the only begotten Son of Elohim. A star was a sign for Yahushua.

"I see Him, but not now; I behold Him, but not near; a Star shall come out of Jacob; a Scepter shall rise out of Yisrael, and batter the brow of Moab, and destroy all the sons of tumult." Numbers 24:17

Here the Messiah is described as a "Scepter," which is a conceptual metaphor revealing that He will be coming to rule.

These are simply examples that are intended to open your eyes, and help you view the Scriptures from a proper perspective. Many westerners have misunderstood and misrepresented the Scriptures, because they fail to view them through an eastern lens.

I hope that this chapter provided some helpful guidance for those seeking truth. It is a journey that will last a lifetime as we continue to draw light from the texts.

Hebrew thought impacts the way we perceive the Creator and His Creation. It impacts how we understand time, and the restoration of time through the Covenant.

The distinction between abstract and concrete carries over to the way we think and understand the Scriptures and our faith. While these cultural distinctions are not so apparent today, due to the pervasiveness of western culture, we are following an ancient path.

The path that leads out of Babylon involves entering into an eastern covenant with YHWH. It is the path of a Hebrew. If we want to know the Covenant and walk in the Covenant then we need to learn to think and live like Hebrews.

That often involves a multi-dimensional paradox shift in the way that we think, and the way we perceive the world around us. We will examine this further in the next chapter as we continue to explore the Hebrew language.

13

The Hebrew Language

In the previous chapter we examined the difference between eastern and western thought. We looked at some examples of how they differentiate, and how those differences impact the way we understand the Scriptures.

They also influence our understanding of the Creator Himself. Read how YHWH is described in one of the Psalms:

"⁶ He only is my rock and my salvation;
My fortress; I shall not be shaken.
⁷ On Elohim rests my salvation and my glory;
My might rock, my refuge is Elohim."
Psalm 62:6-7

Notice again, the concrete descriptions of YHWH as "a rock" and "a fortress." When we read these descriptions, we immediately understand the message being conveyed.

When we describe YHWH as a "mighty rock" we perceive Him as a solid foundation. When we think of Him as "fortress" we understand that He protects us, and He is a refuge in time of trouble. These are vivid images that are easy to understand.

How many of us growing up in western Christianity have heard Elohim described in terms such as: Immutable, Omnipotent, Omniscient and Omnipresent? What on earth do these words even mean?

As a result, many children grow up viewing Elohim in the abstract, because these are abstract terms that don't give us a visual or concrete understanding of the Creator. Imagine a child trying to understand Elohim using those descriptions.

On the other hand, if a child is taught about Elohim from an eastern perspective, it will provide greater understanding. The child will recognize that he or she can run to YHWH for safety and protection.

Now this is just one simple example, but it shows the stark difference between eastern and western thought. It clearly impacts the way that we understand and perceive the Creator.

In English we use the vague term "God" to identify the Creator, while in ancient Hebrew we see "אל" pronounced El.

Recall that the visual of "aleph" (א) is the head of an ox or a bull. This is easily seen in the more ancient script. The aleph represents strength and power. We also see the lamed (ל), representing "a staff of authority," or "a shepherd's staff." So "El" represents a strong power that we must follow and obey. This is a much better understanding than the abstract descriptor God.

Sadly, most westerners have a very abstract understanding of YHWH, and His plan of salvation that we are actually supposed to physically practice and rehearse on a weekly, monthly and yearly basis through the moadim – The Appointed Times commanded in the Scriptures.

The Scriptures provide these rehearsals so that we can learn and rehearse the path of salvation that leads back into the Kingdom. Regrettably, Christians generally do not believe that these times are applicable to them. As a result, they miss the appointments that are supposed to strengthen their relationship with Elohim.

We have already examined the Christian understanding of salvation, which is heavily influenced by western thought. An easterner looks at salvation as an actual physical event, while most Christians view it as a mystical occurrence when you say a prayer, raise your hand, or simply make a decision to believe in Jesus.

They believe that at the moment that they have decided

to "accept Jesus" as their savior that they are immediately saved. It is an internal decision or some simple expression of "belief" that results in salvation.

That leads to another good example of the differences between eastern and western thought – Belief.

I grew up with the understanding that belief was something internal – a thought or decision. Most Christians likely consider their belief in God or Jesus to be a feeling or conviction - a matter of the heart.

In eastern thought, belief is expressed through outward actions. It is something visibly seen in the physical realm. Consider this passage from James:

"14 What does it profit, my brethren, if someone says he has faith but does not have works? Can faith save him? 15 If a brother or sister is naked and destitute of daily food, 16 and one of you says to them, 'Depart in peace, be warmed and filled,' but you do not give them the things which are needed for the body, what does it profit? 17 Thus also faith by itself, if it does not have works, is dead. 18 But someone will say, 'You have faith, and I have works.' Show me your faith without your works, and I will show you my faith by my works. 19 You believe that there is one Elohim. You do well. Even the demons believe - and tremble! 20 But do you want to know, O foolish man, that faith without works is dead? 21 Was not Abraham our father justified by works when he offered Isaac his son on the altar? 22 Do you see that faith was working together with his works, and by works faith was made perfect? 23 And the Scripture was fulfilled which says, 'Abraham believed Elohim, and it was accounted to him for righteousness.' And he was called the friend of Elohim. 24 You see then that a man is justified by works, and not by faith only. 25 Likewise, was not

Rahab the harlot also justified by works when she received the messengers and sent them out another way? ²⁶ For as the body without the spirit is dead, so faith without works is dead also." James 2:14-26

Did you notice that James actually uses Abraham to demonstrate belief? The life of Abraham is marked by a life of obedience, and it is a pattern for our journey out of Babylon. Therefore, we must learn to believe like Abraham believed.

He didn't just say he believed. His actions demonstrated His belief. He left Babylon and moved His family to the land of Canaan. It was a land filled with giants, but that did not stop him.

He trusted in the promises made by YHWH, and he acted on his faith. His belief was demonstrated by outward, visible, concrete action.

So, belief to the easterner involves action that demonstrates, proves and perfects that belief. Your actions make your belief real and tangible.

And this is one of the major issues impacting Christians. They have been led to believe that through "grace" there is nothing they can do except express their belief through words, a thought or a feeling. In fact, some go so far as to say that your attempts to live by the righteous Commandments of Elohim constitute "legalism."

They fail to recognize that obeying the Commandments of the Creator is a good thing, while obeying the commandments of religions and men is "legalism," in the negative sense. Instead, they claim that they don't have to obey the Commandments of Elohim because they are "under grace."

Again, the English word "grace" literally means "thanks." When we "say grace" we give thanks. According to The Miriam-Webster Dictionary, the word "grace" equates to a charming or attractive trait or characteristic.

In the Greek we read "charis." The definition of

"charis" (χάρις) is as follows: "acceptable, benefit, favour, gift or thanks." So consistently, when considering "grace," we see a meaning of "thanks" and "favour" – a gift.

When many Christians speak of grace they are really referring to the "mercy," and the "unmerited favor" of Elohim that provides forgiveness through the shed blood of Yahushua. This equates to "chesed" (חסד) in Hebrew.

The English word "grace" equates to "hen" (חן) in Hebrew. The first time we read about "grace" (חן) in the Scriptures is pertaining to Noah as follows:

"8 But Noah found grace (חן) in the eyes of YHWH. 9 This is the genealogy of Noah. Noah was a just man, perfect in his generations. Noah walked with Elohim." Genesis 6:8-9

From this text we can discern that Noah found "favor" because of the way He lived. He walked with Elohim. That is an important aspect of the grace provided by Elohim. He bestows His favor upon those who desire to please Him and obey Him.

Grace was also used when referring to the Messiah in the New Testament texts.

"And the Child grew and became strong in spirit,
filled with wisdom; and the grace (charis)
of Elohim was upon Him."
Luke 2:40

"And the Word became flesh and dwelt among us,
and we beheld His glory,
the glory as of the only begotten of the Father,
full of grace (charis) and truth."
John 1:14

Again, grace can be a somewhat abstract term, unless you understand it to mean "favor."

Now there is a passage further on in the text of John that becomes a stumbling block for some who grapple with the relationship between the Commandments, often referred to as "The Law," and the favor that YHWH provided through His Son.

Here is what you might read in a common English translation:

"*16 And of His fullness we have all received, and grace for grace. 17 For the Law was given through Moses, but grace and truth came through Jesus Christ. 18 No one has seen God at any time. The only begotten Son, who is in the bosom of the Father, He has declared Him.*" John 1:16-18 NKJV

First of all, when the passage refers to "grace for grace" it is talking about an exchange – a gift for a gift. Not an abolishment, but a fulfillment.

The context of this passage is that Yahushua was the Word from the very beginning of Creation. That Word became flesh and dwelt with mankind. His coming fulfilled the Torah written by Moses as ink on a Scroll.

The Word (Yahushua) was alive before men teaching and leading them on the Covenant path, just like Moses led the Yisraelites.

Did you notice the "but" in verse 17? That "but" becomes a problem for some, because it appears to juxtapose Moses against Yahushua.

If you examine the text closely, you will notice that the "but" is typically in italics in most translations. The reason is because it is a translator insertion. It doesn't exist in the original text.

Here is a better translation of the passage:

"*16 And of His fullness we have all received, and grace for grace. 17 For the Torah was given through*

Moses - grace and truth came through Messiah Yahushua." John 1:16-17

This is much clearer, and more accurate. The written Torah was provided through Moses, but Moses could not supply the fulfillment. He had blood on His hands and he was not from the Tribe of Yahudah.

Yahushua came as the living Torah, the Torah in the flesh. He also provided the atonement that was needed to fulfill to Torah. He offered up His life, as a gift, for the forgiveness of sin.

In fact, Yahushua was the promised one according to Deuteronomy 18:18-19.

"¹⁸ I will raise up for them a Prophet like you from among their brethren, and will put My words in His mouth, and He shall speak to them all that I command Him. ¹⁹ And it shall be that whoever will not hear My words, which He speaks in My Name, I will require it of him.

The Torah was through Moses, and now through Yahushua we have favour and the Torah – the fullness of truth.

So, when we consider the notion of grace we are not talking about some mystical covering that exempts us from the Commandments. It is referring to the free gift of salvation that is offered through the shed blood of the Messiah to those who "repent" from their sins and walk with Elohim – like Noah.

This leads us to the notion of "repentance" which is important to understand from an eastern perspective. Closely linked with belief and salvation, many Christians are led to believe that repentance also simply involves a "decision" or a "prayer."

The Hebrew word for "repent" is "shuv" (שוב), and the act of repentance is often described as "teshuvah" (תשובה).

- 256 -

Repentance is what John the Immerser and Yahushua both preached, so it is obviously important. In fact, it was their first recorded message as adults.

Here is what John said.

"Repent, for the Kingdom of Heaven is at hand!"
Matthew 3:2

And here is what Yahushua said.

"Repent, for the Kingdom of Heaven is at hand."
Matthew 4:17

They both proclaimed the same exact thing! So this is definitely worth examining. Teshuvah literally means "turn," and it involves action. It is intimately tied with the Kingdom of Heaven – the Kingdom of YHWH.

Both John and Yahushua were advising people to turn away from their sins, and turn toward the Kingdom.

This is all about the Torah – the Commandments. Righteous conduct is outlined through the Torah, and sin is defined as "lawlessness," which is not following the Commandments.[236]

So, the act of repentance involves turning away from lawlessness, and turning toward the Commandments. While the act may begin in your heart, it must translate to your outward actions.

It involves acknowledging and confessing your sins, but it doesn't end there. It is not simply a confession or a prayer. Repentance involves action – turning away from sinful conduct, and turning toward righteous conduct.

We repent because we have not been obedient and we ask to receive the unmerited favor - the forgiveness that we cannot earn and do not deserve.

---

[236] *"Whoever commits sin also commits lawlessness, and sin is lawlessness."* 1 John 3:4

Our repentance involves turning toward the Commandments and walking according to them. We acknowledge that we have not lived in accordance with the instructions of Elohim. That deserves punishment. We ask for forgiveness instead of punishment.

We acknowledge that atonement is required, and that atonement involves blood. Those who follow Yahushua understand that He paid the price for the transgression of the Commandments, and provided the needed atonement. We then heed His words and "sin no longer."[237]

These matters are discussed at length in the book titled *Salvation – The Covenant Journey*. They are critical concepts to grasp, because western thinking has distorted a proper Scriptural understanding of them.

Now a westerner would object to this by stating that "we cannot be saved by works," but we're not talking about being saved by our own righteousness. We are talking about being saved by His righteousness, and then following His example on how to live righteously.

YHWH defines the conduct that is acceptable in His Kingdom, and the notion that we are unable to follow His commands is absurd, and contrary to the Scriptures.

Here is what Moses had to say about the issue.

"For this Commandment which I command you today
is not too mysterious for you, nor is it far off."
Deuteronomy 30:11

The phrase "not too mysterious" can also be translated as "not too difficult."

According to John, *"² By this we know that we love the children of Elohim, when we love Elohim and keep His Commandments. ³ For this is the love of Elohim, that we keep His Commandments. And His Commandments are not burdensome."* 1

---

[237] See John 5:14 and 8:11

John 5:2-3

And here is the final Word from Yahushua concerning the Covenant path. *"Because narrow is the gate and difficult is the way which leads to life, and there are few who find it."* Matthew 7:14

He never said it would not be difficult – just not <u>too</u> difficult. So anyone who says that we cannot obey the Commandments is a liar. And if you believe them, you have been deceived.

I can guarantee you that when you stand before Yahushua, He will not condemn you for watching and keeping His Commandments. I can also guarantee you that He will reject you, if you willingly reject His Commands and live in lawlessness.[238]

Yahushua came teaching the Commandments, and specifically stated "follow Me." We must walk as He walked, live as He lived, obey as He obeyed. This is what we must do if He is our Teacher, and our Messiah.

A typical western Christian would proclaim that: "We cannot do anything to aid in our salvation. It's all Jesus!"

Of course, a person cannot earn salvation through works, but we clearly play a part in our salvation. Look at Noah. He had to actually build the ark that would save him and his family. YHWH provided the blueprints and the protection. He provided the "escape plan," but Noah participated in the salvation process.

It is a simple fact that if you do not repent, you cannot be saved, and repentance involves action. While the blood of Yahushua cleanses us from our past sins, upon repentance, we are supposed to stop sinning. That involves living according to His righteous Commandments.

Consider this passage from Acts.

"[17] Yet now, brethren, I know that you did it in

---

[238] Matthew 7:21-23 and Luke 13:24-30

ignorance, as did also your rulers. *¹⁸ But those things which Elohim foretold by the mouth of all His prophets, that the Messiah would suffer, He has thus fulfilled. ¹⁹ Repent therefore and be converted, that your sins may be blotted out, so that times of refreshing may come from the presence of the Master, ²⁰ and that He may send Messiah Yahushua, who was preached to you before, ²¹ whom heaven must receive until the times of restoration of all things, which Elohim has spoken by the mouth of all His set apart prophets since the world began. ²² For Moses truly said to the fathers, 'YHWH your Elohim will raise up for you a Prophet like me from your brethren. Him you shall hear in all things, whatever He says to you. ²³ And it shall be that every soul who will not hear that Prophet shall be utterly destroyed from among the people.' ²⁴ Yes, and all the prophets, from Samuel and those who follow, as many as have spoken, have also foretold these days. ²⁵ You are sons of the prophets, and of the Covenant which Elohim made with our fathers, saying to Abraham, 'And in your seed all the families of the earth shall be blessed.' ²⁶ To you first, Elohim, having raised up His Servant Yahushua, sent Him to bless you, in turning away every one of you from your iniquities." Acts 3:17-26*

This does not mean that our belief should not be followed up with righteous living – obedience. Hebrews express their faith through their actions.

Westerners don't feel the need to obey – they just "believe," and as a result they are lawless. They are without the Torah; without the instructions of Elohim.

Consider the words of James again, whose true name was Jacob: "*¹⁸ But someone will say, 'You have faith, and I have works.' Show me your faith without your works, and I will show you my faith by my works. ¹⁹ You believe that there is one Elohim. You do well. Even the demons believe - and tremble!* [20] *But do you want to know, O foolish man, that faith without works is dead?* [21] *Was not Abraham our father justified by works when he offered Isaac his son on the altar?* [22] *Do you see that faith was working together with his works, and by works faith was made perfect?* [23] *And the Scripture was fulfilled which says, 'Abraham believed Elohim, and it was accounted to him for righteousness.' And he was called the friend of Elohim.* [24] *You see then that a man is justified by works, and not by faith only."* James 2:18-24

Let's repeat that:

> *"You see then that a man is justified by works,*
> *and not by faith only."*

This would seem to directly contradict the proponents of "grace" in the modern Christian religion.

Remember that this was James - the head of the Jerusalem Assembly, and the brother of Yahushua. The tradition is strong that he was hand-picked by Yahushua to carry His message, and lead the sheep. As a result, his words should carry great weight. He provided an eastern understanding of faith amidst the countervailing western notion.

Many people say that they believe in Jesus, but they reject the Commandments. The Commandments of Yahushua are the same as the Commandments of the Father. The Christian notion of faith directly contradicts the faith described in the Scriptures, and we can see that the faith is influenced by language.

It is through the language of the Scriptures that we find the true faith. That faith is the path of restoration through the Covenant. It provides us with an understanding of the Creator, and the instructions for how to live and enter into a relationship with Him. That relationship is defined through a Covenant.

It is a Covenant established, defined, interpreted, lived and fulfilled by Hebrews in an eastern culture and context. To that end, it is important to realize that the Scriptures were originally written in an eastern language, by eastern thinkers.

While many of our New Testament texts are based on the western Greek language, there is significant evidence that some, if not all, of those texts were originally written in Hebrew and Aramaic – both eastern languages.[239]

Thinking like a Hebrew obviously involves an understanding of the Hebrew language. When people from a western background turn to Elohim they often look to a Bible, written in a western language, translated by another westerner from the original eastern language.

This is not always enough, because our language is often at the heart of how we think and perceive the world, as well as Elohim and His Scriptures. We are not getting the full picture of Elohim and His plan if we simply look at Him through a western lens.

As we discussed previously, part of coming out of Babylon involves separating from the cultural influences, and this takes it a step further. We are now talking about changing not just the way we act, but the way that we think, read and speak.

This is an important part of leaving Babylon, and it is possibly one of the hardest and most time-consuming parts of that journey. It is not something that occurs after reading a book, or watching a video. It comes from walking with Elohim, and you cannot fully walk with Him if you do not understand Him and His language.

We already talked about examples of western descriptions of Elohim, such as omniscient, omnipresent, omnipotent, immutable etc. These words don't give you a visual description of the Creator, because they are abstract.

---

[239] The Hebrew Gospels can be examined at www.thehebrewgospels.org

Eastern languages, such as Hebrew, are concrete. We saw a perfect example of this in the Psalms.

"*YHWH is my* **rock** *and my* **fortress** *and my deliverer; my Elohim, my strength, in whom I will trust; my* **shield** *and the* **horn** *of my salvation, my* **stronghold**." Psalm 18:2

Again, words such as rock, fortress, shield, horn and stronghold provide a very real and meaningful description of YHWH as a deliverer, a protector and defender, that even a child can understand.

These differences are not simply limited to descriptions of Elohim. They encompass every aspect of life, and the Scriptures. It is important to understand that the language of the Scriptures was not the modern Hebrew that we see today. Modern Hebrew derives from the Babylonian exile of the House of Yahudah.

The ancient Hebrew language, sometimes referred to as Paleo-Hebrew, consists of pictographs.

<u>22 Ancient Hebrew Pictographs with concrete meanings</u>

1	𐤀	aleph	head, strength, leader
2	𐤁	bet	house, tent floor plan
3	𐤂	gimel	foot, camel, carry, pride
4	𐤃	dalet	door, entry, pathway
5	𐤄	hey	man raised arms, behold, breath
6	𐤅	waw	tent peg, hook, secure, add, and
7	𐤆	zayin	plow, weapon, sickle, cut off
8	𐤇	het	fence, wall, separate
9	𐤈	tet	basket, container, surround
10	𐤉	yud	arm and hand
20	𐤊	kaph	palm, open hand, work, deed
30	𐤋	lamed	shepherd staff, authority, toward
40	𐤌	mem	water, chaos
50	𐤍	nun	sprout, seed, offspring, life

60		samech	hand of staff, prop, support
70		ayin	eye, see, know, experience
80		pey	open mouth, word, speak
90		tsade	hook, desire, need
100		quph	back of the head, divide
200		resh	head, beginning, first
300	w	shin	teeth, consume, destroy
400	X	taw	sign, covenant

This is the written language of Creation that Elohim used to speak Creation into existence. It is important to note that the Hebrew language is a numeric language. In other words, each character also has a numerical value.

It only makes sense that the language of Creation is mathematical. That means every character, and every word, has a numeric value.

Looking at the meaning of the language from a mathematical perspective is sometimes referred to as Gematria. Now I will warn you that Kabbalists can go off the deep end, and turn it into a form of witchcraft. I advise caution, but the fact that people distort things does not diminish their value.

For instance, in John, we read about an interesting encounter between Yahushua and some of His disciples in the Galilee. After the resurrection, the disciples decided left Jerusalem and headed back home. They decided to go fishing, but had no success.

> "[1] *After these things Yahushua showed Himself again to the disciples at the Sea of Tiberias, and in this way He showed Himself:* [2] *Simon Peter, Thomas called the Twin, Nathanael of Cana in Galilee, the sons of Zebedee, and two others of His disciples were together.* [3] *Simon Peter said to them, 'I am going fishing.' They said to him, 'We are going with you*

also.' They went out and immediately got into the boat, and that night they caught nothing. ⁴ But when the morning had now come, Yahushua stood on the shore; yet the disciples did not know that it was Yahushua. ⁵ Then Yahushua said to them, 'Children, have you any food?' They answered Him, 'No.' ⁶ And He said to them, 'Cast the net on the right side of the boat, and you will find some.' So they cast, and now they were not able to draw it in because of the multitude of fish. ⁷ Therefore that disciple whom Yahushua loved said to Peter, 'It is the Master!' Now when Simon Peter heard that it was the Master, he put on his outer garment (for he had removed it), and plunged into the sea. ⁸ But the other disciples came in the little boat (for they were not far from land, but about two hundred cubits), dragging the net with fish. ⁹ Then, as soon as they had come to land, they saw a fire of coals there, and fish laid on it, and bread. ¹⁰ Yahushua said to them, 'Bring some of the fish which you have just caught.' ¹¹ Simon Peter went up and dragged the net to land, full of large fish, one hundred and fifty-three; and although there were so many, the net was not broken." John 21:1-11

Of course, this is a follow-up to the event that occurred when Yahushua was first selecting His disciples. At that time, they caught "*a great number of fish, and their net was breaking.*"²⁴⁰

In the event after His resurrection, the net did not break, which signified that they were ready to complete their mission.

Remember, that Yahushua called them to be "fishers of men." They were supposed to be fishing for men, not for fish. Interestingly, the number of fish are described as "a multitude," and then a specific number is given – 153.

Why the need to give such a precise number? And what

---

²⁴⁰ Luke 5:4-11

is the significance of 153?

Well, when you understand the mathematics of the Hebrew language it all makes sense. You see, in the Hebrew language, the phrase "beni ha'Elohim" (בני האלהים) equals 153. You calculate it as follows:

bet	(ב)	=	2
nun	(נ)	=	50
yud	(י)	=	10
hey	(ה)	=	5
aleph	(א)	=	1
lamed	(ל)	=	30
hey	(ה)	=	5
yud	(י)	=	10
mem	(m)	=	40
Total		=	153

The Hebrew phrase "beni ha'Elohim" means "Sons of Elohim." So this is a powerful message being transmitted through the number of fish caught in the net. Again, they were supposed to be fishing for men – The Sons of Elohim.

It was clearly confirming the fact that the disciples would be the fishermen described by Jeremiah.

"Behold, I will send for many fishermen,
says YHWH, and they shall fish them;
and afterward I will send for many hunters,
and they shall hunt them from every mountain
and every hill, and out of the holes of the rocks."
Jeremiah 16:16

Of course, the reference to "sons of Elohim" brings our attention to the prophecy in Hosea concerning the regathering of the House of Yisrael. Here is a portion of that prophecy that describes the future fate of the House of Yisrael:

"9 Then Elohim said: Call his name Lo-Ammi, for you are not My people, and I will not be your Elohim. 10 Yet the number of the children of Yisrael shall be as the sand of the sea, which cannot be measured or numbered. And it shall come to pass in the place where it was said to them, You are not My people, There it shall be said to them, You are sons of the living El." Hosea 1:9-10

Recall that the Hebrew word "El" is the short form of "Elohim." Of course, Yahushua said that He came for the lost sheep of the House of Yisrael.[241]

Therefore, He was reminding His disciples of their purpose. Their mandate was to fish for those lost sheep who would become Sons of the living Elohim through the renewed Covenant.

Now that is not a message you will hear in many Christian churches, but that is the Good News provided through the Scriptures.

Something else that may go unnoticed in the passage in John 21 is the number of disciples involved in the encounter. At the beginning of this passage we are given the names of some of the disciples, but not all of them. The important thing to notice is the fact that there are seven of them.

Seven is the number often associated with YHWH and "completion." The emphasis on seven began from the very beginning – the first seven words of the Torah found in Genesis 1:1.

Here they are in the Hebrew.

בראשית ברא אלהים את השמים ואת הארץ
7   6   5   4   3   2   1

Here is a transliteration of those seven words.

---

[241] Matthew 15:34

Beresheet bara Elohim et ha'shamayim v'et ha'eretz
 1   2   3   4   5   6   7

In this passage from Genesis 1:1 we read an untranslated word that we have already mentioned pronounced "et" (את). It is the 4th word, and it is affixed to the "vav" (ו), which means "and" at the 6th position.

Again, the word is spelled aleph (א) taw (ת) – "et" (את). In the Ancient Hebrew it looks like this – ✗𝖸. It literally means: "strength of the covenant."

As we saw from the Hebrew language chart above, the aleph (𝖸) is the first character in the Hebrew language and taw (✗) is the last. They encapsulate and surround all of the characters in the Hebrew aleph-bet, and therefore the et (✗𝖸) contains all of the Words - a complete cycle through the aleph-bet.

The "et" (✗𝖸) was present, in the beginning, during Creation, and Creation came into existence through the spoken Word.

Yahushua specifically identifies Himself with the Aleph Taw (✗𝖸),[242] and so did John.

"¹ In the beginning was the Word, and the Word was with Elohim, and the Word was Elohim. ² He was in the beginning with Elohim. ³ All things were made through Him, and without Him nothing was made that was made. ⁴ In Him was life, and the life was the light of men." John 1:1-4

This should make it evident that learning the ancient language helps us better understand the Creator, His Creation, and His Son.

The planet also has been described in many ways, and if you do not understand the nature of the Hebrew language you might take it literally. Remember in the last chapter when we examined the passage describing the Earth as a footstool.

---

[242] See Revelation 1:8, 1:11, 21:6 and 22:13. English translations that derive from the Greek use the Greek "alpha" and "omega," which are the first and last letters in the Greek alphabet. Surely the Messiah of Yisrael, the Word in the flesh, would have spoken the Hebrew letters "aleph" and "taw."

That was a constructive metaphor.

Again, we are not talking about literal furniture. The metaphor is referring to the place that the Earth occupies before the Throne of YHWH.

Like the footstool metaphor, we read other metaphorical descriptions of Creation.

> "It is He who sits above the circle of the earth, and its inhabitants are like grasshoppers, Who stretches out the heavens like a curtain, and spreads them out like a tent to dwell in." Isaiah 40:22

I have seen people teach that because the comparison of grasshoppers is used, then the relative distance of the sun and the moon must be very small. That is really absurd.

Remember that the Yisraelites compared themselves to grasshoppers in the sight of the Nephilim.

> "There we saw the Nephilim (the descendants of Anak came from the Nephilim); and we were like grasshoppers in our own sight, and so we were in their sight." Numbers 13:33

Comparing something to grasshoppers is simply stating that they are very small. I also see people try to gauge the size of the giants by determining the ratio of a grasshopper compared to a man, and then applying that to the giants.

These descriptions weren't necessarily made to scale, nor were they meant to be literal.

Further, the heavens are not literal curtains. They cover the Earth **like** a tent. It's just an expression, not to be taken literally.

How about this Psalm?

> "The Earth and all its inhabitants are dissolved;
> I set up its pillars firmly."

Psalm 75:3

Referring to pillars of the earth does not mean that there are literal pillars under a flat earth. That doesn't even make sense. What are these pillars resting on?

Also, pillars don't hold up a building, they hold up a roof. For instance, we see the two pillars in front of the Temple, on each side of the door.

In fact, the texts also talk about the "Pillars of Heaven." It doesn't mean that there are actual pillars holding up heaven. It is simply giving a concrete example.

How about the description of the circle of the Earth in Isaiah 40:22? Does that passage prove whether the Earth is a disk or globe?

When we look at other planetary bodies from a distance they look like circles. I regularly look at the moon through a telescope, and it is clearly a globe, as are the other planets.

Therefore, it stands to reason that this planet looks like a circle from afar. This does not prove that the earth is a sphere or flat.

The word for "circle" is "hoog" (חוג), and it shares the same root as "hag" (חג). A "hag" is a feast, and YHWH establishes three feasts through a repeating cycle of Appointed Times. These hags revolve through the yearly cycle, and return each year, like the earth turning on its axis and orbit.

So, we see circular motion which is completely consistent with the current theories involving the movement of round planetary bodies. In fact, our time is determined by the corresponding kinesis of two neighboring planetary bodies – the sun and the moon.[243]

None of those passages describing a circle provide proof of a disk, or a sphere. They are simply describing the shape from the perspective of YHWH - Who sits high in the

---

[243] See Genesis 1:14-18. "He made the moon for Appointed Times, the sun knows it's going down." Psalm 104:19

Heavens.

Remember Deuteronomy 32:8 where YHWH is referred to as the "Most High?" *"When the Most High divided their inheritance to the nations, when He separated the sons of Adam, He set the boundaries of the peoples according to the number of the Sons of Elohim."* Deuteronomy 32:8

Now look at these Psalms:

> *"That they may know that You,*
> *Whose Name alone is YHWH,*
> *are the Most High over all the earth."*
> Psalm 83:18

> *"YHWH is great in Tsyon,*
> *and He is high above all the peoples."*
> Psalm 99:2

So, from the heights of the heavens, both a sphere or a disk would look like a circle. It's really that simple. I am saddened to see people grabbing ahold of flat earth concepts, and using Hebrew Scriptures and language to support such an idea, because it definitely does not.

How about the description of the Earth having "four corners?"

> *"He will set up a banner for the nations,*
> *and will assemble the outcasts of Yisrael,*
> *and gather together the dispersed of Judah*
> *from **the four corners of the earth**."*
> Isaiah 11:12

Does this mean that the Earth is a flat square, or a rectangle with four pointed edges? If you took this text literally, you might think so.

The word used here for "corner" is "kanaph" (כנף). The

Hebrew word "kanaph" (כנף) means: "an edge or extremity, a border or a wing."

It is not referring to a 90-degree angle of a square. It is better related to the four directions of north, south, east and west.

Interestingly, when referring to the regathering of the outcasts of Yisrael from the "outermost" parts of the earth, it is the same word used in relation to the "tzitzit," also known as "tassels" or "gadolym."

"You shall make tassels (gadolym)
on the four corners (kanafot) of the clothing
with which you cover yourself."
Deuteronomy 22:12

The ones who are gathered from the four corners are the ones wearing the tzitzit on the four corners of their garments.

This leads us to the concept of Hebrew idioms. These are words or statements that are not intended to be taken literally. Rather, they are expressions that relate an idea, or provide a picture.

For instance, YHWH repeatedly calls the people of Yisrael "a stiff-necked people" – "am-qesheh-oreph." This doesn't mean that the Yisraelites could not bend their necks. It means they were "stubborn," "intractable," "not to be led."

For an agricultural people, this expression was well understood. An ox wore a yoke upon its neck, which was used to guide and direct it. If it was not responsive, it was referred to as hard necked – it is not sensitive to the guidance of the yoke.

YHWH compares His instructions to a yoke that guides and directs His people. People that refuse to be led by His yoke are like "hard-necked" or "stiff-necked" cattle that refuse to respond to the guiding hand of the plowman.

I'm sure you have heard the Promised Land described

as a land "flowing with milk and honey." Of course, there are not literal rivers of milk and honey flowing throughout the Land. That phrase simply means it is a fertile and luscious land.

Again, it is a figure of speech, not to be taken literally. The Scriptures are full of them, and they must be recognized in order to be properly understood.

The New Testament Scriptures also contain idioms and Hebrew figures of speech which points to the fact that they were originally spoken and written in a eastern language.

A good example is when Yahushua stated: *"Do not think that I came to destroy the Torah or the Prophets. I did not come to destroy but to fulfill."* Matthew 5:17

He is not referring to taking a Torah Scroll and burning it. Nor is He talking about doing away with the Torah. That would be preposterous.

The phrase "destroy the Torah" simply means to incorrectly interpret the Torah. Likewise, the phrase "fulfill the Torah" means to correctly interpret the Torah.

When Yahushua made this statement, He had just finished His teaching referred to as "The Beatitudes" during "The Sermon on the Mount."[244] It was all about teaching the Torah.

So, His statement was not about doing away with the Torah. That is unthinkable. It was about His interpretation of the Torah. He was simply stating that He did not come to give a bad interpretation of the Torah. Rather, His teachings would reveal the fullness of the Torah. He would get to the "heart" of the Torah.

Finally, it is important to understand that certain Hebrew words can have different meanings based upon their context.

For instance, the word translated as "Earth" is "eretz" (אֶרֶץ). The Hebrew word "eretz" does not always mean planet

---

[244] See Matthew 5:1-12

Earth. Sometimes it means the entire planet. Sometimes it means "ground" or "land." In fact, it is often used to describe the Covenant "Land" (eretz).

As a result, it is important to look at the context of a passage in order to understand if it is referring to the Covenant Land, the land of another nation, or the entire planet.

I have seen people relate prophecies to the entire planet (eretz), when the context only refers to the Covenant Land (eretz). The same word is used to describe each, so context is critical in order to accurately interpret prophecy.

This can result in incorrect expectations and prophetic interpretations. We will explore this issue further in the chapter titled *Understanding Prophecy*.

Right now we are all still suffering the effects of Babel as the planet and mankind were separated geographically and linguistically. We look forward to the time prophesied through Zephaniah.

> *"For then I will restore to the peoples a pure language,*
> *that they all may call on the Name of YHWH,*
> *to serve Him with one accord."*
> Zephaniah 3:9

Until that time, studying the language, including the characters, the eastern meaning of words, idioms, metaphors, and figures of speech all helps us better understand the Scriptures.

This is not to imply that you must become a Hebrew scholar, because you do not. You simply need to be aware of these differences that have resulted in many false doctrines as people fail to properly translate, interpret and read the Scriptures.

As you begin to think like a Hebrew, the language will become more familiar, and with that will come a better understanding of the Scriptures.

14

Understanding the Scriptures

Thus far, when dealing with Hebrew thought and language, we have examined the "east versus west" paradigm. The point was to emphasize the fact that easterners and westerners speak differently, write differently, and sometimes even think differently.

This impacts the way cultures interact and understand one another. It also creates some serious challenges when translating documents. There are not always precise word-for-word matches in every language to perfectly convey a thought or meaning from another language.

We have talked a lot about the set apart walk, referred to as "halakah." This actually provides another good example of the linguistic differences we are considering.

For instance, the English word "walk" can simply describe the process of putting one foot in front of the other. It can also refer to a brief stroll, as in "I took a walk before breakfast."

The Hebrew word "halakah" (הלך) goes much deeper. When the Scriptures describe the fact that Enoch and Noah "walked" with Elohim, they weren't referring to an afternoon hike. Instead, they are describing the way they lived their lives.[245]

They "walked" in accordance with the instructions of Elohim. They followed His instructions, and lived lives of obedience. Their "walk" was a lifetime journey.

That is why Yahushua didn't tell His disciples to sign

---

[245] See Genesis 5:22, 5:24 and 6:9

up for His teaching seminar, like Him on Facebook, or subscribe to His YouTube channel. He said "Follow Me." He was telling them to "walk" with Him, and follow His instructions. It was a very Hebrew way to call His disciples.

Walking with YHWH by following His Son involves learning how to live righteously. It is quite a change for many who have come out of lawless religious systems that reject the Torah.

Many Christians have been taught that Yahushua "did away with the Law," so the idea of actually following the Commandments is foreign and even offensive to some. I have seen Christians who disdain "the Law," and consider it anathema. They reject the Torah, because they view it as bondage.

I hope by now, it is easy for the reader to see that this is a lie straight from the nachash. It is a deceptive teaching that has led millions, if not billions, to destruction through self-inflicted lawlessness.

In order to be in a Covenant relationship with YHWH, it is important to walk like a Hebrew, not a Greek. The purpose of the walk is so that we are changed. We must become set apart, as a nation of priests.

Much of this involves wisdom, knowledge and understanding. We must be wise as the "nachsash" (serpent) according to Yahushua.[246] We must not fall prey to deception. We do this through knowledge and understanding of the instructions of Elohim.

The Scriptures record that His people perish because they reject the knowledge and forgot His Torah. It was specifically prophesied by Hosea.

"My people are destroyed for lack of the knowledge.
Because you have rejected the knowledge, I also will
reject you from being priest for Me; Because you

---

[246] *"Behold, I send you out as sheep in the midst of wolves. Therefore be wise as serpents and harmless as doves."* Matthew 10:16

have forgotten the Torah of your Elohim, I also will forget your children." Hosea 4:6

Forgetting the Torah brought about a curse for the House of Yisrael. The House of Yisrael was classified as a bunch of "lost sheep," because their predecessors forgot the Torah. They lost their way, and strayed from the Great Shepherd.

That is why we find ourselves in this present condition of exile, separated from YHWH and His Kingdom.

"Therefore My people go into exile for lack of knowledge; their honored men go hungry, and their multitude is parched with thirst." Isaiah 5:13

Yahushua said "Blessed are those who hunger and thirst for righteousness, for they shall be satisfied." That is why we currently see so many waking up to truth. They hungered and thirsted and now they are being satisfied. I like to think of this book as a cold spring in the wilderness.

The problem is that some people are so shocked at the deception they were under, that they spend the rest of their lives turning over rocks and stones to see what else they have missed. This can become an obsession, and a distraction. Acquiring knowledge becomes almost an insatiable quest for many. They hunger and thirst for more truth, which can become a problem for some westerners.

The reason is that knowledge, to a westerner, is likened to acquiring more information. To an easterner it is much different. In fact, knowledge can be a very intimate term in an eastern language like Hebrew.

The Hebrew word for "know" is "yada." In the Scriptures, when a man "knows" his wife, he has sexual relations with her. That is the ultimate intimacy in the special covenant relationship of marriage. Procreation is the result, and that is why sex should be confined within the marriage covenant.

In the same sense, knowing Elohim involves a relationship, and that relationship is defined through the Covenant. Relationships with gods outside of the Covenant is adultery – idolatry.

If you want to "know Elohim" it must be through the Covenant. We express our love through our "walk." It is not through emotions, or some internal thought process. Rather, it is through our actions that we learn to know Him, and He knows us. Again, when a man "knows" his wife, and expresses his affection, he doesn't just think about it. It is a physical act involving both individuals.

In English when you say that you know someone, it could be as simple as the fact that you know their name, or what they look like. Maybe you met them one time in the past. It could infer a relationship, but not necessarily.

So, knowing someone from a western perspective can simply involve internal information, or some superficial acquaintance. Knowing someone from an eastern perspective involves action, and can be intensely intimate.

There are many people who try to know Elohim by acquiring a lot of knowledge. Because they equate knowledge with information they often focus on books, sermons, videos and, of course, the Scriptures to acquire that knowledge.

Some confuse information from written texts with knowledge of Elohim. As they spend their time chasing after ancient and hidden manuscripts, they may find themselves actually straying from the knowledge of Elohim.

You must ask yourself if you are focused on knowing Him, or simply learning about Him, and acquiring more information. That is where some people can stray off the narrow path. Instead of focusing on obeying the clear instructions of Elohim, religious people spend their time talking about Elohim.

We already discussed the terms that westerners apply to Elohim such as "omnipresent, omniscient, immutable, and omnipotent." These are abstract ideas and characteristics used to describe the nature and character of Elohim.

Many people attempt to do the same thing with the book called the Bible. While the Bible contains sacred texts that describe Elohim and His Creation from the beginning, they are texts nonetheless.

Just as we talked about eastern thought and eastern language, it is important to understand how a Hebrew would look at the Scriptures.

First of all, as far as we can discern, Abraham did not have any written texts - yet he is the pattern of the Covenant. His life was actually the Covenant lived out in real time. Again, this is a very Hebrew way of dealing with a covenant. It is not just words on paper, like a contract. It is expressed through living life.

While we read about some of his life, those words are only there to inform us. It was the fact that Abraham actually "walked" with Elohim that is important, and it is **how** he walked.

Read the promise given to Isaac, based upon Abraham's walk.

> "⁴ And I will make your descendants multiply as the stars of heaven; I will give to your descendants all these lands; and in your seed all the nations of the earth shall be blessed; ⁵ because Abraham obeyed My voice and kept My charge, My Commandments, My statutes, and My Torah." Genesis 26:4-5

So how did Abraham know what to obey? He obeyed the voice of YHWH. On several occasions we read about YHWH appearing to him, and speaking to him.[247]

There were also instances when "the Word of YHWH" (דבר-יהוה) came to him.[248] Of course, we know that

---

[247] See Genesis 12:7, 15:17, 17:1
[248] See Genesis 15:1 and 15:4

Yahushua is the Word that became flesh. These could very well be instances of Yahushua visiting with Abraham.[249]

The point is that these were visitations that involved oral instruction to Abraham. He did not pick up a Bible to read the word. He heard the Word.

Abraham and others relied on oral tradition as many ancient cultures continue to do, although it is a waning tradition in this age of information and communication.

Later, when writings and scrolls became more prominent, they would keep special texts separate, and when a person wanted to read a particular text they would retrieve that scroll and read. After they were done, they would roll it up and then return it to its place.[250]

That is why we find a variety of writings in the Dead Sea Scrolls. While there were clearly texts considered to be "sacred," there was no practice of canonizing one complete Bible all combined together like we have today in codex form.[251] That was a western concept developed much later by western Christianity.

There was a generalized grouping of the Torah, the prophets and the writings. But even then, they remained separate – they were not combined into one scroll or book.

The Torah was clearly the foundation, and the most important of them all. It set forth the history and the instructions for the Covenant relationship, and therefore those texts were at the heart of it all.

Now there are some people attempting to distinguish between the Covenant and the Torah in order to justify not following the Torah. Those who do this are trying to apply a different standard to the Melchizedek priesthood, and the Assembly of Yisrael. Their arguments are without merit.

The first time that we read about Melchizedek is

---

[249] As with Abraham, Yahushua came and "walked" out the Covenant through the way He lived.
[250] A good example of this can be seen in Luke 4:16-20 when Yahushua read from the Scroll of Isaiah in the Synagogue at Nazareth.
[251] Codex is the term used to describe a bound text that is the typical for a book in our day.

during the life of Abram, later named Abraham.

"[18] Then Melchizedek king of Salem brought out bread and wine; he was the priest of El Most High. [19] And he blessed him and said: 'Blessed be Abram of El Most High, Possessor of heaven and earth; [20] And blessed be El Most High, Who has delivered your enemies into your hand.' And he gave him a tithe of all." Genesis 14:18-20

We are not given any background information on this Melchizedek, except for the fact that he was a king and a priest. The paying of tithes to Melchizedek makes a powerful statement. Abram acknowledged through his tithing that Melchizedek was the Priest of the El that He served.

It is interesting to note that he tithed before the Torah was written down by Moses at Sinai. It was a practice repeated by his grandson Jacob.[252]

Again, according to Genesis 26:5 *"Abraham obeyed My voice and kept My charge, My commandments, My statutes, and My Torah (instructions)."*

Obeying His voice, His Charge, His Commandments, His statutes and His Torah are all part of the Covenant, and they are found within the "Scroll of the Torah." (Deuteronomy 30:10) So trying to separate the Torah from the Covenant makes no sense since Abraham's obedience to the Torah was an integral part of the Covenant.

You cannot pluck the Torah (instructions) out of the Covenant. The "Scroll of the Torah," and the "Scroll of the Covenant" are the same. This is evident from the incident when Hilkiah found the Scroll in the Temple.

It was called "The Scroll of the Law (Torah)" at 2 Chronicles 34:14 and 15. It was later called "The Word of YHWH" at 2 Chronicles 34:21, and then "The Scroll of the

---

[252] See Genesis 28:22

Covenant (Brit)" at 2 Chronicles 34:30. These were 3 different descriptions of the same Scroll.

Of course, that is a very Hebrew concept and practice. The Hebrew language often uses different words for the same thing. This sometimes poses a problem for those unfamiliar with this ancient language and culture.

In the case of this new Melchizedek doctrine those who ascribe to it erroneously believe that since different words are being used, then there is a different book, scroll, concept, doctrine or covenant being distinguished. That is simply not the case.

A perfect example of the use of different words to present the same concept can be seen through synonymous parallelism in Hebrew poetry. This form of poetry is found in many of the Psalms. We see in Psalm 119 that "the Word of Elohim" is referred to as 14 different Hebrew synonyms translated into 11 different English words in the King James Version.

We can specifically see this prose involving the Law (Torah) and the Covenant (Brit) in Psalm 78:10: *"They did not keep the Covenant (Brit) of Elohim; they refused to walk in His Law (Torah)."* You see here the Law (Torah) and the Covenant (Brit) being used synonymously.

In fact, the Psalms go on to describe many different synonyms for the Covenant. His Covenant is likened to "His Mercy" (Psalm 89:28), "His Crown" (Psalm 89:39), "His Commandments" (Psalm 103:18), "the Word" (Psalm 105:8), "a statute" (Psalm 105:10), and His "testimony" (Psalm 132:12) to name just a few.

This goes along with Hebrew thought, and that is why throughout Hebrew writings we see synonymous parallelism. In fact, we see this style in numerous other passages such as Isaiah 43:2.

"When you pass through the waters, I will be with you; and through the rivers, they will not overflow

*you. When you walk through fire, you will not be
burned, and flame will not scorch you."*

Notice how "the waters" are parallel with "the river"
and "fire" is parallel with "flame." It is not trying to
differentiate and distinguish between the two parallel terms.
Instead, it is trying to emphasize and provide a richer
description using concrete terms that complement one
another.

Consider Isaiah 11:1 which states: *"There shall come forth
a Rod from the stem of Jesse, and a Branch shall grow out of his
roots."* The Rod and the Branch are both descriptions for the
same Messiah, and these descriptions hearken back to the
Exodus from Egypt. You cannot separate the Rod from the
Branch. They are different descriptions for the same
Yahushua, who was also described as "the Word" and "a
Covenant."[253]

Clearly, the Torah cannot, and should not, be separated
and distinguished from the Covenant. They are the same, and
they are intended to show us the path to YHWH. That path
is the Messiah.

Most in modern Christianity have relied on source
texts of Greek and English. They often have looked at the
Torah as more of a history lesson, rather than the foundation
of their relationship with Elohim.

This has led to many of the problems that we have
discussed throughout this book. They fail to "know" Elohim,
because they are not being taught from a proper foundation.

They believe that Jesus came to undo, or abolish, the
Covenant made with Abraham and Yisrael, and start an
entirely brand new covenant with The Church. This has no
basis in the Scriptural texts, but they believe it to be true

---

[253] John 1:1 proclaims: *"In the beginning was the Word, and the Word was with Elohim, and the Word
was Elohim."* Isaiah 42:6 specifically states: *"I, YHWH, have called You in righteousness, and will
hold Your hand; I will keep You and give You as a Covenant to the people, as a light to the Nations."*
Both of these passages are referring to Yahushua the Messiah.

because they fail to rightly divide the word of truth.

We are exhorted in 2 Timothy 2:14 as follows: *"[14] Remind them of these things, charging them before the Master not to strive about words to no profit, to the ruin of the hearers. [15] Be diligent to present yourself approved to Elohim, a worker who does not need to be ashamed, **rightly dividing the word of truth.**"*

The phrase "rightly dividing" is a Hebrew idiom. To "rightly divide" something is referring to properly viewing, understanding and interpreting the texts. It is what Yahushua referred to as "fulfilling the Torah."

The Word of truth referenced in 2 Timothy was the TaNaK - The Torah, the Prophets and the Writings.[254]

They are categorized in order of priority and the Torah is first. Yahushua did not come to abolish or diminish the Torah. He came to fulfill it.

In fact, He specifically stated: *"[17] Do not think that I came to destroy the Torah or the Prophets. I did not come to destroy but to fulfill. [18] For assuredly, I say to you, till heaven and earth pass away, one jot or one tittle will by no means pass from the Torah till all is fulfilled."* Matthew 5:17-18

So He gave room for the Prophets to be fulfilled, but the Torah would not pass away. Remember that "destroy the Torah" is another Hebrew idiom. It does not refer to incinerating a Torah Scroll, or making the instructions obsolete. Rather, it refers to when someone gives a bad interpretation of the Torah. When they teach or interpret a passage in a way that points away from the actual intent, the person is described as "destroying the Torah." The Christian religion destroys the Torah.

So, the foundational texts of the Tanak are not old or irrelevant. They are required reading for understanding the Covenant path that leads us back to Eden through the Messiah.

Here is an example of how Paul explained Yahushua through the Scriptures:

---

[254] Tanak is an acronym – TNK. The "T" stands for Torah. The "N" stands for "Nebi'im" (Prophets), and the "K" stands for "Ketubim" (Writings).

"So when they had appointed him a day, many came to him at his lodging, to whom he explained and solemnly testified of the Kingdom of Elohim, persuading them concerning Yahushua from both the Torah of Moses and the Prophets, from morning till evening." Acts 28:23

If Paul was using the Torah and the Prophets to testify regarding the Messiah, why would we do any different? Those were, and still are, the Scriptures. Amazingly, some actually use Paul as a basis for rejecting the preeminence of those texts.

There were also the writings - the Ketubim. They are essentially the historical documents, including the Psalms and the Proverbs, which are also prophetic.

Just as the Old Testament texts were separate texts, but categorized, we need to keep that in mind when examining the New Testament texts.

Again, we as westerners have grown up with one book called the Bible that has been divided into two sections categorized as "Old" and "New".

Now that alone sets a misleading and destructive framework for the texts, because many simply avoid the "Old," and go straight to the "New." The new is better, right? Or at least more relevant?

That is the general assumption, especially for Christians, but it is upside down and backwards. You cannot properly understand the texts in the "New Testament" without having the foundation of those in the Tanak.

When we examine the texts in the New Testament it is clear that there are certain portions that are more important than others. For instance, the Words of Yahushua should be the highest priority. After all, He is the Messiah, the Word in the flesh, and He was actually teaching the Torah.

As a result, the Gospels should be like the Torah in the hierarchy of those texts. Then we have prophecy, and also the Testimony of Yahushua in the Revelation text.

We then have some history in the Acts, some letters

from "the Pillars" - Peter, James and John.[255] Those should be treated like teachings, sermons that provided clarification and instruction, along with the brief text of Jude.

Finally, we have a variety of letters from Paul dealing with particular conflicts, and issues that specific assemblies were grappling with. It is questionable whether letters should ever have been included in a codex.

They are one sided communications, not always easy to understand in context, and often misapplied and misappropriated by people. Does a letter to someone really rise to the level of Scripture? And how should it be classified and categorized?

Further, while the Gospels record Yahushua selecting and training Peter, James and John, Paul is not mentioned in the Gospels. The only accounts of Yahushua choosing Paul are from Paul's own testimony. Typically you would need two or three witnesses to establish a matter according to the Torah.[256]

Now some hold fast to the fact that the 66 books in the Bible were divinely inspired, and all constitute the inerrant word of God. That assumes that Elohim actually wanted a collection of books bound together, and that the Set Apart Spirit orchestrated the process. Two very big assumptions.

The belief that a certain version of the Bible is the inerrant Word of God completely ignores all of the issues that exist when translating eastern texts into western languages.

Nevertheless, the point of this is not to diminish the significance of the Bible, but rather to provide a balanced perspective on how we handle the texts contained therein.

Compiling all of the texts into one codex, and then summarily categorizing the entire book as the Word of God, creates the illusion that all of the texts are of the same weight and importance. That is clearly not the case, as I hope you can see. Not every word of every text in the Bible is the Word of God, and all texts are not created equal.

---

[255] Paul actually referred to Peter, James and John as "so-called" pillars of the early assembly.
[256] See Deuteronomy 19:15

Even the Torah is apportioned different weights. Read what Yahushua said about the Scribes and Pharisees.

"*Woe to you, scribes and Pharisees, hypocrites! For you pay tithe of mint and anise and cummin, and have neglected the weightier matters of the Torah: justice and mercy and faith. These you ought to have done, without leaving the others undone.*" Matthew 23:23

So the Scribes and Pharisees were focused on the minutia, and they were forgetting the most important matters. There are some aspects of the Torah that are weightier than others, and we must understand that.

In fact, when asked which was the Greatest Commandment in the Torah Yahushua responded:

"*[37] You shall love YHWH your Elohim with all your heart, with all your soul and with all your mind. [38] This is the first and great commandment. [39] And the second is like it: You shall love your neighbor as yourself. [40] On these two commandments hang all the Torah and the Prophets.*" Matthew 22:37-40

This is an amazing teaching. Yahushua was essentially distilling the Torah and the Prophets down to two Commandments. If you can master those two, then you've got it.

The only thing is that you need to learn what love means - from an eastern perspective, not a western perspective. The Hebrew word for "love" is "ahab" (אהב). It is literally the word for "father" (אב) surrounding the "breath" (ה). The ancient pictograph of the "hey" (ה) shows a person with their hands raised (ᗉ), as in worship.

So, when we have the breath of the Father, and He is our life, then we give ourselves completely to Him. Our lives then become a constant act of worship. That is how we love Him.

Now think, for instance, of what Christianity teaches

about loving Elohim, and consider how people conduct themselves during a modern worship service. Back in college ministry, I had a good friend who was a worship leader, and he used to call it the "I'm in pain look."

As people stood in front of a band, hands lifted high, singing with intense looks of their faces, many of them seemed like they were in pain to him. They thought that they were truly expressing love for Elohim, but often they were simply experiencing an emotional high. That's not the brand of love YHWH is looking for.

I'll never forget the first time that I visited the Western Wall in Jerusalem 23 years ago. There was an Orthodox man "davening" (praying) with intensive movements forwards and sideways. It looked like he was pleading and crying while he was praying in deep and profound prayer. I was mesmerized watching this man as it seemed that he was connected straight to the Throne Room.

Then suddenly he stopped, looked down at his watch calmly for a minute, then he restarted his pleading and crying prayers as if nothing had happened. I realized that it was all just a dramatic religious act he was putting on.

We've heard a lot about "fake news" over the past several years. Well this was the definition of "fake prayer." This is not a game, and YHWH sees through all of the religious charades that people put on. It ultimately comes down to the heart, and a proper understanding of love.

The first and great Commandment that Yahushua was referring to is often called "The Shema," found at Deuteronomy 6:4-5. We have talked about it already. It requires us to love YHWH our Elohim with every fiber of our being.

While you might attend a worship service for an hour a week, you are living your normal life the rest of your waking hours. That is when we truly need to learn to love Him.

Here is another similar passage. *"12 And now, Yisrael, what does YHWH your Elohim require of you, but to fear YHWH* *your Elohim, to walk in all His ways and to love Him, to serve YHWH your Elohim with all your heart and with all your soul, ¹³ and to keep the Commandments of YHWH and His statutes which I command you today for your good?"* Deuteronomy 10:12-13

So love, from YHWH's perspective, is not an emotional experience. It is very practical, and it involves obedience. Repeatedly, the Torah links love and obedience together.

YHWH states that He will show mercy to those who love Him, and keep His Commandments.[257]

He does not make mention of showing mercy to someone who made an altar call, raised their hand to "receive Him" in a Church service, or prayed at the Western Wall. We express our love by the way we live our lives every minute of every day. Not by how we feel inside, or appear outside.

Over my years as an attorney I have met with many husbands and wives with marital issues. I have seen and heard the pain of those who were married to an adulterous spouse. They all took vows and made promises to one another, but those words were not enough. Those vows required action, or inaction, in order to support them. As the old saying goes "Talk is cheap."

A husband can say that he loves his wife, but if he gives her a hug and a kiss and then goes off and has an affair, he doesn't truly love her in the way that YHWH defines love. If you love someone you keep your vows and demonstrate it through your conduct.

Indeed, Yahushua specifically said *"If you love Me, keep My Commandments."* John 14:15 Yahushua showed what was important, and it was not a new Commandment. He definitely was not diminishing the Torah. He was elevating it and providing important distinctions that were very easy to understand.

Of course, you cannot compare this teaching of

---

[257] See Exodus 20:6 and Deuteronomy 5:10

Yahushua in the Gospels, to a comment from Paul in one of his letters. For instance, in 2 Timothy 4:13 Paul writes: "Bring the cloak that I left with Carpus at Troas when you come - and the books, especially the parchments."

That sentence is actually in the Bible. The book that some people consider to be the "inerrant Word of God." It's a closing comment in a letter from one person (Paul) to another person (Timothy). Are these the words of God? Not unless Paul is your god.

That is actually the sad truth for some who use Paul's letters to undermine the instructions of the Father, and the Son.

Or how about in Galatians 2:11-19 when Paul accuses Peter of being a hypocrite? He essentially scolds the followers of Yahushua, and then contradicts James. Was that the Word of God? Was it even appropriate to publicly accuse and demean the one who Yahushua selected to carry the Good News to the Nations?[258]

Remember that it was Peter who was given the vision and the revelation regarding the "unclean" foods, and the "unclean" Gentiles described in Acts 10-11. After receiving understanding Peter stated: *"34 . . . In truth I perceive that Elohim shows no partiality. 35 But in every Nation whoever fears Him and works righteousness is accepted by Him."* Acts 10:34-35

Paul's comments were definitely not the Word of God, and we have to wonder what motivated him to write them. After all, it seems as though Paul was constantly vying for the title "Apostle to the Gentiles," but that was clearly given to Peter.

Here is what Peter proclaimed to the Assembly in Jerusalem: *"6 Now the apostles and elders came together to consider this matter. 7 And when there had been much dispute, Peter rose up and said to them: 'Men and brethren, you know that a good while ago Elohim chose among us, that by my mouth the Gentiles (Nations) should hear the word of the Good News and believe.* [8] *So Elohim, who knows the heart, acknowledged them by giving them the Set Apart Spirit, just as He did to us,* [9] *and made no distinction between us and them, purifying their hearts by faith."* Acts 15:6-9

I provide these simple examples to demonstrate that Paul was a man with opinions and teachings. He wrote many letters, most of the time penned by a Scribe, intended to express information and messages to other individuals and groups. They should not the classified as the Word of Elohim. They are the words of Paul. In fact, he even referred to his message as "my gospel" on various occasions.[259]

He owns his message, and it is not appropriate to label his words as "the Word of God." Paul never even made that claim. In the Torah, we constantly read "YHWH said to Moses . . ." or "Thus says YHWH . . ." Those instances clearly provide the Word of YHWH. Paul's letters do not qualify.

This leads us to what I refer to as *The Christian Conundrum.*[260] Without the writings of Paul included within the Bible there would be no question whether or not to obey the Commandments. Of course, we are supposed to obey the Scriptures.

The only way that you could possibly justify not obeying the Commandments is through the writings of Paul. This places people into three general camps on the issue of Paul.

1) The first group includes most Christians who believe that Paul was an Apostle chosen by Yahushua. Therefore, he must be obeyed because of his unique revelation. They interpret his letters as commandments – even higher than the Commandments found in the Torah, because they are

---

[259] See Romans 2:16 and 16:25 as well as 2 Timothy 2:8
[260] *The Christian Conundrum,* written by Todd D. Bennett, is a book that demonstrates the contradiction that exists within modern Christianity that often elevates the confusing words of Paul over the unequivocal words of the Messiah.

newer. They have essentially made Paul their messiah and their god.

2) The second group believes that Paul taught the truth, but his letters have been mistranslated and misunderstood. His teachings are consistent with the Torah when properly examined.

3) The third group believes that Paul was a false prophet who taught a different gospel than the Messiah, He taught a different torah.

Here is what the Torah says about a false prophet. *"¹ If there arises among you a prophet or a dreamer of dreams, and he gives you a sign or a wonder, ² and the sign or the wonder comes to pass, of which he spoke to you, saying, 'Let us go after other gods' - which you have not known - 'and let us serve them,' ³ you shall not listen to the words of that prophet or that dreamer of dreams, for YHWH your Elohim is testing you to know whether you love YHWH your Elohim with all your heart and with all your soul. ⁴ You shall walk after YHWH your Elohim and fear Him, and keep His commandments and obey His voice; you shall serve Him and hold fast to Him."* Deuteronomy 13:1-4

So, YHWH says He will send false prophets to test His people. They will be tested to see if they will walk with YHWH, or whether they will walk away from Him and His Commandments based upon what someone says. So we must always be on guard regarding who we listen to. We do this by holding fast to YHWH, and keeping His Commandments.

That is where many Christians go wrong, and they typically use the writings of Paul to justify their lawlessness. In doing this, they are making Paul a false prophet, regardless of whether or not he was. They are using his words to walk away from the Torah instead of walking out the Torah.

The point of this discussion is not to determine whether or not Paul is a false prophet sent by Elohim. I never met the man myself, and I am therefore unable to assess his character or credibility.

The point is to demonstrate that we are *absolutely never* supposed to stray from the Commandments *no matter who tries to convince us to do so*. If someone does try such a thing, then they are a false prophet, or a false teacher.

So, just because there are letters or writings compiled in a codex by men centuries ago, does not mean that you must do as they say. Even if you think they are telling you not to obey the Commandments - you never walk away from Elohim and His Commandments. Period!

That is why James, when addressing the issue of new believers coming into the Assembly, decided as follows:

"¹⁸ Known to Elohim from eternity are all His works. ¹⁹ Therefore I judge that we should not trouble those from among the Gentiles who are turning to Elohim, ²⁰ but that we write to them to abstain from things polluted by idols, from sexual immorality, from things strangled, and from blood. ²¹ For Moses has had throughout many generations those who preach him in every city, being read in the synagogues every Sabbath." Acts 15: 18-21

In other words, don't require them to learn the entire Torah. That's too much from the start. Get them cleaned up so they can go the Synagogue, and hear Moses being taught every Sabbath. Through this weekly cycle of going through the Torah Scroll they can hear and then obey, which is the very meaning of "shema."

This was a very Hebrew thing to do by the way. James was approaching these "conversions" like an easterner. And, of course, the focus was on Moses as the foundation. He told them to listen to Moses – the Torah. Amazingly, most modern Christians do the exact opposite, because of Paul's letters.

Once you learn the Commandments, those texts are the foundation. They are concrete – they do not change, because YHWH does not change. Remember, He is a Rock.

The purpose of things being written down was to remind us so we don't forget. Scriptural texts are there to help us learn about Elohim. They are supposed to teach us His ways so that we can walk with Him and know Him through His Covenant. That must be the focus.

If your focus or desire is anything else, then you will believe lies, be led astray, and fall into traps that lead to destruction. This is happening to many people today, and it has been happening for centuries as a result of Paul's letters.

Peter warned about it from the very beginning. *"14 Therefore, beloved, looking forward to these things, be diligent to be found by Him in peace, without spot and blameless; 15 and consider that the longsuffering of our Master is salvation - as also our beloved brother Paul, according to the wisdom (sophia) given to him, has written to you, 16 as also in all his epistles (letters), speaking in them of these things, in which are some things hard to understand, which untaught and unstable people twist to their own destruction, as they do also the rest of the Scriptures 17 You therefore, beloved, since you know this beforehand, beware lest you also fall from your own steadfastness, being led away with the error of the wicked; 18 but grow in the grace and knowledge of our Master and Savior Messiah Yahushua."* 2 Peter 3:14-18

Interestingly, Peter takes the high road. Despite Paul's treatment of him, Peter remains gracious. While he referred to Paul's wisdom – sophia, He advised people to grow in the grace (charis), and knowledge (gnosis) of our Master and Savior Yahushua.

So, he is not encouraging people to follow Paul. Indeed, he is revealing that Paul's letters are difficult to understand. He states that people are twisting them, as well as the Scriptures. Notice that he distinguishes between Paul's letters and the Scriptures. According to Peter, some of the fruits of Paul's ministry seem to be chaos and destruction.

That is not a great endorsement from Peter, who is clearly directing people to Yahushua as the Master that we are to obey, because He is the one Who saves us.

So, it all comes down to who you serve and who you will obey – that is who you will know. If it is a lust for power or riches, or just simply knowledge, you will find yourself in trouble. There are untold mysteries of the universe that people are chasing after, but it does not necessarily involve knowing Elohim.

This leads us to another ancient issue that has come back into the forefront due to the recent discovery and translation of the Dead Sea Scrolls.

The Dead Sea Scrolls are a collection of documents and fragments found around the Dead Sea region of Israel and Jordan beginning in 1946. Most of the discoveries continued through to 1956.

They were located in 11 different caves near Khirbet Qumran, written in Hebrew, Aramaic and Greek. They are believed to be dated between 200 BCE and 100 BCE. All tolled there are approximately 900 manuscripts, and over 15,000 fragments that make up the texts in the collection. In 2021 some additional texts were uncovered in a previously excavated cave, called "The Cave of Horror" in the Judean Desert.

The popular assumption is that all of these scrolls are attributed to the same group of people gathered as a community at Qumran, near the Dead Sea. The further assumption is that this group was a sect of Jews called the Essenes.

This is probably not the case, and here's why. The texts found in the Dead Sea region were scatted amongst a variety of caves, and not all of them were at Qumran.

Further, there is historical evidence that the Essenes were a smaller sect of Yisraelites that dwelled among other Yisraelites. In fact, there was an Essene Quarter of Jerusalem. There is also evidence that the Essene Community in the Dead Sea region was at En Gedi, which is quite a distance from Qumran.

I believe that the Yahad community at Qumran was different from the Essenes, and the Scrolls found around the Dead Sea cannot all be attributed to one specific group.

The Yahad Community at Qumran was likely a group of priests who identified as Zadokites, and referred to themselves as "Sons of Light." They were likely the ones who wrote a critique of the Temple[261] and shunned the Temple in Jerusalem.

It is important not to be misled by labels though. Just because they called themselves Zadokites does not mean they were following the Torah. Indeed, they were not. They were interpreting the Torah in an incredibly stringent way.

They actually made the legalism of the Scribes and the Pharisees pale in comparison, and took the "works of the law" to an entirely new level.

The Scrolls do not contain one unified theology, but rather a diverse grouping of texts that may have been weighed differently.

It is possible that the Scrolls were placed in some of the caves by a community in Qumran. It is equally possible that these texts constituted precious texts that were stored away by Jews fleeing the advancing Roman armies prior to 70 CE.

They were clearly hidden, and not just stored. So, they could represent the diverse thoughts and ideas that were pervasive during the centuries leading up to the Messiah.

Again, even if there was a monastery copying texts in the wilderness, there is no evidence that they originated there. The texts that may have actually originated with some secluded sectarian group would have been the Temple Scroll, the War Scroll, the Rule of the Community and the Damascus Document, also referred to as a Zadokite work.

That is where we start to get into complexities, because we have already discussed that after the return of the Yahudim from the Babylonian exile, there was not a complete restoration. Things did not go well. Although the Temple was eventually rebuilt, and the Priesthood re-established, Yahudah

---

[261] See The Temple Scroll 11Q19

had no king seated on the Throne from the Davidic Line.[262]

If you examine history during that period, you see a succession of rulers from Alexander the Great, to the Seleucid Empire, to the Maccabees, the Hasmoneans, the Romans and ultimately the Herodians, who were Edomites. The leadership and priesthood were both corrupted and the position of High Priest ultimately fell to the highest bidder.

As a result of the corruption, as the story goes, the Zadokites who were the true priests went into the desert and established their own celibate community, waiting for the end of the world.

While that sounds very pious, the question is whether YHWH approved or condoned these actions. It is important to understand that there is a difference between the priesthood and the Temple, which was the House of Elohim.

YHWH allowed His House to remain in Jerusalem until it was destroyed by the Romans in 70 CE. As far as we know, He didn't move His address out into the desert, and Yisraelites were still required to gather in Jerusalem at the Appointed Times.[263]

There are many people who have more than one house. While they may not reside full-time in a home, it does not mean it is no longer theirs. YHWH still had a House in Jerusalem, even though He was not necessarily residing there at the time. There was no indication that the Ark, or the "shekinah"[264] was present.

Nevertheless, the text in Luke describes Zechariah as a righteous priest serving in the Temple. He did not abandon his

---

[262] Even though Zerubbabel was from the Davidic line, he was only considered to be a Governor. The reason is because despite some Yahudim having returned from Babylon, they were still subject to the Medo-Persian Empire.

[263] It does not appear that the Ark of the Covenant was in the Holy of Holies, and therefore no Shekina presence of Elohim was in the House> So the question is whether YHWH was even home. Nevertheless, the Command was to meet Him where He placed His Name, and that was still in Jerusalem.

[264] The "shekinah" is often referred to as the presence of YHWH. It comes from the root that means "dwell." "And let them make Me a sanctuary, that I may dwell (shakhan) among them." Exodus 25:8

post, and the Messenger Gabriel actually appeared to him while he was offering incense inside the Temple.[265]

Righteous people still visited the Temple, and attended prayers. The Scriptures describe two special individuals, named Simeon and Anna, who met Yahushua and His parents while they were in the Temple.

Anna was described as a prophetess who lived in the Temple. The reason they met is because Joseph and Mary were presenting offerings in the Temple, according to the Torah.[266]

So what gives? Were these people gathering out in the wilderness doing the right thing? Not necessarily. While John the Immerser was teaching and immersing in the east, that was for a very specific purpose. And He wasn't teaching against Jerusalem and the Temple. He was calling people to repentance in the wilderness, in the same pattern as when Yisrael left Egypt and later crossed the Jordan.

So, we have people attributing the Dead Sea Scrolls to a righteous line of priests, and that assumption leads to other assumptions that the Dead Sea Scrolls must all contain truth. This then draws people to read and follow texts from people that Yahushua was clearly opposed to.

For instance, in the War Scroll, they describe themselves as the Sons of Light. These so-called Sons of Light were separated, and would not have financial dealings with those outside of their group who they referred to as the Sons of Darkness.

This was spiritual arrogance and hypocrisy. It was far removed from the original mandate of Yisrael to be priests to the Nations. Sons of Light are supposed to shine as a light to the Nations, not hide that light in the wilderness.

Yahushua was well aware of these teachings, and clearly opposed them. In contrast to their hermitic and secluded lives, Yahushua was accused of being a glutton and a drunk, because He was often mingling with the so-called

---

[265] Luke 1:5-20
[266] Luke 2:22-24

"Sons of Darkness."

In opposition to their teachings, He specifically taught not to hide your light.

> *"[33] No one, when he has lit a lamp, puts it in a secret place or under a basket, but on a lampstand, that those who come in may see the light. [34] The lamp of the body is the eye. Therefore, when your eye is good, your whole body also is full of light. But when your eye is bad, your body also is full of darkness. [35] Therefore take heed that the light which is in you is not darkness. [36] If then your whole body is full of light, having no part dark, the whole body will be full of light, as when the bright shining of a lamp gives you light."* Luke 11:33-36

That is exactly what some of these groups were doing. They thought they were full of light, yet they were in a "secret place" in the wilderness hiding their light under a basket.

We can further tie this statement to the Yahad, because they were so critical and judgmental that they were involved in a practice called Physiognomic Horoscopes. They would ascertain how a person was composed of various parts "light," and various parts "dark" based upon their physical features. Those ratios of "light" and "dark" parts would then determine the person's future.[267]

This is rather bizarre, and completely contrary to the Scriptures. Regrettably, some people are promoting the notion that the people who wrote the Dead Sea Scrolls were Zadokites and they were teaching truth, in opposition to the Yahudim in Jerusalem.

Well, Yahushua did not reject Jerusalem, and continued to go there for the Appointed Times. He also taught directly against the teachings in the Dead Sea Scrolls.

For instance, the Community Rule Scroll, also known

---

[267] See Dead Sea Scroll fragments 4Q186 and 4Q561

as the Manual of Discipline (1QS) begins by saying that members of the community should be taught to seek Elohim and obey Moses and the Prophets so that "they may love all the sons of light, each according to his lot in Elohim's design, and hate all the sons of darkness, each according to his guilt in Elohim's vengeance."

In direct opposition Yahushua stated: "*⁴³ You have heard that it was said, 'You shall love your neighbor and hate your enemy.' ⁴⁴ But I say to you, love your enemies, bless those who curse you, do good to those who hate you, and pray for those who spitefully use you and persecute you, ⁴⁵ that you may be sons of your Father in heaven; for He makes His sun rise on the evil and on the good, and sends rain on the just and on the unjust. ⁴⁶ For if you love those who love you, what reward have you? Do not even the tax collectors do the same? ⁴⁷ And if you greet your brethren only, what do you do more than others? Do not even the tax collectors do so? ⁴⁸ Therefore you shall be perfect, just as your Father in heaven is perfect.*" Matthew 5:43-48

For centuries, people were puzzled by this passage because they thought Yahushua must have been referring to the Torah, yet there is no Commandment to hate your enemy in the Torah. He was specifically referring to those who wrote the Dead Sea Scrolls.

In the Damascus Document, considered to be a Zadokite work the following instruction is given concerning the Sabbath:

"²² No man shall help an animal in its delivery on the Sabbath day. ²³ And if it falls into a pit or ditch, he shall not raise it on the Sabbath."[268]

In direct contradiction to this admonition Yahushua stated:

"¹¹ What man is there among you who has one sheep, and if it falls into a pit on the Sabbath, will not lay hold of it and lift it out? ¹² Of how much more value then is a man than a sheep? Therefore it is lawful to do good on the Sabbath." Matthew 12:11-12

We could go on and on showing how Yahushua opposed many of the teachings of the Dead Sea Scrolls, and we will look at that more when we consider calendar issues in the next chapter.[269]

This critique was included to steer people away from some of the doctrines promoted in the Scrolls, it was not meant to diminish the significance of their discovery. In fact, aside from some of the doctrines being espoused by certain manuscripts, their discovery was quite profound.

First of all, it reinforced the notion that texts were maintained in separate scrolls, so that they could be treated with different weight. There are also many instances that the Scrolls can be used to validate our modern translations of the Torah, and the Prophets.

Prior to their discovery, the oldest Hebrew manuscript for the Torah was the Masoretic text. The oldest complete Torah is known as the Leningrad Codex, dated to around the 11th Century CE. The oldest Torah was known as the Septuagint. It is a Greek translation of the Torah dated to around the 3rd Century BCE.

So over 1,000 years separated these Torah translations in two different languages. When they did not agree, which one held the authority? The oldest copy in Greek, or the newer translation in Hebrew?

When I first started to learn about the importance of reading the Scriptures in Hebrew, I automatically looked to the Masoretic text. After all, the Greeks were pagan and how could we trust a Torah written in their language?

---

[269] The Dead Sea Scrolls contain a variety of solar calendars that do not conform to the Torah by utilizing both the sun and the moon. See Genesis 1:14-16 and Psalm 104:19

Well, there is much authority to show that the authors of the New Testament actually referenced the Septuagint when they quoted Scripture. The discovery of the Dead Sea Scrolls added a new layer of validation, because they contained Hebrew manuscripts that were 1,000 years older than the Masoretic text.

There was one significant example, found in Deuteronomy 32:8 that helped me in my understanding. Here is an English translation deriving from the Masoretic text:

> *"⁸ When the Most High divided their inheritance to the nations, when He separated the sons of Adam, He set the boundaries of the peoples according to the number of the children of Yisrael."* Deuteronomy 32:8 Masoretic Text

We have already quoted this passage in previous chapters, because it is very significant. It is referring to the Tower of Babel when the Nations were first created from the sons of Adam and divided into different groups, with different languages in different geographical locations.

How on earth did He "set the boundaries of the peoples according to the number of the children of Yisrael?" There were no children of Yisrael at that time.

Here is a common English translation from the Septuagint text:

> *"When the Most High divided the Nations, when he separated the sons of Adam, he set the bounds of the Nations according to the number of the angels of Elohim."* Deuteronomy 32:8 Septuagint Text

Here we read that He set boundaries according to the number of the "angels of Elohim." That starts to make more sense. When we read the passage from the Dead Sea Scrolls, it becomes much clearer.

Here is what we read in the English translation of the Hebrew Dead Sea Scrolls.

"When the Most High divided their inheritance to the nations, when He separated the sons of Adam, He set the boundaries of the peoples according to the number of the Sons of Elohim." Deuteronomy 32:8 DSS

So, according to the oldest Hebrew manuscript, YHWH divided the nations according to the number of the "Sons of Elohim."

Who were the Sons of Elohim? Again, they were a category of beings that interacted with creation.[270] In fact they were present at creation, and Job describes the time: *"When the morning stars sang together, and all the sons of Elohim shouted for joy?"* Job 38:7

Remember that some of these Sons of Elohim rebelled against YHWH's order and had relations with the daughters of Adam. That resulted in the Nephilim corrupting the planet that ultimately ended in judgment through a flood.[271]

That corruption is described in great detail in The Book of the Watchers, contained in the text of 1 Enoch.

1 Enoch is a manuscript that was also found in the Dead Sea Scrolls. Fragments were found in Aramaic, Koine Greek, and even Latin. While its existence was known for centuries, the Dead Sea Scrolls brought renewed interest in the text.

Now it was clearly not written by Enoch, and different

---

[270] There is a text referred to as the Book of Yasher that actually described 70 Sons of Elohim going down to investigate the Tower of Babel. They were the "Us" that went down and scattered the people and they were placed over the nations. (see Genesis 11:5-8) The Book of Yasher is actually mentioned in Joshua 10:13 and 2 Samuel 1:18. It provides some interesting insight and backstory, but should be treated with care and discernment.

[271] *"¹ Now it came to pass, when men began to multiply on the face of the earth, and daughters were born to them, ² that the Sons of Elohim saw the daughters of men, that they were beautiful; and they took wives for themselves of all whom they chose. ³ And YHWH said, My Spirit shall not strive with man forever, for he is indeed flesh; yet his days shall be one hundred and twenty years. ⁴ There were Nephilim on the earth in those days, and also afterward, when the Sons of Elohim came in to the daughters of men and they bore children to them. Those were the mighty men who were of old, men of renown."* Genesis 6:1-4

- 303 -

portions were written at different times. Some consider it all to be Scriptures while others do not. Some portions are clearly more reliable than others, and it is dated to around the First Century BCE.

I consider it to be useful, like the Book of Yasher; especially when it supplements some information in Genesis 6. The beginning of the text describes the trouble when mankind formed relationships with the Fallen Ones in order to obtain knowledge.

This is how Adam and Hawah got into trouble, as well. They interacted with the "nachash," and tried to obtain knowledge that was prohibited to them. They got ahead of YHWH - or at least they tried.

The text of 1 Enoch is useful, but not authoritative for me. This is especially true since the description of the calendar in the Astronomical Book portion directly contradicts the Torah. That is why it is important to wait upon YHWH, and follow His plan. Trust in Him to provide what you need. Start with the foundation, and always keep your feet firmly planted.

We have the Torah, and the Torah contains the instructions that we need to follow Him. Yahushua came teaching the heart of the Torah. He opposed many of the teachings being promoted by the varying sects of Yisraelites. He pointed the way of the straight path, and told us to follow Him.

So, our journey involves a walk that is consistent with the teachings and example set by Messiah Yahushua. We have His words, and we need to focus primarily on them.

While it may be intriguing to seek out further revelation that may be found in ancient texts, it is important to use caution and discernment. We need to cling to Him, and not be led astray by letters and texts, whether they are included in the Bible, the Dead Sea Scrolls or elsewhere.

On that note, YHWH provides specific times when we are supposed to meet with Him, and the express purpose of those meetings is so that we can understand Him better, and build that relationship.

We have mentioned the Appointed Times already. They are not Jewish holidays. Rather, they are Covenant appointments. YHWH schedules these appointments, and the question is whether you care enough to keep them. You cannot properly keep them unless you understand His calendar.

While there are a variety of different solar calendars found among the Dead Sea Scrolls, none of them comply with the clear directives in the Torah for keeping the Appointed Times.

This emphasizes the point that just because a document is ancient, does not mean that it is correct. People have gone astray by using those texts to determine time and the calendar. As a result, that is the subject we will be addressing in the next chapter.

15

Time and the Calendar

Throughout this book, we have been exploring how to think and act like Hebrews, within an eastern-styled covenant. That is because our journey out of Babylon is found on the ancient paths that lead us east.

In the last chapter we talked about the Scriptures, and how we need to view ancient writings in their proper context. This is critical in order to stay on the narrow path where we can know Elohim, and walk with Him.

Of course, I hope it is clear by now that "knowing" does not simply involve acquiring information. It involves relationship and action. In fact, knowing Elohim has more to do with the heart than it does the head. Our walk with Elohim is the way that we know Him. It is a relationship that is forged and perfected through a Covenant.

A sign of that Covenant for every male, is the circumcision in the flesh.[272] It is a sign, because it is a reminder that we ultimately must have our hearts circumcised. What starts with circumcision of the flesh culminates with the circumcision of the heart.

That is the lesson we learn through the Scriptures, but we need to actually live it out in our own lives. The Scriptures provide us with instructions on how to live within the Covenant. Those instructions are not a collection of do's and don'ts intended to put us into bondage.

To the contrary, they are a yoke meant to guide us, and keep us on the Covenant path. They are training for the Bride,

---

[272] Genesis 17:11

to show her how to conduct herself in a relationship with a "holy" (set apart) Elohim.

The Scriptures are all about the Creator, YHWH Elohim, wooing a Bride back to Him. They reveal the "courtship" process, and we can either participate in that or not.

An important part of this process involves the moadim – the Appointed Times. Like planning for a wedding, the Appointed Times are appointments when those in Covenant with YHWH are supposed to meet with Him. We will discuss the annual Appointed Times in the next chapter.

We previously spoke about the weekly appointment, which is also a sign of the Covenant – the Sabbath.[273] That is easy enough to observe - every seventh day. We also discussed that the day begins in the evening, after sunset, and continues through an entire cycle to the following evening. A day is a full cycle. Hebrew thought and action revolve around cycles, as we have also examined.

Now there are some who are bringing confusion into the assembly by promoting notions such as the "lunar Sabbath,"[274] or ideas that the Sabbath only involves the light portion of the seventh day. They teach that a day begins in the morning.

These ideas are usually promoted by people who have gotten too caught up in acquiring knowledge, and they feel the need to keep finding "new" revelation. There comes a point that if you are not living your faith, and actually walking out the Covenant, you will get consumed with the information, and possibly overwhelmed.

While most of the world has been deceived by the

---

[273] Exodus 31:13, 17
[274] The lunar Sabbath doctrine is discussed in the Walk in the Light series book titled The Sabbath. It essentially teaches that the weekly Sabbath is tied to the cycle of the moon. Every month the Sabbath cycle is "reset" according to the sighting of the moon. Of course, the weekly Sabbath is clearly separated from the months and the annual appointed times in Leviticus 23:1-4. These people are "mixing" moadim, which is inappropriate and simply does not work.

religions of men, not everything is a deception. I produced a teaching video that you may find helpful titled, *Understanding a Hebrew Day.*[275]

It is simple to establish through the Scriptures that a day includes both the dark and the light portion of a complete cycle of the sun. It is important that we get these fundamental concepts right, because they form the foundation of our understanding of time.

The Torah is like milk at first. We need to simply allow it to nourish us as infants. Likewise, we simply need to follow the instructions, like children. Later, when we grow up and mature, we can handle meat. Some people want to go straight for the desert, when they should remain on milk.

I have seen this repeatedly over the past decades. People start to learn a little Hebrew and some Torah, and then dive into the Zohar. They start exploring Kabbalah and ultimately reject Yahushua as the Messiah. What a tragedy, since it was their belief in Yahushua that led them back to the Torah in the first place. The nachash is always ready to tempt, distract, deceive and ultimately lead people away from the Tree of Life in their quest for "knowledge."

Obviously, the process of leaving Babylon requires some new information, but the leaving part involves action. It involves living the Torah, not just reading books or watching videos. That is what it means to follow Yahushua.

His example was about being a servant, and the entire point of us leaving the shackles of Babylon is so that we can freely serve in His Kingdom.

In case you didn't realize it, Babylon is a very self-centered culture. It largely seeks to feed the flesh. When we are consumed with material substances, the spirit shrivels up and dies. That is when people fail to bear fruit, and they get cut off.

Part of the turning that we see in repentance involves

---

[275] The video *Understanding a Hebrew Day* is on the Shema Yisrael Teaching YouTube channel at https://youtu.be/qvZwFaSMbcI

turning the attention from ourselves to Him and others. Of course, this is why the weekly Sabbath is so helpful. Here is the promise provided through Isaiah:

> "[13] If you turn away your foot from the Sabbath, from doing your pleasure on My set apart day, and call the Sabbath a delight, the set apart day of YHWH honorable, and shall honor Him, not doing your own ways, nor finding your own pleasure, nor speaking your own words, [14] Then you shall delight yourself in YHWH; And I will cause you to ride on the high hills of the earth, and feed you with the heritage of Jacob your father. The mouth of YHWH has spoken." Isaiah 58:13-14

This is a wonderful promise that requires our observing the Sabbath on the correct day. While people may claim that "every day is the Sabbath" or "Sunday is the new Sabbath," we know that is not correct. In order to keep the weekly Sabbath we only need to count to seven. It is a cycle that repeats every seven days.

The seven-day week cycle ending with the Sabbath has continued perpetually since Creation, and is an integral part of the Torah. It is described as a sign of the Covenant.

> "[12] And YHWH spoke to Moses, saying, [13] Speak also to the children of Yisrael, saying: Surely My Sabbaths you shall keep, for it is a sign between Me and you throughout your generations, that you may know that I am YHWH who sanctifies you. [14] You shall keep the Sabbath, therefore, for it is set apart to you. Everyone who profanes it shall surely be put to death; for whoever does any work on it, that person shall be cut off from among his people. [15] Work shall be done for six days, but the seventh is the Sabbath of rest, set apart to YHWH. Whoever does any work on the

Sabbath day, he shall surely be put to death. [16] *Therefore the children of Yisrael shall keep the Sabbath, to observe the Sabbath throughout their generations as a perpetual Covenant.* [17] *It is a sign between Me and the children of Yisrael forever; for in six days YHWH made the heavens and the earth, and on the seventh day He rested and was refreshed."* Exodus 31:12-19

So, this special day is set apart, and it sets you apart. Your participation in this sign is what makes you "holy" (set apart).

Every seventh day is a recognition of the fact that YHWH created everything, and then rested on the seventh day. If He rested, then how can you do anything but rest on the seventh day?

Through this process, we see a fundamental principle of time, linked with obedience, from the very beginning. It is so important, that the consequence for disobedience was death.

The reason is because the camp of Yisrael was a set apart place where YHWH could "dwell" (shekinah) among His people. As a result, they all needed to observe His set apart day. Disobedience would profane the camp, and prohibit YHWH's presence from the camp.

That is why we are instructed to observe the Sabbath in our "place."[276] If we want YHWH to dwell with us, we need to keep our homes set apart.

So our lives are structured within a pattern that began at Creation. We work six days, and then rest on the seventh day. When we join into this cosmic rhythm, we begin to synchronize our lives with the Creator.

Is it any wonder that Saturday is the busiest day in Babylon? Some people work at their jobs. Most people work in their homes, and it is the ultimate "fun day" to cut loose, enjoy

---

[276] Exodus 16:29

life, and be entertained. Most of Babylon is on a cycle that consists of working five days, and playing for two days. While Sunday is considered to be the Sabbath by Christians, they still do not treat is as a day of rest.

It is a very eastern exercise to look at time in cycles. The other moadim (Appointed Times) require not only the counting of days, but also the counting of months and years. In order to do that, you need to know when a month begins, and when a year begins.

This is where most westerners undergo a serious paradigm shift. Raised on a pagan solar calendar, westerners are used to following a calendar that fits twelve months into a solar year that consists of 365 days, 5 hours, 48 minutes, 45.51 seconds.

This is the period of time required for the earth to make one complete revolution around the sun, measured from one vernal equinox to the next.

The vernal equinox, also known as the spring equinox, is something that most westerners pay little attention to – except for western pagans. In fact, I spent much of my Christian life oblivious to the machinations of the calendar that my life revolved around.

I was content using the current Gregorian calendar, created by the Roman Catholic Church, that simply modified the Julian Calendar used by the Roman Empire. I only had to make sure that I got a new calendar every year. Otherwise I would be lost in time. I had no idea who made these calendars, or how they operated.

It is important to understand that these calendars are strictly solar. They have no interest in using the moon. That is because they are focused on a solar pagan system tracing back to Babylon.

The Scriptures actually tell us that the Creator's Calendar operates using the sun and the moon. Here is what we read in a common English translation:

"¹⁴ Then Elohim said, Let there be lights in the firmament of the heavens to divide the day from the night; and let them be for signs and seasons, and for days and years; ¹⁵ and let them be for lights in the firmament of the heavens to give light on the earth; and it was so. ¹⁶ Then Elohim made two great lights: the greater light to rule the day, and the lesser light to rule the night." Genesis 1:14-16

So time is calculated using two great lights. The word for light is owr (אוֹר), spelled aleph (א), vav (ו), resh (ר). The passage does not actually name the great lights, but we can discern that the two lights being referred to are the sun (shemesh) and the moon (yerach).

They divide the day from the night. The moon is difficult to see in the day, but shines bright in the night. The sun cannot be seen at all during the night, although the sun emits the light that the moon reflects at night.

So, they are intimately related to each other and the Earth, but they have different functions. The key to understanding time is that it is reckoned using light, because light is something that can be seen and observed.

The two great lights are for signs, "seasons,"[277] days and years. In other words, they are visible markers that we can see, and they help us keep track of time.

In America we saw how they operate as signs when a solar eclipse crossed the entire nation in 2017. Another one will be crossing the country in 2024. These events create an incredible sign for the nation as revealed in my video titled *Signs in the Heavens*.[278]

A solar eclipse occurs when the moon covers the sun, and casts a shadow upon the Earth. A lunar eclipse occurs

---

[277] The English word "seasons" is often used to translate the Hebrew word "moadim" which means "Appointed Times." So the sun and the moon are used to determine the Appointed Times of YHWH. This was established from the very beginning of time.
[278] https://youtu.be/_VzmDoXxVps

when the shadow of the Earth covers the moon.

These signs are very predictable, based upon the movements of the sun and the moon in a heliocentric model of the solar system, which is the only model that can explain these signs.

I know that there are people promoting the flat earth theory with the zeal and fervor of a religion, but it cannot explain eclipses, especially a lunar eclipse. Some day we will have the answers to many of the questions of the universe. Until that time, I suggest that we stay focused on the Messiah.

Eclipse events have generally been considered to be signs by all cultures throughout history. In fact, because all major civilizations kept track of these events, we are able to synchronize history using timelines from various civilizations.

The two great lights are also for "seasons." That is the word that we read in most English translations, but it is not really accurate. As previously mentioned, the word "seasons" often makes us think about winter, spring, summer and fall. The four seasons are really confined to the tilting of the earth and the light and heat of the sun upon the planet. That is not what is intended in the passage.

The actual word in Hebrew is "moadim" (מועדים), which means: "appointed times." We will discuss the actual Appointed Times in the next chapter.

For now, it is important to know that the two great lights are for scheduling and determining specific appointments with the Creator. The Scriptures provide us with specific months and days for all of them. All except for one.

In order to determine the timing of the moadim you need to determine months, days and years on the Creator's Calendar. This is when it is important to understand the distinction between the Roman Gregorian solar calendar, and the calendar that the Creator operates under using the two great lights.

The annual Appointed Times are specifically connected with the months. You must know what month it is in order to keep the Appointed Times, which occur between month one and month seven every yearly cycle.

So, once you enter into the cycle of seven days, you then join in with a cycle of seven months.

In Hebrew, we read "ha'chodesh" (החדש) when it refers to "the month." A literal translation of "ha'chodesh" is "the renewal." The question then is: What renewal?

It is well understood that this refers to the renewal of the moon. As a result, "ha'chodesh" is often translated as "new moon."

Now some western thinkers who start delving into Hebrew get confused, because the word "yerach" is not present. They want to see the specific words "new" and "moon," but that is not how the Hebrew language operates. Remember, we are talking about eastern thought.

It is not necessary for a Hebrew to see the word for moon, because we are not dealing with the planetary body, but rather a demarcation in time, that happens to be revealed through the first sliver of light on the moon.

We already mentioned in a past chapter about how there are different descriptions for the Torah. The same holds true here. While the word for the heavenly body called the moon is "yerach" (ירח) in Hebrew, the word for the renewal of the light of the moon as a sign, and for telling time, is different. The beginning of the month is "ha'hodesh." These are two entirely different concepts.

The renewal occurs when the first sliver is sighted. This is without question. Some are following after a false conjunction hypothesis that has no basis in history.[279] Sadly,

---

[279] A lunar conjunction is the event when the earth, moon and sun, in that order, are approximately in a straight line. It is sometimes referred to as the new moon, though traditionally and Biblically new moon refers to observance by earth bound individuals of the first visible crescent of rebuilding moon light. The period of time between two lunar conjunctions is the synodic month.

this has people starting the month too early.

It is important to remember that while the Yisraelites did fall away, there were times when they did things right. We have to use those historical precedents to place the Scriptures in context. We can't just create new theories.

The Yisraelites marked the renewed moon by the visible sighting of the first sliver. That is how the greater light and the lesser light show us the month – through light. Remember that they are referred to as signs. A sign is only a sign if it is visible. The moon, during its conjunction phase is not visible, and it can be dark for up to three days. That is not a sign.

Further, the actual moment when the moon is in conjunction would have been extremely difficult for ancients to calculate. It was nothing that could be seen. Since the darkness lasts more than a day, it simply makes no sense that the conjunction would be the point of a renewal. No one would know it unless they were a math scholar or astronomer

To the contrary, when Yisraelites saw the renewal of light - the first crescent - that is what they would consider the new moon (ha'chodesh). They would blow shofars, and set the day apart.

It is important to remember that the day begins in the evening. An important reason for this is because that is when we sight the first sliver of the new moon.

It is just moments after the setting of the sun that we observe the new moon, and thus we know whether it is day one of a new month or not. From that point onward the sun and the moon work in conjunction to count and mark the days of the month.

You can actually look up at the moon any night and fairly accurately determine what day of the month it is until the moon goes fully dark. It takes practice, but eventually it is like having a calendar above your head, courtesy of YHWH.

Once the moon goes dark, we eagerly anticipate sighting the first sliver of the renewed moon to reveal day one of the next month. So we can easily see how both the lights are used for signs, moadim, and days. The final question is years.

Now because the lunar year is approximately 354 days, it does not synchronize with a solar year, which is approximately 365 days. In order for the sun and the moon to both be used to determine years, the ancient Yisraelites used what is often called "the Rule of the Equinox."

Essentially, after the end of Month 12, the Yisraelites would determine the beginning of Month 1 to be the new moon closest to the vernal equinox.

Now we already mentioned the equinox, which is simply a fancy term for the point when day and night are equal. This occurs two times during the year – at the spring equinox and the autumnal equinox.

We know that the Scriptural year is to begin near the spring equinox, because the order of the Appointed Times dictates that the first moadim, the Passover and the Feast of Unleavened Bread, occur in Month 1.

"³ And Moses said to the people: Remember this day in which you went out of Egypt, out of the house of bondage; for by strength of hand YHWH brought you out of this place. No leavened bread shall be eaten. ⁴ On this day you are going out, in the month the abib. ⁵ And it shall be, when YHWH brings you into the land of the Canaanites and the Hittites and the Amorites and the Hivites and the Jebusites, which He swore to your fathers to give you, a land flowing with milk and honey, that you shall keep this service in this month. ⁶ Seven days you shall eat unleavened bread, and on the seventh day there shall be a feast to YHWH. ⁷ Unleavened bread shall be eaten seven days. And no leavened bread shall be seen among you, nor shall leaven be seen among you in all your quarters. ⁸ And you shall tell your son in that day, saying, This is done because of what YHWH did for me when I came up from Egypt. ⁹ It shall be as a sign to you on your hand and as a memorial between your eyes, that YHWH's Torah may be in your mouth; for with a strong hand YHWH has brought you out of Egypt. ¹⁰ You shall therefore keep this ordinance in its Appointed

Time (mo'ed) from year to year." Exodus 13:3-10

Now notice that these Appointed Times are to occur in "the month of the abib."

Many in the Hebrew Roots movement get distracted by a Karaite tradition which teaches that the condition of the barley crop determines the beginning of the year. This is nothing but a man-made tradition, and it adds to the Torah. The Torah simply states that the two great lights determine years - not a barley crop.

This false tradition goes on to teach that the word "abib" refers to a specific stage of barley maturity. That is a subjective determination that must be made by men. Further, men must also determine whether there are "sufficient amounts" of "abib barley" before the end of Month 12 and the sighting of the new moon in order to declare a Month 1.

Of course, the question should be: "Where is any of this found in the Torah?" The answer is: "It is not."

This tradition requires a number of subjective determinations and decisions that do not comply with the Torah. This tradition is so riddled with errors and additions to the Torah, that it should be obvious to people it is an error.

Sadly, many have adopted this false teaching, because they have not fully examined the Hebrew. In the Hebrew we read "the month of **the** abib" (ha'abib), not "the month of Abib."

Abib was not the name of the month in this passage, but rather a time of year. It was the month of the abib, or rather, the time of the abib.

In the Scriptures the days of the week and the months were simply numbered and counted. They were not named until the Yahudim adopted that tradition in Babylon - literally. So, Month 1 was "the month of the abib."

The word "abib" is not specifically tied to barley as the Karaite tradition teaches. The word for barley is "s'orah" (שערה). While barley is generally the first grain crop to ripen, the time of "the abib" is when many things begin to turn green. The word "aviv" actually means: "green, springing forth and renewal of life."

So, what we need to understand is that the Passover and Unleavened Bread occur in the month of the renewal of life, the time of springing forth - the time of green. It is the time we refer to as spring. Of course that word "spring" carries the same meaning as the Hebrew abib (אבב) - "springing forth."

This is particularly significant when we read the Commandment in Deuteronomy 16:1. Here is a common translation: *"Observe the month of abib, and keep the Passover to YHWH your Elohim, for in the month of abib YHWH your Elohim brought you out of Egypt by night."*

This is not a correct translation. It appears that the Command is instructing Yisrael to observe Passover in a month named Aviv. That is not accurate since at the time this Commandment was given, there were no names given to months. The months were simply numbered.

What we read in the initial Hebrew text is: "shamar et-chodesh ha'abib" (שמור את-חדש האבב). Literally it states: "guard the month (the renewal) of <u>the</u> abib." In other watch for the month of new life springing forth, because in that month you are to celebrate the Passover.

Notice the "et" (את) is attached to the "month" (renewal) of the abib. So the Messiah is intimately connected with this time of renewal and refreshing when new life springs forth. We have a time of shedding blood, while celebrating a renewal - death to life. Yahushua was resurrected in the month of the abib.

The question then is how do we watch, guard and keep the month of the abib? Well, we first must recall the way of telling time and keeping Appointed Times found at Genesis 1:14-16. That text specifically provides:

"14 Then Elohim said, 'Let there be lights in the firmament

of the heavens to divide the day from the night; and let them be for signs and Appointed Times (moadim), and for days and years; [15] and let them be for lights in the firmament of the heavens to give light on the earth"; and it was so. [16] Then Elohim made two great lights: the greater light to rule the day, and the lesser light to rule the night. He made the stars also." Genesis 1:14-16

The two great lights are the sun and the moon. The stars are lights also, but they are not used in determining the Appointed Times. We know this because of the treatment received in the text.

Also, since the Appointed Times must be synchronized with the crops and the rains, the forces that determine the seasons are the sun and the moon – not the stars. Indeed, the way to utilize the sun and the moon to calibrate the crops is through the use of the equinox.

Again, the equinox is defined as "the day when both night and day are equal." There are two equinoxes that occur each year, and they are what divide the two seasons – summer and winter.

All ancient civilizations knew how to determine the equinoxes, and actually built it into their architecture. So we use this predictable and consistent point in time to determine Month 1.

The way that we ensure that the sun and the moon are used to place Month 1 during the time of "the abib," commonly known as spring, is through the Rule of the Equinox. That is a popular name ascribed to the method of using the equinox in order to comply with the Torah. It keeps the Feast of Unleavened Bread "in its season" or "at its Appointed Time from year to year."

The determination of Month 1 is critical, because it will determine every other Appointed Time, and the Scriptures actually provide a framework within which all of the Appointed Times must occur.

Two Scriptures provide us with that framework. Exodus 13 details the first critical requirement in synchronizing the calendar, and the cycle of the Appointed Times. It provides the starting point.

The second Scripture is found in Exodus 34, and provides the end point for the conclusion of the cycle of Appointed Times that span between Month 1 and Month 7.

"⁶ Seven days you shall eat unleavened bread, and on the seventh day there shall be a Feast to YHWH. ⁷ Unleavened bread shall be eaten seven days. And no leavened bread shall be seen among you, nor shall leaven be seen among you in all your quarters. ⁸ And you shall tell your son in that day, saying, 'This is done because of what YHWH did for me when I came up from Egypt.' ⁹ It shall be as a sign to you on your hand and as a memorial between your eyes, that the Torah of YHWH may be in your mouth; for with a strong hand YHWH has brought you out of Egypt. ¹⁰ You shall therefore keep this ordinance in its season (moad) from year to year."
Exodus 13:6-10

The "ordinance" being referred to is the Feast of Unleavened Bread. It must occur "in its season (moad) from year to year." So we can see that it cannot happen in the same year as the previous year. It must occur in a new year, and the new year has been associated with "the abib."

The demarcation point between winter and spring, also known as "the abib," has always been the vernal equinox. The time when day and night are equal.

As was already mentioned, there are technically only two seasons in creation – summer and winter. While we talk about springtime, the ancients did not recognize it as a unique season.

The month of "the abib" was the time we refer to as spring, but it was really the transition between winter and summer in ancient times. We see this distinction in the promise given to Noah:

> "While the earth remains, seedtime and harvest,
>   cold and heat, winter and summer,
>   and day and night shall not cease."
>   Genesis 8:22

The Scriptures are clear that there are only two "seasons" built into creation. We see them listed again in the Psalms.

> "16 The day is Yours, the night also is Yours;
>   You have prepared the light and the sun.
>   17 You have set all the borders of the earth;
>   You have made summer and winter."
>   Psalm 74:16-17

Did you notice how the summer and winter are repeatedly compared to the day and the night? That is because they both follow the same pattern built into creation.

Just as the daily cycle has night and day, the yearly cycle has night and day as well. Winter is the season of cold, darkness and death. Summer is the season of warmth, light and life.

The transition between night and day known as dawn, could be likened to spring. The transition between day and night known as twilight, could be likened to fall. It's not a perfect example, but it reveals the transitions that occur within the cycles of time.

That is why we celebrate the harvest Feast of Sukkot at the "end," also referred to as the "tequfah" or "turn."[280] Summer is ending and winter is beginning around the time of the Feast of Ingathering. There we celebrate the fruit harvest,

---

[280] See Exodus 23:16 and 34:22

and consider all of the bounty that YHWH has provided during the summer harvest.

We have a great celebration, and traditionally pray for rain at the end of Sukkot, as we contemplate plowing and preparing for the next cycle of harvests.

The Yisraelites lives were focused and centered around food. They had to be, and YHWH even pegged His Appointed Times to their harvests. So He was all for it.

He wanted them to work hard, stay on course, and on schedule. That is why it is so important to understand the calendar, because it tells us when the appointments with the Creator will occur.

I spent the first half of my life in a religious system that was completely oblivious to the schedule of the Creator. In fact, my religion specifically placed me out of synch with YHWH, and taught me to keep pagan holy days (holidays). It's all Babylonian centered worship.

We need to get into the rhythm and timing of the Creator, and His Creation, in order to step out of the Babylonian system. This is why it is important to become a Hebrew, and view creation in patterns and cycles, as an eastern thinker.

Just as the Feast of Sukkot occurs around a "turn," so too, the Feast of Unleavened Bread should occur after the "turn" (tequfah) of the vernal equinox, and before the "turn" (tequfah) of the summer solstice.

In order to accomplish this, the Yisraelites developed the "Rule of the Equinox," mentioned previously. The "Rule of the Equinox" always places Day 15 of Month 1 on or after the Hebrew Day of the spring equinox. This is how the sun and the moon (the two great lights) act as "signs" and determine "Appointed Times, days and years."[281]

The entire Hebrew Year is determined from Exodus 13:10, and all of the festivals in the year devolve around this

---

[281] Genesis 1:14

directive. If YHWH would have said to keep the Festival of Sukkot "in its season from year to year" then all of the festivals for the year would devolve around Sukkot. YHWH did not say this so all the festivals of the year devolve around Unleavened Bread.

We then look to the passage in Exodus 34, that sets the outer parameter. "*And you shall observe the Feast of Weeks, of the firstfruits of wheat harvest, and the Feast of Ingathering at the turn of the year (tekufah).*" Exodus 34:22

In Exodus 34:22, YHWH says to keep Sukkot at the turn of the year, or "at the tekufah." We interpret this to mean "around the time of" the fall equinox.

So, when the "Rule of the Equinox" is employed in obedience to Exodus 13:10, Sukkot sometimes occurs entirely in summer.

The Gentile nations of Assyria, Babylon and Persia always placed New Moon 1 (Month 1) on or after the spring equinox, whereas the Creation Calendar, using the "Rule of the Equinox," always places Day 15 of Month 1 on or after the spring equinox according to YHWH's instruction in Exodus 13:10.

This is an important distinction because YHWH warned through Jeremiah "*Do not learn the way of the Gentiles; Do not be dismayed at the signs of heaven, for the Gentiles are dismayed at them.*" Jeremiah 10:2[282]

In summary, according to YHWH in Exodus 12:1-2, the beginning of the Hebrew Year is Month 1, which is the month of the Exodus, the month of the abib, and it is the first month of the year to us.[283]

From the command in Exodus 13:10, we must place Unleavened Bread in spring, which means that Day 15 of Month 1 must be on or after the Hebrew Day of the spring

---

[282] Information in this portion is derived from an article from the TorahCalendar website at torahcalendar.com/PDF/Do_Not_Learn_Way_of_Gentiles.pdf
[283] "' *Now YHWH spoke to Moses and Aaron in the land of Egypt, saying,* ² *This month shall be your beginning of months; it shall be the first month of the year to you.*" Exodus 12:1-2

equinox. This idea is the essence of the Rule of the Equinox, and using it fulfills all of the Torah commands concerning the Appointed Times.[284]

It is important to point out that the current modern Jewish Calendar is another traditional man-made calculated calendar developed by the Pharisees. It was developed by Hillel II hundreds of years after the destruction of the Temple and Jerusalem. It does not use the sun and the moon to determine months and years. Instead, it uses a fixed calculated calendar. As a result, it does not follow the Torah, and it is wrong.

Like the Karaites, it adds to and takes away from the Torah. So, if you are following a Pharisaic or Karaite Calendar then you are not following the Torah. You are following a man-made tradition.

This leads us, once again, back to the Dead Sea Scrolls. As explained in the last chapter, the Dead Sea Scrolls do not contain one unified thought process or theology. Instead, they contain a diverse set of documents containing different belief systems.

One of the categories that revealed both commonality and diversity was the issue of the calendar. There were a variety of calendars expressed in the Dead Sea Scroll texts. They were unified in the sense that they were solar calendars, specifically centered on fitting a yearly cycle into the annual solar cycle. They are diverse in how they accomplished that task.

Of course, we already examined how the moon is for Appointed Times, but these solar calendars completely ignore that fact.

Now again, many assume that since the Temple and Priesthood in Jerusalem became corrupted that the Dead Sea "Zadokite" priests must have been doing things correctly. We already discussed some examples of how Yahushua opposed

---

[284] The information pertaining to the Rule of the Equinox was generously provided by the researchers and developers of torahcalendar.com.

them and their teachings. The same can clearly be extrapolated on the issue of the calendar.

The Appointed Times are not simply about time. They involve being at a particular place at a specific time. The Covenant people were supposed to meet at the House of Elohim at His prescribed Feasts (hagim), using His prescribed method of determining time.

The Zadokites went into the wilderness and separated themselves from Yisrael. They rejected the House and therefore they had no need to be in synchronicity with the Appointed Times, because they were not following the Torah. In fact, they were busy adding to and taking away from the Torah through their rejection of Jerusalem and the Temple.

A fairly recent teaching being promoted is that these Zadokites were the true priests replacing the service in Jerusalem, because the Temple was entirely corrupted. Of course, this notion completely contradicts what we read in the New Testament texts.

We already mentioned Zechariah, the Father of John the Immerser. He was a priest who served in the Temple. Both Zechariah and his wife Elisheva were described as *"righteous before Elohim, walking in all the commandments and ordinances of YHWH blameless."* Luke 1:6

Now there is no way that this could be true, relative to a priest serving in the Temple, if they were on the wrong calendar. The Messenger Gabriel actually appeared in the Temple while Zechariah was performing the incense offering.[285]

Again, it is clear that YHWH was not through with the Temple at that point, and He did not authorize some renegade group of priests to go start up a new system of worship in the wilderness.

Yahushua was brought to the Temple after Mary completed her state of uncleanness. Sacrifices were presented

---

[285] See Luke 1:11-20

on her behalf and while they were there, they met Simeon and Anna.

These two witnesses blessed Yahushua and testified about Him. They were righteous individuals who still went to the Temple[286] and Luke records that Anna *"did not depart from the Temple, but served Elohim with fastings and prayers night and day."* Luke 2:37

Yahushua as a child went to the Temple every year for Passover with Mary and Joseph. He would be in His Father's House conversing, asking questions and answering questions.[287]

Throughout His life He went to Jerusalem and taught in the Temple. He sent people to the Temple[288] and He often cleansed the Temple.[289] Yahushua clearly did not abandon the Temple, Jerusalem, or the Appointed Times. That means He was following the calendar of Yisrael, using the sun and the moon.

Maybe if the so-called Zadokites focused on cleansing the Temple as well, they would have shined as a light to their fellow Yisraelites. Instead, they went in the wilderness and prayed toward the sun every morning. They focused on the wrong light, and while they thought they were light, their light did not shine upon anyone but themselves.

The contrast cannot be more profound. On one hand you had a group of self-righteous individuals spewing hatred toward the world, doing nothing about the darkness that they perceived.

On the other hand, Yahushua all by Himself travelled the Land shining the Light of Life to a dying world. He also taught His disciples to go into all the world and spread the

---

[286] See Luke 2:25-38
[287] See Luke 2:4
[288] Matthew 8:4; Mark 1:44; Luke 5:14, 17:14
[289] Yahushua cleansing the Temple is recorded in Matthew 21:13, Mark 11:17 and Luke 19:46. These descriptions are all deemed to be the same event at the end of His ministry. John 2:13-17 records a similar event at the beginning of His ministry. I tend to think that this may have been a regular occurrence when Yahushua went to Jerusalem.

good news – not to go hide out in the wilderness.

Indeed, His disciples continued to go to the Temple even after His death and resurrection. So, I choose to follow the example set by Yahushua and His disciples, and I encourage you to do the same.

Yahushua foretold when the Temple was finished and He predicted that it would be destroyed in the generation that He was speaking to – not before then. There was still a purpose for Jerusalem and the Temple until the judgment of YHWH ultimately fell upon it through the Romans in 70 CE.

Yahushua reckoned time like all of Yisrael did at the time – using the sun and the moon. If there was an error, He would have pointed it out, but He did not. We can safely assume that it was the correct calendar because He walked, taught and obeyed the Torah according to the popular calendar of Yisrael.

With that understanding we can be certain that the day begins in the evening, after sunset and flows all the way through to the following sunset. We can also be certain that the month begins at the sighting of the first sliver of the renewed moon, not during the darkness of the conjunction.[290]

The calendar in operation at that time of Yahushua was the calendar that He used to fulfill the Torah, as He was born and died on certain Appointed Times. After His resurrection and ascension, the Spirit was sent when Yisraelites were gathered in Jerusalem from many nations to celebrate an Appointed Time.[291]

The Set Apart Spirit thus confirmed the calendar of the time. None of these critical events were being fulfilled in the Dead Sea on their solar calendar, rather in Jerusalem on a calendar using the sun and the moon as prescribed in Genesis 1:14-16.

---

[290] These are two false teachings that get people confused and out of synch with the Creator's Calendar. They are dealt with in more detail in the Walk in the Light series book entitled Appointed Times. It is also discussed more thoroughly in the Time and Calendar video series.
[291] See Acts 2. The Appointed Time referred to as Pentecost in most English Bibles is actually Shabuot – meaning "weeks" in Hebrew.

We will discuss the Appointed Times, and His fulfillment of those Appointed Times next.

16

The Appointed Times

In the last chapter we talked about the Creator's Calendar as provided through Genesis 1:14, which uses the sun and the moon. We also discussed the fact that the two great lights – the sun and the moon - were set in the heavens for signs, for moadim, for days and years.

So, the calendar established by the Creator at Creation uses those two lights – period. If you want to tell time like the Creator, you need to strictly adhere to His method of reckoning.

We have seen that the traditional Jewish calendar, and even the Karaite calendar, both add to and take away from the Torah. The sun and the moon alone are used for determining days and months, and we don't need to examine barley crops in Month 12 to determine whether or not we start the new year. Crops do not determine the calendar. The sun and the moon also determine years, and we use them to intercalate the new year – not barley.[292]

The purpose of understanding the Calendar is so that we can properly keep the moadim – the Appointed Times. The Scriptures are clear that *"He appointed the moon for Appointed Times (moadim)."* Psalm 104:19

A special emphasis is on the moon, because the cycle of the moon represents a month. We visibly observe the passage of a month through the phases of the moon. The Appointed Times are all keyed to specific days of specific months, except for one – Shavout (Shabuot).

---

[292] Intercalation is the process of adding a 13th month. This is necessary at times, because of the difference between the lunar year and the solar year.

The annual cycle of the Appointed Times begins in Month 1. That is why we spent so much time examining how to determine the new year according to the Rule of the Equinox. Day 1 of Month 1 starts a new year, and is commonly referred to as "the month of the abib."

We mentioned that aviv does not exclusively refer to a stage of growth for the barley plant, but rather it refers to a time – a season when life springs forth. In fact, the word "abib" (אבב) is really quite significant.

In previous chapters we talked about how the Hebrew aleph bet includes 22 characters starting from aleph (א) and ending with taw (ת).

All of the characters are encompassed within the aleph taw (את) – the Word that represents the Messiah. All of the characters tell a story through pictures - a story that leads to the Covenant represented by the taw (ת).

We also see a progression of words through the aleph bet. While the first letter in the Hebrew aleph bet is aleph (א). It does not form a word until it is joined with the second letter – bet (ב).

The first word that can be formed in the Hebrew language is spelled "aleph bet." The word is "ab" (אב), which means "father." According to the Klein Etymological Dictionary of the Hebrew language "ab" also means – "young shoot or sprout." It refers to the beginning of life.

The second word that can be formed is spelled "aleph-bet-aleph" (אבא). It is pronounced "aba" and means "father" or "daddy." So the first 2 words in the Hebrew language both refer to the father, the source of the seed, and the beginning of life.

The third word in the Hebrew language that can be formed through the aleph bet is spelled "aleph-bet-bet" (אבב) - "abab" or "abib." According to Klein it means "to bring forth shoots, sprout, the coming of spring, refreshing, renewal."

So the root of "abib" is the third possible Hebrew word in the entire Hebrew language, and it is connected with the father. Of course, the Appointed Times are when we are supposed to connect with the Father by meeting with Him and synchronizing with His Covenant Plan.

The purpose of these meetings is so that we can receive life and direction, and ultimately bear fruit for Him. This should amplify the power and significance of the Appointed Times.

So far, we have mentioned the annual Appointed Times, but we have not provided a complete list of these important appointments. Here they are in chronological order as provided in Leviticus 23:

1)   Passover - Pesach
2)   The Feast of Unleavened Bread - Hag Ha'Matzoth
3)   The Feast of Weeks - Hag Shavuot (Shabuot)
4)   Day of Blasting/Trumpets - Yom Teruah
5)   Day of Atonements - Yom Ha'Kippurim
6)   The Feast of Tabernacles - Hag Sukkot
7)   Shemini Atzeret - the Eighth Day

So, there are seven unique annual Appointed Times spanning over a period of seven months, and three are designated as Feasts (hagim). They are literally Pilgrimage Feasts when those in Covenant with YHWH go to the place where YHWH places His Name.

They all are special times that need to be recognized. While three require travel, Hag Ha'Matzah would naturally include Passover, which occurs one full day before that Feast begins. Likewise, Hag Sukkot would naturally include Shemini Atzeret, which occurs the day after Sukkot ends. So, five of the seven actually occur at the House of YHWH.

Now we don't have the time to examine each one of them in depth. I actually wrote an entire book about them.[293] In this chapter, we will look at the overall message being

---

[293] For a detailed discussion of the Appointed Times please see the Walk in the Light series book entitled *Appointed Times*.

transmitted, along with why they are important for everyone in the Covenant.

As mentioned previously, these are not "Jewish Holidays." The religion of Judaism follows the Rabbinic teachings of the Pharisees, which are often different than the Torah.

They add to and take away from the Torah, which is expressly forbidden.²⁹⁴ They developed their own calendar that does not use the sun and the moon. It is simply a calculation created by men.

So the Jews actually have their own Jewish Holidays that mirror the Appointed Times detailed in the Scriptures, but they celebrate them differently and at different times - based upon their own calendar.

Anyone who follows Yahushua the Messiah should not be following the Torah as taught by the Pharisees. They do not believe in or follow the Messiah. As a result, they are not in the Covenant renewed by the Messiah.

Further, they do not celebrate the Appointed Times recognizing Messiah's past fulfillments, or expecting His future fulfillment. Only those following Yahushua the Messiah understand that He came to fulfill the Torah – literally.

We will discuss that more in the next chapter when we further examine the Renewed Covenant. For now, let's review the timing and purpose of the moadim.

Passover, known as "Pesach" in Hebrew, is observed on Day 14 of Month 1. The Feast of Unleavened Bread, better known as Hag Ha'Matzoth, occurs in Month 1 as well, between Day 15 and Day 21. It is a seven-day celebration with Day 15 being a High Sabbath, and Day 21 being a High Sabbath.

"High Sabbaths" are special Sabbath Days within the annual cycle of Appointed Times that are different from the

---

²⁹⁴ Deuteronomy 4:2 and 12:32; Proverbs 30:6

weekly seventh day Sabbath. This is a critical distinction that must be understood in order to determine when the Feast of Shavuot occurs. More on that in a bit.

The first two Appointed Times are separate, with different purposes, but they are often collectively referred to as Passover.

In order to celebrate Passover at the proper time you must firmly understand the concept of a Hebrew Day. While the Roman Calendar begins a day at the in descript point called midnight, Hebrews use the signs in the heavens to determine time.

The Hebrew day begins after sunset. We understand this from the first week of Creation.[295] We know that Passover occurs on Day 14, and we are to begin our observance "between the evenings," also known as "twilight."

Here is the primary command:

"[1] Now YHWH spoke to Moses and Aaron in the land of Egypt, saying, [2] This month shall be your beginning of months; it shall be the first month of the year to you. [3] Speak to all the congregation of Israel, saying: On the tenth of this month every man shall take for himself a lamb, according to the house of his father, a lamb for a household. [4] And if the household is too small for the lamb, let him and his neighbor next to his house take it according to the number of the persons; according to each man's need you shall make your count for the lamb. [5] Your lamb shall be without blemish, a male of the first year. You may take it from the sheep or from the goats. [6] Now you shall keep it until the fourteenth day of the same month. Then the whole assembly of the congregation of Yisrael shall kill it at twilight (between the evenings). [7] And they shall take some of the blood and put it on the two doorposts and on the lintel of the

---

[295] See Genesis 1 as it describes the passage of each day "and there was evening and there was morning."

houses where they eat it. [8] Then they shall eat the flesh on that night; roasted in fire, with unleavened bread and with bitter herbs they shall eat it. [9] Do not eat it raw, nor boiled at all with water, but roasted in fire - its head with its legs and its entrails. [10] You shall let none of it remain until morning, and what remains of it until morning you shall burn with fire. [11] And thus you shall eat it: with a belt on your waist, your sandals on your feet, and your staff in your hand. So you shall eat it in haste. It is YHWH's Passover." Exodus 12:1-11

All of this is the Passover, and all of it occurs on Day 14 of Month 1. It is very clear from this description that the killing of the Passover Lamb must occur at the beginning of Day 14, because the meal proceeds into the darkness of Day 14.

The term "twilight" is also described as "between the evenings." It refers to the time between sunset and total darkness. Since the day begins at sunset, there can only be one twilight per day, and that occurs at the beginning of the day.

All of the ordinances must be completed before sunrise. What sunrise? Clearly, the sunrise following the night portion of Day 14.

While this may all seem obvious at first glance, the Pharisees have clouded the simplicity of the Commandments. Through their traditions, they have created great confusion by redefining "between the evenings" to refer to an arbitrary period of time spanning from when the sun is at its' zenith until sunset.

That has no basis in the Scriptures. It is a pure Rabbinic fabrication. By redefining "between the evenings" they have pushed the Passover to the end of Day 14. As a result, they end up celebrating most of the Passover ordinances on Day 15 instead of Day 14.

This is typical of the Pharisees. They often add to and take away from the Torah. In doing so, they violate the Torah[296] and end up mucking things up.

As stated, the Scriptural definition of "between the evenings" is equivalent to "twilight."[297] If you follow the Pharisaic tradition, you end up celebrating most, if not all, of the Passover during the first day of the Feast of Unleavened Bread, which is scheduled to occur on Day 15 of Month 1. I hope that the error is obvious.

If you can properly distinguish the first two Appointed Times, then you end up celebrating eight days. This is significant, because the annual cycle of Appointed Times ends in Month 7 with eight days – on the Appointed Time called the Eight Day.

So the Appointed Times of the Covenant with Yisrael are couched within distinctive eight-day celebrations that bracket, or encompass, the Appointed Times. We will discuss the significance of this throughout the remainder of the book.

For now, we proceed on to the third Appointed Time, which is also a Feast, known as Shavuot or Shabuot. Interestingly, Shavuot is the one Feast that does not have a specific day and month assigned to it. Rather, it occurs 50 days after the first barley offering is presented during Hag ha'Matzoth.

Some people try to turn that act of presenting barley into a separate Feast called the Feast of Firstfruits, but that is simply incorrect. The presentation of the barley is called the "resheet" offering, and it is made by the priest before the grain harvest begins. It is the first (resheet), and it is the same word as B'resheet – In Beginning.

So the resheet barley offering is the first of the grain harvest. It occurs during the Feast of Unleavened Bread, and

---

[296] "You shall not add to the word which I command you, nor take from it, that you may keep the commandments of YHWH your Elohim which I command you." Deuteronomy 4:2

[297] For a detailed discussion of "between the evenings" see the article titled *Understanding Between the Evenings* at www.shemayisrael.net.

is not a separate feast within a Feast. It is a special event and offering made within the Feast.

The notion that it is a Feast seems to be the product of Messianic teachers who desperately want to peg that event to the resurrection of Yahushua. Nowhere in the Scriptures is do the barley offering described as a Feast.

The "Feast of Firstfruits" is really Shavuot, which occurs after the counting of seven weeks and fifty days. It is specifically called "the day of the firstfruits," and it is defined as a "Feast."

> *"Also on the day of the firstfruits (bikkurim), when you bring a new grain offering to YHWH at your Feast of Weeks, you shall have a set-apart gathering. You shall do no customary work."* Numbers 28:26

As you can see, the word for "firstfruits" used when describing Shavuot is "bikkurim" (בכורים). The bikkurim is the firstfruits of the wheat that everyone brings with them to Jerusalem, after the wheat harvest.

So, the grain harvest begins during the Feast of Unleavened Bread, and culminates with Shavuot when people bring their firstfruits from throughout the Land to the House of Elohim.

Shavuot will always occur toward the beginning of Month 3. It is not only designated as a Feast (hag), it is also a High Sabbath, because no "customary work" is to be performed.

We begin the count to Shavuot on the "day after the Sabbath" during the Feast of Unleavened Bread. That is when the resheet barley offering is made. Here is the Command: "He shall wave the sheaf before YHWH, to be accepted on your behalf; on the day after the Sabbath the priest shall wave it." Leviticus 23:11

Remember that we do not mix weekly Sabbaths with

the annual High Sabbaths.[298] That is a mistake that the Karaites and Boesthusians have historically made. The Sabbath that is being referred to is the first High Sabbath of the Feast of Unleavened Bread. We can confirm that through history, and it was confirmed by the Set Apart Spirit as described in Acts 2.

That event happened on the Feast of Shavuot in Jerusalem, when Yahudim were gathered from all over. We know that they counted to Shavuot from the day after the High Sabbath of Unleavened Bread, which would be Day 16 of Month 1. As a result, the Spirit confirmed that method of counting to Shavuot.

All of the remaining Appointed Times occur in Month 7. Yom Teruah occurs on Day 1 of Month 7. It is a High Sabbath, which means no work is to be done on this day.

Since it occurs on the first day of the month, people would know exactly when Day 1 of Month 7 occurred by looking up and sighting the first sliver of the new moon.

As mentioned in the last chapter, there are some who believe that a month begins at the astronomical conjunction, but that is not supported by history or the Scriptures.

The "new moon" that you might notice on modern calendars is not the same "new moon" (rosh chodesh) referred to in the Scriptures. The astronomical new moon is based upon the conjunction.

It is important to note that the conjunction is the

---

[298] YHWH makes a clear distinction between the weekly Sabbath and the other Appointed Times in Leviticus 23. Here is how that passage begins: "¹ And YHWH spoke to Moses, saying, ² Speak to the children of Yisrael, and say to them: The Feasts of YHWH, which you shall proclaim to be set apart convocations, these are My feasts. ³ Six days shall work be done, but the seventh day is a Sabbath of solemn rest, a set apart convocation. You shall do no work on it; it is the Sabbath of YHWH in all your dwellings. ⁴ The Feasts of YHWH, set apart convocations which you shall proclaim at their appointed times." Leviticus 23:1-4 Notice how YHWH separates and sets the weekly Sabbath apart from the other Appointed Times through a process called resumptive repetition. That is because the weekly Sabbath is based solely on the weekly day count that started at Creation. All of the other Appointed Times rely upon the sun and the moon. And that is why they have their own Sabbaths on specific days which are dependent upon the moon, which starts every month, at the sighting of the renewed moon – not the darkness of the conjunction.

moment when the moon is aligned with the sun and the earth, while it is already in darkness. The alignment itself is brief, but the moon can be in this dark period called syzygy from 1.5 to 3.5 days. So it requires a calculation to determine the conjunction. You cannot physically observe the conjunction, so it is not a visible sign.

It would be impossible for common people to properly observe this day if only a few select astronomers were using the astronomical conjunction to determine the first day of the month.

Of course, it is obvious that was not the case, and that fact will become clear when we discuss the Messiah's fulfillment of this Appointed Time.

Ten days following Yom Teruah is Yom Kippurim – the Day of Atonements. It is a High Sabbath and a very solemn day. No work is to be done and we are commanded to "afflict our beings." Most spend the day in prayer and fasting. It is a somber day that concludes the traditional forty days of Teshuvah, and the ten "days of awe."

At the conclusion of Yom Kippur we enter the season of joy. By this time the fruits of the land have been harvested – the dates, the figs, the pomegranates, the olives and the grapes. The people will then bring the firstfruits to the place where YHWH places His Name to celebrate Sukkot. The last place was in Jerusalem.

We begin Sukkot on Day 15 of Month 7 and celebrate the Feast of Sukkot for 7 days. Only the first of the seven days is a High Sabbath. During these seven days we are commanded to rejoice while we live in temporary dwellings known as sukkas, or booths.

The seven days conclude on Day 21 of Month 7, often referred to as the Last Great Day – Hoshanna Rabbah. Then, the following Day, the Season of Joy culminates with the seventh and final Appointed Time, which is a High Sabbath known as Shemini Atzereth – the Eighth Day. It actually occurs on Day 22 of Month 7.

So, while Yom Teruah is the aleph (א) of the Seventh Month, Shemini Atzereth is the taw (ת) of the Seventh Month. We can see powerful Messianic significance in these Appointed Times of the Seventh Month.

Just as Passover is separate, but connected with the seven-day Hag Ha'Matzoth, Shemini Atzereth is separate but connected with the seven day Feast of Sukkot

So the entire Cycle of the Appointed Times is bracketed by eight days in Month 1, and 8 days in Month 7, and it all culminates on "The Eighth Day" when we are no longer required to live in Sukkas.

Eight represents new beginnings and the fulfillment of the Covenant promise. That is why the Covenant of Circumcision occurs on the eighth day. While this present creation and time is currently focused on cycles of seven, the Covenant Promise points to a future involving cycles of eight.

Now that we examined the various scheduling issues, let's just take an overall view of these times.

In the last chapter, we discussed the Karaite tradition of looking for aviv barley in Month 12, and basically determining the beginning of a new year based upon the existence or non-existence of sufficient amounts of "aviv" barley in the Land in Month 12 before the sighting of the next new moon.

The reason that they do this is because they know that Passover and the Feast of Unleavened Bread are focused on the beginning of the grain harvest in the Land, and the barley ripens first.

Where they go astray is the assumption that they need "sufficient" amounts of "aviv" barley in Month 12 – prior to Month 1 of a new year, properly referred to as the month of "the aviv."

The first three Appointed Times encompass the grain harvest. They span from the barley to the wheat - the resheet offering made by the Priest to the bikkurim offering brought by the people.

When the people come for Passover they make an offering of blood. During the Feast of Unleavened Bread, when they eat no leaven, the Priest cuts and offers the "first" of the grain offering. That starts the grain harvest, and the count to Shavuot.

"You shall count seven weeks for yourself; begin to count the seven weeks from the time you begin to put the sickle to the grain."
Deuteronomy 16:9

No one can harvest the grain until this offering is made. This is where the Karaite tradition can really wreak havoc. If they make an incorrect judgment call, and prolong the harvest by intercalating a Month 13 because they do not believe that "sufficient amounts of barley" exist in Month 12, that could result in people not being able to harvest ripened crops.

There may, in fact, be times when the barley crops appear very young in Month 12, and then a hot spell occurs in the beginning of the following month, rapidly accelerating the growth of the crops.

The important thing to remember is that you do not need barley to be at a specific stage of maturity in Month 12. You simply need to be able to make a resheet offering on Day 16 of Month 1 - the day following the first High Sabbath of the Feast of Unleavened Bread.

The Yisraelites would want to harvest their crops as soon as possible. So you want Month 1 and the Passover to occur as early as possible – close to the equinox and spring, which is the time of "abib."

The point is for the Priest to make the resheet offering during the Feast, so that people can all go home and begin harvesting their crops. A delay could be devastating to the farmers. The Rule of the Equinox ensures that does not occur.

After the Feast of Unleavened Bread, everyone would return to their homes to harvest the grain – first the barley, then the wheat. They would then return to the House of Elohim for Shavuot with their "Bikkurim" - their first-fruits from the wheat harvest.

So, at Passover they come with the lamb. At Shavuot they come with their wheat. This points to how the Messiah would fulfill these Appointed Times. Yahushua renewed the Covenant at Passover, and later died on Passover Day. He sent the Spirit on Shavuot.

Yom Teruah, on Day 1 of Month 7, was traditionally the time when the Kings of Yahudah would be anointed, and their reigns would be reckoned from that date. We know that Yahushua was born on Yom Teruah, and we expect Him to return on that day as well.[299]

The reason is because we see a vivid picture from the Appointed Times of Month 7 regarding the King coming and judging the Nations on Yom Kippur (Day 10 of Month 7), and providing atonement for those in the Covenant renewed by His blood.

After Yom Kippur, those admitted into the Kingdom can come to the King's Palace with their wine, their fruits, and their offerings. They can rejoice together in temporary dwellings for seven days, and celebrate the Marriage Supper of the Lamb.

Then on Shemini Atzeret they no longer need to live in temporary dwellings. When the Covenant is fulfilled, they can move in with the King on the Eighth Day.

We already talked about how the first seven words in the Hebrew Scriptures provide a framework for time, patterned around sevens. Most understand that mankind is given 6,000 years followed by a 1,000 year millennial reign. After that seventh millennium we look to the new beginnings - the eighth day.

Anyone who has ever read the Scriptures from the

---

[299] For a detailed discussion of the birth, life, death, resurrection and ascension of Yahushua, see the Walk in the Light series book titled *The Messiah*.

beginning realizes that mankind has a problem. Man was originally made in the image of Elohim. The man and the woman were supposed to live in the Garden – Paradise. The Garden was a set apart place. The entire earth was not paradise – only the Garden was described as paradise. It was the headquarters of the Kingdom, and the man and the woman were supposed to populate the planet.

"Then Elohim blessed them, and Elohim said to them, Be fruitful and multiply; fill the earth and subdue it; have dominion over the fish of the sea, over the birds of the air, and over every living thing that moves on the earth." Genesis 1:28

The man and the woman were given instructions and guidance, and they chose to disobey those instructions. As a result, these "images of Elohim" were ejected from the house as rebellious children.

Instead of being clothed with light they were covered by death – literally. They were covered, which is "kippur" in Hebrew.

"Also for Adam and his wife
YHWH Elohim made tunics of skin,
and clothed them."
Genesis 3:21

This verse contains an important Hebrew word play. The word for light is "owr" (אוֹר), spelled aleph (א), vav (ו), resh (ר). The word translated as "skin" is "uwr" (עוּר), spelled ayin (ע), vav (ו), resh (ר).

Instead of starting with an aleph (א) as does "light," the word for skin begins with a "ayin" which represents an "eye." The word for "skin" literally represents an "eye" (ע) "connected" (ו) to the "head" (ר).

We know that the disobedience resulted in their eyes being "opened."

"Then the eyes of both of them were opened,
and they knew that they were naked;
and they sewed fig leaves together
and made themselves coverings."
Genesis 3:7

They were aware of their nakedness, but what on earth does that mean? Just what was this nakedness is the subject of much debate. Interestingly, they sewed fig leaves and made "girdles." They covered their sexual organs.

They tried to use plants to cover themselves, but Elohim made them "tunics of skin."

While the common understanding is that they were covered with animal hides, representing atonement (kippur), there is a deeper meaning here. I believe that they were originally clothed with light, and that light was exchanged for the skin that we all have now.[300]

Thus, they were now covered with skin, and naked having their eyes opened through the sin with the nachash in the Garden. Unlike light, this skin gets dry, old and wrinkled. It wears out, and eventually turns into dust. This is how we see the promised curse upon man being accomplished.

"In the sweat of your face you shall eat bread till you
return to the ground, for out of it you were taken;
for dust you are, and to dust you shall return."
Genesis 3:19

So man came from dust and would now return to dust because of his skin. His container of flesh was going to wear

---

[300] This becomes highly significant when we consider the lights set in the heavens that help us to tell time. The moon does not emanate any light of its own. It reflects light, just as we are supposed to walk in the light so we are clothes in light. That is why the Hebrew word for "full moon" is "kisa," which derives from the word for "cover." Two significant Appointed Times occur at the "full moon" when the moon is "covered" in light, as a reminder that we need to be clothed in light. (see Psalm 81:3)

out and fall apart, and eventually disintegrate.

While he was originally supposed to partake of the fruits of the trees of Garden, he had to toil for bread. Bread comes from grain, and this is the pattern back to the Garden that we see through the Appointed Times

We toil for our bread from Unleavened Bread to Shavuot. Then we look to Month 7, when the King returns and provides atonement. That is when we can enjoy the fruit of the Kingdom, and experience New Beginnings through the renewed Covenant. We receive new bodies when we move out of these "sukkas of flesh," so that we can dwell in the presence of YHWH and move back into the House on the Eighth Day.

We cannot survive in the presence of Elohim in our present physical condition. Man is no longer a perfect image of Elohim, he is infected with death. So mankind has a problem.

The question of the ages has always been "How do we get renewed bodies that can dwell in the Garden? And how do we get back into the Garden?" It's blocked by flaming sword wielding Cherubim.[301]

We are provided the answers and rehearsals through the Appointed Times. We were also given patterns and a demonstration of that plan through Abraham, through Yisrael, and through the Messiah.

The Appointed Times are rich with meaning, and this chapter only scratched the surface. When you first start "rehearsing" you won't always understand why. It is a process that we learn from as we walk the Covenant path.[302]

In the next chapter, we will take a closer look at the renewed Covenant, because unless you understand the promise of renewal and a renewed Covenant you will never fully understand the fulfillment offered by the Messiah.

The Appointed Times bring our focus to the nomadic

---

[301] Genesis 3:24
[302] For a deeper dive into the Appointed Times, you may want to read the Walk in the Light series book titled Appointed Times.

and agricultural lives of the patriarchs. They start with the food of the Bedouins – unleavened bread. They conclude with a focus on living in Bedouin structures – sukkas. In the midst of this is the grain harvest, and the fruit harvest.

This is why so much of the Covenant journey begins in the wilderness. The wilderness is the opposite of Babylon. In the wilderness, none of the luxuries of Babylon matter.

We are forced to rely upon Elohim for everything. That is why the nomadic lifestyle in the wilderness is exemplified through the Appointed Times.

They are rehearsals that we are supposed to participate in each year. They are reminders that we are in a different kingdom, and on a different path. We are sojourners, and we have not yet arrived at our destination.

Remember that Abraham left his house in Babylon, and lived like a nomad. He dwelled in tents the rest of his life. His life was the pattern for leaving Babylon, and YHWH established His Appointed Times so that we remember that fact, and stay grounded.

In fact, the Appointed Times could be considered our annual rehearsal for leaving Babylon. Just as the Yisraelites previously left Egypt and entered into the fullness of the Covenant through the Appointed Times, we can expect the Appointed Times to be our guide out of Babylon as we walk in the Covenant renewed by the Messiah.

17

The Renewed Covenant

You should now have a general understanding of the annual cycle of the Appointed Times. They are meant to teach and guide us on our journey out of Babylon.

We have discussed how they are patterns of the Covenant, and the Plan of Elohim, relative to the restoration of all Creation. They are intentionally and intimately tied to the crops and the cycles of time in order to teach us lessons, and prepare those in Covenant for the promised restoration.

The point is that we synchronize these times with the crops when we present the firstfruits of the Land as well as ourselves as firstfruits. This requires us to understand how to determine time.

The Scriptures clearly provide that the two great lights are for "moadim" - Appointed Times. These lights are also for telling time - for days, months and years. Now they were established on day 4, but this is not the first time that we read about light in creation.

These lights of Day 4 are clearly different from the light that was first spoken into creation on Day 1. We read about that light in Genesis 1:3-4

> *"³ Then Elohim said,*
> *'Let there be light' and there was light.*
> *⁴ And Elohim saw the את-light, that it was good;*
> *and Elohim divided the light from the darkness."*
> Genesis 1:3-4

This Light from the beginning that Elohim spoke into

existence was different from the light emitted by the sun. In verse 4 we read that Elohim saw "אֶת־הָאוֹר," pronounced "et-ha'owr."

The aleph taw (את) is connected with "the light" (ha'owr) of the first day. So the light of the first day is clearly associated with the Messiah.

We talked about Adam and Hawah being clothed with light before they were covered with skin. When YHWH breathed life into the man, it is safe to assume that the breath contained light.

The whole point of light is that it is visible. Elohim is Light, and we are supposed to walk in His Light in order to commune with Him. We are also supposed to emit His light as well.

Light and dark were separated from the beginning, and we cannot live with the Creator if we walk in darkness. Man's light was covered, and that covering of death caused a separation. Light cannot commune with darkness, since they were specifically divided on Day 1.

As a result, we need a renewal in our bodies, and a restoration in the relationship between Elohim and man. Just as the moon renews its light, so too, we need our light renewed. We are reminded of this every month.

That restoration process is "rehearsed" through the Appointed Times, and we are provided with lights to point us to these special meetings with the source of Light. From the beginning we are given patterns of renewal. In fact, evidence points to the fact that man was actually placed in a renewed Earth.

For instance, the Earth that we read about in Genesis 1:2 was in chaos - covered with water.

"The Earth was without form, and void;
and darkness was on the face of the deep."

The Scriptures describe it as "without form and void."

In Hebrew, we read "tohu v'bohu" - literally "tohu and bohu."

The Hebrew word "tohu" (תהו) means: "desolation, confusion, empty place, without form, nothing, (thing of) nought, vain, vanity, waste, wilderness." The Hebrew word "bohu" (בהו) means: "empty, void."

So we read about the Earth in a desolate, empty wasteland. This apparently was not how the earth was originally created.

Read what was spoken through Isaiah:

"For thus says YHWH, Who created the heavens, Who is the Elohim, Who formed the earth and made it, Who has established it, Who did not create it in vain, Who formed it to be inhabited: "I am YHWH, and there is no other." Isaiah 45:18

Notice the phrase "did not create in vain." In Hebrew we read "lo'tohu bara." It literally means: "not in vain create." Again, the phrase "in vain" is "tohu" (תהו), which means "desolation, confusion, empty place, without form, nothing, (thing of) nought, vain, vanity, waste, wilderness."

This passage in Isaiah is saying that "YHWH did not create the earth a desolate condition." So then what we read about beginning at Genesis 1:3 seems to be a renewal when light is restored to the Earth.

It appears that there was a past judgment that resulted in the Earth becoming "tohu v'bohu." Indeed, desolation is a term often associated with the after-effects of judgment.

That would explain all of the apparent evidences that we see of past destructions. There are various hypothesis promoted in the geological scientific communities involving six extinctions on this planet. There are fossil records that would seem to support an old earth.

Those ideas are usually founded upon evolutionary principles. They fail to understand that the "extinctions" could have been judgments, as we saw from the flood of Noah.

In fact, Jeremiah actually describes that "tohu v'bohu" is the effect of judgment, and will be the result of a future judgment. "*I beheld the Earth, and indeed it was without form, and void; and the heavens, they had no light.*" Jeremiah 4:23

The removal of light is a common theme in prophetic passages referring to judgment. We already discussed this in Chapter 12, and will examine it again in Chapter 21, titled *Understanding Prophecy*.

We know that there will be a future judgment and renewal, and the book of Revelation actually describes that process of judgment as well a renewed heaven, and a renewed earth after this judgment.

"Now I saw a new heaven and a new earth,
for the first heaven and the first earth had passed away.
Also there was no more sea."
Revelation 21:1

Isaiah also spoke of the renewed heavens and earth.

"For behold, I create renewed heavens
and a renewed earth; and the former
shall not be remembered or come to mind."
Isaiah 65:17

Now many English translations read "new" heavens and "new" earth, but that does not accurately translate the Hebrew, which reads from right to left.

שָׁמַיִם חֲדָשִׁים וְאָרֶץ חֲדָשָׁה ← Hebrew

English → shamayim chadashim v'eretz chadashah

In Hebrew we read "chadash" (חדשׁ), which is the same spelling as "chodesh" (חדשׁ). Recall that "chodesh" (חדשׁ) refers to the renewal of the cycle of the moon. In the plain Hebrew, without Masoretic vowel points,[303] it is the same as the renewed moon.

In fact, Isaiah talks about how time will continue to be reckoned from one renewed moon to another - **after** the renewed heavens and the renewed earth.

> *"And it shall come to pass that from*
> *one renewed moon to another, and from*
> *one Sabbath to another, all flesh shall come*
> *to worship before Me, says YHWH."*
> Isaiah 66:23

It helps to view creation from a Hebrew perspective, rather than a Greek, or western mindset. That is why we spent chapters exploring the Hebrew language and Hebrew thought. Based upon the evidence, it is possible that our present existence is a renewal.

YHWH Elohim is a Creator and a recycler. He doesn't like to dispose of His handiwork. He desires to salvage, renew and restore as much as possible. Then He burns up all the leftover, and begins afresh.

He operates in cycles and renewals, and notice the continuing significance of the Sabbath in Isaiah. The Sabbath remains an integral part of Creation, and that should send a powerful message, since it is a sign of the Covenant.

YHWH is looking for a people who will work for six days, and then rest on the seventh. That is part of the process of being in the image of Elohim. We mimic what He does. We act like He acts. We become set apart, just as He is set apart.

The fact that the Sabbath Commandment involves working six days should not be lost on us. You see, the traditional view of being saved and then floating on a cloud for

---

[303] Up to this point we have not examined "vowel points" because they are not in original Torah Scrolls. They were inserted by the Masorites to show the pronunciation of words, but I believe that constitutes "adding to the Torah." By altering vowel points, one can alter pronunciation, and even the meaning of a word. The Masoretic vowel points have been included in certain passages so you can see them in operation.

eternity is the exact opposite of what YHWH has planned for His people.

We are all presently on a Covenant "job" interview. We are being tried and tested to see if we have the right stuff to dwell with Elohim in His Kingdom. Again, YHWH Elohim is a Creator, and He wants us to be creators as well. He wants us to work and restore – like Him. That's part of being made in His image.

He is not interested in self-centered, lazy, entertainment driven people who only want to have a good time indulging themselves. He wants people who are ready and willing to work hard.

Now here's the rub. Hard work alone is not enough. The people who built the Tower of Babel worked very hard, but their efforts were in direct contravention to the will of YHWH. They were building a great big "mega-church,"[304] but their building project was the opposite of what YHWH wanted.

Likewise, there are many Christians today who are working hard, and think they are doing it for YHWH, but they are simply building another Tower of Babel.

It is critical that we understand the Covenant that was renewed by the Messiah, so that we are actually living as He intended, and working productively for His Kingdom. Understanding renewal is a critical concept to understand. That is why it was built into creation and time.

The cycle of a day involves renewal, the cycle of the week involves renewal, the cycle of the month involves renewal, and the cycle of the year involves renewal. We even see renewals through the seven-year Shemittah cycle, and the fifty year Jubilee cycle.[305]

YHWH actually provided two great lights in the heavens that renew and provide markers for time. Created

---

[304] It is generally understood that the Tower of Babel was an enormous Ziggurat, which was a sort of Mesopotamian Temple.
[305] See Leviticus 25

time operates in cycles, as do the lives of created men. Mankind lives within a framework involving cycles of days, months and years. The individual life begins lives with dust and ends in dust.

The seed of man would continue to pass through these cycles of renewal. Through the generations of mankind, and time, we see the patterns of renewal and restoration that lead back to the Garden.

We actually see this process lived out through the life of Abram. Abram originated in Babylon. He was uncircumcised when he was given a promise. By faith, he acted on that promise, and literally left Babylon.

Tradition holds that his father Terah was originally an idolater, and that Abram destroyed his idols. While his father, failed to cross over and completely exit Babylon, Abram did. He crossed over, and passed through the waters of the Euphrates east of the Promised Land. That is where we get the meaning of Hebrew as "one who crosses over."

After he crossed over on his way out of Babylon, he had to cross over the Jordan to enter in to the Land. These "crossing over" events have been memorialized through the process known as "immersion." As he left Babylon, he washed Babylon off of him, and as he entered into the Land he immersed in preparation for the Covenant.

A Hebrew is one who hears the voice of Elohim, and is willing to uproot, and go plant new "roots" (shoreshim). A Hebrew is willing to cross boundaries, and pass through the waters to follow YHWH. A Hebrew is a sojourner.

After Abram crossed over the Jordan and began to settle into the land of Canaan, he entered into a blood covenant with YHWH.

Abram first prepared the slaughterings.

"9 So He said to him, Bring Me a three-year-old heifer, a three-year-old female goat, a three-year-old ram, a turtledove, and a young pigeon. 10 Then he brought all

these to Him and cut them in two, down the middle, and placed each piece opposite the other; but he did not cut the birds in two. " And when the vultures came down on the carcasses, Abram drove them away." Genesis 15:9-11

The specific terms of the Covenant were recited:

"*12 Now when the sun was going down, a deep sleep fell upon Abram; and behold, horror and great darkness fell upon him. 13 Then He said to Abram: Know certainly that your descendants will be strangers in a land that is not theirs, and will serve them, and they will afflict them four hundred years. 14 And also the nation whom they serve I will judge; afterward they shall come out with great possessions. 15 Now as for you, you shall go to your fathers in peace; you shall be buried at a good old age. 16 But in the fourth generation they shall return here, for the iniquity of the Amorites is not yet complete." Genesis 15:12-16*

The Covenant was about descendants and land. After the terms were stated, it was formalized:

"*17 And it came to pass, when the sun went down and it was dark, that behold, there appeared a smoking oven and a burning torch that passed between those pieces. 18 On the same day YHWH made a covenant with Abram saying: To your descendants I have given this land, from the river of Egypt to the great river, the River Euphrates 19 the Kenites, the Kenezzites, the Kadmonites, 20 the Hittites, the Perizzites, the Rephaim, 21 the Amorites, the Canaanites, the Girgashites, and the Jebusites." Genesis 15:17-21*

There were clean animals, cut in two with a channel of

blood in the middle. The smoke and the fire passed between the cuttings.

The "smoking oven" in Hebrew is "tannur ashan" (עֲשַׁן תַּנוּר), and is more akin to a firepot. It is used for cooking. The "burning torch" is "esh lapid" (לַפִּיד אֵשׁ) - literally "fire torch."

So you have fire for light in the darkness, and an appliance for cooking. Everything you need for a cookout, or should I say – a covenant meal.

This is the Covenant involving fire that we saw in the very first word of the Torah – Beresheet (בְּרֵאשִׁית). Indeed, this word is simply a combination of the word for "covenant" (בְּרִית), and the word for fire (אֵשׁ).

This was the same smoke and fire that would later lead Yisrael out of Egypt, when they passed through the waters of the Red Sea on their way to the Promised Land. It was a constant reminder of the Covenant made with Abram.

Unlike a normal middle eastern blood covenant, both parties did not pass through the pieces. Abram did not pass through the eight pieces of the sacrifices, and the blood.

Typically both parties would pass through the pieces, symbolizing the fact that the one violating the Covenant would end up dead - like the pieces.

In this case, we can discern that Yahushua, as the Word, passed through and would suffer the penalty of death. By passing through the pieces and the blood, He demonstrated that He would pay the price for breaking the Covenant.

Here is how it reads in modern Hebrew texts:

כָּרַת יְהוָה אֶת־אַבְרָם בְּרִית ← Hebrew

English → "karath YHWH et-Abram brit"

In the Hebrew text we read "cut YHWH et-Abram covenant." The aleph taw (אֵת) stands between YHWH and Abram.

Yahushua the Son of Elohim, represented YHWH and

passed through the blood. He took upon Himself the penalty of death associated with a violation of the Covenant. He assumed the penalty for both parties.

Yahushua passed through the blood while Abram was placed into a "deep sleep." The word is "tardemah" (תרדמה) in Hebrew, and it is the same word used to describe Adam in a "deep sleep" when Hawah was taken out of him.[306]

This was intentional because YHWH was in the process of creating a family to fill His House through this Covenant made by His Son. This was all revealed in the beginning – B'resheet.

A traditional blood covenant involved a meal. You would cook and eat the sacrifice to "seal the deal" so to speak. While the text does not specifically mention a meal, the fact that a fire and a firepot were present seems to imply that the pieces were cooked, consumed and/or burned up.

This event was the basis for the Temple service that Yisrael would later incorporate into their worship of YHWH, after they came out of Egypt in fulfillment of the Covenant.

Interestingly, Abram later rehearsed that promise. He went to Egypt where his bride (Sarai) was taken captive by Pharaoh. Pharaoh was plagued and Abram was delivered from Egypt with great riches, along with Hagar. In Hebrew, the name Hagar literally means "ha'ger" – the stranger.

Hagar was a stranger to the Covenant, but she was grafted in by becoming the woman of Abram. Again, this was a pattern that would later be repeated by Yisrael.

After returning to the Promised Land, we see Abram and Saria receiving new names at the time of the Covenant of Circumcision.

A "hey" (ה) was added to each of their names. The "hey" often represents the "breath" or "spirit" and by each of them receiving a "hey" and a new name, it represents becoming renewed creations by being filled with the Spirit.

---

[306] See Genesis 2:21

They essentially became "new creations" when YHWH entered into the Covenant of Circumcision.

Abram (אברם) was given a new name: Abraham (אברהם). Sarai (שרי) was given a new name: Sarah (שרה).

Through this union would come the promised son of the Covenant. That promised son, Isaac would later be offered up by his father on the mountains of Moriah in the region where Jerusalem is now located.

Of course, he was familiar with that region, because that was where he previously tithed to Melchizedek and received the blessing. Through these patterns we can see how YHWH would solve the problem that plagued man after the fall.

As the Covenant continued through Isaac to His son Jacob, later renamed Yisrael, we could see YHWH continue the patterns of renewal through the cycles of time. The renewal of the Covenant would be revealed through the moadim – the Appointed Times. These times would act as "rehearsals" for a future redemption.

When YHWH was ready to fulfill the Promise made to Abram, He sent a messenger. Moses provided instructions for how to cooperate with YHWH in the plan of Redemption. The Children of Yisrael had to remain set apart, and meticulously follow the instructions if they wanted to be saved.

They were protected from the last seven plagues rendered upon Egypt. The final one being the death of the first born. YHWH protected the first born of Yisrael by the blood of the Lamb at Passover. He then delivered Yisrael through the Feast of Unleavened Bread along with "ha'ger" – the strangers, referred to as a "mixed multitude."[307]

He led them all to Mount Sinai to enter into a Marriage

---

[307] "A mixed multitude went up with them also, and flocks and herds - a great deal of livestock." Exodus 12:38

Covenant at the Appointed Time of Shavuot. This is something I missed during my entire time in the Christian Church. I never realized that Sinai was a wedding ceremony.

While I was taught that "the Church" was the Bride of Christ, I was never taught that Yisrael was the Bride of YHWH. Without that critical piece of information, it is impossible to understand prophecy, and the Covenant plan of Elohim.

The "marriage ceremony" at Sinai included "vows" and obligations. If you have ever gone to a wedding, you probably heard the bride and groom exchange certain promises to one another.

In eastern cultures, those "vows" were actually written as terms of the marriage covenant, often called a "ketubah" (writing). They were not just a bunch of flowery words spoken at a ceremony, and later forgotten. Rather, they were promises that laid the foundation for the relationship, and both parties were expected to fulfill their obligations.

That is why we are given the real-life experience of marriage, so that we can understand, and rehearse, this most significant part of the Covenant with YHWH.

At Sinai, YHWH spoke the Ten Words, and He wrote the ketubah (the marriage contract) on tablets of stone. Yisrael soon broke the Covenant and betrayed her vows by committing adultery/idolatry with the Egyptian gods through the golden calf. She played the harlot while Moses was still mediating the Marriage Covenant. They never got to the honeymoon.

Through Moses, YHWH allowed for the Covenant to be renewed when he descended the last time from Sinai on Yom Kippur (Day of Atonement) with two new tablets. This was not a final and perfect solution though.

All of Yisrael could not enter the House of Elohim – only the Levites, who represented the firstborn of Yisrael. So while the Covenant was renewed, Yisrael would not experience the intimacy originally intended through the marriage.

Another renewal was required to enter into the inner sanctum, the marriage chamber, represented by the Holy of Holies. That would require another Mediator – a different High Priest.

Yisrael eventually entered into the Land, although she was fractured and divided. Through King David the tribes were united into a cohesive Kingdom, but that would only last through his son Shlomo.

Because of the sin of Shlomo, the Kingdom was divided in two: 1) The Northern Tribes – The House of Yisrael, and 2) The Southern Tribes – The House of Yahudah. Those two Kingdoms both fell away from YHWH and sinned. They were punished and exiled separately.

The prophets promised a day when a Son of David would gather the Tribes together and, once again, join the Tribes of Yisrael into a united Kingdom, and back into a Covenant relationship with YHWH.

There is no Husband/Bride relationship outside of the Covenant that originated with Abram, and flowed through Yisrael. That is where Christianity runs afoul. They claim that Jesus came and made a "brand new" covenant with the Christian Church, which has no basis in truth whatsoever.

What was promised through the Prophets was a "renewed Covenant" with Yisrael.[308] Through the Covenant relationship with Yisrael, YHWH made a way for His Son to enter into that Covenant through Yahudah, and later renew that Covenant with all Yisrael. He did that by fulfilling the patterns of the Appointed Times.

We know that He first came on Yom Teruah - Day 1 of Month 7. At the moment of His birth, the Revelation 12 sign was occurring in the heavens over Jerusalem at the sighting of the renewed moon.

---

[308] See Jeremiah 31:31-36

"¹ Now a great sign appeared in heaven: a woman clothed with the sun, with the moon under her feet, and on her head a garland of twelve stars. ² Then being with child, she cried out in labor and in pain to give birth." Revelation 12:1-2

We saw a lot of chatter about a sign on September 23, 2017, but what many failed to realize is that Revelation 12 is talking about the birth of the Son through the woman Yisrael.[309]

That sign occurred at the birth of Yahushua on Yom Teruah - September 11, 3 BCE.[310] Yahushua was actually birthed when the light of the renewed moon was revealed. I hope you can absorb the impact of that truth.

While Yahushua walked and taught with the people of Yahudah it is important to realize that the House of Yisrael was still in exile, although He made it clear that He came for the lost sheep of the House of Yisrael.[311]

Most Christians have no idea what to think of that statement, because they do not understand the history of Yisrael, or the prophecies concerning the House of Yisrael.

Yahushua renewed the Covenant at Passover with twelve disciples present, representing all twelve tribes of Yisrael – both houses.

Some attempt to perform acrobats with the timing of the Last Supper. I have to say that when I first realized that the Last Supper was a Covenant meal, it all began to fall into place. It connected what Yahushua was doing with the ancient Covenant with Yisrael.

That is why He had twelve disciples present, and Judas (Yahudah) would betray Him, just as the House of Yahudah, in large part, rejected Him. Passover was the perfect time to

---

[309] This is discussed in greater detail in my YouTube video titled *Revelation 12 Sign*.
[310] For a detailed description of the signs that occurred surrounding the birth of the Messiah see the Walk in the Light series book titled *The Messiah*.
[311] *"I was not sent except to the lost sheep of the House of Yisrael."* Matthew 15:24

renew the Covenant.

I later came across some teachers who tried to say that the Last Supper was not a Passover meal after all. They wanted desperately for Yahushua to die before the Passover meal, so that He could die when the Passover Lambs were being slaughtered.

It makes for good theater, but that position does not concur with the texts, which all point to the fact that Yahushua prepared for a Passover meal, and conducted a Passover meal.

Read the account in Luke as they prepared for the Passover meal.

"⁷ Then came the Day of Unleavened Bread, when the Passover must be killed. ⁸ And He sent Peter and John, saying, Go and prepare the Passover for us, that we may eat. ⁹ So they said to Him, Where do You want us to prepare? ¹⁰ And He said to them, Behold, when you have entered the city, a man will meet you carrying a pitcher of water; follow him into the house which he enters. ¹¹ Then you shall say to the master of the house, The Teacher says to you, Where is the guest room where I may eat the Passover with My disciples? ¹² Then he will show you a large, furnished upper room; there make ready. ¹³ So they went and found it just as He had said to them, and they prepared the Passover. ¹⁴ When the hour had come, He sat down, and the twelve apostles with Him. ¹⁵ Then He said to them, With fervent desire I have desired to eat this Passover with you before I suffer; ¹⁶ for I say to you, I will no longer eat of it until it is fulfilled in the kingdom of Elohim. ¹⁷ Then He took the cup, and gave thanks, and said, Take this and divide it among yourselves; ¹⁸ for I say to you, I will not drink of the fruit of the vine until the kingdom of Elohim comes. ¹⁹ And He took bread, gave thanks and broke it, and gave it to them, saying, This is My body which is

given for you; do this in remembrance of Me. ²⁰ Likewise
He also took the cup after supper, saying, This cup is the
renewed Covenant in My blood, which is shed for you."
Luke 22:7-20

This was absolutely a Passover meal. It is important to recognize that the terms Unleavened Bread and Passover are used interchangeably. That is because those two moadim are so intimately connected.

There was no mention of Lamb, because Yahushua was the Lamb. He was using the Bread and the wine to demonstrate that fact. The reason why this is significant is because it hearkens back to the ancient covenant procedure. Promises were made, and then a meal consummated the covenant.

Since Yahushua had previously passed through the cuttings while Abram was asleep, Yahushua later allowed Himself to be killed. He bore the penalty of the Covenant that was made before Abram was circumcised. That was appropriate since the House of Yisrael was out of the Covenant, among the nations, in a uncircumcised state.

This was all about renewal with Yisrael, and the twelve disciples representing the twelve tribes. Again, Judas (Yahudah) betrayed Yahushua, and it was the House of Yahudah that specifically rejected Him, and continues to reject Him to this day through their adopted religion of Judaism.

That is why the language of the renewed Covenant treats the House of Yahudah and the House of Yisrael separately. This was fulfilling the promise of a renewal given by Jeremiah.

"³¹ Behold, the days are coming, says YHWH, when
I will make a renewed covenant with the House of
Yisrael and with the House of Yahudah - ³² not
according to the covenant that I made with their
fathers in the day that I took them by the hand to

lead them out of the land of Egypt, My covenant
which they broke, though I was a husband to them,
says YHWH. [33] But **this is the Covenant that I will
make (cut) with the את-House of Yisrael** after those
days, says YHWH: I will put My Torah in their
minds, and write it on their hearts; and I will be
their Elohim, and they shall be My people. [34] No
more shall every man teach his neighbor, and every
man his brother, saying, "Know YHWH,' for they
all shall know Me, from the least of them to the
greatest of them, says YHWH. For I will forgive
their iniquity, and their sin I will remember no more.
[35] Thus says YHWH, Who gives the sun for a light
by day, the ordinances of the moon and the stars for
a light by night, Who disturbs the sea, and its waves
roar (YHWH of hosts is His Name): [36] If those
ordinances depart from before Me, says YHWH,
Then the seed of Yisrael shall also cease from being
a nation before Me forever." Jeremiah 31:31-36

Notice the distinction between the House of Yisrael
and the House of Yahudah? Also, notice the connection with
the ordinances of time?

While Genesis 1:14 only mentioned the two great lights
- the greater light and the lesser light - this passage specifically
identifies those bodies. It names the sun – "shemesh" (שמש) and
the moon – "yerach" (ירח).

These ordinances are there for time and the Appointed
Times, so that Yisrael can meet with YHWH. Again, it all
comes back to the Covenant. The Appointments are for those
in the Covenant.

Yahushua specifically stated that He came for the lost
sheep of the House of Yisrael. So the process of restoring
mankind back to Eden involves a Covenant that is renewed
and refined throughout time.

This is what many Christians completely fail to

understand regarding the Covenant renewed by the Messiah. He was **renewing** the Covenant with the House of Yisrael, and the House of Yahudah.

He was not making a **brand new** Covenant with the Christian Church. There is no mention of a covenant with a new entity called "the Church."

In fact, we can see this clearly from the text, and also by the fact that in Hebrew we read, I will cut a "brit chadashah" – ברית חדשה.

Remember that the word for "covenant" is "brit" (ברית). The Hebrew word "hadashah" means "renewed." It shares the same root of the word "chodesh," which refers to the "renewed moon."

Now it is important to mention that the word "hadash" can also mean new, and in a sense there was a newness to what was happening. For instance, while it is the same moon that we see every month, it is a brand new cycle of the moon when we sight the first sliver. When the day is renewed, it is a brand new day, and different from the previous day – although it is still a day.

Likewise, what Yahushua was doing was new, in the sense that it had never been done before. Yet His renewal still occurred within the framework of the previous Covenant made with Abraham. So when we speak of "renewal" we must remember these distinctions.

While Yahushua was doing something new through His flesh and blood, it still involved the same Covenant terms, and the same Covenant parties - the House of Yisrael and the House of Yahudah.

After renewing the Covenant at the Passover meal, Yahushua then died later on Passover Day, according to the terms of the Covenant that He made with Abram.

He was then resurrected and taken up, after forty days, as described in Revelation:

"She bore a male Child who was to rule all nations

with a rod of iron. And her Child was
caught up to Elohim and His throne."
Revelation 12:5

Yahushua didn't remain permanently here on Earth, because the punishment period for the House of Yisrael had not been completed. There could be no remarriage until the Bride was permitted to return to the Land.

As a result, Yahushua sent the Spirit on Shavuot. Recall, that is the same Appointed Time associated with the giving of the Torah, which included the terms of the original Wedding Covenant at Sinai.

So, Yahushua was equipping the Bride. The Spirit was sent according to the renewed Covenant, so that the Torah could be "in our minds and on our hearts." Now we look forward to returning to a right relationship – the one anticipated before the golden calf event at Sinai.

Never forget that Sinai was a wedding ceremony. That Covenant process was disrupted and broken. While there was a subsequent renewal at Sinai through Moses, that renewal was not the relationship originally desired by YHWH. It was the same terms, written on different stones presented by a man- Moses.

YHWH was interested in the firstborn of Yisrael representing their families before Him. That was how it all began in Egypt, at the Passover.

Moses and Aharon were from the Tribe of Levi. Because the Levites joined with Moses after the sin of the golden calf, YHWH chose the Levites to represent the firstborn as mediators. Since Aharon was involved in the sin, the Levites would serve without a tribal inheritance, different from the others.

We see the pattern of a mediator set in place at Sinai, but the Covenant needed to be renewed and elevated in order to be perfected and restored. In fact, a pattern and prophetic promise involving Moses was provided through Moses.

"15 YHWH your Elohim will raise up for you a Prophet like me from your midst, from your brethren. Him you shall hear, 16 according to all you desired of YHWH your Elohim in Horeb in the day of the assembly, saying, Let me not hear again the voice of YHWH my Elohim, nor let me see this great fire anymore, lest I die. 17 And YHWH said to me: What they have spoken is good. 18 I will raise up for them a Prophet like you from among their brethren, and will put My words in His mouth, and He shall speak to them all that I command Him. 19 And it shall be that whoever will not hear My words, which He speaks in My Name, I will require it of him. 20 But the prophet who presumes to speak a word in My Name, which I have not commanded him to speak, or who speaks in the name of other gods, that prophet shall die." Deuteronomy 18:15-20

Moses is intimately connected with the Torah, so we should expect one speaking and teaching the Torah. That is why we are supposed to **listen** to Him.

Regardless of what Christianity teaches, Yahushua came teaching the Torah. In fact, He was the Torah in the flesh. His words were completely consistent with Moses. In fact, He was taking it to the next level by teaching the heart of the Torah.

Instead of words on stone tablets and scrolls, Yahushua was teaching how the Torah must be "in our minds and on our hearts." That is what Jeremiah prophesied concerning the renewed Covenant.

A good example of this is found in His teachings recorded in Matthew 5:21 – 6:7. Those teachings were couched in between His statement that He did not come to destroy the Torah, and His instructions regarding how to pray. The renewed Covenant was all about the Torah, and He empowered His followers to obey by sending the Spirit.

Not all is fulfilled, and we await the return of Yahushua as a conquering King. He actually revealed Himself to John after the resurrection, and described that fulfillment through the text known as the Revelation.

The Book of Revelation describes the plagues upon the world that will result in the deliverance of the Bride of the Messiah. This will be an "exodus event" on a greater scale than what happened in Egypt, thus fulfilling the pattern of the previous deliverances from Egypt.

This was prophesied by Jeremiah.

> "*14* *Therefore behold, the days are coming, says YHWH, that it shall no more be said, YHWH lives who brought up the children of Yisrael from the land of Egypt, *15* but, YHWH lives who brought up the children of Yisrael from the land of the north (tzephon) and from all the lands where He had driven them. For I will bring them back into their land which I gave to their fathers." Jeremiah 16:14-15*

When we view this future deliverance in the context of the Exodus from Egypt, we see the deliverance occurring through the grain harvest.

Now it is significant to point out that it is believed that the plagues upon Egypt occurred over a period of 6 months prior to the Passover. If that is true, the judgments rendered upon Egypt likely began around Day 10 of Month 7 the year prior - on or around Yom Kippur.

This is something to remember when we consider a future fulfillment of these patterns. The Book of Revelation is actually describing something similar to what happened in Egypt – except on a worldwide scale. It is describing a simultaneous judgment upon the Earth, and a harvesting of the planet.

Of course, as mentioned previously, the Appointed Times are specifically connected with the harvest cycles of the Covenant Land. They are rehearsals and celebrations of a renewal, and the Final Harvest.

This is why the calendar begins in the Month of "the aviv." It is the time of new life springing forth, marking the renewal of the year. Through the patterns of the Appointed Times, and renewal through the cycles of time, we can see the plan of YHWH flowing through the ages and guiding us back to the Garden – the Renewed Jerusalem

Remember that the Garden involved working and dwelling in the presence of Elohim. It also included food. The food in the Garden was the fruit of the trees. Only after being expelled from the Garden did man have to work the ground for food.

> " . . . therefore YHWH Elohim sent him out of the garden of Eden to till the ground from which he was taken." Genesis 3:23

From that point on we see two distinct crops and seasons: 1) grain, and 2) fruit. These are very different crops, and very different harvests.

The grain crops required annual preparation of the soil by tilling and planting. Then you needed the rains to come at precise times – the former and latter rains. When the crops were ready you needed to cut, gather, thresh and winnow. You then needed to store the grain and have seed for the next harvest, because the entire process had to begin again - from scratch.

Obviously, the fruits are much different. They involved trees and vines that were already matured. All you needed to do was watch over them and prune them. That was the situation that was originally presented to Adam in the Garden.

Because of the sin of the garden, mankind must now toil every year for the grain to make the bread that sustains him. YHWH showed that He is willing to free us from that toiling when he provides us with Bread from Heaven – manna That is why Messiah was born in Beit Lechem (Bethlehem) – "house of bread."

Yahushua referred to Himself as "the Bread of Life." Further, the grain harvest begins during the Feast of Unleavened Bread, when the first (resheet) offering is made by the Priest.

"⁹ And YHWH spoke to Moses, saying, ¹⁰ Speak to the children of Yisrael, and say to them: When you come into the land which I give to you, and reap its harvest, then you shall bring a את-omer of the firstfruits of your harvest to the priest." Leviticus 23:9-10

In the Hebrew we read "et-omer resheet" (עמר ראשית-את). This is a hint that Yahushua is the first offering. It begins the grain harvest and He is the first of the harvest that ends with the "bikkurim" (firstfruits) of the wheat from throughout the Land.

I hope you can see the pattern. The barley is considered the lowest of the grains, and is preferably given to animals for feed. It is humble, and represents Yahushua coming as a lowly servant to offer Himself. He can then later collect His wheat.

Remember what John the Immerser said:

"His winnowing fan is in His hand,
and He will thoroughly clean out His threshing floor,
and gather His wheat into the barn;
but He will burn up the chaff with unquenchable fire."
Matthew 3:12

That is why Yahushua gave the parables concerning the wheat and the tares (weeds). His Covenant people are the wheat harvest. The Messiah will reap His people during the wheat harvest. It will be through a renewed cycle of the harvest, but it will be a brand new harvest fulfilled in a brand new way.

> *"⁴ Then I looked, and behold, a white cloud, and on the cloud sat One like the Son of Man, having on His head a golden crown, and in His hand a sharp sickle. ¹⁵ And another messenger came out of the Temple, crying with a loud voice to Him who sat on the cloud, Thrust in Your sickle and reap, for the time has come for You to reap, for the harvest of the earth is ripe. ¹⁶ So He who sat on the cloud thrust in His sickle on the earth, and the earth was reaped."* Revelation 14:14-16

It is later that the rest of the Earth is harvested during the grape harvest leading up to the seventh month.

> *"¹⁷ Then another angel came out of the temple which is in heaven, he also having a sharp sickle. ¹⁸ And another angel came out from the altar, who had power over fire, and he cried with a loud cry to him who had the sharp sickle, saying, Thrust in your sharp sickle and gather the clusters of the vine of the earth, for her grapes are fully ripe. ¹⁹ So the angel thrust his sickle into the earth and gathered the vine of the earth, and threw it into the great winepress of the wrath of Elohim. ²⁰ And the winepress was trampled outside the city, and blood came out of the winepress, up to the horses' bridles, for one thousand six hundred furlongs."* Revelation 14:17-20

This process leads us through the cycle of the Appointed Times that will continue to, and through, the Millennial Kingdom.

Zechariah describes a future time when Messiah rules over the earth.

"⁸ And in that day it shall be that living waters shall flow from Jerusalem, half of them toward the eastern sea and half of them toward the western sea; In both summer and winter it shall occur. ⁹ And YHWH shall be King over all the earth. In that day it shall be - YHWH is one, and His name one." Zechariah 14:8-9

That is why Zechariah emphasizes Sukkot – The Feast of Tabernacles.

"And it shall come to pass that everyone who is left of all the Nations which came against Jerusalem shall go up from year to year to worship the King, YHWH of hosts, and to keep the Feast of Tabernacles (sukkot)." Zechariah 14:16

This Feast is a seven-day Feast that does not get completely fulfilled until the end of the 1,000 year Millennial Reign – the Sabbath Reign.

It is important to understand that the Appointed Times are not completely fulfilled until the end of time as we know it – the end of the Millennial age. Some people try to simplify things by saying that Yahushua fulfilled the Spring Feasts during His first appearance, and then will fulfill the Fall Feasts at His second coming. That is not completely correct.

He was born on Yom Teruah so that was a partial fulfillment of that Appointed Time on Day 1 of Month 7. He also did not completely fulfill the so-called Spring Feasts.

There is more to come for all of them, and only when the Millennial reign is concluded are the Appointed Times of the Seventh Month completely fulfilled. That is when the New (Renewed) Jerusalem ultimately sets down on the planet.

"Then I, John, saw the set apart city, New Jerusalem,
coming down out of heaven from Elohim,
prepared as a Bride adorned for her Husband."
Revelation 21:2

At that final Sukkot we end on the Seventh Day - Hoshanah Rabah (The Last Great Day), which then progresses to the Eighth Day (Shemini Atzeret) - The Final Appointed Time.

Again, this Eighth Day actually occurs on Day 22 of Month 7. The Appointed Times of the Seventh Month begin on Day 1 – aleph (א), and continue to Day 22 - taw (ת).

So the focus of the Seventh Month is on the Messiah - the aleph taw (את) - literally, the First and the Last. It then shifts from seven to eight. This is the fulfillment of the Covenant of Circumcision, and the Renewal of the Covenant by Messiah

The number eight represents a fence, or separation in the ancient script. In some cases it appeared as a ladder or DNA strand. It represents "new beginnings" when the Bride and her Husband can finally dwell with one another and consummate the marriage on a renewed Earth.

These patterns of fulfillment and cycles of renewal are very Hebrew, and that is how the Elohim of the Hebrews helps us to learn His ways, and walk His path. It is critical that we learn to think, walk and live like an Hebrew, so that we can fully understand the Covenant renewed by the Messiah.

As we already mentioned, that Covenant is made with Yisrael. In order to be in that Covenant you must be a part of the Assembly of Yisrael. That is why an important part of leaving Babylon involves finding your identity in Yisrael.

18

Finding Your Identity in Yisrael

In the last chapter we discussed the process of renewal patterned through the life of Abraham, and rehearsed through the Appointed Times. Understanding these cycles of time is critical in order to fully comprehend the Covenant renewed by Yahushua the Messiah.

We also talked about the fact that Yisrael represents the set apart Assembly – the only party to this Covenant. Many people confuse the Covenant Assembly of Yisrael with the Jews, because of the fact that the House of Yisrael was exiled and seemingly "lost" forever.

This left the House of Yahudah, which is where we derive the word "Jew." Although they were exiled a second time, they never lost their identity like the House of Yisrael did.[312]

Many people use the word Jew and Jewish Roots, along with Messianic Judaism to identify with Yisrael. That is a very big mistake. It is both confusing and inaccurate, as we will discuss in this chapter.

At best, the people who call themselves Jewish are the descendants of the House of Yahudah. No one knows for sure if this connection actually exists.[313]

---

[312] See Hosea 1:1-11 concerning the progressive distancing that would take between YHWH and the House of Yisrael. Ultimately, there would be a regathering until they are called Sons of the Living El.
[313] There have been various groups identifying with Yisrael throughout history. We currently see the Jewish people claiming direct descendancy with ancient Yisrael, but that is not necessarily the case. Before the destruction of Jerusalem in 70 CE, the Yahudim were mixed and even ruled by Edomites. With the passage of 2,000 years and the mixing with other peoples, it is doubtful that many could actually prove a pure bloodline. In any event, the future

It is important to remember that Yahudah was only one tribe. David and Shlomo both belonged to the Tribe of Yahudah, and they reigned over the individual tribes in a united Kingdom.

After the death of Shlomo, the Kingdom was divided. That is when the House of Yahudah was reborn,[314] and that kingdom included other tribes, namely Yahudah, Benjamin and Levi. There were also likely people from all of the other tribes who joined in with Yahudah, as a result of King Jeroboam corrupting the worship in the north.

So you could use the term Yudea to refer to the land under the control of the Kingdom of Yahudah. You could use the word Yudean, or Yahudi to describe someone who lived within the Kingdom of Yahudah. The most accurate usage would apply to someone who belonged to the Tribe of Yahudah. This demonstrates how the term has become interchangeable and sometimes muddled.

We have spent a lot of time talking about the Covenant, and the cycles of renewal. It is the Covenant that distinguished "the chosen people" from all others. The point was not to select an ethnic group, and then treat them special because of their DNA.

YHWH desires to draw people to Him from all the Nations. He chose Abram and his seed to accomplish that task. He would do it the easy way, if the people obeyed, or the hard way, if the people were stubborn and stiff-necked.

Well, the Covenant people chose the hard way, and it is through their disobedience and punishment that YHWH will draw the Nations back to Him, through His Son.

That's the big picture, and you must understand the big picture, otherwise you might get caught up idolizing the modern State of Israel, and treating people special because they claim to be Jewish.

---

plan of Elohim involves the Nations, and the important thing is whether you are in the renewed Covenant. This matter will be explored further in the book titled *The Israel Dilemma*.
[314] Prior to the uniting of the tribes, David reigned over the House of Yahudah for seven years.

The bottom line is Yisrael was a special people when YHWH dwelled in their midst, and they conducted themselves as a Royal Priesthood. If the obeyed, they could remain in that special station, and dwell in the Land. If they disobeyed, they would be outcasts.

That is exactly what happened to the ten Northern Tribes first. They were removed by the Assyrians around 721 BCE and exiled for a long time – 2,730 years. Their punishment period has recently ended and they are now freed to return when YHWH decides to gather them.[315]

The House of Yahudah was later exiled by the Babylonians around 586 BCE, and some returned after the punishment of seventy years was concluded. That is why we saw a "Jewish" presence in the Promised Land when Yahushua came looking for the lost sheep of the House of Yisrael.

They were lost and needed to be found, although that task was just getting started when Yahudah was once again punished and exiled. This time in 70 CE by the Romans.

The Yahudim should have been focusing on the Covenant, and the renewal of the Covenant by Yahushua. Instead, the priests and elders largely rejected Yahushua, so YHWH rejected them.

That creates even more confusion, since it was primarily the Pharisees who survived, and they created a brand new religion with Rabbis in charge, instead of Priests. That new religion is called Judaism, and people who adhere to that religion are referred to as Jewish.

So the term Jew carries many different, and sometimes contradictory, usages. Now add to the mix the declared Jewish State named Israel, with citizens called Israelis. Now you've got a real mess!

For instance, how about the Arab Muslim who is an

---

[315] The punishment period can be determined by Ezekiel 4 and Leviticus 26. While it was scheduled to expired somewhere around 2009 to 2014, that does not mean that they will immediately return. YHWH typically works with generations. So it is safe to say that we are in the generation that will see the return of the House of Yisrael.

Israeli citizen? They aren't in the Covenant, but claim a right to live in the Covenant Land. How about an Israeli citizen whose mother was Jewish, and whose father was Christian? Neither of them are in the Covenant with Yisrael renewed by Yahushua, if they are not obeying what He Commanded. Are they entitled to live in the Covenant Land?

How about a Jewish atheist? Someone who rejects the Covenant all together? Are they permitted to live in the Covenant just because they identify as being Jewish?

Well, the Jewish State says these are all okay, but YHWH says differently. So, currently there are a bunch of people, claiming to be Israelis who do not qualify, according to the Scriptures. They are defiling the Land by worshipping false gods and rejecting YHWH, all while claiming rights to His Land. That won't go on much longer.

I hope it is apparent that it is not proper to use the blanket term "Jew" when referring to the Covenant Assembly of Yisrael. So let's take a moment and examine the Covenant Assembly.

We know from the beginning that YHWH Elohim had a relationship with Adam that involved terms and boundaries. We are not given a list, but it is safe to assume that YHWH expected the same level of righteousness from His Creation from the very beginning.

The terms of Adam's tenancy in the Garden were violated, and the special relationship was severed. Once sin (disobedience) entered creation, it spread like a virus. Through successive generations, mankind continued to rebel until we see a great reset occur. Punishment was rendered, although YHWH chose Noah and his family to survive the flood.

Those eight people on the ark would be a "new beginning," and that is why the number eight holds a special place in the Covenant, and the process of renewal.

We see with Noah, that YHWH did not change anything in His plan for man. Noah was chosen because He "walked with Elohim."

"This is the genealogy of Noah. Noah was a just man, perfect in his generations. Noah walked with Elohim." Genesis 6:9

You walk with Elohim when you live according to His instructions. The reason why the word "walk" is used is because it is an active relationship - you live your life on the righteous path prescribed by His Instructions. This is a very simple concept that has been clouded by religion and traditions.

You see, the Scriptures record that Noah was a "just" man. An English speaker might think that Noah was a "fair" guy, but the Hebrew is much more specific. In the Hebrew the word is "tzadik" (צדיק), which means "righteous." You are "righteous" when you walk on the righteous path.

The text also describes Noah as "perfect." Again, a English speaker might think this meant he never did anything wrong, but that is not necessarily the case. The word for "perfect" in the Hebrew is "tamiym" (תמים) which means: "integrity, truth - without blemish, complete, full, perfect, sincerely (-ity), sound, without spot, undefiled, upright(-ly), whole."

It is the same word used to describe an acceptable sacrifice. Since a sacrifice was intended to represent the "nefesh" of the person offering the sacrifice, that means we are supposed to be "tamiym" as well.[316]

It doesn't mean that you are "perfect" in the sense that you never did anything wrong. It can mean that you are "perfect" in your walk with YHWH. You are on the path, and are not veering to the right or the left.

This is similar to someone claiming to have a "perfect" driving record. They have followed the signs, the directions

---

[316] *"And whoever offers a sacrifice of a peace offering to YHWH, to fulfill his vow, or a freewill offering from the cattle or the sheep, it must be perfect to be accepted; there shall be no defect in it."* Leviticus 22:21

and the rules of the road. They may have made some mistakes, but they don't have any "marks" on their license.

The way of YHWH is perfect, and when we remain on it, our way is perfect. You might not have been on the path your entire life, but the point is that you are on it now and that you remain on it.

> *"[31] As for Elohim, His way is perfect (תמים); The word of YHWH is proven; He is a shield to all who trust in Him . . . [33] Elohim is my strength and power, and He makes my way perfect (תמים)."* 2 Samuel 22:31 and 33

We know that YHWH revealed a way for Noah to save his family, and he chose it. He was told to build a ark.

> *"Make yourself an ark of gopherwood;*
> *make rooms in את-the ark,*
> *and cover it inside and outside with pitch."*
> Genesis 6:14

Do you see the aleph taw (את) connected to the ark? The ark would provide protection and salvation from the waters of judgment, but Noah had to follow the instructions. This was a pattern for the future salvation provided through the Son, the aleph taw (את). He would provide the salvation, but we need to follow His instructions.

After the flood, Noah entered into a covenant with YHWH. We are then able to trace a line from Noah, through Shem to Terah, and his son Abram. This is the line that YHWH chose to continue His Covenant. The Covenant was intended to find a remnant through time, who could fill the Kingdom.

The Covenant promise found its way to Babylon. As was mentioned in the very first chapter, while the focus turns to Abram, it appears that his father Terah was first told to leave. He never crossed over the Euphrates, and died on the border of Babylon.

Thereafter, Abram was called out of Babylon, and he heeded the call. He walked with Elohim.

We talked about the name change that occurred with Abram during the Covenant of Circumcision. The first time that we read the name Abram in the Scriptures is Genesis 11:26, it is prefaced by the aleph taw (את), along with his two other brothers.

So we see the aleph taw (את) connected with Abram from the very beginning – et-Abram (את-אברם). The Name Abram is spelled aleph (א), bet (ב), resh (ר), mem (ם).[317]

Remember when we were examining the month of the abib, and the fact that aleph bet – "ab" (אב) is the first word that can be spelled in the Hebrew language? The word spelled aleph bet is "ab" (אב). It means "father," but is also means: "young shoot or sprout."

The word spelled bet resh is "bar" (בר), which means "son." So the word for "son" (בר) is in the middle, surrounded by aleph mem – em (אם).

The Hebrew word "em" (אם) means "a mother" in the sense of the bonding of a family. It is the root of "emah" which is the common Hebrew word for "mother."

So, right in the name Abram we have the emphasis on "a sprouting family." This is important because it hints that through this man Elohim would make a Covenant to build a family through the Messiah.

Remember the "Covenant House for the Son" that we saw in the beginning, from the word B'resheet? Abram would be used to fill that Covenant House.

Abram was called a Hebrew, because he passed through the waters. He took the plunge, which we repeat through immersion. He washed away the residue of Babylon, which we

---

[317] You might notice the differences in the "mem" (ם) in the name of Abram, which was a "mem sofit" (ם), otherwise known as a "final" mem. Some Hebrew characters are written differently when they end a word.

must do as well.

He crossed over on his way from Babylon to the Land of Canaan. This is significant, because he was always a Hebrew. Even when His name was later changed to Abraham and he was circumcised, he was still not Jewish. He was never a Jew.

The Covenant of Circumcision was a good example of renewal. Remember, when Abram entered into the original blood Covenant, he was uncircumcised, and did not bear the penalty for breaking the Covenant.

During the Covenant of Circumcision, his flesh was cut, and his blood was shed. It was a new thing, in the sense that he now had to shed blood and bear the mark. It was a renewal, in the sense that it was the same Covenant, with the same parties, and the same promises.

Here is how that Covenant is prefaced:

"When Abram was ninety-nine years old, YHWH appeared to Abram and said to him, I am Almighty Elohim; walk before Me and be blameless (tamayim)." Genesis 17:1

Did you notice the word for "blameless," which is "tamiyim" (תמים) in Hebrew? It is the same word used to describe Noah. So, YHWH was instructing Abraham to be circumcised, walk with Him and be "perfect" or "blameless" – just like Noah.

YHWH requires the same conduct from all Covenant participants. Walk with Him, and follow His righteous instructions. Again, that is why Yahushua said "follow Me." He teaches us how to walk with Elohim.

A covenant involves "cutting." That is the symbolism provided through circumcision. Flesh is removed from the male organ, and the seed of the male then passes through the cutting of the Covenant. At the first Covenant ceremony, with the uncircumcised Abram, the Seed of YHWH passed through the cuttings.

Only after Abraham and Sarah had their names changed at the Covenant of Circumcision did the Covenant seed pass from Abraham into the Covenant womb of Sarah. Isaac was thereafter circumcised on the eighth day, so his seed could then pass through the cutting, resulting in Esau and Jacob.

Even though Esau was the firstborn, completely out of the womb, Jacob's hand reached out first. As a result, his life was framed by his struggle to take hold of the Covenant promise. He negotiated the right of the firstborn from Esau, but then he deceived his father to receive the blessing.

As with Abram, Jacob also experienced a name change. We read about it in Genesis 32:28.

> "And He said, 'Your name shall no longer be called Jacob, but Yisrael; for you have struggled with Elohim and with men (anashim), and have prevailed.'" Genesis 32:28

In the Hebrew, a profound message is seen.

וַיֹּאמֶר לֹא יַעֲקֹב יֵאָמֵר עוֹד שִׁמְךָ
כִּי אִם־יִשְׂרָאֵל כִּי־שָׂרִיתָ עִם־אֱלֹהִים וְעִם־אֲנָשִׁים וַתּוּכָל

In English we read: "your name shall no longer be called Jacob but, em-Yisrael (אֵם־יִשְׂראל). Because you have struggled with am-Elohim (עִם־אֱלֹהִים), and am-anashim (אֲנָשִׁים־עִם)."

This is a good example of a Hebrew word-play. There is a message for the reader, but it doesn't translate into other languages. The term "em-Yisrael" contains the "aleph mem" (אֵם). Again, the word "em" (אֵם) is actually the root of "mother" – "emah" (אִמָּה).

Remember the "em" (אֵם) in the name "Abram" (אַבְרָם)?

It is the same word that surrounds the "son" – "bar" (בר) in the name Abram.

Well, there is a word play going on, because the "em" attached to Yisrael is contrasted against the "am" spelled "ayin mem" (עם). The "ayin mem" (עם) is attached to Elohim, and anashim (men).

The Hebrew word "am" (עם) means: "a people (as a congregated unit); specifically, a tribe (as those of Israel); hence (collectively) troops or attendants; figuratively, a flock."

So, we are seeing that "em"-Yisrael would be "am" Yisrael. A people - a nation of tribes through the Covenant made with Abram. That Covenant would connect a people to Elohim.

This name change occurred prior to Jacob "crossing over" at Peniel. The Hebrew word "peniel" means: "Face of El." It was there that he wrestled with Elohim and lived. It was, quite possibly the same place where Abram previously crossed over and became a Hebrew.

Jacob was travelling with his family and children to the Land of Promise. He was returning to his inheritance, unless Esau decided to kill him for it. After he crossed over he camped at a place called Sukkot. That word should be familiar because it is the name of the Appointed Time of the seventh month.

Here is what we read in the text:

"And Jacob journeyed to Sukkot,
built himself a house, and made sukkas for his livestock.
Therefore the name of the place is called Sukkot."
Genesis 33:17

Interestingly, he built a house for himself – "beit" (house). He built sukkot for his "miqneh" (מקנה) - commonly translated as flocks, livestock – anything "acquired." We will examine the significance of that word further in this discussion. So his belongings, the things he acquired, went in sukkas – temporary dwellings, while he lived in a house.

That is the transition that we long to make, and that is what we celebrate at Sukkot, when those who belong to Elohim – those "acquired" by the blood of Yahushua, can move out of their temporary dwellings, and move into the House of Elohim.

Interestingly, we later read about the man Yisrael at Bethel, which means the "House of Elohim." It is here that we read about his new name a second time.

> "⁹ Then Elohim appeared to Jacob again, when he came from Padan Aram, and blessed him. ¹⁰ And Elohim said to him, Your name is Jacob; your name shall not be called Jacob anymore, but em-Yisrael shall be your name. So He called his אֶת-name Yisrael. ¹¹ Also Elohim said to him: I am El Shaddai. Be fruitful and multiply; a nation and a company of nations shall proceed from you, and kings shall come from your body. ¹² The land which I gave Abraham and Isaac I give to you; and to your descendants after you I give this Land. ¹³ Then Elohim went up from him in the place where He talked with him. ¹⁴ So Jacob set up a pillar in the place where He talked with him, a pillar of stone; and he poured a drink offering on it, and he poured oil on it. ¹⁵ And Jacob called the אֶת-name of the place where Elohim spoke with him, Bethel." Genesis 35:9-15

Be fruitful and multiply? Isn't that the same Command given to Adam, at the very beginning?[318] That is because the plan of YHWH did not change, it simply continued through a Covenant people.

In that passage, we again read his name as em-Yisrael and in verse 10, where it is translated "so He called his name Yisrael," we read "et-shem Yisrael." The Messiah was involved in the naming, and the name of the place in verse 15.

---

[318] Genesis 1:22

The point is that through Yahushua, the aleph taw (את), the restored and renewed Yisrael will dwell in the House of Elohim.

So, Yisrael would become the Nation that the Messiah would use as a conduit for the restoration of mankind through the Covenant. Now, instead of starting in the Garden, the chosen line will begin in Babylon, and make their way back to the Garden – into the House of Elohim.

But why the name Yisrael? What does Yisrael actually mean? A basic definition is found in the text of Genesis 32:28 during the naming process. This is often the case in the giving of a Hebrew name. Sometimes the name describes the circumstances of the birth.

Here, we see Jacob become a new man – born again. His name describes his journey – "You have struggled with Elohim, and with men, and have prevailed." "Ki-sarit am-Elohim" is the focus, since Elohim was the one providing the name.

Remember that Yisrael is spelled "yud, sin, resh, aleph, lamed" (ישראל). The Hebrew word for "struggled" is "sarit" spelled "sin, resh, yud, taw" (שרית). El (אל) is the short form of Elohim. So YHWH created a new name from the description that He provided.

Interestingly, the name Yisrael begins with "yud" (י), which represents an arm in the ancient Hebrew script (ᗉ). The existence of "sar" (שר) in the name refers to the seed of "royalty." The name of Abram's wife was Sarai, which literally means "princess." The word "sar" (שר) means "prince."

The "em" affixed to Yisrael places the emphasis on the mother binding the family together, and this mother is royalty. Remember the promise given to Sarai at the Covenant of Circumcision when their names were changed?

"*¹⁵ Then Elohim said to Abraham, As for Sarai your wife, you shall not call her name Sarai, but Sarah shall be her name. ¹⁶ And*

I will bless her and also give you a son by her; then I will bless her, and she shall be a mother of Nations; kings of peoples (amim)shall be from her." Genesis 17:15-16

This is an important point to remember that the Covenant of circumcision involved a cutting on the man's flesh, but that was to prepare him for emitting seed into the womb of the chosen woman.

Both Abraham and Sarah were integral parties to the Covenant of Circumcision that would lead to the promise and creation of Yisrael - establishing a Royal Covenant Family of Elohim. The future fulfillment will involve the marriage between the Messiah, and His set apart Bride Yisrael. Both the Bride and the Bridegroom are significant players in this Covenant relationship.

So we see Yisrael as the Royal Arm of Elohim. The Royal Family representing the Kingdom on this planet. Adam and Hawah were originally supposed to be the King and Queen of this Kingdom, but they failed. Now through Abraham and Sarah that process would be renewed through Yisrael, leading to the marriage of Messiah and His Bride.

We have talked about Gematria already. Some people turn it into a mystical practice, and that can be dangerous. On the other hand, there is a very practical reality that Hebrew is a mathematical language, and every word has a mathematical value. There is no denying that fact, and there is value in examining the mathematical connections.

The numerical value of Yisrael is 541, and so were the "sheaves" (almutikim) in Joseph's Dream that bowed to his sheaf described in Genesis 37:7.

The "unleavened bread" (ha'matzoth) when YHWH described the Feast of Unleavened Bread also equals 541.

> *"So you shall observe את-ha'matzoth (Unleavened Bread), for on this same day I will have brought your armies out of the land of Egypt. Therefore you shall*

observe this day throughout your generations as an
everlasting ordinance." Exodus 12:17

Interestingly the Hebrew word for "feast" (hag) is not found in this passage. Instead, the "et" (את) is attached to the matzot, representing Yahushua.

There are many others that help paint a picture of the plan and purpose of Yisrael. The point is that in the Hebrew text we see important principles that can only be seen and understood through the Hebrew language.

Yisrael had twelve sons who became twelve tribes. These twelve tribes eventually went down to Egypt as seventy beings.

"*¹ Now these are the names of the children of Yisrael who came to Egypt; each man and his household came with Jacob: ² Reuben, Simeon, Levi, and Yahudah; ³ Issachar, Zebulun, and Benjamin; ⁴ Dan, Naphtali, Gad, and Asher. ⁵ All those who were descendants of Jacob were seventy persons (for Joseph was in Egypt already).*" Exodus 1:1-5

The number seventy is significant, because it represents the Nations. That is how the peoples were divided after the flood of Noah. So we see the focus on twelve becoming seventy. This is the pattern of restoration fulfilled through Yisrael.

The purpose of Yisrael is the Nations. This is why Yahushua first send out twelve, and then sent out seventy. He was demonstrating that He was fulfilling the mandate of Yisrael.[319]

This is the pattern of redemption and Restoration - Yisrael and the Nations. Yisrael was not meant to be some exclusive privileged ethnic group called the Jewish People.

---

[319] See Luke 9:1 to 10:23

That is a twisted understanding of the Covenant, the Scriptures, and even history.

Yisrael was chosen to draw the Nations back to Elohim – into His Family. Those seventy beings who entered into Egypt willingly, were later enslaved in Egypt. While in Egypt they grew into a might people – a Nation.

That Nation was now ready to absorb the Nations that were separated from YHWH since the Tower of Babel. That absorption and assimilation began at the Passover. The Covenant people were delivered from Egypt along with "a mixed multitude" of peoples – representing the Nations.

"A mixed multitude went up with them also,
and flocks and herds - a great deal of livestock."
Exodus 12:38

Remember that during the famine in Joseph's time the Nations came to Egypt for food, and Egypt was probably filled with people from all around the known world. When they saw the wrath of the Elohim of the Hebrews, they decided that they wanted to follow that Elohim.

In fact, the Book of Exodus is called Shemot in Hebrew, which means "Names." One of the focal points of the text is how YHWH would reveal His Name to Egypt, and the entire world.

Now mind you, He could have just "raptured" Yisrael out of Egypt if all He wanted to do was remove them, but that was not the point.

The point was that through His wrath and judgments upon Egypt, and the gods of Egypt, He would demonstrate His Power, Might and Name to the Nations. This is something to remember when we consider the end of the age.

Many people are expecting to be raptured as an escape, but that does not square with the way YHWH delivered Yisrael from Egypt. It doesn't fit the pattern. While He surely will separate and protect His people, He is not likely to remove them. At least not until He has gathered them all from the Nations while judging the Nations.

In the future, when YHWH judges the entire planet, He will deliver His people and a remnant from the Nations who join with Him. Through that process He will test them and refine them.

So YHWH not only brought the Children of Yisrael out of Egypt, He also delivered the foreigners – the ger (גֵר). Of course, this was the pattern of Abram and Hager (הָגָר) – "the stranger."

Yisrael was always about the Nations. That is why they were mandated to be a Kingdom of priests.

"And you shall be to Me
a Kingdom of priests and a holy (set apart) Nation."
Exodus 19:6

They were supposed to mediate the Covenant between YHWH and the Nations. They were supposed to teach the ways of YHWH to the Nations, and lead the Nations back to YHWH.

This task would be accomplished either through obedience or disobedience. If they chose to obey they would shine as a light to the surrounding Nations. If they disobeyed they would be an example to the Nations that they were exiled into.

They were supposed to reveal the blessings of the Covenant as they were planted in the Covenant Land, and they were supposed to bear fruit.

In fact, Yisrael is often referred to as: "The Planting of El." That is because of the word spoken through Isaiah:

"That they may be called trees of righteousness,
the planting of YHWH, that He may be glorified."
Isaiah 61:3

This is another aspect of Yisrael. They were a people intended to be planted in a specific Land, that was supposed to represent the return to the Garden.

Consider the following passages:

"¹ We have heard with our ears, O Elohim, Our fathers have told us, the deeds You did in their days, in days of old. ² You drove out the Nations with Your hand, but them You planted." Psalm 44:1-2

"Yet I had planted you a noble vine, a seed of highest quality." Jeremiah 2:21

"You have planted them, yes, they have taken root; They grow, yes, they bear fruit." Jeremiah 12:2

"For YHWH of hosts, who planted you . . ." Jeremiah 11:17

Again, they were planted in the Covenant Land. This represented the restoration of Adam and Hawah to the Garden. Once in the Land, the Torah is the rule of the Land, and obedience is a condition precedent for Yisrael living in the Land.

This is why it is imperative to understand the Covenant and the Covenant Assembly.

YHWH wants to restore all of the Nations to Him, and they will be restored through obedience to the Covenant. While they are not perfect, they decide to walk perfect. And the way they walk perfect is revealed through the Torah.

As a result, there is only one Torah for all people. YHWH did not create the Torah for the Jewish People – He created it for all the Nations.[320]

---

[320] The religion of Judaism promotes the notion that only Jewish People can obey the Torah and that the Nations cannot obey the Torah. They say it is prohibited, and claim that the Nations are only supposed to obey the Noahide Laws, which are a Pharisaic creation. So the

He simply revealed it to the Nations through Yisrael. And the Assembly of Yisrael does not equate to the Jewish people.

> *"One Torah shall be for the native-born*
> *and for the stranger who dwells among you."*
> Exodus 12:49

> *"One Torah and one custom*
> *shall be for you and for the stranger*
> *who dwells with you."*
> Numbers 15:16

> *"You shall have one Torah*
> *for him who sins unintentionally,*
> *for him who is native-born among the children of Yisrael*
> *and for the stranger who dwells among them."*
> Numbers 15:29

The message was clear. There is one standard of righteousness for anyone who desires to dwell in with YHWH.

The stranger refers to one not born into the Covenant, like Hagar. She was a stranger from Egypt, but she became part of Abram's family.

The pattern of Hagar is consistent with the notion that the stranger was always welcome into the Covenant. They came into the Covenant by following the Torah – the same Torah that Yisrael followed.

Today we see Rabbinic Judaism trying to promote the idea of the "Seven Noahide Laws;" as if only those in the religion of Rabbinic Judaism can or should obey the Torah.

The important thing to remember is that when they refer to the Torah – they are talking about their man-made

---

religion of Judaism actually keeps the Torah from the Nations, which is opposite from the mandate of opposite from the mandate of Yisrael.

torah – the oral torah that was created and developed by the Pharisees.

They have added to and taken away from the Torah through their traditions - the Noahide Laws being one of those traditions. There is no such thing as Noahide Laws, and we are not supposed to become "Sons of Noah." We are supposed to become Sons of Elohim.

The Rabbis are attempting to create a barrier between the Covenant assembly and the Nations, which is not supposed to exist. The amazing thing is they do this when they aren't even in the Kingdom themselves.

This is exactly what the Pharisees did in Yahushua's day, and that is why He stated:

> "But woe to you, scribes and Pharisees, hypocrites! For you shut up the Kingdom of Heaven against men; for you neither go in yourselves, nor do you allow those who are entering to go in." Matthew 23:13

So the Pharisees are continuing their nonsense to this day, trying to keep people away from the Torah and out of the Kingdom. Is it any wonder that He said they are of their father the devil?[321] Attempting to steer people away from the Torah is the exact opposite of what Yisrael is supposed to do. It is sheer evil.

That is why when Yahushua was cleansing the Temple He quoted Isaiah,[322] which states the following:

> "³ Do not let the son of the foreigner who has joined himself to YHWH speak, saying, YHWH has utterly separated me from His people; Nor let the eunuch say, Here I am, a dry tree. ⁴ For thus says YHWH: To the eunuchs who keep My Sabbaths, and choose what pleases Me, and hold fast My

---

[321] John 8:44
[322] See Matthew 21:12-13, Mark 11:15-17 and Luke 19:45-46

*Covenant, ⁵ Even to them I will give in My House
and within My walls a place and a name better than
that of sons and daughters; I will give them an
everlasting name that shall not be cut off. ⁶ Also the
sons of the foreigner who join themselves to YHWH,
to serve Him, and to love the Name of YHWH, to
be His servants - Everyone who keeps from defiling
the Sabbath, and holds fast My Covenant ⁷ Even
them I will bring to My set apart mountain, and make
them joyful in My House of prayer. Their burnt
offerings and their sacrifices will be accepted on My
altar; For My House shall be called a house of prayer
for all Nations."* Isaiah 56:3-7

It is easy to gloss over the enormity of this promise if
you are unfamiliar with the rules of being set apart. The
promise in this passage is profound. It is speaking to people
who were prohibited from coming near the Altar, because of
their particular status.

The point is that anyone can join the Covenant.
Everyone is invited to the House. If you love the Name of
YHWH, you must cling to YHWH, and not let anyone tell
you that you don't belong. No matter what, you must "hold
fast to the Covenant."

That is, after all, a hallmark of Yisrael. Striving with
Elohim and not letting go. Consider the naming event of
Yisrael in context.

*"²⁴ Then Jacob was left alone; and a Man wrestled
with him until the breaking of day. ²⁵ Now when He
saw that He did not prevail against him, He touched
the socket of his hip; and the socket of Jacob's hip was
out of joint as He wrestled with him. ²⁶ And He said,
'Let Me go, for the day breaks.' But he said, "I will
not let You go unless You bless me! ²⁷ So He said to
him, "What is your name? He said, 'Jacob.' ²⁸ And He*

said, 'Your name shall no longer be called Jacob, but
אם-Yisrael; for you have struggled with עם-Elohim and
with עם-men, and have prevailed.'" Genesis 32:24-28

Jacob's entire round trip had been a struggle with men, beginning with, and ending with his brother Esau. At that moment, he literally prevailed in his physical struggle with Elohim, that prepared him for the moment that he dreaded for the last 20 years.

Immediately preceding this "wrestling event," Jacob divided his house into two camps. That was prophetic.

Over two centuries later, when Yisrael left Egypt and entered into the Land, they were divided into twelve tribes, but ultimately ended up consolidating into two houses - the Northern Tribes and the Southern Tribes – two camps.

Ephraim became the dominant Tribe of the Northern Tribes – called the House of Yisrael. Yahudah became the dominate Tribe of the Southern Tribes, known as the House of Yahudah.

After the period of the Judges, when David became King, he first ruled over the House of Yahudah for seven years, as was previously mentioned. He then became the King of the House of Yisrael, thus uniting both Houses under one King into one Kingdom.

That union did not last long. After the death of David's son Shlomo, the Kingdom was divided into two kingdoms.

Shlomo's son Rehoboam ruled over the Southern Tribes, and Jeroboam ruled over the Northern Tribes. Both houses sinned and were exiled because they broke the Covenant.

The House of Yisrael was exiled first, because their sin was particularly egregious. Jeroboam constructed two golden calves, and set up a false sacrificial system at none other than Beth El – the House of Elohim.

As a result of that, the House of Yisrael was totally removed from their land in the North through a series of invasions and exiles carried out by the Assyrians.

Their sin was so offensive that YHWH actually divorced them.

> "Then I saw that for all the causes for which backsliding Yisrael had committed adultery, I had put her away and given her a certificate of divorce; yet her treacherous sister Yahudah did not fear, but went and played the harlot also." Jeremiah 3:8

The House of Yahudah watched all of this happen, and instead of drawing closer to YHWH, they too fell away.

Jeremiah indicated that the House of Yahudah would be exiled for seventy years. A year of exile for every year that they did not keep the Shemittah year, so that the Land could have its' Sabbath rest. Their return was conditioned upon their obedience.

Read what YHWH declared through Jeremiah.

> "[10] Many rulers have destroyed My vineyard, they have trodden My portion underfoot; They have made My pleasant portion a desolate wilderness. [11] They have made it desolate; Desolate, it mourns to Me; The whole land is made desolate, because no one takes it to heart. [12] The plunderers have come on all the desolate heights in the wilderness, for the sword of YHWH shall devour from one end of the land to the other end of the land; no flesh shall have peace. [13] They have sown wheat but reaped thorns; they have put themselves to pain but do not profit. But be ashamed of your harvest because of the fierce anger of YHWH. [14] Thus says YHWH: Against all My evil neighbors who touch the inheritance which I have caused My people Yisrael to inherit - behold, I will pluck them out of their land and pluck out the House of Yahudah from among them. [15] Then it shall be, after I have plucked them out, that I will return and have

compassion on them and bring them back, everyone to his heritage and everyone to his land. ¹⁶ And it shall be, if they will learn carefully the ways of My people, to swear by My Name, as YHWH lives, as they taught My people to swear by Baal, then they shall be established in the midst of My people. ¹⁷ But if they do not obey, I will utterly pluck up and destroy that Nation, says YHWH." Jeremiah 12:10-17

Both Yahudah and the surrounding Nations who led Yahudah astray would be plucked out of the Land. They would be allowed to return, but they needed to swear by the Name of YHWH, not Baal.

In other words, they needed to make YHWH their Master and follow His ways. Otherwise, they would be "utterly plucked up and destroyed."

This is critical to understand, because while they were allowed to return from Babylon, most did not. Those who returned ended up falling away from YHWH, being subject to the Roman Empire, and ruled by the Edomite King Herod.

Their King Messiah arrived exactly as provide by Gabriel to Daniel, and as testified by John the Immerser. Nevertheless, the leaders of Yahudah rejected Him. Yahushua prophesied the utter destruction of Jerusalem, and it happened in 70 CE when the Romans destroyed Jerusalem and the Temple.

So both houses were punished and exiled. The prophet Ezekiel demonstrated their punishment period in dramatic fashion.

"⁴ Lie also on your left side, and lay the iniquity of the house of Yisrael upon it. According to the number of the days that you lie on it, you shall bear their iniquity. ⁵ For I have laid on you the years of their iniquity, according to the number of the days, three hundred and ninety days; so you shall bear the

*iniquity of the House of Yisrael. ⁶ And when you
have completed them, lie again on your right side;
then you shall bear the iniquity of the House of
Yahudah forty days. I have laid on you a day for each
year."* Ezekiel 4:4-6

In Leviticus 26 Moses warned that if Yisrael failed to
repent their punishment would be multiplied seven times.
That is exactly what happened. While the House of Yahudah
retained their identity, the House of Yisrael completely lost
their identity due to the divorce as described in Jeremiah 3 and
Hosea 1.

There was also a promise that they would be restored
and reunited, but YHWH promised that He would reunite
them under one head.

Ezekiel provided a powerful picture of that reunion in
the prophecy of the Two Sticks.

*"¹⁵ Again the word of YHWH came to me, saying,
¹⁶ As for you, son of man, take a stick for yourself
and write on it: For Yahudah and for the children of
Yisrael, his companions. Then take another stick
and write on it, For Joseph, the stick of Ephraim, and
for all the House of Yisrael, his companions. ¹⁷ Then
join them one to another for yourself into one stick,
and they will become one in your hand. ¹⁸ And when
the children of your people speak to you, saying,
Will you not show us what you mean by these? ¹⁹ say
to them, Thus says YHWH Elohim: Surely I will
take the stick of Joseph, which is in the hand of
Ephraim, and the tribes of Yisrael, his companions;
and I will join them with it, with the stick of
Yahudah, and make them one stick, and they will be
one in My Hand. ²⁰ And the sticks on which you
write will be in your hand before their eyes. ²¹ Then
say to them, Thus says YHWH Elohim: Surely I*

will take the children of Yisrael from among the Nations, wherever they have gone, and will gather them from every side and bring them into their own Land; [22] and I will make them one nation in the Land, on the mountains of Yisrael; and one King shall be king over them all; they shall no longer be two nations, nor shall they ever be divided into two kingdoms again. [23] They shall not defile themselves anymore with their idols, nor with their detestable things, nor with any of their transgressions; but I will deliver them from all their dwelling places in which they have sinned, and will cleanse them. Then *they shall be My people, and I will be their Elohim* [24] David My servant shall be king over them, and they shall all have one shepherd; they shall also walk in My judgments and observe My statutes, and do them. [25] Then they shall dwell in the Land that I have given to Jacob My servant, where your fathers dwelt; and they shall dwell there, they, their children, and their children's children, forever; and My servant David shall be their prince forever. [26] Moreover I will make a Covenant of Peace (Shalom) with them, and it shall be an everlasting Covenant with them; I will establish them and multiply them, and I will set My sanctuary in their midst forevermore. [27] My Tabernacle also shall be with them; indeed *I will be their Elohim, and they shall be My people.* [28] The Nations also will know that I, YHWH, sanctify Yisrael, when My sanctuary is in their midst forevermore." Ezekiel 37:15-28

Notice the language "For Yahudah and for the children of Yisrael, his companions." That is because many from the House of Yisrael headed south after Jeroboam set up his false system of worship.

So Yahudah became mixed with all of the tribes. Even so, Yahudah was still punished, because she went and played the harlot as well.

The first restoration of the House of Yahudah after the seventy year exile in Babylon was detailed through the texts of Nehemiah and Ezra.

Restoration to the Torah was integral in this process of returning, restoring and rebuilding. This was obvious because the exile was the result of their disobedience.

Notice the phrase *"Then they shall be My people, and I will be their Elohim?"* That's Covenant language.

It was critical that if they wanted to remain in the Covenant and in the Land – they needed to remain obedient. This is something completely lost in the Christian understanding of a covenant.

While Yahudah was still in the Land, the Messiah came through the House of Yahudah to repair the separation between YHWH and the House of Yisrael.

That is why He stated: *"I was not sent except to the lost sheep of the House of Yisrael."* Matthew 15:24 He renewed the Covenant as prophesied by Jeremiah, and we spoke of that renewal at length in the last chapter.

It is very important to understand the fact that we must be involved in this renewed Covenant if we want the be operating in the Kingdom, and the renewed Covenant is with Yisrael.

When Yisrael was in Egypt, the people needed to listen to Mosheh and His instructions to participate in the redemption and deliverance from Egypt. They couldn't go backwards in the Covenant and just say we are going to follow Noah or Abraham.

Moses was there telling them the plan of Elohim and they needed to walk in it. But remember that Moses himself was kept out of the Promised Land. The message was loud and clear that Moses alone could not get you into the Land. Only Joshua (Yahushua) could actually bring you into the fullness of the Covenant.

That is why YHWH sent one like Moses. His Son specifically named Yahushua – not Jesus. We need to listen to Him in order to be in the Covenant. If you don't follow Him – you are not in the renewed Covenant. And again, the renewed Covenant is with Yisrael.

It doesn't matter if your mother was Jewish, or if you were born in Jerusalem. And that leads us back again to the issue of the modern State of Israel. Just how does this fit into the plan of Elohim? Is this a fulfillment of prophecy, or something else? A deception, or a distraction?

When considering the modern State of Israel, many Evangelical Christians will cite a single verse from Isaiah as follows:

"Who has heard such a thing? Who has seen such things? Shall the earth (or land) be made to give birth in one day? Or shall a nation be born at once? For as soon as Tzion was in labor, she gave birth to her children." Isaiah 66:8

Since the modern State of Israel was authorized by a vote of the United Nations, some attribute the Partition Plan vote in 1947 to this prophecy.

Others look to the later declaration on May 14, 1948, when David Ben-Gurion, the head of the Jewish Agency, proclaimed the establishment of the State of Israel.

Again, the question is whether this declaration of a Jewish State was a fulfillment of Isaiah 66?

Well, you need to read the entire passage to understand the context. The verse is preceded by the following, which we already partially analyzed:

"¹ Thus says YHWH: Heaven is My throne, and earth is My footstool. Where is the house that you will build Me? And where is the place of My rest? ² For all

those things My hand has made, and all those things exist, says YHWH. But on this one will I look: On him who is poor and of a contrite spirit, and who trembles at My word. ³ He who kills a bull is as if he slays a man; He who sacrifices a lamb, as if he breaks a dog's neck; He who offers a grain offering, as if he offers swine's blood; He who burns incense, as if he blesses an idol. Just as they have chosen their own ways, and their soul delights in their abominations, ⁴ So will I choose their delusions, and bring their fears on them; Because, when I called, no one answered, when I spoke they did not hear; But they did evil before My eyes, and chose that in which I do not delight. ⁵ Hear the word of YHWH, You who tremble at His word: Your brethren who hated you, who cast you out for My name's sake, said, 'Let YHWH be glorified, that we may see your joy. But they shall be ashamed. ⁶ The sound of noise from the city! A voice from the Temple! The voice of YHWH, Who fully repays His enemies! ⁷ Before she was in labor, she gave birth; Before her pain came, she delivered a male child."
Isaiah 66:1-7

This is about wrath and judgment, not the founding of the Jewish State. And it is focused on the birth of Yahushua – not the founding of a Jewish State that rejects the Son and the renewed Covenant.

This becomes even clearer as we continue further with the passage.

"¹⁵ For behold, YHWH will come with fire and with His chariots, like a whirlwind, to render His anger with fury, and His rebuke with flames of fire. ¹⁶ For by fire and by His sword YHWH will judge all flesh; and the slain of YHWH shall be many. ¹⁷ Those who sanctify themselves and purify themselves, To go to

the gardens after an idol in the midst, eating swine's flesh and the abomination and the mouse, shall be consumed together, says YHWH. [18] For I know their works and their thoughts. It shall be that I will gather all nations and tongues; and they shall come and see My glory. [19] I will set a sign among them; and those among them who escape I will send to the nations: to Tarshish and Pul and Lud, who draw the bow, and Tubal and Javan, to the coastlands afar off who have not heard My fame nor seen My glory. And they shall declare My glory among the Nations. [20] Then they shall bring all your brethren for an offering to YHWH out of all Nations, on horses and in chariots and in litters, on mules and on camels, to My set apart mountain Jerusalem, says YHWH, as the children of Yisrael bring an offering in a clean vessel into the house of YHWH. [21] And I will also take some of them for priests and Levites, says YHWH. [22] For as the new heavens and the new earth which I will make shall remain before Me," says YHWH, So shall your descendants and your name remain. [23] And it shall come to pass That from one New Moon to another, and from one Sabbath to another, all flesh shall come to worship before Me, says YHWH. [24] And they shall go forth and look upon the corpses of the men Who have transgressed against Me. For their worm does not die, and their fire is not quenched. They shall be an abhorrence to all flesh." Isaiah 66:15-24

The formation of the modern State of Israel does not fit within the context of this passage, unless the point is that it is going to be judged and destroyed.

Of course, it appears that judgment would be in order since the modern State of Israel is occupying the Land while not in Covenant with YHWH. They are dwelling in the Land in a state of defiance and disobedience to the Covenant.

Remember that the House of Yahudah was previously sent into exile for seventy years, because they did not keep the Sabbath year? Well, the Land has not been enjoying a Sabbath every 7 years, as a whole.[323]

If the formation of the modern State of Israel was truly a restoration event, then they are accruing punishment since they do not keep the Shemitah Year either. That is unless YHWH has temporarily suspended the Torah, which is not the case.

Further, the people who returned were previously thrown out for rejecting the Messiah. They continue to reject Him, so how can they possibly return without repentance? If rejecting the Messiah is acceptable, then why were they exiled to begin with?

What I see happening in the modern State of Israel does not follow the pattern of a prophetic restoration that is supposed to occur through the Son of David.

First of all, the motivation for the formation of the modern State of Israel was the political movement of Zionism. It is a secular movement based upon a common ethnicity called Jewish. It is critical to understand that being ethnically Jewish does not equate to being in the Covenant Assembly of Yisrael.

The founders of the Jewish State were admittedly secular, and the state was grounded on socialist and communist principles – not the Torah. The governmental structure is a parliamentary democracy – not a Theocracy or Monarchy ruled by a King and a High Priest.

In fact, it is ruled by oligarchs with underlying support from Illuminati forces such as the Masons, the Rothchilds, and the Rockefellers to name a few.

Again, this is a Jewish State that has essentially hijacked the name of Israel. If they claimed to be the descendants of the House of Yahudah, then they should have

---

[323] It should be pointed out that there are certain Orthodox vineyards and farms that are observing a Shemittah year, although no one has been able to reliably reconstruct the Jubilee or Shemitah Cycle at this point in time.

used the name Yahudah. By using the name Israel, people become thoroughly confused, and unable to distinguish between reality, fiction and prophecy.

Remember that the term Jew can refer to someone from the Tribe of Yahudah, or from the Kingdom of Yahudah – the Southern Kingdom. Neither of these definitions equates to all Yisrael.

Being in Yisrael is about being in a Covenant relationship with YHWH, and since the Covenant relationship was severed when each house was exiled, the only way to rejoin that Covenant is through a renewal.

There is no indication that the modern State of Israel had or has any intention of entering into a renewed Covenant with YHWH. So calling the Jewish State - Israel is simply dishonest, and completely inappropriate.

The modern State of Israel does not recognize the renewed Covenant. Instead, Jews simply try to trace their ethnic identity through their mother, to justify their presence in the Land. Of course, that is completely backwards. According to the Scriptures, the seed comes from the father, and tribal identity would flow from the father.

Further, they fail to recognize that the House of Yisrael still needs to be reunited and returned to the Land. In fact, they are actively excluding Joseph. By attempting to restrict the Covenant Land to ethnic Jews, they are attempting to exclude those who identify as Torah observant Yisraelites.

There are people who want to come home to the Covenant Land, but the Land is closed to them. This is much like the sibling rivalry of the past when the brothers of Joseph expelled him from the Land.

Later, Joseph was hidden from them while they stood before him in Egypt. Once their eyes were opened and they recognized him they repented and were restored.

The same holds true today. There needs to be true recognition, repentance and restoration and that must occur through the Messiah. That will happen when YHWH is ready for His people Yisrael to return to the Land. Until then, we wait with anxious anticipation.

Right now, the modern State of Israel does not recognize the Covenant renewed and established by Yahushua. In fact, it is very much opposed to Yahushua. Followers of Yahushua are generally prohibited from becoming citizens, and often times followers of Yahushua who try to remain in the Land are persecuted, and expelled. Israel also has laws against proselytizing. They are more than willing to suppress free speech if it pertains to Jesus or Yahushua.

Whether or not the Jewish people actually descend from the House of Yahudah is a question. Even if they could prove that they were from the House of Yahudah, that alone does not mean that they are allowed to return.

Yahushua was the last One to render judgment against Yahudah. He cursed the fig tree, and the message was that it would be cut down and thrown into the fire, because it was not bearing fruit.[324] When you throw wood into a fire, it incinerates.

That was exactly what happened in 70 CE, and unlike the previous exile from Babylon, there was no time given for another return. Indeed, it would be entirely unfair to allow Yahudah to return, again, while the House of Yisrael was still in exile. This is especially true in light of their egregious sin of rejecting the Messiah. That makes two golden calves pale in comparison.

Even if they were allowed to return, they would have to recognize that they are only a portion of Yisrael, and they need to make way for the House of Yisrael to return to their allotted Land. Like I said, they are actively blocking attempts to return.

Yisrael always was inclusive of anyone. The only test

---

[324] John the Immerser said the following: "*[8] Therefore bear fruits worthy of repentance, and do not begin to say to yourselves, "We have Abraham as our father.' For I say to you that God is able to raise up children to Abraham from these stones. [9] And even now the ax is laid to the root of the trees. Therefore every tree which does not bear good fruit is cut down and thrown into the fire.*" Luke 3:8-9

was whether they would follow the Torah. Remember that there was one Torah for everyone. That is not the case in the modern State of Israel. The official religion of the modern State of Israel is Rabbinic Judaism – which derives from the Pharisees. They impose the oral torah, their man-made rules, traditions and religion that Yahushua was absolutely opposed to.

The Rabbis rule, or at least try to rule, over all areas of religious life. Just like the Pharisees, they place a heavy yoke upon the people

While I was writing this book, an issue arose in Israel involving the authority to provide Kosher certificates to restaurants. The Chief Rabbinate wanted to wield exclusive power to determine whether restaurants conform to their rules of kashrut.

A High Court ruling allowed the use of other sources, but the Chief Rabbinate is threatening fines to restaurants who don't submit to their authority. Of course they no longer have exclusive power, but they are still trying to intimidate people.

As I was finishing edits on this book, Prime Minister Netanyahu was attempting to stack the Supreme Court with Conservatives, resulting in massive protests. If he succeeds, that would surely strengthen the power and authority of the Rabbis.

Interestingly, if you want to become a citizen, and you can't prove your Jewish identity, you must convert to the religion of Judaism and deny Yahushua. But if you can prove that you are Jewish, it doesn't matter what you believe.

In fact, most of Israel is secular, many are atheists, some are Muslims. They hold rave dance parties in the desert with people using drugs, and dancing around a golden calf. Prostitution, child trafficking and pornography are rampant.

Tel Aviv hosts the largest gay pride parade in the region, and the LGBTQ agenda is flaunted and promoted throughout the land, along with all sins of the flesh.

In Jerusalem, a variety of lawless religions are found

within her gates, and she is being profaned as we speak. It is a pagan city consumed by the religions of Babylon.

Could this really be the restoration prophesied in the Scriptures? I say no.

In fact, the Book of Revelation refers to it as Sodom and Egypt. "*And their dead bodies will lie in the street of the great city which spiritually is called Sodom and Egypt, where also our Master was crucified.*" Revelation 11:8

How about the fact that the State of Israel adopted the ancient cultic symbol of Saturn, often referred to as the Star of David? The Supreme Court building even contains a pyramid on top.

Archaeologists are raising obelisks that are supposed to be knocked down and destroyed. The cultic symbols are everywhere to be seen, and YHWH is surely not pleased with this so-called "restoration."

I could go on and on. The point is not to disparage anyone, but simply point out the reality that the formation of the modern State of Israel is not the restoration of both Houses under One righteous King.

It is still the Covenant Land, but currently occupied by strangers who are not in the Covenant renewed by the Messiah. They are not keeping the Torah, as walked and taught by the Messiah, all while blocking true Covenant keepers from moving in.

In fact, the spirit that controls the modern State of Israel is the same spirit that sought to kill Yahushua in the past. That is why they continue to opposed Him, and seek to blot out His Name and memory.[325]

I suspect that this hatred derives from the fallen Son of Elohim that originally ruled over the Canaanites, and was "dethroned" by Yisrael under the leadership of Joshua

---

[325] In Israel, the Rabbis refer to Yahushua as "Yeshu." It is an acronym for a curse. The name Yeshu is an abbreviation of "Yimach Shmo Uzichro," which means: "may his name and memory be blotted out." So much for the shared Judeo-Christian values that so many Evangelical Christians espouse.

(Yahushua). That being is now back in power – temporarily.

So what do we make of the modern State of Israel? Is it part of the plan? Surely, if YHWH allowed it to happen it is. Is it what people expected? Definitely not.

There is nothing in the Scriptures that would ever lead us to believe that Yisrael was cast out of the Land due to disobedience, but would somehow get a free pass in the end to return and remain in disobedience for over seventy years.

That doesn't make any sense, and does not fit with the prophesies and the work of the Messiah. Sadly, I see many Christian leaders almost worshipping the modern State of Israel, because they fail to understand history and the Scriptural Covenant plan.

Remember Ezekiel? This is a description of the restoration we are looking for:

> "24 David My servant shall be king over them, and they shall all have one shepherd; they shall also walk in My judgments and observe My statutes, and do them. 25 Then they shall dwell in the Land that I have given to Jacob My servant, where your fathers dwelt; and they shall dwell there, they, their children, and their children's children, forever; and My servant David shall be their prince forever. 26 Moreover I will make a Covenant of Shalom with them, and it shall be an everlasting Covenant with them; I will establish them and multiply them, and I will set My Sanctuary in their midst forevermore. 27 My Tabernacle also shall be with them; indeed I will be their Elohim, and they shall be My people. 28 The Nations also will know that I, YHWH, sanctify Yisrael, when My Sanctuary is in their midst forevermore." Ezekiel 37:24-28

That is the true description of restored Yisrael. The only way for Yisrael to be in Covenant with YHWH after the

Covenant was broken at Sinai was through the Covenant renewed by Moses. Likewise, after the Covenant was broken by both Houses, it needs to be renewed as prophesied in Jeremiah 31.

Yahushua came and renewed the Covenant as a suffering servant - Messiah ben Joseph. He will return as a conquering king – Messiah ben David. Therefore, in order to be in Yisrael we must be part of the Covenant He renewed. The two sticks must be brought together, yet the rulers of the modern State of Yisrael are doing everything in their power to keep them apart.

The Covenant of Shalom means a covenant that is finally completed and fulfilled. Since the House of Yisrael was divorced, there needs to be another wedding. This is why the first recorded miracle of Yahushua was at a wedding. And this is why Yahushua repeatedly provided parables about weddings.

I grew up in Christianity thinking that Christians were the Bride of Christ. I later discovered that Yisrael is the Bride.

The promise given to the adulterous wife was literally lived out through the prophet Hosea. After describing the punishment there will be restoration through another exodus event where the Bride would be brought into the wilderness.

> "*14 Therefore, behold, I will allure her, will bring her into the wilderness, and speak comfort to her. 15 I will give her her vineyards from there, and the Valley of Achor as a door of hope; She shall sing there, as in the days of her youth, as in the day when she came up from the land of Egypt. 16 And it shall be, in that day, says YHWH, That you will call Me 'My Husband,' and no longer call Me 'My Master,' 17 For I will take from her mouth the names of the Baals, and they shall be remembered by their name no more. 18 In that day I will make a covenant for them with the beasts of the field, with the birds of the air, and*

with the creeping things of the ground. Bow and sword of battle I will shatter from the earth, to make them lie down safely. ¹⁹ I will betroth you to Me forever; Yes, I will betroth you to Me in righteousness and justice, in lovingkindness and mercy; ²⁰ I will betroth you to Me in faithfulness, and you shall know YHWH. ²¹ It shall come to pass in that day that I will answer, says YHWH; I will answer the heavens, and they shall answer the earth. ²² The earth shall answer with grain, with new wine, and with oil; they shall answer Jezreel. ²³ Then I will sow her for Myself in the earth, and I will have mercy on her who had not obtained mercy; then I will say to those who were not My people, You are My people! And they shall say, You are my Elohim!"
Hosea 2:14-23

To fully understand this passage, you need to recall the even that occurred at the Valley of Achor. Remember that the Valley of Achor was the place where Achin, from the Tribe of Yahudah, hid items after the destruction of Jericho which caused the Yisraelites to be cursed. He profaned the camp by essentially stealing from YHWH, and bringing Babylon into the Camp.

When you consider what the modern State of Israel is bringing into the Land, the sin of Achin pales in comparison.

According to Hosea, there is a direct correlation between the Valley of Trouble in the past, and the Future Door of Hope. Remember that Yahushua said *"I am the door."*[326]

This is the door He was referring to, and as we consider the door of hope that He provides, we must remember that promise in the context of the Valley of Trouble (Achor).

Achin lusted after the things of Babylon. The text specifically states: *"When I saw among the spoils a beautiful*

---

[326] *"I am the door. If anyone enters by Me, he will be saved, and will go in and out and find pasture."* John 10:9

Babylonian garment, two hundred shekels of silver, and a wedge of gold weighing fifty shekels I coveted them and took them. And there they are, hidden in the earth in the midst of my tent, with the silver under it." Joshua 7:21

He lusted after Babylonian "stuff" – described as accursed things. As a result of his coveting he lost everything. Read his punishment:

> "²⁴ *Then Joshua (Yahushua), and all Yisrael with him, took* את*-Achan the son of Zerah,* את*-the silver,* את*-the garment,* את*-the wedge of gold,* את*-his sons,* את*-his daughters,* את*-his oxen,* את*-his donkeys,* את*-his sheep,* את*-his tent, and* את*-all that he had, and they brought them to* את*-the Valley of Achor. ²⁵ And Joshua said, Why have you troubled us? YHWH will trouble you this day. So all Yisrael stoned him with stones; and they burned them with fire after they had stoned them with stones.*" Joshua 7:24-25

It is a very dramatic event, amplified by the existence of the aleph taw (את) twelves times. The Messiah is all over this punishment event meted out by Joshua (Yahushua).

It is also a very sad event, because this man made it into the Promised Land. He and his family were right on the verge of finally making it to their new homes in the Promised Land, and Achin lost it all because he lost his focus. He lusted after Babylon instead of obeying YHWH and Joshua (Yahushua).

The message is clear that YHWH does not condone Babylon in His Camp. He is going to destroy every vestige of Babylon in His Land, along with those who try to conceal it and profane the Land.

The promise, through Hosea, would be that Valley of Achor would be a door of hope.³²⁷ Instead of silver, gold, clothes and possessions, we have the promise of a restoration

---

³²⁷ "*Sharon shall be a fold of flocks, and the Valley of Achor a place for herds to lie down, for My people who have sought Me.*" Isaiah 65:10

through a wedding, and a covenant with Yisrael.

That restoration occurs through the aleph taw (את) – the Messiah, not through a Jewish State called Israel.

That wedding will be to a faithful Bride as specifically provided in Hosea. "*I will betroth you to Me in faithfulness, and you shall know YHWH.*" It will not be to a bunch of Jewish people who deny Him, and curse Him.

As we conclude this discussion on identifying with Yisrael, there has been some overlap and repetition. That is because the identity of Yisrael has been so clouded and veiled by men and religions. It often takes time to untangle the web of confusion that has been spun over this most important subject.

The nachash has attempted to keep mankind out of the Garden from the very beginning. His deception continues, by trying to keep people from joining the Covenant Assembly of Yisrael.

I trust that it is now clear. Yisrael is the conduit for the Covenant people to return to YHWH and His paradise, thanks to the work of the Son, Who renewed the Covenant through His blood.

With that understanding we can now examine how the true Covenant Assembly of Yisrael will be gathered, and restored according to the Scriptures. That will be the subject of the next chapter – the continuing relevance of the Covenant Land.

19

Understanding the Covenant Land

As we have seen so far, leaving Babylon is a process of separating ourselves from the systems of the world. As we turn our backs against Babylon, we turn our face toward YHWH and then walk on His path. His path is lit by His instructions.

This course change often involves a complete paradigm shift for many, and it can impact all areas of our lives - from the way we think, the way we act, to the we way we speak. Of course, it is the transformation process that prepares us to become fruitful and productive members of the Kingdom of Elohim.

As we discussed in the last chapter, that Kingdom is populated by a Covenant family of Yisrael. Yisrael is the Covenant Assembly, and consists of those in the Covenant renewed by Yahushua – not the Christian Church or Rabbinic Judaism.

I hope that it is clear that if you have joined in the Covenant renewed by the Messiah, then you are part of Yisrael. You are not part of some new religion founded by the Roman Empire. And you are not part of some entity called The Christian Church.

It should also be clear that you don't have to be Jewish, or be in the religion of Judaism to be part of Yisrael. Since the Covenant was broken by both the House of Yisrael and the House of Yahudah, the only way to be in Covenant with YHWH is through the Covenant renewed by Yahushua.

So, the point is not to be classified as Jewish. Just being Jewish does not mean you are in the Covenant. In fact, many who claim to be Jewish may not even derive from the Tribe of Yahudah at all, and the religion of Judaism does not get them in the Covenant. This is a mixed-up tangled mess that has caused enormous confusion for people desiring to follow YHWH.

Ultimately, the answer comes from understanding Yisrael. The goal is to become part of Yisrael whether you can discover that you have Jewish ancestry or not. That's not what matters. What does matter is whether you are willing to become a faithful and obedient bride.

We also talked about how the modern State of Israel was established as a Jewish State. This Jewish State lays claim to all of the Land promised to ancient Yisrael, including the Land allotted to the House of Yisrael. The modern State of Israel will not allow any returning lost sheep of the House of Yisrael to permanently move back in the Land, even though their punishment period has expired.

So they claim the Land apportioned through Joshua,[328] according to the Covenant promise given to Abraham, but they are attempting to exclude all of Yisrael. They also claim the Land according to the Covenant, but they are not in the Covenant renewed by the Messiah. This is definitely going to be resolved through judgment, and the righteous King Yahushua.

While I grew up as a Christian, and believed that I was in a "new" Covenant instituted by Jesus, I was never taught that it was actually a "renewed" Covenant. Nor was I told that the renewed Covenant involved Land. I was always told that I was going to Heaven, because I was saved. I think that this is universally taught in Christianity.

As a result, most Christians are not overly interested in the Land. They may like to visit, because they can identify with certain places and events that they read about in their Bibles, but they do not feel vested in the Land. They don't view

---

[328] I continue to use the popular English name of the Patriarch Joshua in order to avoid confusion with the Messiah Yahushua.

it as a final destination. That is because they fail to understand that it is part of the Covenant renewed by the Messiah.

As a result, they have essentially relegated the Promised Land to the Jewish People, and even support the Jewish position that lays claim to all of the Land. By doing so, they are forfeiting their inheritance, like Esau. Some actually despise their birthright.[329]

Sadly, this flawed understanding of the Scriptures and the Covenant has permeated into the Messianic and Hebrew Roots movements, which are supposedly focused on Torah observance.

Instead of going to the Covenant Land, and Jerusalem to observe the Feasts, many gather at various places around the world, because they don't see the eternal significance of the Covenant Land.[330]

In the last chapter, we discussed how the Covenant with Yisrael involves a family. The very name Abram (אברם) includes the family – Father (אב), mother (אם) and at the very heart - son (בר).

The Covenant with Abram started with a promise of descendants, and land.

> *"¹ Now YHWH had said to Abram: 'Get out of your country, from your family and from your father's house, to a land that I will show you. ² I will make you a great nation; I will bless you and make your name great; and you shall be a blessing. ³ I will bless those who bless you, and I will curse him who curses you; and in you all the families of the earth shall be blessed.'"* Genesis 12:1-3

---

[329] See Genesis 25:29-34
[330] Now I understand that some people are financially limited, but YHWH provides a way through our tithes to attend His Feasts. Sadly, most do not even consider the possibility, and do not even try. It is an amazing thing to visit the Land of our inheritance. While the House of YHWH is no longer here, He has plans to rebuilt in the future. And He will not be residing in anything built by the Pharisees.

While Abram wanted descendants more than anything, that promise could not be fulfilled in Babylon. It required that Abram leave Babylon, and travel to a specifically designated Land.

Only when he actually crossed over and entered the Land did He actually enter into a Covenant. Until he left Babylon, it was only a promise. He had to act.

This is a critical fact. Many people "name it and claim it," but they never act on the promises. A covenant involves two individuals, and they both have responsibilities, and obligations.

Abram had to provide and prepare all of the elements for the Covenant. This would set the stage for the priesthood, and it was a lot of work. We already examined the Covenant ceremony, but it bears repeating here.

> "*9 So He said to him, 'Bring Me a three-year-old heifer, a three-year-old female goat, a three-year-old ram, a turtledove, and a young pigeon.' 10 Then he brought all these to Him and cut them in two, down the middle, and placed each piece opposite the other; but he did not cut the birds in two. 11 And when the vultures came down on the carcasses, Abram drove them away. 12 Now when the sun was going down, a deep sleep fell upon Abram; and behold, horror and great darkness fell upon him. 13 Then He said to Abram: 'Know certainly that your descendants will be strangers in a land that is not theirs, and will serve them, and they will afflict them four hundred years. 14 And also the nation whom they serve I will judge; afterward they shall come out with great possessions. 15 Now as for you, you shall go to your fathers in peace; you shall be buried at a good old age. 16 But in the fourth generation they shall return here, for the iniquity of the Amorites is not yet complete.' 17 And it came to pass, when the sun went down and it was*

dark, that behold, there appeared a smoking oven and a burning torch that passed between those pieces. [18] On the same day YHWH made a covenant with Abram, saying: 'To your descendants I have given this land, from the river of Egypt to the great river, the River Euphrates - [19] the Kenites, the Kenezzites, the Kadmonites, [20] the Hittites, the Perizzites, the Rephaim, [21] the Amorites, the Canaanites, the Girgashites, and the Jebusites.'" Genesis 15:9-21

What if Abram ignored the command to get the animals? What if he failed to slaughter them, shed their blood and place them opposite one another? Do you see my point? He had to participate in the process that was focused primarily on the promise of Land, and I can assure you, it was a lot of work.

We talked in a previous chapter how Yahushua passed through the blood. In doing so, Yahushua revealed that He would shed His blood to pay the price for Abram's descendants breaking the Covenant.

So, while Abram's descendants were ejected from the Land, ultimately, they would be able to return through Yahushua, since He paid the price. Abram's efforts did not provide the solution, he was simply participating in the process. But his participation was vital.

We see this again when YHWH appeared to Abram, and changed His name to Abraham. Now, the focus was on the promise of a descendant. That is why the Covenant of Circumcision was focused on the male organ, the source of the seed.

Abraham was required to circumcise his flesh, and the flesh of all the males in his household. Here are the terms of the Covenant.

"[2] And I will make My Covenant between Me and you, and will multiply you exceedingly. [3] Then Abram fell on

his face, and Elohim talked with him, saying: ⁴ As for Me, behold, My Covenant is with you, and you shall be a father of many Nations. ⁵ No longer shall your name be called Abram, but your name shall be Abraham; for I have made you a father of many Nations. ⁶ I will make you exceedingly fruitful; and I will make Nations of you, and kings shall come from you. ⁷ And I will establish My את-Covenant between Me and you and your descendants after you in their generations, for an everlasting Covenant, to be Elohim to you and your descendants after you. ⁸ Also I give to you and your descendants after you את the land in which you are a stranger, את all the land of Canaan, as an everlasting possession; and I will be their Elohim." Genesis 17:2-8

Like the Covenant with Abram, it dealt with Land that would pass to his descendants. That Land and that Covenant are specifically associated with the Messiah, as we can see from the aleph taw (את).

Now, instead of the Nations being blessed by him, we read that Nations will actually come from him. That is far different from his original desire for a child, and a piece of land. Three times, YHWH mentioned that Abraham would be the father of Nations – many Nations.

As with any blood Covenant, blood needed to be shed. This time, instead of the blood of animals, it would be the blood of the males. Here is a description of that process.

"⁹ And Elohim said to Abraham: "As for you, you shall keep My את-Covenant, you and your descendants after you throughout their generations. ¹⁰ This is My את Covenant which you shall keep, between Me and you and your descendants after you: Every male child among you shall be circumcised; ¹¹ and you shall be circumcised in the flesh of your foreskins, and it shall be a sign of the *covenant between Me and you.* [12] *He who is eight days old among you shall be circumcised, every male child in your generations, he who is born in your house or bought with money from any foreigner who is not your descendant.* [13] *He who is born in your house and he who is bought with your money must be circumcised, and My Covenant shall be in your flesh for an everlasting Covenant.* [14] *And the uncircumcised male child, who is not circumcised in the flesh of his foreskin, that person shall be cut off from his people; he has broken My Covenant."* Genesis 17:9-14

Abraham and all of His descendants of this Covenant would shed their blood. Only when Abraham was circumcised would his seed pass through the cutting of the Covenant. This would result in the promised son, who could then inherit the Promised Land.

Of course that is a picture of Yahushua, the Promised Son, passing through the cutting of the Covenant while Abram slept.

Now again, what if Abraham said "I'm afraid." "What if my knife slips?" "Anywhere but there YHWH!"

If he failed to diligently obey, the pattern would not be established, and the Covenant could not be fulfilled through the Promised Son.

Speaking of the Promised Son, remember that after Isaac was born, YHWH commanded Abraham as follows: *"Then He said, Take now your son, your only son Isaac, whom you love, and go to the land of Moriah, and offer him there as a burnt offering on one of the mountains of which I shall tell you."* Genesis 22:2

That event provided the pattern for the Promised Son to be the sacrifice, only it would not be Isaac. Rather YHWH Himself would provide the sacrifice. He provided His Son Yahushua the Messiah.

This event was critical for our understanding of the Messianic fulfillment of the Covenant. It set the stage for Yahushua to come and die for those in the Covenant. What if Abraham refused to obey? What if he said, no way YHWH, you promised me this child?"

Again, his participation was critical, and certainly difficult. But YHWH was testing Him, and He tests all of us.[331] So, the next time someone says "We can't obey the Instructions" you should tell them they are a liar, and they should stop spreading lies.

Point them to Noah. He wasn't perfect, but he walked with YHWH. He had to build an ark. Direct them to Abraham. Abraham wasn't perfect either, but he obeyed. He trusted YHWH, and that was accounted as righteousness. The reason is that the Commandments are the very definition of righteousness. So when you obey, you are walking righteously.

Notice that there appear to be different dimensions of the Land. Uncircumcised Abram's descendants were promised Land from the Nile to the Euphrates. Those in the Covenant of Circumcision appear to be focused exclusively on the Land of Canaan.

Could this be a pattern for a future people who have circumcised hearts? They are the ones permitted closer to YHWH. They have the more intimate relationship.

Whenever you see a change of name, it is significant. We talked about the first naming of Yisrael at Peniel. We saw the word play between em-Yisrael, am-Elohim, and am-anashim.

The mother, Yisrael would provide a womb for a people for Elohim – a people from men. Well, that Covenant family needs a home, and that is why the second naming of Yisrael occurred at Beth El - the House of Elohim.

At Beth El, Yisrael was commanded: "be fruitful and multiply." Again, that was the same Command given to Adam

---

[331] See Genesis 22:1. For a discussion of the issue of testing see the articles titled *The First Test in Wilderness* and *Bread in the Wilderness* on the shemayisrael.net website.

in the Garden. So, Yisrael in the Land had the same mandate as Adam did in the Garden. Take dominion.[332] Start with the Covenant Land, and spread the truth of YHWH to the Nations.

The Covenant Land represented the Garden of Eden. YHWH prepared it for His people, just like He prepared the Garden of Eden for Adam and Hawah.

> *"[10] So it shall be, when YHWH your Elohim brings you into the land of which He swore to your fathers, to Abraham, Isaac, and Jacob, to give you large and beautiful cities which you did not build, [11] houses full of all good things, which you did not fill, hewn-out wells which you did not dig, vineyards and olive trees which you did not plant - when you have eaten and are full - [12] then beware, lest you forget YHWH who brought you out of the land of Egypt, from the house of bondage. [13] You shall fear YHWH your Elohim and serve Him, and shall take oaths in His name. [14] You shall not go after other gods, the gods of the peoples who are all around you [15] (for YHWH your Elohim is a jealous Elohim among you), lest the anger of YHWH your Elohim be aroused against you and destroy you from the face of the earth."*
> Deuteronomy 6:10-15

Everything was provided for them. It was a "turn-key operation." All they needed to do was follow the rules of the house. That is something any parent would expect from their children. Every parent has likely said it at some point. "It's my house and these are my rules."

The Yisraelites were provided with the choice of blessings or curses after they entered the Promised Land under Joshua, whose Hebrew name was Yahushua. Of course it is no

---

[332] Genesis 1:26-28

coincidence that Joshua, was the one who led Yisrael into the Land.

When Joshua left Egypt his name was Hoshea, which means "salvation." Before he entered the Land with the 12 Spies his name was changed to Yahushua – "Yah Saves" or "Yah is salvation."

He later led this nation of Yisrael as they "crossed over" into the Land of Canaan, as part of this Hebrew Covenant. They crossed over near Jericho. It was, in fact, a corporate immersion.

Once they crossed over, Joshua oversaw the circumcision of the males at Gilgal. They then kept the Passover in the Land, and proceeded to Shechem, where the Covenant from Sinai was renewed.

Of course, this was a pattern for Yahushua the Messiah Who was immersed at the same place in the Jordan. He came to renew the Covenant at Passover, and circumcise our hearts.

Moses had previously described the process that would occur when they renewed the Covenant after entering the Land. They were clearly told the blessings for disobedience and the curses for disobedience as described in Deuteronomy 28.

The point was to obey, and remain in the Land. Just like Adam and Hawah – they failed. As a result they were divided and punished. They failed to stay on the straight Covenant path.

Jeremiah described what happened. *"15 Because My people have forgotten Me, they have burned incense to worthless idols. And they have caused themselves to stumble in their ways, from the ancient paths, to walk in pathways and not on a highway, 16 To make their land desolate and a perpetual hissing; Everyone who passes by it will be astonished and shake his head. 17 I will scatter them as with an east wind before the enemy; I will show them the back and not the face in the day of their calamity."* Jeremiah 18:15-17

Here Jeremiah describes the curse of disobedience that

befell Yisrael because they forgot Elohim. Both the House of Yisrael and the House of Yahudah strayed from the "ancient paths." They were supposed to walk on the "highway," which is "derech" (דרך) in Hebrew.

A "derech" is a "way" to a known destination. If you stay on it, you will arrive at your destination. If you stray, you may get lost.

We have already talked about the abominations of Jeroboam. He constructed two golden calves. The House of Yisrael slaughtered to the one at Beth El, and surely burned incense to them both. Jeroboam also moved the dates of the Appointed Times.

As a result, the House of Yisrael was removed first by the Assyrians. They completely lost their identity, according to Hoshea. They were totally removed from the Land, and scattered to the four corners of the Earth according to Isaiah.[333]

They mixed with the Nations, and multiplied while they were in exile. There were promises made concerning their restoration, and it is critical that you see and read these promises so that they become real and relevant.

As a result, I am going to include many lengthy Scripture passages. These promises are the terms of the Covenant, so it is important to review them, if you want to be in the Covenant, and participate in those promises.

When I have clients come in to review their estate planning documents, I give them plenty of time to review them. Please take the time to review these prophecies, because they are about your future inheritance, if you are in the renewed Covenant.

Isaiah prophesied that there would be a regathering by a Rod – the root of Jesse. Read the following passages to get a more complete understanding of these prophetic promises.

"¹ There shall come forth a Rod from the stem of

[333] See Isaiah 11:12

Jesse, and a Branch shall grow out of his roots. ² The
Spirit of YHWH shall rest upon Him, The Spirit
of wisdom and understanding, The Spirit of counsel
and might, The Spirit of knowledge and of the fear
of YHWH. ³ His delight is in the fear of YHWH,
and He shall not judge by the sight of His eyes, Nor
decide by the hearing of His ears; ⁴ But with
righteousness He shall judge the poor, and decide
with equity for the meek of the earth; He shall strike
the earth with the rod of His mouth, and with the
breath of His lips He shall slay the wicked. ⁵
Righteousness shall be the belt of His loins, and
faithfulness the belt of His waist. ⁶ The wolf also
shall dwell with the lamb, the leopard shall lie down
with the young goat, the calf and the young lion and
the fatling together; and a little child shall lead them.
⁷ The cow and the bear shall graze; their young ones
shall lie down together; and the lion shall eat straw
like the ox. ⁸ The nursing child shall play by the
cobra's hole, and the weaned child shall put his hand
in the viper's den. ⁹ They shall not hurt nor destroy
in all My Set Apart mountain, for the earth shall be
full of the knowledge of YHWH as the waters cover
the sea. ¹⁰ And in that day there shall be a Root of
Jesse, Who shall stand as a banner to the people; for
the Nations shall seek Him, and His resting place
shall be glorious. ¹¹ It shall come to pass in that day
that Adonai shall set His hand again the second time
to recover the remnant of His people who are left,
from Assyria and Egypt, from Pathros and Cush,
from Elam and Shinar, from Hamath and the
islands of the sea. ¹² He will set up a banner for the
nations, and will assemble the outcasts of Yisrael,
and gather together the dispersed of Judah from the
four corners of the earth. ¹³ Also the envy of Ephraim
shall depart, and the adversaries of Judah shall be

cut off; Ephraim shall not envy Judah, and Judah shall not harass Ephraim. ¹⁴ But they shall fly down upon the shoulder of the Philistines toward the west; together they shall plunder the people of the East; They shall lay their hand on Edom and Moab; and the people of Ammon shall obey them. ¹⁵ YHWH will utterly destroy the tongue of the Sea of Egypt; with His mighty wind He will shake His fist over the River, and strike it in the seven streams, and make men cross over dryshod. ¹⁶ There will be a highway for the remnant of His people who will be left from Assyria, as it was for Yisrael in the day that he came up from the land of Egypt." Isaiah 11:1-16

This is an incredible promise, and I encourage you to re-read it if necessary. It says that He will raise up a banner, and set His hand **a second time**, to assemble the outcasts of Yisrael and the dispersed of Yahudah from the four corners of the Earth.

Just because both Yahudah and Ephraim failed, does not mean that YHWH was finished with them, or the Covenant Land.

I deal with parents who are involved with some terrible situations involving their children. Even when they need to invoke "tough love," they still love their children.

Look at the precedent set by Hosea. Even though he lived with an adulterous wife, he still showed love and the willingness to forgive and restore the relationship.

Just because the man and the woman were evicted from the Garden does not mean YHWH still does not want mankind to dwell in Paradise. Of course He does. That is the point of the Covenant.

In fact, Jeremiah prophesied that both Houses would be restored through the renewed Covenant.

"⁷ For thus says YHWH: Sing with gladness for Jacob, and shout among the chief of the nations; Proclaim, give praise, and say, O YHWH, save Your people, the remnant of Yisrael! ⁸ Behold, I will bring them from the north country, and gather them from the ends of the earth, among them the blind and the lame, the woman with child and the one who labors with child, together; A great throng shall return there. ⁹ They shall come with weeping, and with supplications I will lead them. I will cause them to walk by the rivers of waters, In a straight way in which they shall not stumble; for I am a Father to Yisrael, and Ephraim is My firstborn. ¹⁰ Hear the word of YHWH, O nations, and declare it in the isles afar off, and say, He who scattered Yisrael will gather him, and keep him as a shepherd does his flock. ¹¹ For YHWH has redeemed Jacob, and ransomed him from the hand of one stronger than he. ¹² Therefore they shall come and sing in the height of Tzyon, streaming to the goodness of YHWH - for wheat and new wine and oil, for the young of the flock and the herd; Their souls shall be like a well-watered garden, and they shall sorrow no more at all. ¹³ Then shall the virgin rejoice in the dance, and the young men and the old, together; for I will turn their mourning to joy, will comfort them, and make them rejoice rather than sorrow. ¹⁴ I will satiate the soul of the priests with abundance, and My people shall be satisfied with My goodness says YHWH."
Jeremiah 31:7-14

Again, do you see the emphasis on Ephraim as a firstborn? Remember that Ephraim was elevated to the firstborn status by the man Yisrael, while he was in Egypt. Ephraim represents the House of Yisrael, not the Jewish people. Ephraim has been in exile for thousands of years. But YHWH Who scattered them will gather them as a shepherd does a flock.

Sheep know the voice of their shepherd. As they graze throughout the day, they will spread out, each looking for the best food to eat. When the shepherd calls out, they will all turn and return to his voice. The same will occur to the House of Yisrael.

How will this happen? Through repentance and a return to the Land.

"16 Thus says YHWH: Refrain your voice from weeping, and your eyes from tears; For your work shall be rewarded, says YHWH, and they shall come back from the land of the enemy. 17 There is hope in your future, says YHWH, That your children shall come back to their own border. 18 I have surely heard Ephraim bemoaning himself: You have chastised me, and I was chastised, like an untrained bull; Restore me, and I will return, for You are YHWH my Elohim. 19 Surely, after my turning, I repented; and after I was instructed, I struck myself on the thigh; I was ashamed, yes, even humiliated, because I bore the reproach of my youth. 20 Is Ephraim My dear son? Is he a pleasant child? For though I spoke against him, I earnestly remember him still; Therefore My heart yearns for him; I will surely have mercy on him, says YHWH. 21 Set up signposts, make landmarks; Set your heart toward the highway, the way in which you went. Turn back, O virgin of Yisrael, Turn back to these your cities. 22 How long will you gad about, O you backsliding daughter? For YHWH has created a new thing in the earth - a woman shall encompass a man." Jeremiah 31:16-22

And what is the renewed Covenant? It is provided through Jeremiah, and bears repeating here.

"27 Behold, the days are coming, says YHWH, that I

will sow the House of Yisrael and the House of Yahudah with the seed of man and the seed of beast. [28] And it shall come to pass, that as I have watched over them to pluck up, to break down, to throw down, to destroy, and to afflict, so I will watch over them to build and to plant, says YHWH. [29] In those days they shall say no more: The fathers have eaten sour grapes, and the children's teeth are set on edge. [30] But every one shall die for his own iniquity; every man who eats the sour grapes, his teeth shall be set on edge. [31] Behold, the days are coming, says YHWH, when I will make a renewed Covenant with the House of Yisrael and with the House of Yahudah - [32] not according to the Covenant that I made with their fathers in the day that I took them by the hand to lead them out of the land of Egypt, My Covenant which they broke, though I was a Husband to them, says YHWH. [33] But this is the Covenant that I will make with the house of Yisrael after those days, says YHWH: I will put My Torah in their minds, and write it on their hearts; and I will be their Elohim, and they shall be My people. [34] No more shall every man teach his neighbor, and every man his brother, saying, Know YHWH, for they all shall know Me, from the least of them to the greatest of them, says YHWH. For I will forgive their iniquity, and their sin I will remember no more." Jeremiah 31:27-34

This restoration and return is all about knowing Elohim, and having His Torah within us - so we can obey. Our broken relationship with Him is restored through the Renewed Covenant. Only when you are in Covenant with Him are you considered to be "His people."

Right now, His people are scattered throughout the world – like lost and scattered sheep. This is because they were punished and exiled into the Nations. But remember, it was for a purpose. When He gathers His people out of the Nations,

He will use that as an opportunity to draw the Nations to Him.

Ultimately, His people will be united under one King, after they are gathered. We already reviewed this promise from Ezekiel, but it bears repeating.

> "[21] Then say to them, Thus says Adonai YHWH: Surely I will take the children of Yisrael from among the nations, wherever they have gone, and will gather them from every side and bring them into their own land; [22] and I will make them one nation in the Land, on the mountains of Yisrael; and one king shall be king over them all; they shall no longer be two nations, nor shall they ever be divided into two kingdoms again. [23] They shall not defile themselves anymore with their idols, nor with their detestable things, nor with any of their transgressions; but I will deliver them from all their dwelling places in which they have sinned, and will cleanse them. Then they shall be My people, and I will be their Elohim. [24] David My servant shall be king over them, and they shall all have one shepherd; they shall also walk in My judgments and observe My statutes, and do them. [25] Then they shall dwell in the land that I have given to Jacob My servant, where your fathers dwelt; and they shall dwell there, they, their children, and their children's children, forever; and My servant David shall be their prince forever. [26] Moreover I will make a Covenant of Peace with them, and it shall be an everlasting covenant with them; I will establish them and multiply them, and I will set My את-sanctuary in their midst forevermore. [27] My tabernacle also shall be with them; indeed I will be their Elohim, and they shall be My people. [28] The nations also will know that I, YHWH, sanctify את-Yisrael, when My sanctuary is in their midst forevermore." Ezekiel 37:21-28

This is all a Messianic promise of an everlasting Covenant established by YHWH through David, a prince. It is no coincidence that Yahushua is known as "the Prince of Peace" and the "Son of David." Did you notice that the sanctuary that will be in their midst is connected with the Messiah? In Hebrew it is "et-miqdash" (אֶת-מִקְדָּשׁ).

Notice again that *"I will take the children of Yisrael from among the nations, wherever they have gone, and will gather them from every side and bring them into their own land."* They will leave the places where they were scattered, and they will be transplanted into the Covenant Land. He will sanctify אֶת-Yisrael through the Messiah.

The children of Yisrael are those in a Covenant relationship with YHWH. That is why the text refers to a Covenant of Peace – a "Brit Shalom" in Hebrew. It is also referred to as an Everlasting Covenant, which is "Brit Olam" – a covenant through the ages.

This is the same as the Renewed Covenant described by Jeremiah. The Covenant of Peace is what He brings when the wrath of Elohim is abated. And we read about a Covenant of Peace in Numbers as well.

> *"¹⁰ Then YHWH spoke to Moses, saying: ¹¹ Phinehas the son of Eleazar, the son of Aaron the priest, has turned back My wrath from the children of Yisrael, because he was zealous with My zeal among them, so that I did not consume the children of Yisrael in My zeal. ¹² Therefore say, Behold, I give to him My Covenant of peace; ¹³ and it shall be to him and his descendants after him a Covenant of an everlasting priesthood, because he was zealous for his Elohim, and made atonement for the children of Yisrael."* Numbers 25:10-13

YHWH will pour out His wrath on the world in the future. The world ruled by the Babylonian Beast system, and represented by the anti-messiah. It will be like the time when

He poured out His wrath on the beast of Egypt, represented by Pharaoh.

While He is judging and punishing the Beast, and all the Nations within her, YHWH will have mercy on His children and deliver them through His Covenant of Peace.

"For the mountains shall depart and the hills be removed,
but My kindness shall not depart from you,
nor shall My Covenant of Peace be removed,
says YHWH, who has mercy on you."
Isaiah 54:10

Ezekiel tells how the Covenant of Peace will involve placing the House of Yisrael into their own bountiful land.

"²⁰ Therefore thus says Adonai YHWH to them: 'Behold, I Myself will judge between the fat and the lean sheep. ²¹ Because you have pushed with side and shoulder, butted all the weak ones with your horns, and scattered them abroad, ²² therefore I will save My flock, and they shall no longer be a prey; and I will judge between sheep and sheep. ²³ I will establish one shepherd over them, and he shall feed them - My servant David. He shall feed them and be their shepherd. ²⁴ And I, YHWH, will be their Elohim, and My servant David a prince among them; I, YHWH, have spoken. ²⁵ I will make a Covenant of Peace with them, and cause wild beasts to cease from the land; and they will dwell safely in the wilderness and sleep in the woods. ²⁶ I will make them and the places all around My hill a blessing; and I will cause showers to come down in their season; there shall be showers of blessing. ²⁷ Then the trees of the field shall yield their fruit, and the earth shall yield her increase. They shall be safe in their land; and they shall know that I am YHWH, when I have broken

the bands of their yoke and delivered them from the hand of those who enslaved them. ²⁸ And they shall no longer be a prey for the nations, nor shall beasts of the land devour them; but they shall dwell safely, and no one shall make them afraid. ²⁹ I will raise up for them a garden of renown, and they shall no longer be consumed with hunger in the land, nor bear the shame of the Nations anymore. ³⁰ Thus they shall know that I, YHWH their Elohim, am with them, and they, the House of Yisrael, are My people, says Adonai YHWH." Ezekiel 34:20-30

For those who grew up in the Christian Church, I hope it is clear how these promises are applicable to a future people who follow King Messiah. A people known as the House of Yisrael. I also hope it is clear how wrong Christian eschatology has been concerning the people of YHWH, and His Plan of restoration.

There is no new and different covenant that involves sending lawless Christians to heaven. They will definitely be sent somewhere by the King, if they do not repent.[334]

There is, on the other hand, a plan to restore His people to the Covenant Land, through His Covenant of Peace. If you desire to be part of that Covenant, then you had better be ready to move if you are not currently dwelling in His Promised Land. You must be prepared to leave Babylon.

Abram was told: *"Get out of your country, from your family and from your father's house, to a land that I will show you."* Genesis 12:1 He had to leave Babylon in order to enter into a Covenant relationship with YHWH. Again, what if he decided he was too comfortable, or simply had too many things? What if he said it was too difficult? Or, it wasn't a good time to sell due to the real estate market?

---

[334] See Matthew 7:21-23

Abram had to move out of Babylon, just like Yisrael had to move out of Egypt. They all had to live in tents and keep following YHWH as He directed their path.

We are no different, if we expect to live in a Covenant, where the final destination is the Covenant Land. In fact, I am writing this chapter while I am in Jerusalem celebrating the Feast of Sukkot. Remember the Feast where we are commanded to dwell in sukkas (sukkot) for seven days? There is a specific reason for why we dwell in sukkas.

> "*41 You shall keep it as a Feast to YHWH for seven days in the year. It shall be a statute forever in your generations. You shall celebrate it in the seventh month. 42 You shall dwell in sukkas (sukkot) for seven days. All who are native Yisraelites shall dwell in sukkas (sukkot), 43 that your generations may know that I made the children of Yisrael dwell in sukkot when I brought them out of the land of Egypt: I am YHWH your Elohim.*" Leviticus 23:41-43

We still rehearse the Feast by dwelling in temporary dwellings. That means we have not yet seen the fulfillment of this Appointed Time.

Immediately following Sukkot, is a separate but connected Appointed Time known as "The Eighth Day" or "Shemini Atzeret." That Appointed Time points to a future fulfillment when we can come out of our temporary dwellings and finally move into our permanent home with YHWH. It is the final Appointed Time that lands of Day 22 of Month 7. It is a High Sabbath and represents the fullness of the Covenant through the Covenant of Peace.

In order to get to that point, there must be a final gathering. Besides the texts already mentioned, the prophets repeatedly speak of this promise. Here are some further examples:

"He will lift up a banner to the nations from afar,
and will whistle to them from the end of the earth;
Surely they shall come with speed, swiftly."
Isaiah 5:26

"I will whistle for them and gather them, for I will redeem them;
and they shall increase as they once increased."
Zechariah 10:8

Those passages always make me think of my childhood, especially during the summer. All the kids on my street would gather and play manhunt, or hide-and-go-seek, in the evening. We would scatter all over the neighborhood trying to hide and not be found out.

We would always lose track of time, but our father was always keeping track of time. When it got to the "appointed time," my father would go outside and whistle for us. You could hear it throughout the neighborhood. When my sister and I heard it, we knew it was time to return home to our father. We would run all the way home where dinner was ready and waiting for us. There was a meal prepared for us at the appointed time. What an amazing picture that YHWH gave me as a real-life example!

So, there will be a future great regathering, as YHWH mobilizes His people from the four corners of the Earth.

"Behold, I will bring them from the north country,
and gather them from the ends of the earth,
among them the blind and the lame,
the woman with child and the one who labors with child,
together; a great throng shall return there."
Jeremiah 31:8

Jeremiah described why they were removed in the first place, as well as the promise of a miraculous return. It will be so incredible, that they will no longer talk about the deliverance from Egypt. It will be truly miraculous!

"*11* then you shall say to them, Because your fathers have forsaken Me, says YHWH; they have walked after other gods and have served them and worshiped them, and have forsaken Me and not kept My את-Torah. *12* And you have done worse than your fathers, for behold, each one follows the dictates of his own evil heart, so that no one listens to Me. *13* Therefore I will cast you out of this Land into a land that you do not know, neither you nor your fathers; and there you shall serve other gods day and night, where I will not show you favor. *14* Therefore behold, the days are coming, says YHWH, that it shall no more be said, YHWH lives who brought up the children of Israel from the land of Egypt, *15* but, YHWH lives who brought up the children of Yisrael from the land of the north and from all the lands where He had driven them. For I will bring them back into their Land which I gave to their fathers. *16* Behold, I will send for many fishermen, says YHWH, and they shall fish them; and afterward I will send for many hunters, and they shall hunt them from every mountain and every hill, and out of the holes of the rocks. *17* For My eyes are on all their ways; they are not hidden from My face, nor is their iniquity hidden from My eyes. *18* And first I will repay double for their iniquity and their sin, because they have defiled My land; they have filled My inheritance with the carcasses of their detestable and abominable idols. *19* O YHWH, my strength and my fortress, my refuge in the day of affliction, The Nations shall come to You from the ends of the earth and say, Surely our fathers have inherited lies, worthlessness and unprofitable things. *20* Will a man make gods for himself, which are not gods? *21* Therefore behold, I will this once cause them to know,

*I will cause them to know My hand and My might;
and they shall know that My Name is YHWH."*
Jeremiah 16:11-21

This text reveals that the people were exiled because
they forsook YHWH, and His Torah. Did you notice the
aleph taw (אֵת) affixed to Torah? This is a powerful message
that we need to follow the Torah as taught by the Messiah.

For those who repent and turn back to the אֵת-Torah,
He will bring them back into their Land which He gave to
their fathers.

The return of the people from the Nations will first
involve an awakening amongst the Nations. The people of
YHWH will reject the lies that they inherited from their
fathers, including the religion of their fathers. They will learn
the Name of YHWH, and they will return to Him and His
ways.

Did you notice the promise of fishermen? This is why
Yahushua called His disciples to be fishers of men.
Interestingly, Yahushua went to Bethsaida to recruit some of
His disciples.[335] Bethsaida in Hebrew is "Beit-tzaida," which
means "House of Fishing" and "House of Hunting."

Coincidence? I think not. Yahushua was revealing that
He was fulfilling the prophecy in Jeremiah, which states that
He will send out fishers first, and then hunters.

The fishermen have been casting out their nets for
centuries, gathering in the "Sons of Elohim." That was the
resounding message that was sent to His disciples when He
appeared to them after the resurrection, and they caught 153
fish in nets that did not break.[336]

Yahushua will send out hunters who will track down
individual people. That is part of what Yahushua described
when He returns. *"[30] Then the sign of the Son of Man will appear
in heaven, and then all the tribes of the earth will mourn, and they*

---

[335] *"Now Philip was from Bethsaida, the city of Andrew and Peter."* John 1:44
[336] See John 21:1-13

will see the Son of Man coming on the clouds of heaven with power and great glory. *³¹ And He will send His messengers with a great sound of a shofar, and they will gather together His elect from the four winds, from one end of heaven to the other.*" Matthew 24:30-31

Again, this will make the deliverance from Egypt pale in comparison. In fact, Jeremiah further describes this event occurring through the Messiah as the Shepherd of the lost sheep of the House of Yisrael.

> "*¹ Woe to the shepherds who destroy and scatter the sheep of My pasture! says YHWH. ² Therefore thus says YHWH Elohim of Yisrael against the shepherds who feed My people: You have scattered My flock, driven them away, and not attended to them. Behold, I will attend to you for the evil of your doings, says YHWH. ³ But I will gather the remnant of My flock out of all countries where I have driven them, and bring them back to their folds; and they shall be fruitful and increase. ⁴ I will set up shepherds over them who will feed them; and they shall fear no more, nor be ~ dismayed, nor shall they be lacking, says YHWH. ⁵ Behold, the days are coming, says YHWH, That I will raise to David a Branch of righteousness; A King shall reign and prosper, and execute judgment and righteousness in the earth. ⁶ In His days Judah will be saved, and Yisrael will dwell safely; Now this is His name by which He will be called: YHWH OUR RIGHTEOUSNESS. ⁷ Therefore, behold, the days are coming, says YHWH, that they shall no longer say, As YHWH lives who brought up the children of Yisrael from the land of Egypt, ⁸ but, As YHWH lives who brought up and led the descendants of the House of Yisrael from the north country and from all the countries where I had driven them. And they shall dwell in their own land.*" Jeremiah 23:1-8

I hope by now it is obvious, but it bears repeating - YHWH is the Elohim of Yisrael, and Yahushua renewed the Covenant with Yisrael. If you are in that renewed Covenant, then you need to identify with Yisrael, and you should desire to live with the King in His Land.

The text specifically states that people will no longer be talking about the Exodus from Egypt, but rather *"As YHWH lives who brought up and led the descendants of the House of Yisrael from the north country and from all the countries where I had driven them. And they shall dwell in their own land."*

Well, at the recent Passover, we were still talking about the deliverance from Egypt. That would lead me to believe that we have yet to see this prophecy fulfilled. Of course, the House of Yisrael has not been gathered back into their Land. It is currently being occupied by Christians, Muslims and Jews – all people outside of the Covenant renewed by Yahushua, according to Jeremiah 31.

The repeated mention of the deliverance from Egypt seems to be telling us that the future deliverance, sometimes referred to as the Greater Exodus, might also occur at Passover.

As with the Passover in Egypt, we should expect to be teaching and bringing "a mixed multitude" with us.[337] It's all part of prophecy, and the patterns provided through the Appointed Times.

"YHWH Elohim, who gathers the outcasts of Yisrael,
says, Yet I will gather to him others
besides those who are gathered to him."
Isaiah 56:8

That is why it is important that we understand and rehearse all of the Appointed Times. While some people teach

---

[337] See Exodus 12:38

that the Spring Feasts are all fulfilled, and only the Fall Feasts remain to be fulfilled, that is not correct.

While they had past fulfillments, they also have future fulfillments. So, there will be a great regathering and return to the Land heralded by the Messiah, and this will be the actual fulfillment of the Appointed Times.

Remember in the last chapter we talked about Isaiah 66? How many interpret this as a prophecy about the modern State of Yisrael?

If you examine the text in its entirety, it is talking about the birth of Tzyon as YHWH destroys His enemies. It is all about Him being glorified, not a Zionist State that ignores Him.

Tzyon is not a group of people looking to found a Jewish state, promoting a political agenda called Zionism.

YHWH specifically says in Isaiah 66:2 that He will look upon *"him who is poor and of a contrite spirit, and who trembles at My Word."* We don't see many people trembling at the Word of YHWH today in the modern State of Israel.

In fact, the majority of the people don't even consider His Word. Instead of humility, you see t-shirts and slogans exalting the power and might of the IDF (Israeli Defense Force). I see pride. I don't see much humility.

Also, it is important to remember that through the partition of the Ottoman Empire after World War 1 many Nations were "born" or created spontaneously. Those nations include Turkey, Saudi Arabia, Yemen and the modern Arab World.

French Mandates of Syria and Lebanon resulted in the formation of those countries, and British Mandates of Mesopotamia and Palestine ultimately resulted in the formation of the modern State of Israel.

So, while the formation of a Jewish State was an incredible historical event, it was not the only nation birthed after World Wars I and II through various negotiations and treaties. These nations technically all appeared "in one day" when the mandates were formalized.

Of course, using the word Zionism to label the movement that led to the development of the Jewish State further confuses the issue, because Tzyon is specifically defined as the City of David in the Scriptures.

"Nevertheless David took the stronghold of Tzion
(that is, the City of David)."
2 Samuel 5:7[338]

It is important to understand that Tzyon is not the same as Jerusalem. It is where the King lives, and reigns with his family. Even though YHWH departed, He will, once again return, and establish a home there.

"Thus says YHWH: I will return to Tzyon, and dwell in the midst
of Jerusalem. Jerusalem shall be called the City of Truth, The
Mountain of YHWH of hosts, The Holy (Set Apart) Mountain."
Zechariah 8:3

"Rejoice greatly, O daughter of Tzyon!
Shout, O daughter of Jerusalem!
Behold, your King is coming to you;
He is just and having salvation, lowly and riding
on a donkey, a colt, the foal of a donkey."
Zechariah 9:9

So, Tzyon is where YHWH resides in the midst of Jerusalem. This was represented by the Temple in the past.

It is the closest to the King. Only recently has great focus and attention been placed on the City of David, which was largely ignored and forgotten for centuries. In fact, if you go to Jerusalem today, they still don't even recognize the City of David as Tzyon. They call the western hill Mount Zion

---

338 See also 1 Kings 8:11, 1 Chronicles 11:5, 2 Chronicles 5:2

The point of all this is that Isaiah 66 refers to a birthing of Tzyon, and the wrath of the King which has not yet occurred. Zionism sought the Covenant Land without the Covenant. The final restoration will involve Tzyon - those in the Covenant.

The text in Isaiah 66 ends by describing the King, and all of the Nations going to Jerusalem to worship YHWH.

> "*[18] For I know their works and their thoughts. It shall be that I will gather all nations and tongues; and they shall come and see My glory. [19] I will set a sign among them; and those among them who escape I will send to the nations: to Tarshish and Pul and Lud, who draw the bow, and Tubal and Javan, to the coastlands afar off who have not heard My fame nor seen My glory. And they shall declare My glory among the Gentiles. [20] Then they shall bring all your brethren for an offering to YHWH out of all nations, on horses and in chariots and in litters, on mules and on camels, to My holy (set apart) mountain Jerusalem, says YHWH, as the children of Yisrael bring an offering in a clean vessel into the house of YHWH. [21] And I will also take some of them for priests and Levites, says YHWH. [22] For as the new heavens and the new earth which I will make shall remain before Me, says YHWH, So shall your descendants and your name remain. [23] And it shall come to pass That from one New Moon to another, and from one Sabbath to another, All flesh shall come to worship before Me, says YHWH."*
> Isaiah 66:18-23

This text is talking about a time in the future – not 1948 when the modern State of Israel was established. It shows the continuing importance of the Land, and where the King will set up His Throne. Anyone who serves the King should surely desire to see the King, and live near the King. So there will be a return to the Land, and people in Covenant should be prepared for that return.

Isaiah described that reconnect in Isaiah 62

"¹ For Tzyon's sake I will not hold My peace, and for Jerusalem's sake I will not rest, until her righteousness goes forth as brightness, and her salvation as a lamp that burns. ² The Nations shall see your righteousness, and all kings your glory. You shall be called by a new name, which the mouth of YHWH will name. ³ You shall also be a crown of glory in the hand of YHWH, and a royal diadem in the hand of your Elohim. ⁴ You shall no longer be termed Forsaken, Nor shall your land any more be termed Desolate; But you shall be called Hephzibah, and your land Beulah; For YHWH delights in you, and your land shall be married. ⁵ For as a young man marries a virgin, so shall your sons marry you; and as the bridegroom rejoices over the bride, so shall your Elohim rejoice over you. ⁶ I have set watchmen on your walls, O Jerusalem; They shall never hold their peace day or night. You who make mention of YHWH, do not keep silent, ⁷ And give Him no rest till He establishes and till He makes Jerusalem a praise in the earth. ⁸ YHWH has sworn by His right hand and by the arm of His strength: Surely I will no longer give your grain as food for your enemies; And the sons of the foreigner shall not drink your new wine, for which you have labored. ⁹ But those who have gathered it shall eat it, And praise YHWH; Those who have brought it together shall drink it in My holy (set apart) courts. ¹⁰ Go through, Go through the gates! Prepare the way for the people; Build up, Build up the highway! Take out the stones, lift up a banner for the peoples! ¹¹ Indeed YHWH has proclaimed to the end of the world: Say to the daughter

of Tzion, Surely your salvation is coming; Behold, His reward is with Him, and His work before Him. [12] And they shall call them The Holy (Set Apart) People, The Redeemed of YHWH; and you shall be called Sought Out, A City Not Forsaken." Isaiah 62:1-11

Notice the focus here – Tzyon, Jerusalem, a set apart people. They are set apart because of the righteous instructions and they shine that light to the Nations, which was the original mandate of Yisrael. This is a restored Yisrael under the rulership of YHWH.

The highways are built up to lead the people to Tzyon, and through the gates to the King. That city and those gates are the Renewed Jerusalem that descends upon the planet as described by John in the Revelation.

"[2] Then I, John, saw the Set Apart City, Renewed Jerusalem, coming down out of heaven from Elohim, prepared as a bride adorned for her husband. [3] And I heard a loud voice from heaven saying, Behold, the tabernacle of Elohim is with men, and He will dwell with them, and they shall be His people. Elohim Himself will be with them and be their Elohim." Revelation 21:2-3

This is all occurs through renewed Covenant, and it is a fulfillment of the Land Covenant.

So, Yahushua is coming in the clouds to gather the elect from the four corners of the Earth where they are still presently scattered, but He is not rapturing them to live in Heaven for eternity.

Rather, He will gather them together, and prepare them to live, serve and reign here on Earth. The Messiah is returning to stay this time. He will possess the Land, and restore and rule over the entire planet. The original mandate of Adam and Hawah will be fulfilled through Yahushua and His Bride.

It is important to understand that not everyone in the Kingdom is the Bride. That is an important distinction that we will talk about in the next chapter as we discuss the issue of entering the Kingdom.

20

Entering the Kingdom

Many in Christianity perceive the Abrahamic Land Covenant as something exclusively for the Jewish people, because they fail to understand that Messiah was actually renewing the Land Covenant originally made with Abram.

Indeed, it was the same Covenant that YHWH exclusively entered into with Abram while he was still uncircumcised.[339] Abram was a Hebrew when that Covenant was made, and he remained a Hebrew when his name was changed to Abraham.

In neither case was a Covenant made with a group of people called Jews. It was made with the descendants of Abraham, which refers to those people who walk in the Covenant path – those who are in the House of Abraham.

You can be a physical descendant of someone but, not be in their house. Remember that everyone in Abraham's house was circumcised, not just his children. This was a pattern for the future.

The Covenant is for all those who believe in the Promised Son, and walk in the Covenant path blazed by Abraham.

So, anyone who believes in and follows Yahushua should be very interested in the Land promised to the descendants of Abraham, because it ultimately belongs to YHWH and will be claimed by the Promised Son.

It does not belong to a group of Jewish people, and it

---

[339] Refer to prior discussion of the blood Covenant in Chapters 3 and 17.

never did belong to them. While the Yisraelites were permitted to dwell in the Land as long as they obeyed the Covenant, they were expelled when they disobeyed. So, the Land never belonged to them either. By now you should fully understand the distinction.

The Covenant Land is where Yahushua will establish His Kingdom, and this is where He will reign with His Bride from the renewed Jerusalem once it descends from the heavens following the Sabbath Millennium.

This becomes more obvious when we look at the patterns of the Covenant. While Abram was in Babylon he was given a promise. He initially believed. He then "turned" his back on Babylon, and his face toward YHWH.

He began to walk toward the Promised Land, and on his way, he "crossed over." His belief was proven by his actions – he obeyed the voice of YHWH.

Notice the similarity of following Yahushua – believe, repent, and be immersed. It is the same journey – the journey of a Hebrew.

Abram had to leave Babylon at the Euphrates River - which was east of the Promised Land. When he crossed over and entered the Land he went to Shechem and built an altar. Then he camped near Beth El and built an altar there.

He later travelled south and went to Egypt during a famine. He left the Promised Land. While he was in Egypt, Pharaoh was plagued, Abram was enriched and he left from the Nile region, and returned back with Hagar. Her name is the same root as "the ger" which literally means "the stranger."

It was only after this journey of crossing over from the East – the Euphrates, and then from the west – the Nile that he returned to the Land and met with the King of Salem – Melchizedek. The Nile and the Euphrates are the boundaries for the Land of Promise. Abram came from Babylon, and then brought the stranger with him from Egypt.

The encounter with Melchizedek was very significant. Here is a common translation:

"[18] Then Melchizedek king of Salem brought out bread and wine; he was the priest of El Most High. [19] And he blessed him and said: 'Blessed be Abram of El Most High, possessor of heaven and earth; [20] And blessed be El Most High, Who has delivered your enemies into your hand.' And he gave him a tithe of all." Genesis 14:18-20

Melchizedek was a "cohen" of El Most High. There is a depth to this passage that many people miss. There are two blessings here. The first was to Abram of El Most, "possessor of heaven and earth." The second was to El Most High, Who delivered the enemies into Abram's hand.

The first one to Abram seems so enormous, that many translators fail to ascribe it all to Abram. Possessor of heaven and Earth? This must be referring to Elohim.

The Hebrew is clearly referring to Abram. The Hebrew word for "possessor" is "qanah" (קָנָה), which means to "acquire, to buy, or to purchase." Did Abram buy heaven and earth – shamayim v'eretz?

This is an interesting parallel to the first sentence in the Torah where is describes "in the beginning Elohim created et ha'shamayim v'et ha'eretz." In Genesis 1:1 we read about the et (אֵת) creating, while in Genesis 14:19 we read about Abram "acquiring heaven and earth."

Do you remember the first recorded miracle of Yahushua? He turned water into wine at Cana (Qanah), which literally means: "acquire." He chose a wedding to perform this miracle, because He was connecting the two events in Genesis, and revealing that He was the Melchizedek High Priest coming to "acquire" His bride. It's easy to miss these things if you don't read the Hebrew texts.

You see Adam was entrusted with the Land, and lost it due to the fallen Sons of Elohim, who also lost their positions in the shamayim. So the Land needed to be reacquired, and the shamayim needed to be replenished and refreshed with Sons of Elohim. According to Melchizedek, both of these would be accomplished through the Covenant with Abram.

Abram and his descendants would "acquire" both Land, and a place in the shamayim through this Covenant. The ultimate fulfillment and "purchase price" would be provided through the Promised Son -Yahushua. He was the first of the Sons of Elohim that would fill the shamayim. This is very deep stuff, that most people completely fail to understand.

So, Melchizedek blessed both parties to the blood covenant that would soon follow. We already talked about this Covenant of eight pieces, and how Yahushua was the only One who passed through the blood – thus He bore the penalty for that Covenant being broken.

Now we know that the Land grant in that Covenant spanned from the Nile to the Euphrates – Egypt to Babylon.

"[18] . . . To your descendants I have given this land, from the river of Egypt to the great river, the River Euphrates - [19] the Kenites, the Kenezzites, the Kadmonites, [20] the Hittites, the Perizzites, the Rephaim, [21] the Amorites, the Canaanites, the Girgashites, and the Jebusites." Genesis 15:18-20

This is a very large swath of land – much larger than the modern State of Israel, or even ancient Yisrael for that matter.

This Land is intimately associated with the Messiah and there will be a future time when He fills it all.

"[10] And in that day there shall be a Root of Jesse, Who shall stand as a banner to the people; For the Gentiles shall seek Him, and His resting place shall be glorious. [11] It shall come to pass in that day that Adonai shall set His hand again the second time to recover the remnant of His people who are left, from Assyria and Egypt, from Pathros and Cush, from Elam and Shinar, from Hamath and the islands of the sea. [12] He will set up a banner for the nations, *and will assemble the outcasts of Yisrael, and gather together the dispersed of Yahudah from the four corners of the earth. [13] Also the envy of Ephraim shall depart, and the adversaries of Judah shall be cut off; Ephraim shall not envy Judah, and Judah shall not harass Ephraim. [14] But they shall fly down upon the shoulder of the Philistines toward the west; together they shall plunder the people of the East; they shall lay their hand on Edom and Moab; and the people of Ammon shall obey them. [15] YHWH will utterly destroy the tongue of the Sea of Egypt; with His mighty wind He will shake His fist over the River, and strike it in the seven streams, and make men cross over dryshod. [16] There will be a highway for the remnant of His people who will be left from Assyria, as it was for Yisrael - In the day that he came up from the land of Egypt."* Isaiah 11:10-16

This is the great regathering that we discussed previously when *"Adonai shall set His hand again the second time"* and gathers His people from the four corners of the Earth – from the entire planet.

Notice the highway from Assyria. This was the land formerly called Babylon. We also read that highway spanning the entire Covenant Land in Isaiah 19.

"[23] In that day there will be a highway from Egypt to Assyria, and the Assyrian will come into Egypt and the Egyptian into Assyria, and the Egyptians will serve with the Assyrians. [24] In that day Yisrael will be one of three with Egypt and Assyria - a blessing in the midst of the land, [25] whom YHWH of hosts shall bless, saying, 'Blessed is Egypt My people, and Assyria the work of My Hands, and Yisrael My inheritance." Isaiah 19:23-24

Now that is not a prophetic verse that you hear many people talk about. Sure Yisrael is His inheritance, but Egypt His people? Assyria the work of His Hands? What's up with that?

It is very important to recognize that the Covenant Land for the uncircumcised Abram spanned from Egypt to Assyria. This represents the Nations who will be drawn to YHWH.

We then see the Covenant of Circumcision narrowed to the Land of Canaan.

> "⁷ And I will establish My את-Covenant between Me and you and your descendants after you in their generations, for an everlasting Covenant, to be Elohim to you and your descendants after you. ⁸ Also I give to you and your descendants after you the land in which you are a stranger, all the land of Canaan, as an everlasting possession; and I will be their Elohim. ⁹ And Elohim said to Abraham: 'As for you, you shall keep My covenant, you and your descendants after you throughout their generations. ¹⁰ This is My covenant which you shall keep, between Me and you and your descendants after you: Every male child among you shall be circumcised; ¹¹ and you shall be circumcised in the flesh of your foreskins, and it shall be a sign of the covenant between Me and you. ¹² He who is eight days old among you shall be circumcised, every male child in your generations, he who is born in your house or bought with money from any foreigner who is not your descendant." Genesis 17:7-12

Notice that this is a את-Covenant. The "descendants" being referred to are those who are in this Covenant, that is ultimately renewed by the Messiah.

So with the uncircumcised Abram, the Land spanned

between two great rivers and then, when Abraham became circumcised, and spilled his own blood and the blood of his household, the Covenant Land became smaller and more focused.

We then see patterns continue to emerge through his covenant seed. Jacob went east back across the Euphrates to Paddam Aram, which is Haran. He went back to where Abram began his journey out of Babylon.

There he raised a family and then retraced the journey of Abram. He brought his family across the Euphrates and then across the Jordan where he camped at Sukkot.

We talked about Sukkot as an Appointed Time, but to Jacob, it was a place along the journey. In fact, it says he built a house for himself, and sukkas for his animals.

"And Jacob journeyed to Sukkot, built himself a house, and made booths for his livestock. Therefore the name of the place is called Sukkot." Genesis 33:13

A nomadic person typically lives in a tent while the animals remain outside. A sukka is a temporary dwelling that they reside in during the winter months. It provides a little more protection than a tent. So, moving from a sukka to a house meant he planned on settling down for a while.

After Sukkot, he then went to Shechem and then back to Bethel (the House of El) where He finally became the newly named man Yisrael.

Later, the descendants of Yisrael moved west into Egypt at the Nile River. When they were delivered from the west, they camped at Sukkot before proceeding toward the Promised Land.[340] This was not the same place that Jacob camped when he entered the Land from the east. The Yisraelites were still in Egypt preparing to leave.

This connection provides us with an incredible

---

[340] Exodus 12:37

prophetic picture of how the Covenant Land will be filled from the Nile to the Euphrates through Sukkot – the Appointed Time of the Seventh Month.

We later see David uniting the divided tribes of Yisrael into one Kingdom. He made Jerusalem the capital of the Kingdom, and established his throne in Tzyon – the City of David where He also set up the Tabernacle of YHWH.

Interestingly, they have recently uncovered what is referred to as the Melchizedek Temple in the City of David. It is an ancient Temple in what was called Shalem, where Melchizedek reigned.[341]

David knew that this place was the beginning of the Covenant in the Land, and we see that the Kingdom is set up in degrees. The closer you get to Tzyon, the closer you get to the King. While some will visit at Appointed Times, others will dwell there permanently.

This journey to Tzyon is a picture of the restoration back to the Garden. Remember that Eden was like the Promised Land, and there was a Garden planted east of Eden – like Jerusalem.

The Garden contained the Tree of Life, just like the renewed Jerusalem will, once again, contain the Tree of Life for those who are permitted entry.

"Blessed are those who do His Commandments, that they may have the right to the Tree of Life, and may enter through the gates into the city." Revelation 22:14

The Renewed Jerusalem is for Yisrael, those who are in Covenant, and obey the Commandments.

Remember how we previously mentioned Isaiah 66:8, and how many people try to apply that text to the formation of the modern State of Yisrael? That is simply not accurate.

---

[341] Genesis 14:18 and Hebrews 7:1. Shalem is the same Hebrew root as Shalom.

Isaiah 66 is talking about the birthing of children from Tzyon through the Messiah. He will ultimately judge and establish the Kingdom resulting in renewed Heavens and a renewed Earth. After all, He created them and Abram acquired them through the Covenant. The very Covenant that Yahushua paid the price for being broken.

Let that sink in for a minute, because this is all very legal. Yahushua has now acquired all of the promises of the Covenant.

Many refer to the 1948 formation of the modern State of Israel as the fulfillment of the question: "Shall a nation be born at once?" They fail to recognize that the question is preceded with the question: "Shall the earth be made to give birth in one day?"

The prophecy in Isaiah goes far beyond the formation of a modern state. The word for "nation" is "goy," and goy typically refers to a heathen nation. There is an interesting word play in the Hebrew – "echad em-yeled goy p'am echat."

The phrase is surrounded by echad/echat which mean: "one" or "unified." We then see the contrast between "em" and "am" surrounding the birth of the child. This was the same thing that we saw with the renaming of Jacob to Yisrael

The text of Isaiah then goes on to state: "For as soon as Tzyon was in labor, she gave birth to her sons." In Hebrew we read "she gave birth to her את-sons." So these sons are the Sons of Elohim brought into the Kingdom by the Messiah – Sons of Tzyon.

This will be accomplished through the Messiah – not the United Nations. This is not some political movement or group that claims their mother was Jewish. And remember that Tzyon is the City of David - it is the heart of Jerusalem. It is where the Bride will dwell with the King. It will be a set apart place – qodesh! That is not what we have today.

We actually are given a beautiful picture of the Bride in Tzyon through Isaiah 4.

"¹ And in that day seven women shall take hold of one man, saying, We will eat our own food and wear our own apparel; Only let us be called by your name, to take away our reproach. ² In that day the Branch of YHWH shall be beautiful and glorious; and the fruit of the earth shall be excellent and appealing for those of Yisrael who have escaped. ³ And it shall come to pass that he who is left in Tzyon and remains in Jerusalem will be called set apart - everyone who is recorded among the living in Jerusalem. ⁴ When Adonai has washed away the filth of the daughters of Tzyon, and purged the אָ-blood of Jerusalem from her midst, by the spirit of judgment and by the spirit of burning, ⁵ then YHWH will create above every dwelling place of Mount Tzyon, and above her assemblies, a cloud and smoke by day and the shining of a flaming fire by night. For over all the glory (esteem) there will be a covering. ⁶ And there will be a Tabernacle (Sukka) for shade in the daytime from the heat, for a place of refuge, and for a shelter from storm and rain."
Isaiah 4:1-6

The Hebrew gives us more clarity as we read that Jerusalem will be washed by אָ-blood – the blood of the Messiah. Of course, Yahushua is "the Branch of YHWH."³⁴²

The glory will be a covering is - "Al-Kol-Kavod-Chuppa." It means: "Over all - The Kavod will be a Chuppa."

The Kavod is the glory, the esteem, of YHWH. It is the same cloud and the fire that was over the Tabernacle. The tent of YHWH in the wilderness will now be a Chuppa over every dwelling place on Mount Tzyon.

The chuppa is the covering provided by a husband over his bride during a wedding. A traditional Hebrew wedding takes place under a chuppa. Amazingly, in the Hebrew we read that this Tabernacle that provides shade is actually a Sukka!

---

³⁴² Isaiah 11:1; Jeremiah 23:5 and 33:15; Zechariah 3:8 and 6:12

So we see a picture of the Bride dwelling on Mount Tzyon – Under the Sukka - covered by the chuppa of the Messiah – the Branch. I believe that the chuppa is the renewed Jerusalem sitting in the heavens, before it finally descends upon Tzyon.

Now remember that a sukka is a temporary dwelling. Isaiah is referring to a temporary situation until the final fulfillment of Sukkot, when the renewed Jerusalem comes down on the Earth.

It ends where Revelation 21 begins.

"[1] Now I saw a new heaven and a new earth, for the first heaven and the first earth had passed away. Also there was no more sea. [2] Then I, John, saw the holy city, New Jerusalem, coming down out of heaven from Elohim, prepared as a bride adorned for her husband. [3] And I heard a loud voice from heaven saying, Behold, the tabernacle of Elohim is with men, and He will dwell with them, and they shall be His people. Elohim Himself will be with them and be their Elohim . . . [9] Then one of the seven messengers who had the seven bowls filled with the seven last plagues came to me and talked with me, saying, Come, I will show you the Bride, the Lamb's wife. [10] And he carried me away in the Spirit to a great and high mountain, and showed me the great city, the Holy (Set Apart) Jerusalem, descending out of heaven from Elohim, [11] having the glory (esteem) of Elohim. Her light was like a most precious stone, like a jasper stone, clear as crystal. [12] Also she had a great and high wall with twelve gates, and twelve angels at the gates, and names written on them, which are the names of the twelve tribes of the children of Yisrael: [13] three gates on the east, three gates on the north, three gates on the south, and three gates on the west. [14] Now the wall of the city had twelve foundations, and on them were the names of the twelve apostles of the Lamb." Revelation 21:1-14

This is Tzyon finally descending through a renewed Heaven to a renewed Earth fulfilling the Land Covenant, and it is all about the Messiah and His Bride.

This is describing the restoration brought by Messiah through the renewed Covenant. It will result in the restoration of mankind to the Garden with access to the Tree of Life.

> *"In the middle of its street,*
> *and on either side of the river,*
> *was the Tree of Life, which bore twelve fruits,*
> *each tree yielding its fruit every month.*
> *The leaves of the tree were*
> *for the healing of the nations."*
> Revelation 22:2

Remember that access is only granted to those who obey.[343] It is the same as we saw in the Garden. Those who are in the Covenant can enter in and partake.

Now this is where it is important to stay focused on the Messiah. Remember that the Covenant was broken by both Houses of Yisrael. They were expelled from the Land because of their disobedience.

They can only return to the Land through a renewed Covenant. Just like when Yisrael broke the Covenant at Sinai and Moses had to act as a mediator and renew the Covenant. Both houses need a Mediator – like Moses. It was promised that there would one who would come like Moses.

> *"[18] I will raise up for them a Prophet like you from among their brethren, and will put My words in His mouth, and He shall speak to them et (את) all that I command Him. [19] And it shall be that whoever will not*

---

[343] Revelation 22:14

hear My words, which He speaks in My Name, I will require it of him" Deuteronomy 18:18-19

This was referring to Yahushua the "et" – the aleph taw (את). He came and spoke all the Words. Like Moses, He renewed the Covenant.

If you want into the Covenant, into the Kingdom, and into the House, then you need to pass through the door covered by the blood of the Lamb – His Blood. That is the only את-blood that will wash Jerusalem and cover the Bride of Tzyon.

Again, the Kingdom is a matter of degrees - Yahushua made that clear.

"17 Do not think that I came to destroy the Torah or the Prophets. I did not come to destroy but to fulfill. 18 For assuredly, I say to you, till heaven and earth pass away, one jot or one tittle will by no means pass from the Torah till all is fulfilled. 19 Whoever therefore loosens one of the least of these Commandments, and teaches men so, shall be called least in the Kingdom of Heaven; but whoever does and teaches them, he shall be called great in the Kingdom of Heaven. 20 For I say to you, that unless your righteousness exceeds the righteousness of the scribes and Pharisees, you will by no means enter the Kingdom of Heaven." Matthew 5:17-20

This is a profound statement. Your position in the Kingdom actually depends on your obedience, and the Pharisees are not getting in.

I know many people who come into the realization that they need to obey the Torah, and then they look to Rabbinic Judaism. That is a grave mistake. Yahushua said that they are not getting into the Kingdom, and your righteousness must exceed theirs if you want to get in.

Rabbinic Judaism traces directly back to the Pharisaic sect. It is absolutely unthinkable that anyone who believes and follows the Messiah would look to them for guidance. Especially after what He said about them.

Just read a few lines in Matthew 23.

"² The scribes and the Pharisees sit in Moses' seat. ³ Therefore whatever they tell you to observe, that observe and do, but do not do according to their works; for they say, and do not do. ⁴ For they bind heavy burdens, hard to bear, and lay them on men's shoulders; but they themselves will not move them with one of their fingers. ⁵ But all their works they do to be seen by men. They make their phylacteries broad and enlarge the borders of their garments. ⁶ They love the best places at feasts, the best seats in the synagogues, ⁷ greetings in the marketplaces, and to be called by men, 'Rabbi, Rabbi.' ⁸ But you, do not be called 'Rabbi'; for One is your Teacher, the Messiah, and you are all brethren." Matthew 23:2-8

In other words, when they speak the words of Moses – do that. But don't do what they do, because they add to and take away from the Torah. They are hypocrites.

In fact, Yahushua went on to state: *"But woe to you, scribes and Pharisees, hypocrites! For you shut up the Kingdom of Heaven against men; for you neither go in yourselves, nor do you allow those who are entering to go in."* Matthew 23:13

That is exactly what Rabbinic Judaism is doing to people from the lost tribes seeking to return. They tell people that they cannot obey the Torah unless they are Jewish. That is a lie.

And again, Yahushua told them *"for you neither go in yourselves."* They are not getting into the Kingdom. He called them fools, hypocrites and blind guides.

He said *"²⁷ . . . For you are like whitewashed tombs which indeed appear beautiful outwardly, but inside are full of dead men's bones and all uncleanness. ²⁸ Even so you also outwardly appear righteous to men, but inside you are full of hypocrisy and lawlessness.*" Matthew 23:27-28

Yahushua summed up His assessment of them by stating: "*Serpents, brood of vipers! How can you escape the condemnation of hell?*" Matthew 23:33

So, Yahushua essentially judged them and declared their sentence. If you want to follow them, you do so at your own risk. You have been duly warned.

One of their major problems is that they appear to obey the Torah, but they do not. They have created their own "oral torah" by adding to, and taking away from the Torah of Elohim. This is expressly forbidden.[344]

They follow their traditions and by doing so they transgress the Commandments. That is why Yahushua asked: "*Why do you also transgress the Commandment of Elohim because of your tradition?*" Matthew 15:3

He also stated "[6] . . . *Well did Isaiah prophesy of you hypocrites, as it is written: 'This people honors Me with their lips, but their heart is far from Me.* [7] *And in vain they worship Me, Teaching as doctrines the commandments of men.'* [8] *For laying aside the Commandment of Elohim you hold the tradition of men - the washing of pitchers and cups, and many other such things you do.* [9] *He said to them, All too well you reject the commandment of Elohim, that you may keep your tradition.*" Mark 7:6-9

This described the Pharisees in the times of Yahushua, and it describes the religion of Rabbinic Judaism now. They lay aside the Commandments of Elohim, and replace them with their traditions.

Therefore, those in Judaism must repent and leave their Babylonian, man-made religion and traditions just like Christians must do. They are not part of some special selected class of Chosen People who are exempt from the renewed Covenant.

There is no side door that opens via a Jewish DNA test. They need Messiah, and must enter through the door covered

---

[344] "*You shall not add to the word which I command you, nor take from it, that you may keep the commandments of YHWH your Elohim which I command you.*" Deuteronomy 4:2

by His blood.

As a result, we should not look to Judaism for guidance. We have only One Teacher, the Messiah. If you claim to believe in Yahushua then you must heed His words, and look to Him for guidance. He is the Covenant. He is the Door - The Gate - the Way back in to the Garden where we commune with the Father.

He meant it when He said: "*I am the way, the truth, and the life. No one comes to the Father except through Me.*" John 14:6 So, you only come into the Kingdom through Messiah, but not everyone in the Kingdom is the Bride.

Remember the Parable of the Ten Virgins in Matthew 25? All desired to go to the wedding, but only five were wise. They were the ones with extra oil. They were able to keep their lamps lit so they could be ready for when the bridegroom came.

Once they went in, the door was shut. So not everyone will dwell in Jerusalem or Tzyon. Not everyone will have the deep intimacy and relationship as those in Tzyon. This is important to understand as we consider entering into the Kingdom and dwelling with Elohim.[345]

Only when we grasp these concepts can we fully appreciate the enormity of the Covenant that leads us into the Kingdom, and the amazing fulfillment of the Covenant as provided through the Prophets.

Many people fail to comprehend the prophecies contained in the Scriptures, because they do not understand their proper context within the overall plan of Elohim.

In the next chapter we will examine some of the issues that have hindered people from properly interpreting and understanding prophecy.

---

[345] For more detail on this subject see the article titled *There will be Weeping and Gnashing of Teeth* on the shemayisrael.net website.

21

Understanding Prophecy

We have spent a lot of time in this book examining and adjusting our paradigm – the way we view our existence, the world, the Scriptures, and the way that we walk out our faith.

An important part of Leaving Babylon involves understanding the plan of Elohim, and how we fit into that plan. The way we look at the future is critical for our walk, because every journey requires a destination, which exists somewhere and sometime in the future.

The Covenant path provides the direction that we all must take when we leave Babylon, otherwise we get distracted in Haran, or we get mired in the wilderness. That is why I spend so much time examining the Covenant in my various teachings.

Sadly, much of the world and the religions of man utterly fail to understand the Covenant. Christianity has specifically separated itself from the Covenant with Yisrael, and attempts to create a brand-new Covenant separate and apart from Yisrael. I hope by now that you understand that to be a clear error.

Much of the problem is that western Christianity has detached itself from the eastern culture and the language. It has also misappropriated the Scriptures and elevated letters from Paul above the clear and unequivocal words of YHWH, Yahushua, Moses and the Prophets.

The words of Peter are just as true today as they were nearly 2,000 years ago when they were first written. When referring to Paul's writings in 2 Peter 3:16 he stated:

"as also in all his epistles, speaking in them of these things, in which are some things hard to understand, which untaught and unstable people twist to their own destruction, as they do also the rest of the Scriptures."

The main reason why people twist Paul's writings, and the Scriptures, is typically because they fail to understand how to treat the Scriptures. Often times, passages are "cherry picked" in order to suit the needs of a teaching or doctrine. That is extremely problematic, and potentially destructive. It is imperative that we place every text and passage into its appropriate context.

We already discussed this in a previous chapter titled *Understand in the Scriptures*, and that is the primary focus of the Walk in the Light Book titled *The Scriptures*. It is critical that we take off our Christian lenses, and examine the underlying theme that flows from Genesis to Revelation.

The overwhelming thrust of the Scriptures is the restoration of Creation. Through that process, YHWH is seeking a people to establish a Covenant with. Adam and Hawah were placed in the Garden without a choice, they chose to disobey and were ejected. We now can choose whether to return.

YHWH created a covenant path for those who would choose Him and His ways. Through this Covenant family He would redeem and restore mankind to dwell with Him in His House. The Scriptures describe that Covenant process from Abraham through Isaac and Jacob to Yisrael.

We read about how Yisrael broke the Covenant, and was divided into two Houses. The Northern Tribes became known as the House of Yisrael, and the Southern Tribes became known as the House of Yahudah.

Each of these two Kingdoms fell away from YHWH. The Northern Kingdom was completely removed from the

Land by the Assyrians. Their exile would end up lasting for 2,730 years as described by Ezekiel and Moses.[346]

The Southern Kingdom was conquered by the Babylonians and partially exiled. It is during that event when the House of Yahudah and the people of Yahudah were compared to figs by the prophet Jeremiah. We read in Jeremiah that the good figs were those who were exiled to Babylon. The bad figs were the ones who stayed in Jerusalem and also the ones who went to Egypt to avoid punishment.[347]

Jeremiah described that the exiled individuals would be allowed to return after seventy years. He also described that Babylon would be punished after seventy years.[348] The Book of Daniel takes place during that seventy years exile. In fact, the specific context of Daniel 9 is after he witnessed the punishment of Babylon and sought to know when the seventy year exile would be over so that they could return.

While praying, repenting and fasting He was visited by Gabriel and given a timeline of seventy weeks. We read about that timeline in Daniel 9 which gave a schedule for the return from exile, the rebuilding of Jerusalem and the Temple, and the appearance of Messiah - followed by the subsequent destruction of the Temple.

Daniel had previously been told to seal up a vision, and we read about the unsealing by Yahushua in the Book of Revelation. Much of the Book of Revelation was meant for specific Assemblies that existed while John was still alive. Some of the text refers to the end - which is the culmination of the Covenant through the final harvest of the planet that will occur through the Appointed Times.

Sadly, many in Christianity have failed to interpret the

---

[346] Ezekiel described that the House of Yisrael would be punished for 390 years (Ezekiel 4:4-5). Moses explained that a punishment could be multiplied seven times if the people failed to repent and return (Leviticus 26:18). That is where we come up with a 2,730 year of punishment for the House of Yisrael.

[347] See Jeremiah 24. From this, we can deduce that the House of Yahudah was represented by a fig tree, and those who constituted that House were either good "ripe" fruit or bad "rotten" fruit.

[348] Jeremiah 25:11-12 and 29:10

prophets and Revelation in their proper context. They often ignore the fact that these prophecies were given thousands of years ago, directly to people who lived thousands of years ago. They do not understand that many of those prophecies had a specific application to the generation that heard them, and therefore many prophecies have already been fulfilled.

Instead they apply numerous prophecies to the future, and to the Christian Church, when the context of most of the prophets involved the punishment upon the two houses of Yisrael and Yahudah, and the promise of the regathering and restoring them through the Messiah.

As a result, some Christian eschatology is misplaced and misapplied. When we read the prophets, it is critical to understand the context within which they were given. For instance:

* Was the prophet to Yisrael, or another nation? If so, during what time period?

* Was Yisrael still united or was it divided? If divided, then which Kingdom were they prophesying to?

* Were both Kingdoms still in the Land, or had one or both been sent into exile?

* Or was it after the seventy year exile when the House of Yahudah had been allowed to return to the Land, and the House of Yisrael was still in exile?

These are questions that must be addressed before examining a prophet, and this is a primary reason why so many people fail to understand the prophecies in Daniel, particularly the so-called "Seventy Week Prophecy."

Daniel was in Babylon after Babylon had destroyed the Temple, and exiled many from the House of Yahudah. He was one of the "good figs" that was taken to Babylon. He knew that Jeremiah had prophesied a seventy year exile, and he was praying when that would end.

We read about this in chapter 9 of the book of Daniel.

Daniel 9:1-21 provides us with context, and then at Daniel 9:22 we begin to read about a visitation from Gabriel.

Here is the passage in its entirety:

"*¹ In the first year of Darius the son of Ahasuerus, of the lineage of the Medes, who was made king over the realm of the Chaldeans - ² in the first year of his reign I, Daniel, understood by the scrolls the number of the years specified by the word of YHWH through Jeremiah the prophet, that He would accomplish seventy years in the desolations of Jerusalem. ³ Then I set my face toward El-Adonai the Elohim to make request by prayer and supplications, with fasting, sackcloth, and ashes. ⁴ And I prayed to YHWH my Elohim, and made confession, and said, "O Adonai, great and awesome El, Who keeps His covenant and mercy with those who love Him, and with those who keep His Commandments, ⁵ we have sinned and committed iniquity, we have done wickedly and rebelled, even by departing from Your precepts and Your judgments. ⁶ Neither have we heeded Your servants the prophets, who spoke in Your Name to our kings and our princes, to our fathers and all the people of the land. ⁷ O Adonai, righteousness belongs to You, but to us shame of face, as it is this day - to the men of Yahudah, to the inhabitants of Jerusalem and all Yisrael, those near and those far off in all the countries to which You have driven them, because of the unfaithfulness which they have committed against You. ⁸ YHWH, to us belongs shame of face, to our kings, our princes, and our fathers, because we have sinned against You. ⁹ To Adonai our Elohim belong mercy and forgiveness, though we have rebelled against Him. ¹⁰ We have not obeyed the voice of YHWH our Elohim to walk in His Torah, which He set before us by His servants the prophets. ¹¹ Yes, all*

Yisrael has transgressed Your את-Torah, and has departed so as not to obey Your voice; therefore the curse and the oath written in the Torah of Moses the servant of the Elohim have been poured out on us, because we have sinned against Him. [12] And He has confirmed His words, which He spoke against us and against our judges who judged us, by bringing upon us a great disaster; for under the whole heaven such has never been done as what has been done to Jerusalem. [13] As it is written in the Torah of Moses, all this disaster has come upon us; yet we have not made our prayer before YHWH our Elohim, that we might turn from our iniquities and understand Your truth. [14] Therefore YHWH has kept the disaster in mind, and brought it upon us; for YHWH our Elohim is righteous in all the works which He does, though we have not obeyed His voice. [15] And now, O Adonai our Elohim, who brought Your people out of the land of Egypt with a mighty hand, and made Yourself a name, as it is this day - we have sinned, we have done wickedly! [16] O Adonai, according to all Your righteousness, I pray, let Your anger and Your fury be turned away from Your city Jerusalem, Your holy mountain; because for our sins, and for the iniquities of our fathers, Jerusalem and Your people are a reproach to all those around us. [17] Now therefore, our Elohim, hear the prayer of Your servant, and his supplications, and for the Adonai's sake cause Your face to shine on Your sanctuary, which is desolate. [18] O my Elohim, incline Your ear and hear; open Your eyes and see our desolations, and the city which is called by Your Name; for we do not present our supplications before You because of our righteous deeds, but because of Your great mercies. [19] O Adonai, hear! O Adonai, forgive! O Adonai, listen and act! Do not delay for Your own sake, my Elohim, for Your city and Your people are called by Your

Name. ²⁰ Now while I was speaking, praying, and confessing my sin and the sin of my people Yisrael, and presenting my supplication before YHWH my Elohim for the set apart mountain of my Elohim, ²¹ yes, while I was speaking in prayer, the man Gabriel, whom I had seen in the vision at the beginning, being caused to fly swiftly, reached me about the time of the evening offering. ²² And he informed me, and talked with me, and said, O Daniel, I have now come forth to give you skill to understand. ²³ At the beginning of your supplications the command went out, and I have come to tell you, for you are greatly beloved; therefore consider the matter, and understand the vision: ²⁴ Seventy weeks are determined for your people and for your set apart city, to finish the transgression, to make an end of sins, to make reconciliation for iniquity, to bring in everlasting righteousness, to seal up vision and prophecy, and to anoint the Most Set Apart Place. ²⁵ Know therefore and understand, that from the going forth of the command to restore and build Jerusalem until Messiah the Prince, there shall be seven weeks and sixty-two weeks; the street shall be built again, and the wall, even in troublesome times. ²⁶ And after the sixty-two weeks Messiah shall be cut off, but not for Himself; and the people of the prince who is to come shall destroy the city and the sanctuary. The end of it shall be with a flood, and till the end of the war desolations are determined. ²⁷ Then He shall "champion" (גְּבִיר) a covenant with many for one week; But in the middle of the week He shall bring an end to sacrifice and offering. And on the wing of abominations shall be one who makes desolate, even until the consummation, which is determined, is poured out on the desolate." Daniel 9:1-27

He was given a timeline of seventy weeks by Gabriel

that were fulfilled through the Messiah. He was told that in the seventieth week, the Covenant would be renewed, and that the Messiah would be cut off.

Now here is a point of prophecy that many fail to understand. They attribute the "covenant" to a future anti-christ, and they believe that there must be a seven-year tribulation period, with three and a half years of a Great Tribulation after a future Temple has been rebuilt, and then sacrifices will cease.

This is a grave mistake and misunderstanding of the text. Part of this derives from the fact that most Christians utterly fail to understand how Yahushua fits into the Covenant plan of YHWH. That is because most generally ignore the foundational Covenant. They think it has been done away with, and replaced by a brand new Covenant. They do not recognize the need to enter into a Covenant relationship with YHWH if they are to be "saved" from the sting of death.

As a result, even though the clear context of this seventy week plan is about the return to the Land and the restoration of Jerusalem and the Temple, people take the seventieth week out of that context, and place it in the future.

The seventieth week of Daniel was actually fulfilled in the final "week" of Yahushua's life when He "confirmed," or better yet, "championed," "elevated," and "made great" a Covenant for one week. Those are the meanings reflected by the Hebrew word "gibbowr" (גִּבּוֹר), found in the text.

Here is the passage rendered in Young's Literal Translation – "*And He hath strengthened a covenant with many – one week.*"

This was a literal week when Yahushua came into Jerusalem as a King, He renewed the Covenant at the Passover meal – often referred to as the Last Supper - through His Body and Blood and was "cut-off" (crucified) in the middle of that week (on a Wednesday), and then resurrected on the final day of the week – The Sabbath.349

This was the "New Covenant" that Christianity refers to. It is actually the renewal, or the elevating of the Covenant that had been broken with Yisrael. It was new, in the sense that it was perfected and fulfilled by Yahushua as the mediator, instead of Moses. Instead of the blood of animals to atone, the blood of Yahushua can provide cleansing and forgiveness. Instead of a Levitical High Priest, Yahushua was acting as the Melchizedek High Priest.

Incredibly, there are many people actually attributing this fulfillment by the Messiah in the past, to the anti-christ at some future date.

As a result, we have countless Christians expecting a chain of events to occur in the future that already occurred in the past. That is because they don't understand Yisrael, the Covenant and Messiah's role in renewing the Covenant provided through the Appointed Times.

Moses and the prophets foretold that Yisrael would be punished, but that there would also be a renewal through the Covenant. Yahushua specifically came to renew the Covenant. There was never a mention of the end of that Covenant, or the selection of a new group of people to enter into a brand new Covenant with Elohim.

Again, the Covenant was meant to draw the Nations back to YHWH through Yisrael. The Nations would either learn about YHWH's instructions through Yisrael's obedience and blessings, or through Yisrael's disobedience and curses.350

Yisrael chose to disobey, they were cursed and exiled, and the House of Yisrael was actually divorced from YHWH. As a result, they needed a renewal into the Covenant through a re-marriage. That is the context of the Messiah's coming, and that is the context of His return.

---

349 For a detailed discussion of the timing of the final week of Yahushua's life including the crucifixion and resurrection see the Walk in the Light series book titled *The Messiah*.
350 See Deuteronomy 28-29

He specifically stated that He came for the lost sheep of the House of Yisrael,[351] and the fulfillment of His return will involve the gathering and marriage with His flock. He came the first time to pay the penalty for that Covenant being broken. He will return again to claim what He "acquired" (qanah) as part of that Covenant.

Without that context of the past, it is difficult to understand the future. And this is where most Christians run into trouble. Much of modern Christianity has relied on source texts of Greek, Latin and English. These are texts written in western languages that describe the renewal of a covenant that originated in an eastern culture, and originally transmitted in an eastern language.

Needless to say, they have missed much from eastern Hebrew texts, including the context. We have discussed some of those differences in previous chapters. Aside from these problems, most Christians have also been steeped in western religious systems that have been influenced by Replacement Theology.

They have been taught that a new entity called "The Church" has replaced Yisrael. As a result, many have a flawed view of history, prophecy and the future. They regularly misapply prophecies intended for Yisrael to the Christian Church. They filter the texts through their inherited traditions. Therefore, most Christians are left with a deficient understanding of Scriptural prophecy, and an erroneous expectation of things to come.

For instance, I grew up believing and expecting a seven-year tribulation with a final three and a half year "Great Tribulation." I was then given a choice of a pre-trib, mid-trib or post-trib Rapture The seven-year tribulation was so steeped in my faith that it was an assumed fact, as was the rapture, although neither of these ideas have any real support in the Scriptures.

---

[351] *"But He answered and said, I was not sent except to the lost sheep of the house of Yisrael."* Matthew 15:24

I was taught to believe that the Temple had to be rebuilt and sacrifices had to be resumed in order for the anti-christ to come and stop them in the middle of the seven-year tribulation. As a result, we needed to find the ashes of the Red Heifer, and the Ark of the Covenant, in order to rebuild the Temple, so that Jesus could return.

Now you may have learned something similar to this, or a variation on the theme. I'm not going to spend much time looking at the source of these beliefs except to say that they primarily derived from placing a future emphasis on certain prophecies in Daniel and Revelation that were most likely fulfilled in the past.

As a result, I was intrigued by the search for the Ark of the Covenant and the ashes of the Red Heifer, because I wanted the Temple to be rebuilt. I wanted sacrifices to get started again, so we could ultimately usher in the return of Messiah. Again, I wanted to see all of these things happen because I was taught to believe that the anti-christ was going to then make a seven-year covenant with the Jews, and that covenant would be broken and the sacrifices would be stopped.

These beliefs were based upon inherited assumptions and traditions – not necessarily an accurate view of history and the Scriptures. Amazingly, there are many Messianic and Hebrew roots people who espouse these same ideas. Most came out of Christianity. As a result, they are so rooted in that eschatological framework that they fail to recognize the error.

This is the problem with tradition - it often clouds the truth and becomes our reality. Therefore, we have many people watching, and waiting for the fulfillment of prophecies that have long past been fulfilled, and events that are simply not going to happen at all. We also have people teaching these things.

The point of leaving Babylon is to shed these inherited traditions, and walk in unadulterated truth, so that we are found ready for the Master's return. This involves understanding the Covenant plan provided through the

Appointed Times, and the Prophets. We also need to understand the purpose of prophecy.

For instance, so many people look at prophecies as a way of telling the future, but that was typically not the primary purpose of a prophet. A prophet usually came to warn the people to repent.

When the people strayed from the Covenant path, the prophet's job was to point out the error, and often warn of the punishment associated with disobedience. The prophet would also often provide encouragement, if the people would repent and return.

Hosea, for instance, lived out the process of what would happen to the House of Yisrael if they continued to play the harlot. He actually was joined with a harlot, and had children by her. He literally lived out the pain and frustration of having an unfaithful bride, just as YHWH was experiencing with the House of Yisrael.

The text of Hosea then described that process, through the birth and naming of three children that he had through Gomer.

Here is the account in the Scriptures:

"² When YHWH began to speak by Hosea, YHWH said to Hosea: Go, take yourself a wife of harlotry and children of harlotry, for the land has committed great harlotry by departing from YHWH. ³ So he went and took את-Gomer the daughter of Diblaim, and she conceived and bore him a son. ⁴ Then YHWH said to him: Call his name Jezreel, for in a little while I will avenge the bloodshed of Yezreel on the house of Yehu, and bring an end to the kingdom of the House of Yisrael. ⁵ It shall come to pass in that day that I will break the bow of Israel in the Valley of Jezreel. ⁶ And she conceived again and bore a daughter. Then said to him: Call her name Lo-Ruhamah, for I will no longer *have mercy on the house of Yisrael, but I will utterly take them away. ⁷ Yet I will have mercy on the house of Judah, will save them by YHWH their Elohim, and will not save them by bow, nor by sword or battle, by horses or horsemen. ⁸ Now when she had weaned Lo-Ruhamah, she conceived and bore a son. ⁹ Then Elohim said: Call his name Lo-Ammi, for you are not My people, and I will not be your Elohim. ¹⁰ Yet the number of the children of Yisrael shall be as the sand of the sea, which cannot be measured or numbered. And it shall come to pass in the place where it was said to them, 'You are not My people,' There it shall be said to them, You are sons of the living El. ¹¹ Then the children of Yahudah and the children of Yisrael shall be gathered together, and appoint for themselves one head; and they shall come up out of the land, for great will be the day of Yezreel!" Hosea 1:2-11*

This is a highly significant passage that is critical to understand if you want to know the future. Hosea was called to prophesy to the House of Yisrael, after the Kingdom of Yisrael was divided into two houses.

Through the life of this prophet we see the steady decline of the House of Yisrael as they became distant and detached from YHWH until they were "Not His People." That means they were no longer in the Covenant.

The word "Yizreel" (יזרעאל) is a play on Yisrael, and means: "Elohim sows" or "the scattered of Elohim." Remember that Yisrael means: "the planting of Elohim."

So, through their falling away and punishment, the House of Yisrael would become scattered and sown to the four corners of the Earth, awaiting the future harvest described in the text of Revelation 14.

Through their scattering into the Nations, the Nations would eventually be drawn back to YHWH, because of the restorative work of Yahushua – the "one head," (echad rosh), also known as the "rosh pina."[352]

The incredible promise in Hosea is that the House of Yisrael would be restored with the House of Yahudah, and they would be called "Sons of the Living El," also known as "Sons of Elohim."

So the point is that the House of Yisrael would be punished, but there was hope for those who repented. In fact, the House of Yisrael would multiply while they were in exile, just as Yisrael multiplied while they were in Egypt.

The House of Yisrael would not return from Egypt though. Instead they would be sown into the Nations, and then delivered from all the Nations.

It grieved YHWH to treat the House of Yisrael in such fashion. Read how Hosea describes the situation.

> "*¹ When Yisrael was a child, I loved him, and out of Egypt I called My son. ² As they called them, so they went from them; They sacrificed to the Baals, and burned incense to carved images. ³ I taught Ephraim to walk, taking them by their arms; but they did not know that I healed them. ⁴ I drew them with gentle cords, with bands of love, and I was to them as those who take the yoke from their neck. I stooped and fed them. ⁵ He shall not return to the land of Egypt; But the Assyrian shall be his king, because they refused to repent.*" Hosea 11:1

Isn't that an amazing description of the tender and gentle love shown by YHWH to Ephraim - the House of Yisrael? Nevertheless, Ephraim betrayed that love and failed to walk the narrow path of obedience. When warned, they refused to repent.

Hosea was revealing what would happen to the House of Yisrael if they did not turn back to YHWH. Of course, we

---

[352] See Psalm 118:22, Matthew 21:42, Mark 12:10, Luke 20:17, Acts 4:11, 1 Peter 2:6

know that they did not heed the warnings, and continued in their sin.

The point of this is to show that the real focus of a prophet was to point out sin, and encourage people to repent. That is why John the Immerser came preaching repentance.

> *"¹ In those days John the Immerser came preaching*
> *in the wilderness of Yudea, ² and saying,*
> *Repent, for the Kingdom of Heaven is at hand!"*
> Matthew 3:1

Yahushua called John the greatest of the Prophets.

> *"¹¹ Assuredly, I say to you, among those born of*
> *women there has not risen one greater than John the*
> *Immerser; but he who is least in the Kingdom of*
> *Heaven is greater than he. ¹² And from the days of*
> *John the Immerser until now the Kingdom of Heaven*
> *suffers violence, and the violent take it by force. ¹³ For*
> *all the prophets and the Torah prophesied until John."*
> Matthew 11:11-13

Not only was John's message about repentance, his immersion was described as an immersion of repentance. *"John came immersing in the wilderness and preaching an immersion of repentance for the remission of sins."* Mark 1:4

Since John focused so powerfully on repentance, clearly repentance was at the top of their priority list. Yahushua came as the Prophet like Moses preaching repentance as well.

> *"From that time Yahushua began to preach and to say,*
> *Repent, for the Kingdom of Heaven is at hand."*
> Matthew 4:17

Of course, repentance involves turning back to

YHWH, and walking in the righteous path that He established through His Torah.

Sadly, most "prophecy teachers" and modern "prophets" completely miss that, and instead act more like sooth-sayers. Trying to determine future events can become a great deception, if you are not grounded in obedience.

Now clearly some prophets provided information regarding future events. Yahushua foretold the destruction of Jerusalem and the Temple, and He also foretold His return. As a result, those of us who believe in the Messiah are looking forward to His return, and the end of the age.

It is important to understand that time is segmented into ages. As many look to the future they are anticipating "The End" – period. But the end of an age is not necessarily the end of all time, or the end of creation.

The end of an age is more like the transitioning into a renewal. Specifically the renewal of YHWH's plan to restore His Creation through His Covenant.

We are currently living in a time when many sense that we are at the end of this age. As such, people are looking to prophecies for clues, signs and indicators to help them better understand the times.

Sadly, because of the lack of a solid understanding of history, and the failure to place particular prophecies into their proper historical context, many are going to be caught by surprise.

I was raised in a traditional mainline Christian denomination, and then moved into an evangelical Christian setting that tended to apply a future fulfillment to most prophecies. As a result, I would have been classified as a "futurist."

As I began to examine and test the traditions that I inherited, I realized that I had to place all Scriptures within their proper historical context

I learned that futurism was developed with an agenda. In fact, I learned that the futurist interpretation of Bible prophecy was invented by the Jesuit, Francisco Ribera during the counter-reformation. I also learned that the preterist interpretation of Bible prophecy was invented by the Jesuit, Luis del Alcázar during the counter-reformation.

So, major prophetic lines of thought were actually molded and invented by Jesuits. The Jesuits are often considered to be The Pope's Army, although their real allegiance lies with the Jesuit General, also known as The Black Pope.

They are a nefarious group whose mission is to deflect people's attention from the fact that the Pope is the anti-christ. He claims to be the Vicar of Christ – the earthly representative of Christ sitting in the place of Christ. That is the very definition of anti-christ. The current Pope happens to be a Jesuit, so it would appear that "the stars have aligned" in the Catholic Church.

By creating confusion concerning the interpretation and application of prophecies, people would not necessarily look at the present-day papacy. After all, if prophecies concerning the anti-christ were fulfilled in the past, how could they apply to the Pope and the Roman Catholic Church, which remains in existence? Likewise, if prophecies concerning the anti-christ were in the future, how could is apply to the present-day Pope?

By inventing two, seemingly disparate prophetic interpretation models, they skillfully directed peoples' attention away from the present, and into the past and the future.

As I began to intensely study the Scriptures within their actual historical context, I realized that many prophecies were given at specific times, and in specific contexts. As a result, many had actually already been fulfilled.

Regrettably, those who believe that certain prophecies were fulfilled in the past are often classified as "preterists," even though they believe some prophecies still must be fulfilled. Some believe that all prophecy points to the future. I believe that it is not so black and white. Each prophetic passage must be weighed according to our knowledge of history.

I discuss this issue in my Walk in the Light series book titled *The Final Shofar*, and it is extremely important that people looking for answers in the Scriptural texts understand this distinction.

Now the problem with labels is that they tend to pigeon-hole people into different categories. While some people are strictly futurists and others are strictly preterists, I happen to believe that there is room in the middle.

People always try to place a label on things, and by doing so it makes it easier to dismiss a particular position. I reject taking on labels and prefer to simply call myself a "contextualist."

Clearly, there are prophecies that were fulfilled in the past, but there are also certain prophecies that remain unfulfilled. Therefore, when reading the Scriptures, and particularly prophecies, we should always be aware of the time in history that they were written, the context in which they were given, as well as the person speaking the word and to whom it was spoken and whether the events being described actually happened.

We also need to consider any translation issues concerning the passage. I recently heard a Christian commentator quote a prophetic passage regarding "the Day of the LORD." He proceeded to state with certainty that because the prophecy mentioned the Day of the LORD, then it was clearly referring to the second coming of Jesus. This is a mistake that many people make.

First of all, "the Day of the LORD" is better known as "the Day of YHWH." Second, while the return of the Messiah, named Yahushua, may indeed coincide with the Day of YHWH, the Day of YHWH is not a one-time future event.

Rather, it typically describes a time when prophecy is fulfilled, and that often involves judgment. There have been many "Day of YHWH" occurrences in the past.

For example, some believe that events described in Amos 5 may be one of the earliest references to the Day of YHWH.[353] We know from Amos 1 that the prophecy was given at a time when Yisrael was divided into two kingdoms after the death of King Solomon.

The prophecy begins by stating: *"concerning Yisrael in the days of Uzziah king of Yahudah, and in the days of Jeroboam the son of Joash, king of Yisrael, two years before the earthquake."* Amos 1:1.

The text in Amos 5 that later describes the Day of YHWH specifically addresses the Northern Kingdom. *"Hear this word which I take up against you, a lamentation, O House of Yisrael."* Amos 5:1

So the Day of YHWH spoken of by Amos involved the judgment that would befall the House of Yisrael by the Assyrians - it was specifically given to the Northern Kingdom. Other prophets would prophesy concerning the destruction that would befall the House of Yahudah, the Southern Kingdom.

That judgment and the destruction of Jerusalem by the Babylonians was also considered to be a Day of YHWH event (see Lamentations 2:21). The subsequent fall of Babylon by the Persians was described as the Day of YHWH by Isaiah in what certainly sounds like the end of the world (see Isaiah 13). And it basically was, for those falling under the judgment of YHWH.

From these few examples we see that it is important to understand the historical context of the prophecies and recognize that they were accomplished in the past. While we can learn about a future Day of YHWH from these passages, they clearly had a previous fulfillment.

Another good example of contextual and translation analysis can be found in the book of Zephaniah, which has no

---

[353] Clearly, this was not the first Day of YHWH event that occurred in history. The Flood during Noah's time and the destruction of Sodom, Gomorrah, Admah and Zeboiim surely fell into that category.

less than five specific references to the Day of YHWH. Let us read the first three verses of Zephaniah, in the New International Version (NIV), which set the stage for the rest of the text.

> *"¹ The word of the LORD that came to Zephaniah son of Cushi, the son of Gedaliah, the son of Amariah, the son of Hezekiah, during the reign of Josiah son of Amon king of Judah: ² 'I will sweep away everything from the face of the earth,' declares the LORD. ³ 'I will sweep away both man and beast; I will sweep away the birds in the sky and the fish in the sea - and the idols that cause the wicked to stumble. When I destroy all mankind on the face of the earth,' declares the LORD."* Zephaniah 1:1-3

Now according to this text, it initially appears that we are reading about a final judgment when all living things are destroyed from the entire planet.

If we look at the context of the prophecy we know that it was given during the reign of King Josiah – King of Yahudah. From this portion of the text we know that his father was Amon, and from the Book of Kings we learn *"Josiah was eight years old when he became king, and he reigned in Jerusalem thirty-one years. His mother's name was Jedidah daughter of Adaiah; she was from Bozkath."* 2 Kings 22:1

As a result, we can discern that he reigned from around 640 BCE to 609/608 BCE.[354] Therefore, when this prophecy was given, the House of Yisrael had already seen their Day of YHWH event that had been prophesied by Amos. That judgment culminated around 722 BCE when Samaria, the capital of the House of Yisrael, fell to the Assyrians.

So the context of the Zephaniah prophecy was after the fall of the Northern Kingdom, and it was given prior to the fall of the Southern Kingdom, when Jerusalem was subsequently

---

[354] See 2 Chronicles 34; 2 Chronicles 35:1-25

destroyed by the Babylonians.

Despite that context, the text still seems to be talking about a judgment upon the entire world, until we examine the translation. If we look at the word translated as "world" in the Hebrew we see that it is "adamah" (אדמה) which can mean "ground or land." Later, the Hebrew word "eretz" (ארץ) is used, which also refers to "land."

The prophecy is clearly talking about the "land" of Yahudah, and the surrounding region. When you read further this becomes evident. Therefore, it is a very specific prophecy to the royal family of Yahudah, the people of Jerusalem, the Kingdom of Yahudah, and neighboring peoples well over 2,000 years ago.

So Zephaniah is not talking about a future event, or the end of the world, but rather the Day of YHWH, which was a past judgment rendered upon the Land of Yahudah.

The point of all this is that we must carefully examine the texts when we look to the future. Many people have misplaced expectations concerning the return of the Messiah, because they have inherited poor eschatological teachings.

They are expecting certain events to occur that have already happened long ago. As such, many may be found unprepared and caught off guard when the Day of YHWH actually arrives "as a thief in the night."

Peter described a future Day of YHWH as follows: "But the Day of YHWH will come as a thief in the night, in which the heavens will pass away with a great noise, and the elements will melt with fervent heat; both the earth and the works that are in it will be burned up." 2 Peter 3:10.

Apparently, many will be unprepared, because they will be sleeping. The Messiah described His future return when He spoke the parable of the Ten Virgins (see Matthew 25). They all slumbered and slept and when they were awakened by a midnight cry only half of them were prepared for the wedding. Now is the time to get ready and stay alert.

Many are currently sleeping and slumbering, because

they erroneously believe that certain events must occur before we begin a seven year countdown or a three and a half year countdown, but their expectations may be misplaced.

In fact, I find that many have completely misunderstood the context of Matthew 24, and that is the reason for their complacency. They believe that all of the warnings given by Yahushua during the Olivet Discourse[355] are meant for our future when in fact most, if not all, were intended for His disciples, and that generation.

Yahushua was actually describing a Day of the YHWH, that would occur at the end of that age. The Day of YHWH refers to a time when YHWH no longer withholds His wrath. It is a time of judgment.

Remember that the House of Yahudah previously received punishment for their failure to repent. YHWH used the Babylonian empire to destroy Jerusalem and the Temple in 586 BCE. That event was the Day of YHWH for the House of Yahudah.

After the seventy year exile prophesied by Jeremiah[356] was completed they were permitted to return and rebuild. When that seventy year period was up, Daniel prayed and Gabriel appeared as an answer to that prayer. He gave Daniel a schedule that would include the rebuilding of Jerusalem and the Temple, along with the coming of the Messiah in a mysterious period of seventy weeks.[357]

Despite being permitted back into the Land, many of the Yahudim chose to stay in Babylon. Those who returned became divided and corrupted. Ultimately, most rejected their promised Messiah. As a result, they would be judged again.

This was the context of the Matthew 24 Olivet

---

[355] The Olivet Discourse is the term often ascribed to the words spoken by Messiah on the Mount of Olives after He stated that the Temple would be destroyed. The Olivet Discourse is found in Matthew 24 and Mark 13. Some also include Luke 21 as also occurring on the Mount of Olives but it is possible that those were were spoken in the Temple, thus creating an important distinction when we consider the questions being answered by Yahushua.
[356] Jeremiah 25:11-12 and Jeremiah 29:10
[357] Daniel 9:24-27

Discourse passage when Yahushua left the Temple, and foretold its destruction. Many people interpret the words of the Messiah in Matthew 24 as a future prophecy for our present generation, because they fail to read the passage in its proper context.

When we place Matthew 24 in context, we see that Yahushua had already ridden into Jerusalem in a donkey. He cleansed the Temple, and there was every indication that He was the promised King who had come to set up His Throne in Jerusalem and restore the Kingdom.

In Matthew 23 we read about Yahushua calling down the woes upon the Scribes and Pharisees and then saying:

> "31 Therefore you are witnesses against yourselves that you are sons of those who murdered the prophets. 32 Fill up, then, the measure of your fathers' guilt. 33 Serpents, brood of vipers! How can you escape the condemnation of hell? 34 Therefore, indeed, I send you prophets, wise men, and scribes: some of them you will kill and crucify, and some of them you will scourge in your synagogues and persecute from city to city, 35 that on you may come all the righteous blood shed on the earth, from the blood of righteous Abel to the blood of Zechariah, son of Berechiah, whom you murdered between the temple and the altar. 36 Assuredly, I say to you, all these things will come upon this generation." Matthew 23:31-36

So He is calling down judgment on "this generation." While overlooking the city He then stated:

> "37 O Jerusalem, Jerusalem, the one who kills the prophets and stones those who are sent to her! How often I wanted to gather your children together, as a hen gathers her chicks under her wings, but you were not willing! 38 See! Your house is left to you desolate; 39 for I say to you, you shall see Me no more till you say,

Blessed is He who comes in the Name of YHWH"
Matthew 23:37-39[358]

Immediately after making this statement we transition into Matthew 24 and we read the following: *"¹ Then Yahushua went out and departed from the Temple, and His disciples came up to show Him the buildings of the Temple. ² And Yahushua said to them, Do you not see all these things? Assuredly, I say to you, not one stone shall be left here upon another, that shall not be thrown down."* Matthew 24:1-2

He said it was all going to be destroyed. He then went up to the Mount of Olives, which was directly across from the entire Temple Complex. While sitting there, staring at the Temple that He just said would be destroyed, His disciples come to him with three questions:

1) Tell us, when will these things be?
2) And what will be the sign of Your coming,
3) And of the end of the age?

When you read the following passage you must ask yourself which question was Yahushua answering. And then you compare the context against Luke 21 which took place earlier in the Temple, and dealt exclusively with two questions:

1) Teacher, but when will these things be?
2) And what sign will there be when these things are about to take place?

We can figure out what statements applied to the destruction of the Temple in 70 CE, and what applies to end of the age. Of course, the end of the age could refer to the end of that age, and the Kingdom of Yahudah, or the end of this

---

[358] Recall the previous discussion concerning the condition of the Earth at the beginning of creation. The use of the word "desolate" speaks of judgment.

age when the Messiah returns. Can you see the distinctions? This is neither preterism or futurism. It is simply analyzing the context.

Now many read Matthew 24 and, because of the apocalyptic language they think it all applies to the future. What they fail to understand is that some of that apocalyptic language was used in the past to describe the end of a kingdom or empire.

In this context Yahushua was using it to apply to the coming judgment, and the end of the House of Yahudah. Here is what he said:

> "Immediately after the tribulation of those days
> the sun will be darkened, and the moon will not give
> its light; the stars will fall from heaven, and the
> powers of the heavens will be shaken."
> Matthew 24:29

Now many people, because of their assumptions about "The Great Tribulation" automatically assume that Yahushua is talking about a future tribulation for us, when He was actually referring to a future tribulation upon the House of Yahudah and Jerusalem within that generation.

As with all prophecy, it is critical to understand the time that the words were spoken, and the context within which it was spoken.

When we place the focus on the judgment of Jerusalem we see that this is the same terminology used by Isaiah to describe the fall of Babylon to the Medes in 539 BCE.

Here is what the Prophet proclaimed:

> "¹ The burden against Babylon which Isaiah the son of
> Amoz saw. . . ⁹ Behold, the Day of YHWH is coming,
> cruel, with fury and burning anger, To make the land a
> desolation; And He will exterminate its sinners from it.
> ¹⁰ For the stars of heaven and their constellations will not

flash forth with their light; The sun will be dark when it rises, and the moon will not shed its light." Isaiah 13:1, 9-10

This is language similar to prophecy's concerning the destruction of other kingdoms such as Samaria by Amos (Amos 8:9), the nations by Isaiah 34:1-6, and Egypt by Ezekiel (Ezekiel 32:2, 7-8). We also see similar language in Joel 2 concerning "The Day of YHWH" as judgment brought about through conquering armies.

So, the language in Matthew 24:29 was meant to describe the judgment and fall of Yahudah in 70 CE, after the tribulation that occurred during the siege and destruction of Jerusalem and Judea. Yahushua repeatedly referenced the impending judgment that was about to befall the Yahudim.[359] That is why Yahushua had just recently cursed the fig tree.

Remember that Yahudah was referred to as figs by Jeremiah. The good figs were the ones taken to Babylon and the bad figs were the ones who remained in the Land.[360] The ones who returned from Babylon and were planted back in the Land were not bearing fruit – the fruit of the Kingdom.

John the Immerser came warning the Yahudim to repent because: "*. . . even now the ax is laid to the root of the trees. Therefore, every tree which does not bear good fruit is cut down and thrown into the fire.*" Matthew 3:10

John was telling people to bear good fruit. He was preparing the way for the Messiah.

This is also the context for the Parable of the Fig Tree

---

[359] Here are just 2 examples: "*²¹ Woe to you, Chorazin! Woe to you, Bethsaida! For if the mighty works which were done in you had been done in Tyre and Sidon, they would have repented long ago in sackcloth and ashes. ²² But I say to you, it will be more tolerable for Tyre and Sidon in the day of judgment than for you. ²³ And you, Capernaum, who are exalted to heaven, will be brought down to Hades; for if the mighty works which were done in you had been done in Sodom, it would have remained until this day. ²⁴ But I say to you that it shall be more tolerable for the land of Sodom in the day of judgment than for you.*" "*O Jerusalem, Jerusalem, the one who kills the prophets and stones those who are sent to her! How often I wanted to gather your children together, as a hen gathers her chicks under her wings, but you were not willing!*" Matthew 23:37
[360] See Jeremiah 24

- 484 -

spoken by Yahushua:

"⁶ A certain man had a fig tree planted in his vineyard, and he came seeking fruit on it and found none. ⁷ Then he said to the keeper of his vineyard, 'Look, for three years I have come seeking fruit on this fig tree and find none. Cut it down; why does it use up the ground?' ⁸ But he answered and said to him, 'Sir, let it alone this year also, until I dig around it and fertilize it. ⁹ And if it bears fruit, well. But if not, after that you can cut it down.'"
Luke 13:6-9

Yahushua was speaking specifically to the Yahudim living in the Land, and this is why He specifically stated during the Olivet Discourse:

"³² Now learn this parable from the fig tree: When its branch has already become tender and puts forth leaves, you know that summer is near. ³³ So you also, when you see all these things, know that it is near - at the doors! ³⁴ Assuredly, I say to you, this generation will by no means pass away till all these things take place. ³⁵ Heaven and earth will pass away, but My words will by no means pass away." Matthew 24:32-35

Yahushua was therefore describing the judgment that was about to befall those in the House of Yahudah that had returned from Babylon and were living in the Land.

That was the context of His statement. When He referred to "this generation" He was talking about the generation that was alive when He made the statements. He was not describing some future event for our present generation nearly 2,000 years later called "the fig tree generation."

He was speaking to that generation. That was the "fig tree generation." In fact, everything prior to Matthew 24:37 is in response to the question concerning the Temple.[361]

It would take volumes of books to address all of the issues of prophetic interpretation. We obviously don't have time for that, but I hope that this has given you some guidance and advice to make your study of prophecy more productive and accurate.[362]

While there is always the possibility of multiple and layered fulfillments of prophecy, it is always best to understand the original and intended application first.

The important thing to recognize when considering prophecy is that the Scriptures are focused on the Covenant Assembly, and most prophecies must be read within that context.

In the next and final chapter we will discuss the fulfillment of the Covenant, which is actually the culmination of all prophecy.

---

[361] Similarly, Luke 21:5-36 which was probably spoken in the Temple, not on the Mount of Olives, was focused exclusively on the Temple.
[362] For an in depth analysis of prophecy and the end of the age I recommend the Walk in the Light series book titled *The Final Shofar*.

22

The End of the Journey

It has been my pleasure to accompany you on your journey out of Babylon. I hope that this book has been a helpful guide for you, your friends and your loved ones. While this book may be coming to a conclusion, our journey continues on.

Just as every journey has an end, so too – this journey has a final destination. It should be clear by now that the journey out of Babylon leads to the Kingdom of Elohim. While the Kingdom is seated in another dimension, it is manifested here on earth through us, and Mount Tzyon is the seat of the Kingdom. That is why we revere Jerusalem, and continue to see the significance of the Covenant Land.

Abraham left his house in Babylon and lived the rest of his life in a tent. He was given a future promise of Land, when his descendants could ultimately settle down and build houses. Until that time, his people would dwell in temporary structures. He understood and accepted that fact as he provided the pattern of the Covenant, and the walk of faith.

While he was alive, the Land was still controlled by the Canaanites, and filled with giants. Not much has changed. As Shlomo is attributed as saying: *"That which has been is what will be, that which is done is what will be done, and there is nothing new under the sun."* Ecclesiastes 1:9 The same Nephilim that operated in the Land in his day are active and present today. In fact, Babylon has spread throughout the entire planet.

We have already talked about the fact that the Appointed Times are like a road map on our journey. They are waypoints that keep us headed in the right direction. They are also important rehearsals preparing us for a future event – the Marriage of the Lamb.

Our journey out of Babylon began with a wedding invitation. That journey involves timing, planning and coordination. We need to get to the wedding at the right place and time, fully prepared to attend. This is why the Appointed Times are also called "miqra qadosh" (מִקְרָא-קֹדֶשׁ) – set apart rehearsals.

We talked about the ancient Hebrew wedding model as a pattern for our relationship with YHWH. We saw from the beginning, that the woman would come from the man, and they would join together and procreate. From the two would come children.

All of creation is meant to multiply and increase. It is all about a family, and we were made by a Creator Who desires for us to be in His family.

The continuous theme throughout the Scriptures is that YHWH will provide a home for us. If we simply obey "the rules of the house" we can dwell with Him. He will provide us with all of our needs. He will fill the pantry with food, and our closets with the clothes that we need. The thing is, He does not always give us everything we want. That is where the problems begin.

We get seduced by Babylon, and we stray from the straight path because of our wants and desires. Remember Achin? He saw the gold, the silver and the Babylonian clothes, and he just had to have them, despite the Commandment forbidding it. He didn't think of the consequences. He just needed to satisfy his lust to possess the things of Babylon.

Well, these same lusts eventually infected Yisrael. The disobedience of Shlomo resulted in the Kingdom being divided.

The House of Yisrael worshipped YHWH as a bull, which was the same likeness as the Canaanite god Ba'al. It may have seemed harmless, since Joseph was compared to a bull,[363] but in the eyes of YHWH it was serious.

That got them a certificate of divorce from YHWH.[364] Remarriage was prohibited according to the Torah under these circumstances,[365] and one of the parties needed to die because of the broken Covenant. Yahushua paid the price.

The House of Yahudah was treacherous and unfaithful as well. She deserved to drink the bitter waters of jealousy.[366] If found to be guilty, her unfaithfulness would result in her inability to reproduce.

Yahushua took the cup of the unfaithful wife, and He died so that there could be a remarriage. This is all in accordance with the Torah. He did not bear children in the flesh, or reproduce. He would have defiled Himself with an unfaithful bride.

That is why He is returning for a unblemished obedient Bride, purified by His blood. So we await His return, and in the meantime, we continue to rehearse and prepare. We stay pure and undefiled by obeying His righteous instructions. It's the least that we can do.

In fact, we should view the Appointed Times as our preparation for the return of the King and the Bridegroom. We need to take them that seriously. We come to the Land now to rehearse, even though YHWH is not dwelling in a tent, or a house.

We long for the day when He moves back in, although this time His House will not be built by a bunch of Pharisees who rejected His Son. The building will be part of the restoration that occurs after judgment is rendered. And believe me, the people currently in the Land are going to be judged.

No discussion on leaving Babylon would be complete

---

[363] "16 With the precious things of the earth and its fullness, and the favor of Him who dwelt in the bush. Let the blessing come "on the head of Joseph, and on the crown of the head of him who was separate from his brothers. 17 His glory is like a firstborn bull, and his horns like the horns of the wild ox; Together with them he shall push the peoples to the ends of the earth; They are the ten thousands of Ephraim and they are the thousands of Manasseh." Deuteronomy 33:16-17

[364] Jeremiah 3:8

[365] Deuteronomy 24:1-4

[366] Numbers 5:1-31

without mentioning what happened to the Southern Kingdom after her exile. On several occasions we have spoken of the division of the Kingdom of Yisrael, because it is such a critical event with prophetic implications.

The House of Yisrael was taken captive by the Assyrians, and removed from the Land. Their exile was complete around 721 BCE. The Assyrians were later conquered by the Babylonian Kingdom. Babylon was the Kingdom used to judge the Southern Kingdom, also known as The House of Yahudah.

Babylon attacked Yahudah and took many captives. Ultimately, around the year 586 BCE Babylon, under the rulership of Nebuchadnezzar, conquered Jerusalem and destroyed the Temple.

This period of activity actually triggered two seventy year periods of judgment, both prophesied by Jeremiah. The House of Yahudah would be punished in exile for seventy years.[367] Also, the Kingdom of Babylon would be punished after a seventy-year period.[368] While they were concurrent with one another, they didn't necessarily begin and end at the same time.

This is what led up to Daniel's prayer concerning the seventy weeks. Remember, he was one of the "good figs" spoken of by Jeremiah.[369] While in exile, he was praying about the end of the seventy years.

> "*1 In the first year of Darius the son of Ahasuerus, of the lineage of the Medes, who was made king over the realm of the Chaldeans – 2 in the first year of his reign I, Daniel, understood by the books the number of the years specified by the word of YHWH through Jeremiah the prophet, that He would accomplish seventy years in the desolations of Jerusalem.*" Daniel

---

[367] Jeremiah 20:11 and Jeremiah 29:10
[368] Jeremiah 25:12
[369] Jeremiah 24:5

We already discussed the fact that due to His prayer, the messenger Gabriel appeared to him, and provided what is known as the "Seventy Week Prophecy." As with all prophecies, we need to consider the context. It was an answer to prayer, so what was Daniel praying about?

Well, he was primarily praying about when the people could go back to Jerusalem, and restore the city. He got more than he asked for. Gabriel also provided the promise of Messiah the Prince. Not only was Daniel told that the city would be rebuilt, but that it would also be destroyed again.[370]

The modern Christian understanding of that passage has baffled people because they view it from a western – linear perspective. They also apply a futurist interpretation to the so-called seventieth week.

Cyrus, the King of Persia, permitted the return, and slowly, some from the House of Yahudah returned to the Land to rebuild. It is generally understood that most of the remnant who returned were poor. After all, they had nothing to lose. The wealthy and the content stayed in Babylon. After all, once Babylon wraps you in its tentacles, its hot easy to get free.

Imagine that! Most of the Yahudim stayed in Babylon. That is how powerful the allure of Babylon is. The sad truth is that most people would rather remain in the comforts of Babylon, than to return to the Land and rebuild. They lacked the same spirit and character as Abram, when he left Babylon.

What about you? Could you heed the call and leave everything behind?

Well, the return of Yahudah was not off to a very good start. Instead of a complete exodus from Babylon, like we saw from Egypt, it was just a trickle. Those who actually returned had a difficult time.

Their efforts were hindered and stalled. They

---

[370] Daniel 9:24-27

eventually became apathetic and complacent. They were excited at first, but they brought Babylon with them. They focused on their own lives, and building their own personal kingdoms. They neglected the House of Elohim, and instead built houses for themselves.

The House of Elohim, which was supposed to be the motivation for their return, remained unfinished until YHWH spoke through the Prophet Haggai. He pointed out the error of their ways and encouraged them to complete the work. The people "repented" by returning their focus to YHWH, and building His House.

Ultimately it was finished as a house of wood. It wasn't pretty. In fact, those who could remember the former Temple built by Solomon wept when they saw it. Others rejoiced though.[371]

That original structure is referred to as the Temple of Zerubbabel. It was likely completely renovated and replaced by the Temple built by Herod. That was the building that Yahushua stated would be torn down.

"And Yahushua said to them,
Do you not see all these things?
Assuredly, I say to you,
not one stone shall be left here upon another,
that shall not be thrown down."
Matthew 24:2

That is exactly what happened in 70 CE. The Romans were used by YHWH to judge the House of Yahudah . . . again. This time there was no prophet like Jeremiah to provide a duration for their exile, or another return and restoration. There was no plan for Yahudah to rebuild.

So we see that YHWH is not interested in houses built by men. He reigns from Mount Tzyon, in the heavens.

---

[371] See Ezra 3:10-13

Someday, He will bring a heavenly home to this earth.

That is why we still rehearse. We still go to the Covenant Land, and we still dwell in sukkas to remind us of that fact. It is a yearly rehearsal focused on leaving Babylon.

We live in tents, just as Abraham lived in a tent his entire life. We live in tents just as the Yisraelites lived in tents when they left Egypt. We live in tents, because YHWH also chose to live in a tent - the Tabernacle.

Of course, Sukkot is just a rehearsal, that points to a time when we move out of our temporary dwellings and return to a permanent home. I suspect things will look a lot different when that time ultimately comes, but this is nothing new in the course of time and the progression of the Covenant of restoration.

The process of restoration often involves destruction and tearing down, in order to make way for rebuilding and renewal. How intriguing then, that The Appointed Times conclude with what the Torah simply describes as the Eighth Day - Shemini Atzeret.

It is described in the text of Leviticus as follows:

"On the eighth day you shall have a miqra qadosh, and you shall offer an offering made by fire to YHWH. It is an atzeret, and you shall do no customary work on it." Leviticus 23:36

Now since it follows the seven days of Sukkot, many make the mistake of thinking that it is part of Sukkot. It is not. Sukkot is specifically set within seven days.

While it is connected to Sukkot, it has its own unique significance. It is a special day because it is the conclusion of the cycle of the Annual Appointed Times and it is specifically focused on eight, which is the number of the Covenant of Circumcision. It refers to a Renewal and New Beginnings.

While Shemini Atzeret is associated with the number eight, it actually lands on Day 22 of Month 7, and that has great prophetic significance.

It is the final Appointed Time in the cycle that began in Month 1. Now we see an end to that cycle in Month 7. Notice that it is not the end of the year, which would either be in month 12 or 13, but it is the end of the cycle of Appointed Times.

Interestingly it occurs at a time known as "the end of the year" when Sukkot is referred to as The Feast of Ingathering.

> *"*[14] *Three times you shall keep a Feast to Me in the year:* [15] *You shall keep the Feast of Unleavened Bread (you shall eat unleavened bread seven days, as I commanded you, at the time appointed in the month of the Abib, for in it you came out of Egypt; none shall appear before Me empty);* [16] *and the Feast of Harvest, the firstfruits of your labors which you have sown in the field; and the Feast of Ingathering at the end of the year, when you have gathered in the fruit of your labors from the field.*" Exodus 23:14-16

How can Sukkot, also known as the Feast of Ingathering occur at the end of the year, when it is only in month seven? The reason is because the main harvest season has essentially ended. The work of gathering is over, and it is time to start preparing for the next grain harvest.

So, when you consider it within the context of the harvest cycles, it makes sense. Another text that refers to Sukkot as the Feast of Ingathering provides some additional information.

> *"And you shall observe the Feast of Weeks,*
> *of the firstfruits of wheat harvest,*
> *and the Feast of Ingathering at the year's end.*"
> Exodus 34:22

The phrase "at the years end" is "tequfet ha'shanah" in

Hebrew. Literally – "the turn of the year." So, there is a turning or shifting that occurs at the "tequfah." The tequfahs (tequfot) are understood to be the "turns" of the equinoxes, when day and night are equal. So the Feast of Ingathering should occur around the "turn" (tequfah) of the autumnal equinox. We already discussed that in depth in Chapter 15.

Just as the beginning of the cycle of the Appointed Times starts around the tequfah referred to as the Spring Equinox, we see the cycle end around the tequfah referred to as the Autumnal equinox. It is important to remember that YHWH built these turns into Creation. The pagans often revere these times, because they understand their significance.

Those who follow the One Who actually intentionally created them should recognize their significance as well. The calendar that Elohim established at the beginning of time is important, and the subject of much debate.

It is important to recognize that He created two great lights, the sun and the moon, specifically for reckoning time. Make sure you do not get led astray by some solar calendar, or YHWH forbid, the Rabbinic Calendar. Simply follow the lights as signs.

So, even though Shemini Atzeret occurs on Day 22, it is called the Eighth Day. Eight is the number of the Covenant. Eight is equivalent to the letter "het" (ח), which represents a fence or a wall. This can be seen in the Paleo-Hebrew representation of "het" (ﬡ).

Remember that the Garden is "gan" (גן) in Hebrew, which means "enclosed space." That is why there is a wall around the Renewed Jerusalem. I actually completed the video series that resulted in this book on Shemini Atzeret in Jerusalem. I was outside the walls of the Old City of Jerusalem filming, and I could only enter in through one of the gates.

This is what we see through the "het." And the eight day is a day of separation, and distinctions. It points to a Covenant that is represented by a City that has a wall and twelve gates. The fulfillment of that Covenant is the New

Jerusalem, which is the destination of this journey out of Babylon

Now when we look at the Gematria of the number eight we see many important connections. The first time that we read a word with a value of 8 is in Genesis 4:26.

> "*And as for Seth, to him also a son was born;*
> *and he* את*-named him Enosh.*
> אז *Then men began to call on*
> *the Name of YHWH.*"
> Genesis 4:26

How amazing that this clue is provided to us when men began to "call on the Name of YHWH." Here is the word "az" (אז) as seen in modern Hebrew and here it is in Paleo-Hebrew (𐤆𐤀). Aleph (𐤀) numerically equals 1, and Zayin (𐤆) equals 7.

Remember that aleph looks like a bull, and means "strength." Zayin looks like a weapon, a sickle, a plow or a pruning hook. You can clearly see that in the modern Hebrew depiction of "zayin" (ז).

Of course these were interchangeable because in times of peace the instruments would be used for the harvest. and in times of war they would be converted into swords and weapons.

We read this conversion in preparation for war in Joel.

> "⁹ *Proclaim this among the nations: Prepare for war!*
> *Wake up the mighty men, Let all the men of war draw*
> *near, let them come up.* ¹⁰ *Beat your plowshares into*
> *swords and your pruning hooks into spears; Let the*
> *weak say, I am strong.*" Joel 3:9-10

We also read about a conversion back, after the time of war described in Joel, when YHWH reigns from Tzyon.

"² Now it shall come to pass in the latter days that the mountain of YHWH's House shall be established on the top of the mountains, and shall be exalted above the hills; and all Nations shall flow to it. ³ Many people shall come and say, Come, and let us go up to the mountain of YHWH, to the house of the Elohim of Jacob; He will teach us His ways, and we shall walk in His paths. For out of Tzyon shall go forth the Torah, and the word of YHWH from Jerusalem. ⁴ He shall judge between the nations, And rebuke many people; They shall beat their swords into plowshares, And their spears into pruning hooks; Nation shall not lift up sword against nation, neither shall they learn war anymore." Isaiah 2:2-4

So, this first word in the Torah that numerically equals eight carries quite a message. And the imagery of the "zayin" is profound when we consider the harvest and war cycles that will ultimately culminate in peace.

We long for the time when all swords are turned into sickles to harvest the bounty that YHWH provides us in peace. Currently, as I finish this book, war is looming throughout the world.

Notice that *"they shall learn war no more."* The book of I Enoch describes that Azazel, a fallen Son of Elohim, actually taught mankind how to make weapons and conduct war.[372] The fallen Sons of Elohim learned that they would be judged and die like men.[373]

YHWH had a plan to replace them and replenish His Kingdom with new Sons of Elohim. That is the destiny of those who follow the Son Yahushua. That explains the battle that is currently raging in the spirit realm. Those jealous fallen Sons are trying to keep us from "filling their slots." They want to take as many down with them as they can, and keep us from

---

[372] I Enoch, *Book of the Watchers 8:1*
[373] Psalm 82:7

obtaining our "new beginnings" as Sons of Elohim.

In Genesis 15, when it describes the Covenant with Abram, we read about eight pieces of slaughterings that were placed across from one another. Later, when YHWH entered into the Covenant of Circumcision, we read specifically about an event that occurs on the eighth day.

"He who is eight days old among you shall be circumcised, every male child in your generations, he who is born in your house or bought with money from any foreigner who is not your descendant." Genesis 17:12

We later read about Isaac, the first child recorded to be circumcised on the eighth day.

"Then Abraham circumcised his son Isaac
when he was eight days old,
as Elohim had commanded him."
Genesis 21:4

The next time we see a word that equals eight is related to that Promised Son, circumcised on the eighth day. Here is the passage:

"Then He said, Take now your את-son, your את-only son את-Isaac, whom you love (אהב), and go to the land of Moriah, and offer him there as a burnt offering on one of the mountains of which I shall tell you." Genesis 22:2

Can you guess the word that equals eight? I included it in the Hebrew. It is spelled aleph (א), hey (ה), bet (ב). Aleph equals 1, hey equals 5, and bet equals 2. The Hebrew word "ahab" (אהב) means "love."

Of course, those same characters rearranged spell "ha'ab" (האב) which means: "the Father." So "the Father" also equals eight in the Hebrew language.

We can clearly see the focus on love, the Father and the promised Son of the Covenant in this passage, represented by the aleph taw (את), and connected with eight. And remember that circumcision on the eighth day is a "sign" of the Covenant. Of course, the fulfillment of that sign will be the circumcision of our hearts. I believe that will also be the fulfillment of the Eighth Day Appointed Time.

In this 22nd Chapter, I felt it was important to connect the conclusion of this journey with the significance of the number eight.

These are just a few examples, but you can see how eight is so important to the Covenant path that leads us out of Babylon. It represents the transition from an end to a beginning, or rather – a new beginning.

And by no coincidence Shemini Atzeret is a Sabbath. Remember the command:

> *"On the eighth day you shall have a miqra qadosh, and you shall offer an offering made by fire to YHWH. It is a atzeret, and you shall do no customary work on it."*
> Leviticus 23:36

Every seventh day is a Sabbath. We rehearse that pattern every week. It operates on a different cycle than the annual Appointed Times, but here we see the mystery getting clearer.

While the Seventh Day is a Sabbath, so is the Eighth Day. We also see two Sabbath years in a row at the time of the Jubilee. The Jubilee Year follows the 49th year, or the seventh Shemitah year. Did you catch that?

Remember that every seventh year is a Sabbath year. After the seventh Sabbath year is a Jubilee year. That is a Sabbath year and is likened to the eight year. After the Jubilee, the count begins anew at year one in the first Shemitah cycle. So the Eighth Day is also connected with the Jubilee.

As a result, we would anticipate seeing the fulfillment of the Eighth Day rehearsal in a Jubilee Year. So we can see how this will culminate at the end of the Sabbath reign – the millennial reign of Messiah.

It means new beginnings and this is when the planet and the Kingdom will be renewed. It is when the Renewed Jerusalem will descend upon the Renewed Heavens and the Renewed Earth as we read about in Revelation 21.

"Then I, John, saw the set apart city, Renewed Jerusalem,
coming down out of heaven from Elohim,
prepared as a bride adorned for her husband."
Revelation 21:2

Yahushua said: *"In My Father's house are many mansions; if it were not so, I would have told you. I go to prepare a place for you."* John 14:2

Right now the Messiah is preparing the renewed Jerusalem. Like the Covenant, it will be a new thing, within the original Covenant framework. That is why He was described as a "builder" (tekton) in the Scriptures.[374] He is still building. He is building a new House for Himself and His Bride to dwell in here on Earth, after the ingathering.

Landing this Eighth Day Appointed Time on Day 22 of Month 7 is extremely significant. Seven is the number of creation and time, as we saw from the first sentence in the Hebrew Scriptures.

1	2	3	4	5	6	7	8

B'resheet bara Elohim את ha'shamyim v'את ha'eretz v'ha'eretz

Of course from those seven words we saw the entire plan of Elohim laid out like a map of time – 7,000 years. Did you notice the eighth word? It is interesting to point out that

---

374 Mark 6:3

the eighth word in the Torah is also ha'eretz. It is pointing to a renewed Earth.

The number 22 is also significant because it also represents an end. Just as this 22nd Chapter is the conclusion of our journey, the "taw" (ת) is the 22nd, and final letter of the Hebrew aleph bet. In fact, it is the conclusion of the aleph bet.

The aleph (א) is the First, and the taw (ת) is the Last. Another way of saying it is that the aleph (א) is the beginning, and the taw (ת) is the end that leads to a new beginning in the cycle of time.

The Hebrew language is built into Creation, and it is important to view this walk as a Hebrew journey. Hebrew thought is cyclical, as is Creation. The end of a day leads to a renewal - the beginning of another day, and so on . . .

So "the end" in Hebrew thought is not the same as "the end" in western thought. When a western thinker considers "the end," they think that "it's all over," "it's done," or "it's concluded," - "the end of the line."

There is a sense of finality there, like the end of a movie or a book. There is nothing beyond "the end." It's almost hopeless.

A good Hebrew, on the other hand, recognizes that the end leads to renewal. Take for instance the monthly cycle. The month begins with the light of the first crescent moon. The moon is "birthed" from the darkness of the womb. It increases in brightness until it is "full," and then it begins to wane into old age when it finally goes dark, representing death.

But that begs the question: "Is the darkness the time in the womb, or the time in the grave - sheol?" Is it the end or leading to a new beginning? Do you understand the significance of that question?

I hope so. Because if you do, then that means you are becoming a Hebrew. And that is a prerequisite for following the path of Abram the Hebrew on the journey out of Babylon.

The walk of a Hebrew involves understanding the cycles of life. Remember, the Word that represents the

Messiah is the aleph taw (את), and Yahushua specifically identified Himself with the aleph taw (את).

We can discern this from the book of Revelation. In a common English translation of Revelation 1:8 we read:

"I am the Alpha and the Omega,
the Beginning and the End, says the Master,
who is and who was and who is to come, the Almighty."

It is important to understand that Yahushua wasn't speaking Greek – He was speaking Hebrew. He actually said:

"I am the Aleph and the Taw, (את)
the Beginning and the End, says the Master,
who is and who was and who is to come – El of Hosts."

So, Yahushua is not only stating that He is "El of Hosts" - He is saying that He has been here since Creation, and He is coming back. He is also identifying Himself as "the Word."

The "et" (את) is the Word - aleph (א) and taw (ת). The "aleph" (א) means strength, while the "taw" (ת) represents the mark of a covenant, as can be seen in the Paleo-Hebrew rendering of the "taw" (✕). The aleph taw (את) is the "strength of the Covenant." It contains, and passes through, all 22 Hebrew letters that lead to the Covenant.

As a result, the death of the aleph taw (את) was not the end, because there was resurrection, and new life that followed.

So as we reach the conclusion of the Appointed Times each year, we recognize that we are operating in cycles. We live in the present, while we prepare for the future. We have not reached a termination point as westerners view the end, with a sense of finality.

We are Hebrews, and we recognize that the end leads to a renewal – a new beginning. We live in cycles, and we learn and draw closer to Him through the rehearsals of the Appointed Times. This is how the Bride prepares herself. It is a perpetual refining process.

We continue to rehearse until we finally reach the consummation of the Wedding and the Marriage Supper rehearsed during Sukkot.

After dwelling in temporary dwellings for seven days we look forward the Eighth Day, when we no longer dwell on Sukkas. The Eighth Day points to the fulfillment of the Covenant Journey.

Here is that Renewal described in Revelation after the resurrection and judgment when the Covenant people no longer live in sukkas

> "20:11 Then I saw a great white throne and Him who sat on it, from whose face the earth and the heaven fled away. And there was found no place for them. 12 And I saw the dead, small and great, standing before Elohim, and books were opened. And another book was opened, which is the Scroll of Life. And the dead were judged according to their works, by the things which were written in the books. 13 The sea gave up the dead who were in it, and Death and Hades delivered up the dead who were in them. And they were judged, each one according to his works. 14 Then Death and Hades were cast into the lake of fire. This is the second death. 15 And anyone not found written in the Scroll of Life was cast into the lake of fire. 21:1 Now I saw a new heaven and a new earth, for the first heaven and the first earth had passed away. Also there was no more sea. 2 Then I, John, saw the Holy (Set Apart) City, Renewed Jerusalem, coming down out of heaven from Elohim, prepared as a bride adorned for her husband. 3 And I heard a loud voice from heaven saying, Behold, the tabernacle of Elohim is with men, and He will dwell

with them, and they shall be His people. Elohim Himself will be with them and be their Elohim. [4] And Elohim will wipe away every tear from their eyes; there shall be no more death, nor sorrow, nor crying. There shall be no more pain, for the former things have passed away. [5] Then He who sat on the throne said, Behold, I make all things new. And He said to me, Write, for these words are true and faithful. [6] And He said to me, It is done! I am the Aleph (א) and the Taw (ת), the Beginning and the End. I will give of the fountain of the water of life freely to him who thirsts. [7] <u>He who overcomes shall inherit all things, and I will be his Elohim and he shall be My son.</u>" Revelation 20:11-21:7

There it is. We will become sons - Sons of Elohim. This will occur when Yahushua "acquires" us, and our place in the Kingdom. That is exactly what we saw when Melchizedek blessed Abram and El Most High. It is the fulfillment of the Covenant and the Prophets, and it is all accomplished through the Son - the strength of the Covenant - the aleph taw (את).

He will restore the Tabernacle (sukka) of David as prophesied in Amos.

"*On that day I will raise up the את-sukka of David, which has fallen down, and repair its damages; I will raise up its ruins, and rebuild it as in the days of old.*" Amos 9:11

David united the tribes, and moved the Ark of the Covenant to Jerusalem. He placed it in a sukka – a temporary dwelling. Amos refers to raising up the את-sukka. The aleph taw (את) will build this sukka, not the Pharisees, the Rabbis or the Jewish People, who deny Yahushua.

This is where the Messiah and His people will dwell

until He finally brings down the Renewed Jerusalem from the heavens. That will be the culmination of the Eighth Day in a future Sukkot at the end of the Sabbath Millennium.

And as we discussed the significance of eight with the letter het (ﬡ), we see that the Renewed Jerusalem has great walls and gates. It is laid out precisely like the camp of Yisrael in the Wilderness.

Here is the description:

> ""¹² Also she had a great and high wall with twelve gates, and twelve angels at the gates, and names written on them, which are the names of the twelve tribes of the children of Yisrael: ¹³ three gates on the east, three gates on the north, three gates on the south, and three gates on the west." Revelation 12:12-13

The Renewed Jerusalem is for the Assembly of Yisrael, and Yisrael consists of those who are in Covenant with YHWH. Since the Covenant was previously broken, the only way back in is through the Covenant renewed by the Messiah.

So, we see that the Seventh Month is all about the Messiah, and His fulfillment of the Appointed Times, which results in a renewal of all Creation through that Renewed Covenant

That Covenant is a Hebrew Covenant best understood in the Hebrew language, and in the context of a Hebrew marriage covenant. The Words and the Hebrew language are important to guide us Hebrews on our journey.

As we have discussed, the ancient Hebrew language is closely connected with agricultural concepts, and the nomadic lifestyle. Therefore, it is important that we view this journey as Hebrews, not western Babylonian city dwellers.

We must become nomadic tent dwellers on this journey - living in temporary structures. Ready to move when YHWH directs. I know that is contrary to everything that you have been taught by Babylon, but it is the only way out.

We have been conditioned to build and plant roots outside of the Covenant Land. As a result, most will not return, even when given a chance, because they don't want to leave their comfort zones.

We are no different from our ancient predecessors. Until we can finally move back into the home that YHWH has prepared for us, we dwell in sukkas. Babylon wants you to build your own kingdom and plant roots in Babylon. While there may have been a time for that – that time is not now.

Here is what Jeremiah told the House of Yahudah as they were going into exile:

"He has sent this message to us in Babylon: It will be a long time. Therefore build houses and settle down; plant gardens and eat what they produce." Jeremiah 29:28

Contrary to that moment in time, those of us in the House of Yisrael are coming out of our punishment. In fact, the punishment and exile of the House of Yisrael is over. We should be getting ready to leave Babylon.

While we are still in Babylon, I suggest we start praying like Daniel did when he was in Babylon. We need to be asking YHWH - "When?" And remember that the promise of the renewed Covenant to the House of Yisrael was different from the previous renewal offered to the House of Yahudah.

"But this is the Covenant that I will make with the House of Yisrael after those days, says YHWH: I will put My Torah in their minds, and write it on their hearts; and I will be their Elohim, and they shall be My people." Jeremiah 31:33

Only those who have the testimony of Yahushua, <u>and</u> keep the Commandments of Elohim will be in the Covenant renewed by Yahushua. (Revelation 12:17 and 14:12)

We have talked about the importance of understanding

Hebrew Language and thought. And this becomes abundantly clear when we look at the Hebrew word for "commandments," which is "mitzvot."

As with the word "Torah," the English does not necessarily provide us with a full translation of the word "mitzvot." When we consider the Commandments, we typically think of a list of do's and don'ts that have penalties associated with breaking them.

According to Jeff Benner, the word "mitzvot" Hebraically means: "the directions given to guide one on the journey."[375]

Of course, the first time we read the Hebrew word "mitzvot" is in Genesis 26 when YHWH told Isaac to dwell in the Land promised to Abraham, and He confirmed the promises because Abraham obeyed.

> "[2] *Then YHWH appeared to him and said: Do not go down to Egypt; live in the land of which I shall tell you.* [3] *Dwell in this land, and I will be with you and bless you; for to you and your descendants I give all these lands, and I will perform the oath which I swore to Abraham your father.* [4] *And I will make your descendants multiply as the stars of heaven; I will give to your descendants all these lands; and in your seed all the nations of the earth shall be blessed;* [5] *because Abraham obeyed My voice and kept My charge, My* **Mitzvot**, *My statutes, and My Torah."* Genesis 26:2-5

Abraham blazed the Covenant path and succeeded, because He believed the promises, and his belief was demonstrated by his actions. He moved his tent and followed the instructions

The Torah is a roadmap, and the Commandments

---

[375] Ancient Hebrew Research Center at ancient-hebrew.org

(mitzvot) are directions on this precarious journey out of Babylon, that ultimately leads to the Promised Land. That roadmap provides waypoints for us to calibrate our passage through the Appointed Times.

When man was in the Garden he partook of the fruits. Only after he was expelled from the garden was he required to toil in the soil for his food. It is no coincidence that the Appointed Times begin with the grain harvest, and end with the fruits. They point the way back to the Garden, where we can leave our plows and sickles behind, and once again, partake of the fruit of the Garden.

While our journey began in Babylon, we are on the same covenant path as our ancestors - trying to find our way back in to the Garden. It is in the Garden where we find the fruit, and it is in the Garden that we find true rest.

As stated previously, I actually finished filming the video series that resulted in this book while in Jerusalem on Shemini Atzeret. It was my 22nd Shemini Atzeret in the Covenant Land. That is both significant, and profound.

As I spent the seven days of Sukkot in Jerusalem dwelling under a sukka, it reminded me of the separation that still exists between YHWH, and His Covenant Assembly Yisrael.

As we left our sukkas after the seventh day of Sukkot, and began to rehearse the time of renewal of the Eighth Day – I felt that ancient longing for the day when our journey ends, and we no longer have to rehearse Sukkot and dwell in sukkas.

While we rejoice during the Feast, we realize that the true joy comes for those in the Covenant when the rehearsals are over. When the journey comes to an end, we can finally experience true peace - shalom.

In fact, that is really the definition of "shalom." The root of "shalom" is the same as "shalem." It means to be whole or sound, and this leads to translations that speak of completeness, wholeness, well-being, welfare and peace.

When we finish our journey, and arrive at our destination whole and complete, that is the essence of shalom.

Of course, that is why the culmination of the Covenant is referred to as the Covenant of Shalom.[376] It will literally be fulfilled in the City of Peace (Shalem).

> "In Shalem also is His tabernacle,
> and His dwelling place in Tzyon."
> Psalm 76:2

Well, it has been my pleasure helping to guide you out of Babylon. This is an ancient journey that has been blazed by many before us, and will continue until the fulfillment of the Eighth Day moadim.

Our journey out of Babylon will not be complete until we finally return to the Garden with our Master and Bridegroom Yahushua. He provided the way back by renewing the Covenant with His broken body and shed blood. That is what allowed the way for a remarriage with unfaithful Yisrael and Yahudah.

Yahushua showed us how to walk the path, and He sent the Spirit to teach us, guide us, and strengthen us along the way.

He also instructed: *"¹³ Enter by the narrow gate; for wide is the gate and broad is the way that leads to destruction, and there are many who go in by it. ¹⁴ Because narrow is the gate and difficult is the way which leads to life, and there are few who find it."* Matthew 7:13-14

I encourage you to find the ancient path and walk perfectly. Do not veer off to the right or to the left. The way to Life offered through the Messiah is the way out for those intent on Leaving Babylon.

Safe travels and shalom!

---

[376] Numbers 25:12, Isaiah 54:10, Ezekiel 34:25 and 37:26

Appendix A

The Walk in the Light Series

Book 1   Restoration – A discussion of the pagan influences that have mixed with the true faith through the ages which has resulted in the need for restoration. This book also examines true Scriptural restoration.

Book 2   Names – Discusses the True Name of the Creator and the Messiah as well as the significance of names in the Scriptures.

Book 3   The Scriptures – Discusses the ways that the Creator has communicated with Creation. It also examines the origin of the written Scriptures as well as the various types of translation errors in Bibles that have led to false doctrines in some mainline religions.

Book 4   Covenants – Discusses the progressive covenants between the Creator and His Creation as described in the Scriptures which reveals His plan for mankind.

Book 5   The Messiah – Discusses the prophetic promises and fulfillments of the Messiah and the True identity of the Redeemer of Yisrael.

Book 6   The Redeemed – Discusses the relationship between Christianity and Judaism and reveals how the Scriptures identify True Believers. It reveals how the Christian doctrine of Replacement Theology has caused confusion as to how the Creator views the Children of Yisrael.

Book 7   The Law and Grace – Discusses in depth the false doctrine that Grace has done away with the Law and demonstrates the vital importance of obeying the commandments.

Book 8   The Sabbath – Discusses the importance of the Seventh Day Sabbath as well as the origins of the tradition concerning Sunday worship.

Book 9	Kosher – Discusses the importance of eating food prescribed by the Scriptures as an aspect of righteous living.
Book 10	Appointed Times – Discusses the appointed times established by the Creator, often erroneously considered to be "Jewish" holidays, and critical to the understanding of prophetic fulfillment of the Scriptural promises.
Book 11	Pagan Holidays – Discusses the pagan origins of some popular Christian holidays which have replaced the Appointed Times.
Book 12	The Final Shofar – Examines the ancient history of the earth and prepares the Believer for the deceptions coming in the end of the age. Also discusses the walk required by the Scriptures to be an overcomer and endure to the end.

The series began as a simple Power point presentation which was intended to develop into a book with twelve different chapters, but it ended up being twelve different books. Each book is intended to stand alone, although the series was originally intended to build from one section to another.

For free newsletters, announcements, additional teachings, or to make a donation go to: www.shemayisrael.net

Appendix B

The Shema
Deuteronomy (Debarim) 6:4-5

Traditional English Translation

Hear, O Israel: The LORD our God, the LORD is one!
You shall love the LORD your God with all your heart, with all
your soul, and with all your strength.

Corrected English Translation

Hear, O Yisrael: YHWH our Elohim, YHWH is one (unified)!
You shall love YHWH your Elohim with all your heart, with
all your soul, and with all your strength.

Modern Hebrew Text

שְׁמַע ישראל יהוה אלהינו יהוה אחד
ואהבת את יהוה אלהיך בכל‑ לבבך ובכל‑ נפשך ובכל‑ מאדך

Ancient Hebrew Text

Hebrew Text Transliterated

Shema, Yisra'el: YHWH Elohenu, YHWH echad!
V-ahavta et YHWH Elohecha b-chol l'vavcha u-b-chol
naf'sh'cha u-b-chol m'odecha.

The Shema has traditionally been one of the most important prayers in
Judaism and has been declared the first (resheet) of all the Commandments.
(Mark 12:29-30).

Appendix C

Tanak Hebrew Names

Torah - Teaching

English Name	Hebrew	English Transliteration
Genesis	בראשית	Beresheet
Exodus	שמות	Shemot
Leviticus	ויקרא	Vayiqra
Numbers	במדבר	Bemidbar
Deuteronomy	דברים	Debarim

Nebi'im – Prophets

Joshua	יהושע	Yahushua
Judges	שופטים	Shoftim
Samuel	שמואל	Shemu'el
Kings	מלכים	Melakhim
Isaiah	ישעיהו	Yeshayahu
Jeremiah	ירמיהו	Yirmeyahu
Ezekiel	יחזקאל	Yehezqel
Daniel	דניאל	Daniel
Hosea	השוע	Hoshea
Joel	יואל	Yoel
Amos	עמוס	Amos
Obadiah	עבדיה	Obadyah

Jonah	יונה	Yonah
Micah	מיכה	Mikhah
Nahum	נחום	Nachum
Habakkuk	חבקוק	Habaquq
Zephaniah	צפניה	Zepheniyah
Haggai	חגי	Chaggai
Zechariah	זכריה	Zekaryah
Malachi	מלאכי	Malachi

Kethubim – Writings

Psalms	תהלים	Tehillim
Proverbs	משלי	Mishle
Job	איוב	Iyob
Song of Songs	שיר השירים	Shir haShirim
Ruth	רות	Ruth
Lamentations	איכה	Eikhah
Ecclesiastes	קהלת	Qohelet
Esther	אסתר	Ester
Ezra	עזרא	Ezra
Nehemiah	נחמיה	Nehemyah
Chronicles	דברי הימים	Dibri haYamim

Appendix D

Shema Yisrael

Shema Yisrael was originally established with two primary goals: 1) The production and distribution of sound, Scripturally based educational materials which would assist individuals to see the light of Truth and "Walk in the Light" of that Truth. This first objective was, and is, accomplished through Shema Yisrael Publications; and 2) The free distribution of those materials to the spiritually hungry throughout the world, along with Scriptures, food, clothing and money to the poor, the needy, the sick, the dying and those in prison. This second objective was accomplished through the Shema Yisrael Foundation and through the Foundation people were able to receive a tax deduction for their contributions.

Sadly, through the passage of the Pension Reform Act of 2006, the US Congress severely restricted the operation of donor advised funds which, in essence, crippled the Shema Yisrael Foundation by requiring that funds either be channeled through another Foundation or to a 501(c)(3) organization approved by the Internal Revenue Service. Since the Shema Yisrael Foundation was relatively small and operated very "hands on" by placing the funds and materials directly into the hands of the needy in Third World Countries, it was unable to effectively continue operating as a Foundation with the tax advantages associated therewith.

As a result, Shema Yisrael Publications has essentially functioned in a dual capacity to insure that both objectives continue to be promoted, although contributions are no longer tax deductible. To review some of the work being accomplished you can visit www.shemayisrael.net and go to the "Missions" section.

We gladly accept donations, although they will not be tax deductible. To donate, please make checks payable to "Shema Yisrael Publications" and mail to:

Shema Yisrael
123 Court Street • Herkimer, New York 13350

You may also visit our website or call (315) 866-6648 to make a donation or receive more information.

Made in the USA
Middletown, DE
19 September 2023